Programming the Web Using
ASP.NET

Dave Mercer

InformationTechnology

McGraw Hill **Technology Education**

Boston   Burr Ridge, IL   Dubuque, IA   Madison, WI   New York   San Francisco   St. Louis
Bangkok   Bogotá   Caracas   Kuala Lumpur   Lisbon   London   Madrid   Mexico City
Milan   Montreal   New Delhi   Santiago   Seoul   Singapore   Sydney   Taipei   Toronto

McGraw Hill Technology Education

iPROGRAMMING THE WEB USING ASP.NET
Published by McGraw-Hill/Technology Education, a business unit of The McGraw-Hill Companies, Inc., 1221 Avenue of the Americas, New York, NY, 10020. Copyright © 2004 by The McGraw-Hill Companies, Inc. All rights reserved. No part of this publication may be reproduced or distributed in any form or by any means, or stored in a database or retrieval system, without the prior written consent of The McGraw-Hill Companies, Inc., including, but not limited to, in any network or other electronic storage or transmission, or broadcast for distance learning. Some ancillaries, including electronic and print components, may not be available to customers outside the United States.

This book is printed on acid-free paper.

1 2 3 4 5 6 7 8 9 0 DOC/DOC 0 9 8 7 6 5 4 3

ISBN   0-07-291809-8

Editor in chief: *Bob Woodbury*
Publisher: *Brandon Nordin*
Senior sponsoring editor: *Donald J. Hull*
Developmental editor   *Lisa Chin-Johnson*
Manager, Marketing and Sales   *Paul Murphy*
Producer, Media technology: *Greg Bates*
Senior project manager: *Jean Lou Hess*
Senior production supervisor: *Rose Hepburn*
Designer: *Adam Rooke*
Supplement producer: *Lynn Bluhm*
Senior digital content specialist: *Brian Nacik*
Cover image: (©) *2003 Corbis Images*
Typeface: *10/12 New Baskerville*
Compositor: *Black Dot Group*
Printer: *R. R. Donnelley*

Library of Congress Control Number: 2003110724

www.mhhe.com

McGraw-Hill Technology Education

At McGraw-Hill Technology Education, we publish instructional materials for the technology education market, in particular computer instruction in post-secondary education—from introductory courses in traditional four-year universities to continuing education and proprietary schools. McGraw-Hill Technology Education presents a broad range of innovative products—texts, lab manuals, study guides, testing materials, and technology-based training and assessment tools.

We realize that technology has created and will continue to create new mediums for professors and students to use in managing resources and communicating information to one another. McGraw-Hill Technology Education provides the most flexible and complete teaching and learning tools available as well as offers solutions to the changing world of teaching and learning. McGraw-Hill Technology Education is dedicated to providing the tools for today's instructors and students, which will enable them to successfully navigate the world of Information Technology.

- McGraw-Hill/Osborne—This division of The McGraw-Hill Companies is known for its best-selling Internet titles, Harley Hahn's *Internet & Web Yellow Pages*, and the *Internet Complete Reference*. For more information, visit Osborne at **www.osborne.com**.

- Digital Solutions—Whether you want to teach a class online or just post your "bricks-n-mortar" class syllabus, McGraw-Hill Technical Education is committed to publishing digital solutions. Taking your course online doesn't have to be a solitary adventure, nor does it have to be a difficult one. We offer several solutions that will allow you to enjoy all the benefits of having your course material online.

- Packaging Options—For more information about our discount options, contact your McGraw-Hill/Irwin sales representative at 1-800-338-3987 or visit our website at **www.mhhe.com/it**.

McGraw-Hill Technology Education is dedicated to providing the tools for today's instructors and students.

Preface

To The Student

This text is a basic but comprehensive introduction to Microsoft's exciting new .Net Framework and Active Server Pages.Net (ASP.Net). In this book is everything you need to begin learning how easy it is to program basic to complex, full-featured Web applications and Web Services with ASP.Net, using Visual Studio.Net. Whether you are taking just one or two programming classes or are a computer-science major, you will find this book indispensable for working with any type of Web-based applications.

Traditional Web programming was more like an afterthought, with clunky scripting languages and few full-featured development tools available. ASP.Net goes a long way toward making Web application development a smooth and efficient process. Any student should find the built-in objects and programming model easy and fun to master, especially when using Visual Studio.Net in conjunction with ASP.Net. This book covers many basic programming concepts and how they are related to ASP.Net, the basic ASP.Net objects, and the Visual Basic.Net language and many other interpreted and compiled languages that play a part in modern Web applications, database design and Structured Query Language (SQL), application design, optimization, and some of the many wizards, application templates, and built-in form controls you'll find in VS.Net. By the end of the book, after having completed the exercises and projects, you will feel very comfortable with any task that calls for a Web application or Web Service.

The design of ASP.Net makes it very straightforward to build the next great ecommerce application, or hot new Web site. And because it's so easily accessible but powerful at the same time, you will use it, or interact directly with those who do, many times in your career. You can write ASP.Net applications from your own computer, load them on a properly configured server, and run them from the Web through just about any browser. Existing ASP applications can either run side-by-side with ASP.Net applications or be modified and updated with ASP.Net. The projects and exercises in this book will take you step-by-step through everything you need to know about ASP.Net, and the projects in this book give a great practical demonstration of how ASP.Net works.

PREFACE

To The Teacher

This text provides a straightforward and hands-on approach to the introduction of basic Web application and programming concepts. Although Active Server Pages.Net (ASP.Net) is a very powerful technology for creating all types of Web applications, it is simple enough for beginners to use, especially since we use Visual Studio.Net (VS.Net) as the development platform. In VS.Net, Web applications can be created from the included templates with practically no in-depth technical understanding of how programming or applications work. Even non–computer science students will find a course including this book exciting and interesting, while computer science majors will appreciate the efficiency of ASP.Net objects used with VB.Net, ADO.Net, and VS.Net.

Each chapter outlines fundamental programming and application development concepts and demonstrates their use with ASP.Net. Small applications are created starting with the very first chapter, and progress to complete, complex applications with XML Web Services and SQL Server databases in the final chapters. The Hands On Projects at the end of every chapter are fun and useful in their own right, not just demo projects. The book covers all the basic concepts required to build these applications, but does not dwell on them or stray too far into the technical side. The purpose of the book is to provide a solid introduction and leave students interested in finding out more if they choose, but with the tools to make Web applications if they go on to other pursuits.

The chapters in this text progress easily from one to the next, with Web applications used as exercises from the start. Each chapter includes relevant topics followed by Quick Check Questions to reinforce learning, exercises for hands-on practice with ASP.Net, discussions to highlight topical points, and larger, more complete projects that demonstrate the topics covered in the chapter with actual Web applications and Web Services built with ASP.Net in VS.Net. The first few chapters cover basic programming concepts; installation and setup of the IDE; ASP.Net objects and their methods, properties, and events; and so forth. In the middle and later chapters, SQL Server databases and Web Services are introduced so that more complex applications can be built. Finally, a complete distributed application is designed and created. Following is a short outline of the contents of the chapters.

- **Chapters 1–3** cover the basics of Active Server Pages and ASP.Net, the main IDE used in the book (Visual Studio.Net), HTTP Requests and Responses, and the ASP.Net Web Application template. Chapter 1 reviews ASP.Net, provides a tour of Visual Studio.Net, and shows how easy it is to get started making an application. Chapter 2 discusses HTTP and the Request and Response objects, as these are fundamental to interactivity online, as well as how classes, object, properties, methods, and events are intertwined. Chapter 3 discusses common files that can be found in ASP.Net applications, and

- **Chapters 4–6** over coding languages, the concept of applications and sessions, and important user interface considerations, all key ingredients of complete Web applications. Chapter 4 covers markup languages (such as HTML, XHTML, and the XML specification), interpreted languages (such as VBScript and Javascript), and programming languages (such as Visual Basic.Net). While not a programming text, this book covers essentials such as variables, data types, operators, and expressions, so students will have a fundamental understanding of how programming works in an ASP.Net application. Chapter 5 covers the concept of state as related to the Application and Session objects in ASP.Net and the role of the Global.asax file and discusses the ViewState property available to ASP.Net. Chapter 6 covers the concept of interface and the importance of user-friendly interface design for online applications and discusses how scope affects programming in ASP.Net applications using VB.Net, as well as the basics of application configuration with Web.config files. Upon completing these chapters, students will be familiar and comfortable with markup, interpreted, and programming languages as used in ASP.Net and will understand the importance of state and how to manage it in an online environment. Students also will have a basic roadmap for creating user interfaces, and a firm understanding of how configuration files affect ASP.Net Web applications.

- **Chapters 7 and 8** are primarily concerned with the design and use of databases, and SQL Server databases are used to demonstrate many common application-related database requirements. Chapter 7 covers the creation of tables, fields, and views in SQL Server, while Chapter 8 introduces ADO.Net and the many objects available for working with databases in ASP.Net applications. Upon completion of these chapters students will understand relational database concepts, basic SQL queries such as SELECT and INSERT, and ADO.Net objects such as the Connection and Command objects and the ADO.Net DataAdapter and DataSet objects.

- **Chapters 9 and 10** cover XML Web Services and ASP.Net Web application debugging. Chapter 9 covers UDDI, WSDL, SOAP, and important Web Service design considerations, while Chapter 10 covers performance tuning basics and how to use Trace features of ASP.Net and the debugging tools available in VS.Net. Upon completion of these chapters students will be ready to design, program, debug, and deploy their ASP.Net Web applications.

- The accompanying CD contains answers for all Quick Check Questions and Exercises, and all code examples from throughout the chapters and Hands On Projects. Note that printed code examples are for illustration only and should not be copied manually; the code examples and the project files on the CD were copied directly from the server and work properly, and should therefore be used for all in-class demonstrations.

Acknowledgments

My thanks to the McGraw-Hill team: Lisa, Dan, and all the editors and production staff who worked so hard to get this book into shape on a short timeline. Particular thanks go to Dan Silverburg, who acquired the project, and Lisa Chin-Johnson, who managed it. The entire team, from proofreading to production, was very professional. The academic reviewers and professional programmers who reviewed each chapter offered many suggestions that made this a better textbook. Jeff Davis at UCSD provided a very competent technical review in a very short space of time, and a great deal of expertise during the writing process.

Finally, thanks to David Fugate at Waterside Productions. Dave, I've said it before and I'll say it again: You're the best!

Brief Contents

1. ASP.NET   1
2. The ASP.Net Template   47
3. HTTP Classes   81
4. ASP.Net and Languages   115
5. Applications & Sessions   153
6. The User Interface (UI)   181
7. Databases and SQL   209
8. Introduction to ADO.Net   243
9. XML Web Services   289
10. ASP.Net Optimizing and Debugging   319

Contents

CHAPTER 1

ASP.NET   1

Learning Objectives   1

Introduction   1

What Is Active Server Pages.Net?   2
- How ASP and ASP.Net Are Processed   2
- Web Application Development   4
- Before Installing ASP.Net   8

What Does ASP.Net Do?   9
- ASP.Net Objects   9
- Building and Hosting ASP.Net Web Applications   11

Discussion—ASP.Net Web Applications   13

The Visual Studio.Net IDE   14
- Installing and Configuring VS.Net   14
- The .Net Framework   14
- VS.Net Features   15
- A Tour of VS.Net   15

How Examples Are Organized in This Book   27

Discussion—VS.Net Features   28

Creating an ASP.Net Web Application in VS.Net   29
- Solutions and Projects   29

> Quick Check Questions   30
> Summary   30
> Exercise   31
> Hands On Project   31
> Alerts and Advice   44
> Key Terms   45
> Review Questions   45

CHAPTER 2

The ASP.Net Template   47

Learning Objectives   47

Introduction   47

Differences between ASP and ASP.Net   48
- .NET Structures and Languages   48
- Migrating from ASP to ASP.Net   49

ASP.Net Web Application Files   50
- ASP.Net Web Application Structure   51
- ASP.Net Page Processing   63

Discussion—The VB.Net ASP.Net Template   65

ASP.Net Directives   65
- Coding Directives   66

Discussion—ASP.Net Directives   68

> Quick Check Questions   68
> Summary   69
> Exercises   69
> Hands On Project   72
> Alerts and Advice   79
> Key Terms   79
> Review Questions   79

CHAPTER 3

HTTP Classes 81

Learning Objectives 81

Introduction 81

Internet Communications and HTTP 82
- HyperText Transport Protocol (HTTP) 83

Objects, Properties, Methods, and Events 85
- Object-Oriented Programming (OOP) 86
- Base Classes and Objects 87
- Properties 88
- Methods 88
- Events 89
- Control Objects and ASP.Net 89

Discussion—Controls in ASP.Net Applications 92

The HttpContext Class 92
- HttpContext Properties 92

The HttpRequest Class 93
- HttpRequest Properties 93
- HttpRequest Methods 99

The HttpResponse Class 100
- HttpResponse Properties 100
- HttpResponse Methods 102

The HttpServerUtility Class 103
- The HttpServerUtility ScriptTimeout Property 103
- HTTPServerUtility Methods 103

Discussion—HTTP Classes 104

- Quick Check Questions 105
- Summary 105
- Exercise 113
- Hands On Project 106
- Alerts and Advice 113
- Key Terms 113
- Review Questions 114

CHAPTER 4

ASP.Net and Languages 115

Learning Objectives 115

Introduction 115

Web Sites and Web Applications 116
- How Traditional Web Sites Work 116
- How Web Applications Work 117

Programming Language Basics 118
- Markup, Interpreted, and Compiled Languages 118

Markup Languages and Specifications 119
- HTML and SGML 119
- XML and XHTML 121

Scripting (Interpreted) Languages 125
- Php and VBScript 125
- Javascript 125

VB.Net and Other Compiled Languages 126
- Compiled Language Features 126

Discussion—Markup, Interpreted, and Compiled Programming Languages 132

The Concept of Scope 133
- Scope in VB.Net 134

Discussion—Scope 136

- Quick Check Questions 136
- Summary 136
- Exercises 137
- Hands On Project 138
- Alerts and Advice 150
- Key Terms 151
- Review Questions 152

CHAPTER 5: Applications & Sessions 153

Learning Objectives 153

Introduction 153

State 154
- ASP.Net Web Application State 154

Applications and Sessions 157
- Application and Session Events 157
- The Global.asax File 158
- The Intrinsic Application and Session Objects 160
- ASP.Net Sessions 162

Discussion—Applications and Sessions 164

- Quick Check Questions 165
- Summary 165
- Exercises 166
- Hands On Projects 167
- Key Terms 180
- Review Questions 180

Validation 189
- ASP.Net Validation Controls 190
- Server-Side and Client-Side Validation 190
- Regular Expressions 191

Discussion—User Interfaces 191

Caching ASP.Net Applications 192
- Output Caching 192
- Data Caching 193

Discussion—Caching 194

Configuring ASP.Net Web Applications 194
- ASP.Net Web.config Configuration Files 195

Discussion—Application Configuration 198

- Quick Check Questions 198
- Summary 199
- Exercises 199
- Hands On Projects 200
- Key Terms 208
- Review Questions 208

CHAPTER 6: The User Interface (UI) 181

Learning Objectives 181

Introduction 181

The User Interface (UI) 182
- Basic UI Requirements 183
- User Interface Design 183
- User Interface Development 185

The Page Object and Control Objects 188
- Page Events and the Control Execution Lifecycle 188

CHAPTER 7: Databases and SQL 209

Learning Objectives 209

Introduction 209

Databases 210
- Databases in Ecommerce Applications 211
- Designing a Database 211

Discussion—Designing Databases 214

Structured Query Language (SQL) 215
- SQL Database Queries 215
- Joining Tables in SQL Queries 219

Aggregate Queries   220
Stored Procedures   221

Discussion—SQL   221

Practical Database Design   222
Basic OMPGame Application Requirements   222
Database Tables for OMPGame Application   222

Database Engines   224
Selecting a Database Engine   224
Microsoft Access   224
Microsoft SQL Server   225

Discussion—SQL Server   225

> Quick Check Questions   227
> Summary   227
> Exercise   228
> Hands On Projects   229
> Alerts and Advice   241
> Key Terms   242
> Review Questions   242

CHAPTER 8 Introduction to ADO.Net   243

Learning Objectives   243

Introduction   243

Data Providers   244
Database Engines   244
Middleware   244

ADO.Net   246
Making Database Connections   246
Running Database Commands   248
The DataReader   248
The DataAdapter   248

Discussion—ADO.Net   250

OMPGame Business Process   250
Registration   251
Login   251
Game Selection and Start Notification   251
Game Play   252

> Summary   253
> Hands On Project   253
> Alerts and Advice   287
> Key Terms   287
> Review Questions   287

CHAPTER 9 XML Web Services   289

Learning Objectives   289

Introduction   289

XML Web Services and ASP.Net   290
XML Web Services Development Process   290

Discussion—XML Web Services Design   291

XML Web Services Protocols   292
Specific Problems Facing XML Web Service Developers   292
Web Services Description Language (WSDL)   294
Simple Object Access Protocol (SOAP)   299

Discussion—WSDL and SOAP   299

Building Web Services   300
Building XML Web Services Manually   300
Using VS.Net to Build Web Services   300

> Quick Check Questions   301
> Summary   301
> Exercise   301
> Hands On Project   302
> Key Terms   318
> Review Questions   318

CHAPTER 10: ASP.Net Optimizing and Debugging 319

Learning Objectives 319

Introduction 319

Optimizing an ASP.Net Web Application 320

    ASP.Net Specific Performance Improvements 320

    Measuring Web Application Performance 321

    ASP.Net Web Application Testing Tools 322

ASP.Net Web Application Debugging 325

    The Debugging Process 325

    ASP.Net Debugging Tools in VS.Net 327

Discussion—Debugging 327

Deploying an ASP.Net Web Application 328

    Quick Check Questions 328
    Summary 329
    Exercises 329
    Hands On Project 333
    Key Terms 345
    Review Questions 346

ASP.NET

CHAPTER 1

LEARNING OBJECTIVES

Upon completion of this chapter, you will be able to:

1. Briefly explain where Active Server Pages (ASP) originated.
2. Describe how ASP works in a Web page.
3. Understand how ASP and ASP.Net differ.
4. Download ASP.Net executables on the Microsoft site.
5. Check your server to see if ASP or ASP.Net is loaded.
6. Create a simple ASP application manually.
7. Run your ASP application.
8. Review VS.Net features.
9. Create the basis for an ASP.Net application from a VB.Net template.
10. Discuss the fundamental file types for ASP.Net applications.

INTRODUCTION

Active Server Pages.Net is really composed of two parts: Microsoft's Active Server Pages technology and Microsoft's .Net Framework technology. Microsoft created the Active Server Pages (ASP) technology as a response to the need for easier integration of markup language code with server-based scripting languages. The name ASP reflects how the technology makes Web pages "active" via programming that runs on the server.

The .Net Framework technology is a foundation for developing applications that work well over the Internet. .Net is not limited to ASP; rather, it is part of the operating system and is available to many programming languages and applications. Combined with ASP, it brings ASP to the next level for building Web applications.

Although ASP.Net applications can be built by hand (with ordinary text editors), it is much easier to build working applications with Visual Studio.Net. For this book we will use VS.Net extensively. The bulk of our exercises and projects will be built in VS.Net, but the fundamental ASP.Net programming is still done manually (but is also easier done in VS.Net's Source Code Editor).

The overall purpose of this textbook is to familiarize you with the many built-in ASP.Net objects and cover fundamental programming and Web application development using ASP.Net. The exercises and projects in this book are done using ASP.Net, and most of the code is written in Visual Basic Scripting Edition (VBScript) or Visual Basic.Net, but we also make use of other tools, application programs, and programming languages.

In this chapter we introduce ASP and ASP.Net, discuss the server requirements and development environments you may use with ASP.Net, discuss when ASP or ASP.Net is an appropriate technology to solve a particular application requirement, and create some simple Web applications.

What Is Active Server Pages.Net?

ASP.Net is Microsoft's next generation of **Active Server Pages (ASP)**, but although some of the code is similar it is really a whole new technology relying on the **.Net Framework**. Notice we refer to both ASP and **ASP.Net** as technologies rather than as programming languages or applications. Neither ASP nor ASP.Net is a programming language, but developers familiar with them know that they are accessed via programming language calls. Think of ASP as a combination of HTML and ASP objects (such as the **Request and Response objects** mentioned in the following example) connected by some interpreted or compiled programming language. ASP.Net works much the same way as ASP, but whereas the connecting language in ASP is often VBScript (an interpreted programming language), the connecting language in ASP.Net is often **Visual Basic.Net** (a compiled programming language).

How ASP and ASP.Net Are Processed

In ASP, you can write code directly between HTML or include HTML in your responses. The ASP code is processed before the HTML code is returned to the user's browser (unless the code is set to run specifically on the client side). The user's browser sees only finished HTML plus any client-side code. In ASP.Net, you create the Web page part of it in one file (very similar to a standard Web page written using HTML), and in another file (called the *code-behind* file) you write programming code. When you are finished and the first page of the application is called for the first time, the entire set of files making up the Web page (the HTML, ASP.Net object calls, and programming language code) is turned into an object that responds as though it were a Web page, thus resulting in faster execution and greater efficiency. This separation of the display (the HTML or XHTML code) from the processing (the VB.Net code in the code-behind page) is one of the great improvements of ASP.Net over ASP.

During your career as a developer, you'll probably encounter ASP and/or ASP.Net in code as well. For example, in ASP, to respond to user input you might write

```
<html>
<head><title>My Web Page</title></head>
<body>
<% Response.Write "<b>Hello</b>" %>
</body>
</html>
```

Notice that the ASP code is contained within HTML tags, and is also placed inside percent-sign delimiters. While all the HTML will be returned to the user, only the HTML tags for Bold (`<b>` and `</b>`) and the word "Hello" will be returned because the ASP is processed on the server.

This code would have to be written in a file with an ending (filename extension) of .asp, and the file would have to be running on a Web server (such as IIS) that is capable of executing code containing calls to ASP objects (meaning that the ASP technology has been loaded onto the server). The call to Request is a reference to an object representing the way communications occur using HTTP (the standard Web communications protocol) and we'll explain HTTP in greater detail in Chapter 3.

If this environment had been properly set up (it's easy to do by default when installing Windows 2000), then when the user connected with the site via any browser and hit the ASP file, the user would see as a response "Hello" in their browser. Making very simple responses is really no more difficult than that.

The "Response" part of the code above is not a programming language command; it is a call to the ASP "Response" object. Let's add some VBScript code so we can tell where one starts and the other leaves off. Here's an example that accepts form input and responds according to the input submitted:

```
<%
If Request.Form("name") = "Jim" Then
   Response.Write "Hello"
Else
   Response.Write "Goodbye"
End If
%>
```

In this example we've added some VBScript code that forms a control flow structure. If the user submits (via an HTML form field named "name") the name "Jim", the application responds by saying "Hello". If the user submits anything else, the application responds by saying "Goodbye". The VBScript code is distinct from the ASP objects in use (Response and Request), but the two are intermingled.

In ASP.Net there are **objects** similar to the Request and Response objects. Later in this book we'll list and give details about the ASP.Net objects that are available when ASP.Net is installed on your server, as well as much of the VB.Net language keywords, functions, structures, and so forth.

Since many applications have already been written using ASP, it is important to note that if both ASP and ASP.Net have been installed on your server, both ASP and ASP.Net applications can run side by side. They are processed by the asp.dll and aspnet_isapi.dll, respectively. By the way, one quick means of checking your server to see which has been loaded is to run files with the .asp or .aspx extension and see if they are processed by the server.

So to answer the question "What is ASP.Net?", it is a technology designed to make creating dynamic **Web applications** and XML Web services easier and more efficient. By way of comparison, if you were to write from scratch all the code required to capture user input from a Web page form and respond to that input, it would be possible but would take much more time and effort.

Web Application Development

If you are very familiar with your own computer, you know that it is made from pieces of hardware, such as a hard disk drive, a video card, a CD-ROM drive, a motherboard, and so forth. When you turn it on, software embedded in the motherboard (the BIOS) runs through a series of checks to make sure all the basic hardware is connected and working. Next, the typical computer will boot up the operating system (typically some form of Windows, Mac OS, or Linux). Once these things have been done, the computer is ready to do useful work.

For many years, useful work has been performed by desktop **application programs**. For example, you might run Microsoft Excel to create and use spreadsheets. Interestingly, Excel lets you create any type of spreadsheet you want, and once you've created a spreadsheet suitable for a particular purpose, you might then give it to someone else for data entry or report creation.

The rise of the Internet and the World Wide Web has made online or Web-based applications more appealing. Like desktop applications, Web applications receive input, process data, and produce output. But unlike desktop applications, Web applications can coordinate the input of many users in real time and can connect to other data sources in real time. This makes them much more powerful than stand-alone desktop applications. While not every application needs to be Web-enabled, there are good reasons to think that the bulk of applications will be eventually.

So one way to categorize applications is into Windows (desktop) and Web applications. Web applications typically use your browser as the user interface, while Windows applications use forms that run in ordinary windows from the desktop. The development process for either type of application is quite similar, although there are some issues and concerns that are different. Actually programming the two types of applications used to be quite different, but lately even that is becoming similar. The next few sections discuss the development process and development tools, and the following diagram (Illustration 1.1) shows how the process generally works.

Application Development

Applications, whether Windows or Web, do a few basic functions: accept input, process data, and produce output. Applications intended for use by humans have some kind of user interface, while applications intended for use by machines have interfaces that may be difficult or impossible for people to use. The primary considerations developers face, aside from such things as the actual features of the application, are size, speed, reliability, and security. Other important considerations are robustness, ease of use, maintainability, and so on. As an application developer, your development cycle also may be affected by the amount of time and money available for the project. And, of course, at some point you will need to focus on the actual features your application must have to perform its intended functions.

Applications typically start as an idea, perhaps occurring to you, or perhaps occurring to your boss, your client, upper management, the marketing department, or your friends. The first step in creating an application from an idea (assuming the decision makers feel the idea is worth the effort) is to build a project plan.

For business applications, the project plan should outline the background of the idea, why it is considered valuable and worth making into an application (the business need), how it will integrate into existing business processes, how it answers the primary considerations mentioned in the previous paragraph, and the time and money to be devoted to it. It also should contain a proposed development solution, although it's not necessary to spell out in detail every programming aspect of the application.

The project plan also should indicate the features and functions expected of the application, in enough detail that developers will be able to program them. Typically, the project plan also will indicate whether the client or sponsor of the application expects it to be a Web application, or Web-enabled.

From that point the project plan is a working document that may be modified as the project proceeds. Large-scale tasks that appear in the project plan may

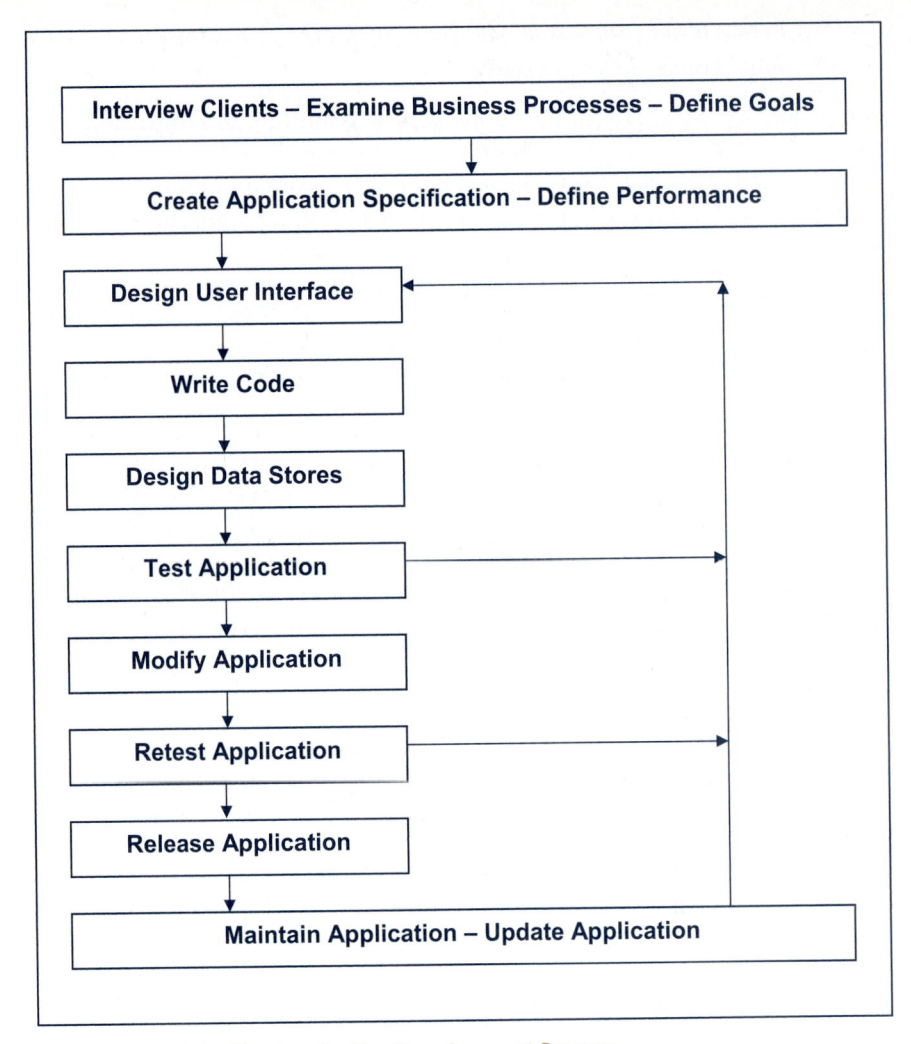

```
┌─────────────────────────────────────────────────────────┐
│  Interview Clients – Examine Business Processes – Define Goals │
└─────────────────────────────────────────────────────────┘
                            ↓
┌─────────────────────────────────────────────────────────┐
│    Create Application Specification – Define Performance │
└─────────────────────────────────────────────────────────┘
                            ↓
┌──────────────────────────┐
│   Design User Interface  │ ←───────────────────┐
└──────────────────────────┘                     │
                            ↓                     │
┌──────────────────────────┐                     │
│        Write Code        │                     │
└──────────────────────────┘                     │
                            ↓                     │
┌──────────────────────────┐                     │
│    Design Data Stores    │                     │
└──────────────────────────┘                     │
                            ↓                     │
┌──────────────────────────┐                     │
│     Test Application     │ ───────────────┐     │
└──────────────────────────┘                 │     │
                            ↓                 │     │
┌──────────────────────────┐                 │     │
│    Modify Application    │                 │     │
└──────────────────────────┘                 │     │
                            ↓                 │     │
┌──────────────────────────┐                 │     │
│    Retest Application    │ ───────────────┘     │
└──────────────────────────┘                       │
                            ↓                       │
┌──────────────────────────┐                       │
│    Release Application   │                       │
└──────────────────────────┘                       │
                            ↓                       │
┌─────────────────────────────────────────────────┐ │
│   Maintain Application – Update Application     │─┘
└─────────────────────────────────────────────────┘
```

ILLUSTRATION 1.1 The Application Development Process

be broken down into much finer tasks in a project management program, and the project management program may be used to manage the development project. Or perhaps, on smaller development projects, a single developer will just program the entire application in a few days and then review it with the project sponsor, debugging and making changes along the way. Either way, the finished project is likely to be somewhat different than the initial project plan specified, and as it is being tweaked many compromises will be made. One thing to keep in mind: regardless of what was initially specified, the application is successful only when users agree that "it works."

An Example Business Application Suppose you work for a company that sells travel, specifically cruise ship packages. Cruise lines offer discounts if a group has more than eight paying customers. As the Web application developer for the company, you might want to create an application that does the following:

- Advertises available cruises to users.
- Provides them an opportunity to register as a group for specific cruises.
- Accepts payments online.
- Tracks the number of registered users in their group.
- Notifies them when they reach the discount number.
- Notifies if anyone in their group drops off and they lose their discount.

A Web application that performs these functions is perfectly feasible on the Web but would be difficult to create as a stand-alone desktop application. This application could periodically poll the travel company, the cruise line, the registered customers, and so on to manage its activities, while a desktop application would not be able to perform these online functions efficiently (unless the desktop application were actually connected to the Web, but that's another story).

Application Programming Tools

A good computer, the appropriate operating system, and the appropriate technologies are fundamental requirements for application development, but even with this foundation in place there are quite a variety of tools available to help in the development process. While code can be written with simple text-editing tools, and (depending upon the type of application under construction) a compiler may be required, developing applications with only these tools is no longer considered very efficient.

For many years, application developers have been relying more and more on specialized application development tools. Tools include **Integrated Development Environments (IDEs)**, specialized source code editors, debuggers, template files, and built-in objects and features that eliminate much of the routine, boring, tedious, and error-prone aspects of development.

Visual Studio.Net (VS.Net) is our IDE of choice. We use it in this book for developing ASP.Net applications. The ASP.Net application template files that come with VS.Net make it easy to quickly put together an application. We could build these files from scratch, but that wouldn't make us better programmers; it would just take longer. Of course, there are some parts of the template files we'll need to examine and understand, because there might be a time when we need to eliminate or modify these parts, or add new parts. But mostly these templates just eliminate having to hand-code the exact same parts over and over each time we create a new ASP.Net application.

Before Installing ASP.Net

Like any software, ASP.Net is installed as a package, and in order to develop applications with ASP.Net, certain hardware and software requirements must be met. These consist of requirements for the CPU, hard disk drive space, RAM, operating system (OS), and supporting Web server and data component software.

ASP.Net System Requirements

The operating systems on which ASP.Net runs include Windows 2000 and Windows XP. To deploy ASP.Net applications, a Web server is required, such as Microsoft's Internet Information Server (IIS). And there are requirements associated with Visual Studio.Net, such as Microsoft Data Access Components (MDAC) 2.7. We also run Microsoft SQL Server as a data provider, although you can use many other database applications with ASP.Net.

At the time of this writing, Microsoft is recommending the following minimum hardware and OS for Visual Studio.NET:

- Computer/processor—PC with a Pentium II–class processor, 450 megahertz (MHz)
- Operating system—Microsoft Windows XP Professional/Home Edition, 2000 Professional/Server, NT 4.0 Workstation/Server
- Minimum RAM requirements—Windows® XP Professional: 160 megabytes (MB) of RAM; Windows® 2000 Professional: 96 MB of RAM; Windows 2000 Server: 192 MB of RAM; Windows NT 4.0 Workstation: 64 MB of RAM; Windows NT 4.0 Server: 160 MB of RAM
- Hard disk—Standard Edition, 2.5 gigabytes (GB) on installation drive, which includes 500 MB on system drive; Professional and Enterprise Editions, 3.5 GB on installation drive, which includes 500 MB on system drive
- Drive—CD-ROM or DVD-ROM drive
- Display—Super VGA (800 × 600) or higher-resolution monitor with 256 colors
- Input device—Microsoft mouse or compatible pointing device

Acquiring ASP.Net

Visual Studio.Net comes with the ASP.Net package, and you also can find the download for ASP.Net (it's included with the .Net Framework download) online at the Microsoft MSDN site, as well as at www.asp.net (version 1.1 came out as this book was being written). Installing this package on a machine running the appropriate hardware and software will prepare you for developing ASP.Net applications.

There is also a freely available development environment named Web Matrix available at the asp.net site, as well as developer's tools and kits for many application types, including mobile applications. And while we use SQL Server and Access files for database application development, Microsoft offers a free download of MSDE (a database type) from the asp.net site for anyone to use.

What Does ASP.Net Do?

Loading ASP.Net on your server doesn't mean there's another application program there that you can open up and interact with in a visual way, like Microsoft Word or Microsoft Access. By itself, ASP.Net is just part of the .Net Framework, and the objects in ASP.Net are available for use in ASP.Net Web Applications.

So what's included? ASP.Net includes a number of objects that simplify user interactions across the Web, such as the Request and Response objects. ASP.Net also includes a facility for writing code that runs at the application level, meaning you can preserve data across the entire application, as well as across sessions. And unlike ASP, ASP.Net code is compiled so it runs faster, while at the same time any changes you make are immediately picked up and included the next time files containing those changes are accessed. ASP.Net settings are contained in one or more configuration files, allowing you fine-grained control over Web application configuration. And there are a number of programming, security, and performance features built in to ASP.Net to make it easy to build and fine-tune your Web applications.

ASP.Net Objects

There are quite a few objects in ASP.Net that will be familiar to developers who've written Web applications with ASP, such as the HttpRequest and HttpResponse objects (derived from their respective classes in the .Net Framework). We'll list some of them here, and in later chapters we'll cover them in depth. You can find a great deal of reference material on all classes available on the MSDN site. The documentation in this site is arranged in hierarchical fashion, so look in .Net Development|.Net Framework SDK|.Net Framework|Reference|ClassLibrary|System Web.

- **HttpRequest**—Objects derived from this class read the incoming HTTP values sent by a client (submitted from an HTML form in a browser, for example). In your code, you would call this object and examine its Form collection (a collection of name–value pairs corresponding to the names of the HTML form fields and the values submitted by a user) to pick out the value submitted by the user for each field. This object also contains values submitted with a query string (attached to the end of a URL in a link that has been clicked), cookies value, server variable values, and so forth. See Chapter 3 for more information.

- **HttpResponse**—Objects derived from this class send data back to the user in the HTTP response from the server. Plain text can be sent, or text formatted as HTML, Javascript, and so forth. The Write method sends text to the user's browser, so in your code you would call this object and the Write method to send back any responses you wish to the user. This object also supports redirecting the user to another Web page, writing cookies, and so forth. See Chapter 3 for more information.
- **HttpContext**—This class provides access to the intrinsic Request, Response, and Server objects for the current request.
- **HttpServerUtility**—The intrinsic **Server object** can be used to create other objects, retrieve and clear errors, encode and decode HTML, and so on.
- **HttpCookie**—Objects derived from this class can be used to retrieve or set the names and values of cookies, set their expiration, find out whether a cookie has subkeys, and so forth.
- **HttpBrowserCapabilities**—Objects derived from this class can be used to get data about the browser the user is using to access the Web application. These data may play a role in the construction of HTML and Javascript sent back to the user in subsequent responses. For example, there are Browser, Major, and Minor properties that contain the name of the browser (i.e., Internet Explorer), major version (i.e., 6), and minor version (i.e., 2800).

Using ASP.Net Objects

With the objects we've listed here, and what we know about programming with Visual Basic and markup languages such as HTML, what kind of Web applications could we create? First off, to illustrate the difference between ordinary Web pages on a Web site and a dynamic Web application, let's discuss how the ordinary Web site works:

1. Following the development of a specification for the look and feel (the graphics, colors, page layout, and text and image content) of the Web site, the graphic designer (often also proficient with HTML and Web page design) creates a basic template for the pages of the Web site. This includes the graphics, the HTML, and perhaps some example starting text and images.

2. The template is then used by the Web site construction team to create basic Web pages using HTML files, one for each page on the Web site. Once the content is entered, it is changed by opening the HTML file (usually in an HTML editor) and manually changing the text content. The graphics and page layout remain the same, or with very minor modifications.

3. Users click on links or enter URLs in the address bar of their browser to browse to the Web site's pages.

4. As users browse, the Web server simply copies out to them the pages they've requested, with no changes to the HTML or text content.

In contrast, Web applications follow a different development and usage pathway:

1. A specification for both the look and feel and the application functions of the Web site is designed. The graphic designer still designs the overall look and feel, but the application functions are now developed by programmers and database designers.

2. When the templates for the look and feel are delivered, the application developers incorporate elements of the template into all the pages the user sees.

3. Rather than the Web site being composed of static HTML pages, one for each page the user might view, the server responds to user requests by running code, connecting to databases, processing user input, and creating responses containing HTML, text, and graphics based on the results of the processed input.

4. As users browse, what they see might be entirely new and different from what any other user is seeing. Additionally, changes in content are often made by administrative users changing database content, rather than anyone making changes to HTML files.

So with the ASP.Net objects listed above, a working knowledge of HTML, and some Visual Basic .Net programming, we could create an application that does the following:

- Check to see what browser the user is using to view the Website.
- Deliver a home page coded in HTML to render well on the user's browser.
- Set a cookie on the user's browser that distinguishes that user from other users, so the site could remember them the next time they visit.
- Capture values submitted by the user from an HTML form (or from a link the user clicked).
- Perform data processing functions on those values and deliver to the user different HTML, text, or image content based on the results.

Building and Hosting ASP.Net Web Applications

The difference between Web applications and ordinary desktop Windows applications is diminishing. Both types of application have a Windows-based user interface, and both often use databases for data storage, with data processing in between to manage the application and produce the desired results. The following diagram (Illustration 1.2) gives an idea of the relationship between personal computers, operating systems, Windows applications, Web servers, and Web applications.

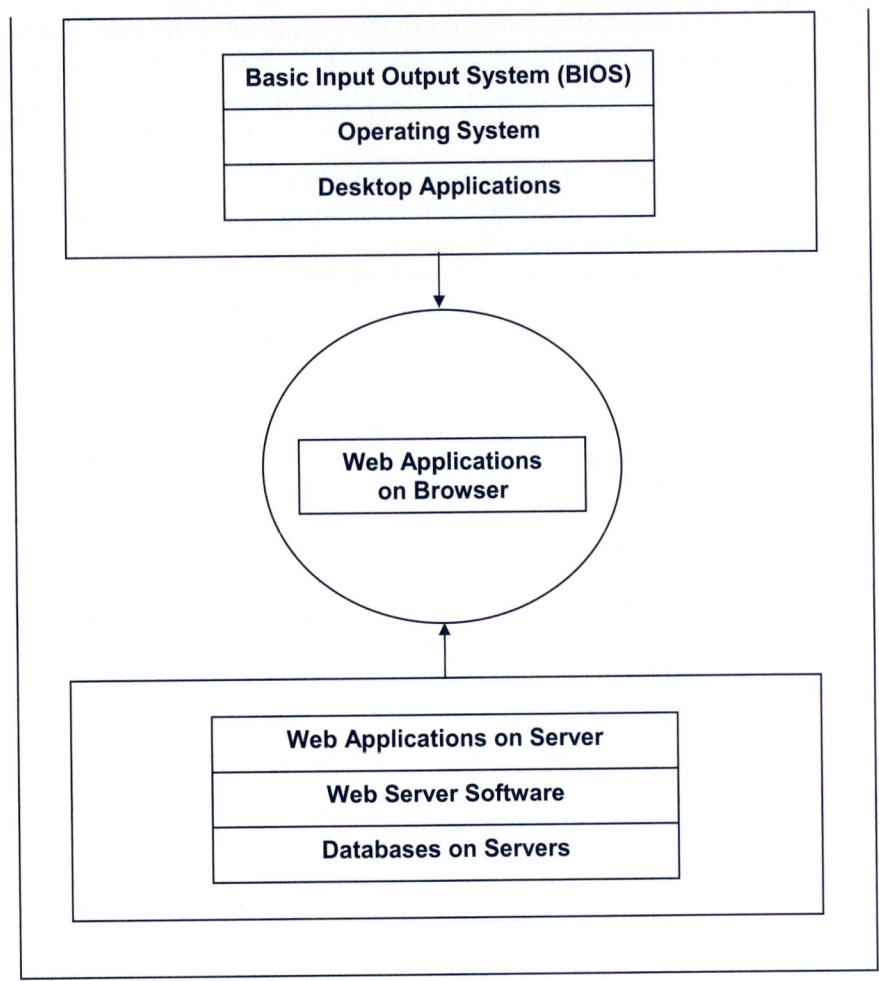

ILLUSTRATION 1.2 The Relationship between Computers, Servers, and Applications

Windows applications are generally self-contained, meaning they come with all the user interface, processing logic, and back-end data built in, and run locally on your computer. Web applications, in contrast, rely on your browser to render the user interface, must be connected to the Internet to run, and may have their processing logic and data stores distributed anywhere on the Internet. Due to their distributed nature, Web application development is a bit more complex, and hosting issues are a greater concern.

Hosting Web Applications
Since most of the processing takes place on the server, and the server may be servicing multiple users (sometimes thousands) at any given time, the hardware and software making up the server must be very robust. Server comput-

ers often contain multiple processors and a large amount of RAM, as well as plenty of hard disk drive space. Sometimes servers have a RAID (redundant array of inexpensive drives) system for redundant data storage, and sometimes the servers are grouped into "server farms," in which multiple servers serve a single application. Another key consideration for servers is the amount of bandwidth available to the server. Running short of processor power or of bandwidth can greatly affect a server's ability to support a Web application.

Web server software for ASP.Net applications will generally be Internet Information Server (IIS), while Web applications running on Unix variations are often supported by Apache. Web server software manages incoming HTTP requests and outgoing HTTP responses, and mediates the data processing and database connections taking place in between.

Developing Web Applications

While we use Visual Basic.Net as our language of choice, developers often use the language (or languages) they are most familiar with to write the processing logic for Web applications. Languages such as VBScript (often used with ASP), Php and Perl (often used on Linux servers), Visual Basic.Net and C# (used on Windows servers with .Net), C++, Python, and so forth are commonly used to build Web application programming logic. Fortunately, ASP.Net can be used in conjunction with many of these languages, so long as a compiler is available to turn their code into the Intermediate Language state for the **Common Language Runtime** employed by the .Net Framework. This makes the development process smoother and reduces the learning curve of skilled developers.

Discussion—ASP.Net Web Applications

Application programs are the workhorses of today's computers. While BIOS and operating systems make our computers ready to run, and server software supports many computer-to-computer interactions, application programs are what people deal with to get work done. Examples of application programs are Microsoft Word, Excel, and Access.

One way to categorize application programs is as Desktop Windows applications and Web applications. Windows applications are for the most part self-contained and come with their user interface, processing logic, and data. Web applications follow a more distributed model, with the user interface provided by the user, the processing logic running on one or more servers somewhere on the Internet, and data stored in one or more databases or other data structures, also located somewhere on the Internet.

ASP.Net is a Microsoft technology (not a programming language) that provides objects facilitating common tasks that Web applications must perform.

ASP.Net works closely with the .Net Framework to make the development of Web applications easier, and to make the resulting applications more efficient while running and easier to maintain. Developing Web applications using ASP.Net means some basic system requirements must be met, and the finished applications are affected by the same variables (processor performance and available bandwidth) that any Web applications face.

The Visual Studio.Net IDE

Developing ASP.Net Web applications can be done by hand, meaning you can use nothing more complicated than a plain text editor (such as Notepad) to write all the files making up your application (except perhaps the graphics and other resources of this type). So long as you store the Web application files in the proper folders on an Internet-connected computer running the right operating system and Web server software, your application should run.

Efficient Web application development is another story. Many of the files, including their names and extensions as well as their actual content, are the same or similar for all your ASP.Net Web applications, and much of the code you'll write falls into the same basic categories of syntax and content. What this means is that the developer who uses an Integrated Development Environment (IDE) such as Visual Studio.Net (VS.Net) will have a big advantage over the developer who tries to hand-code all the content. That's why we use VS.Net extensively in this book.

Installing and Configuring VS.Net

VS.Net is an application program like any other, and it has its own set of hardware and software requirements (noted in the system requirements). In this book we run VS.Net on the same server upon which our Web applications run.

Installation

Installing VS.Net begins with putting the CD disks in; you are prompted for typical answers during the installation process. If your system needs certain Windows components, your installation disks will supply them, in particular Microsoft Data Access Components. The correct version of these components is crucial for your ASP.Net Web applications that are database driven.

The .Net Framework

You may notice that during installation the .Net Framework was installed (if it was not already present on your computer). ASP.Net is part of the .Net Framework. The Framework itself is essentially a set of classes and a programming model that .Net-enabled Windows and Web applications can take advantage of.

One of the major parts of the .Net Framework is the Common Language Runtime (CLR). The CLR is the basis of .Net, and supports language integration (because developers can write applications in several languages), security, memory management, and process and thread management.

Another major part of the .Net Framework is the base classes. Among the base classes are

- ADO.Net classes—for data management
- SQL classes—for SQL-based data management
- XML classes—for working with XML documents and Web services
- ASP.Net classes—for Web applications
- Windows Forms classes—for Windows applications

When you are developing Web applications with ASP.Net in VS.Net, you will use many of these classes, no matter which language you use. Your applications will automatically take advantage of the .Net Framework while running, relieving you of many common application chores that developers find tedious.

VS.Net Features

VS.Net contains, as its name implies, many visual tools that let you see something close to what your applications are going to look like in use and allow you to drag and drop elements onto your application forms. You also can format, arrange, size, and align elements on your forms with your mouse and change their properties in the **Properties window**. VS.Net writes the code reflecting your changes automatically, making the entire process much more intuitive.

VS.Net also contains code editors suited to specific types of code, such as HTML, XML, VB.Net, and C#. These editors help you find the right keywords, elements, and attributes; offer tips to help you write functions properly; and complete code blocks properly for you. These editors go far beyond ordinary text editors in helping write clean code quickly.

Finally, VS.Net contains a number of highly useful debugging tools that make analyzing your code and fixing errors less of a burden and less time-consuming. You can examine variable values, set breakpoints, and build and rebuild your application quickly to see the effects of your changes.

A Tour of VS.Net

Like any desktop application, VS.Net opens in a window, has menus and toolbars to control the action, and works on a variety of file types to accomplish your goals. The menus and toolbars are context sensitive, meaning that the choices on them are displayed or become active depending upon what file type you are working with or what part of an operation you are currently involved in. For example, with VS.Net open but no solutions, projects, or files open, the menu choices are fairly limited, and even those displayed are sometimes "grayed out" or inactive.

Merely opening VS.Net without opening anything to work on does produce a limited menu, and the choices available are common to most desktop applications. For example, there is a File menu in which you can create new files, projects, and solutions; open existing ones; and save them. There is an Edit menu that lets you undo and redo actions, as well as cut, copy, and paste selected text and objects. The following sections discuss these and other main menu choices in more detail and a few of the tools we'll use as we build ASP.Net Web applications.

Opening VS.Net

Opening VS.Net is as simple as clicking Start|Programs|Microsoft Visual Studio.Net|Microsoft Visual Studio.Net from your Windows desktop. The application should resemble Figure 1.1 the first time you open it.

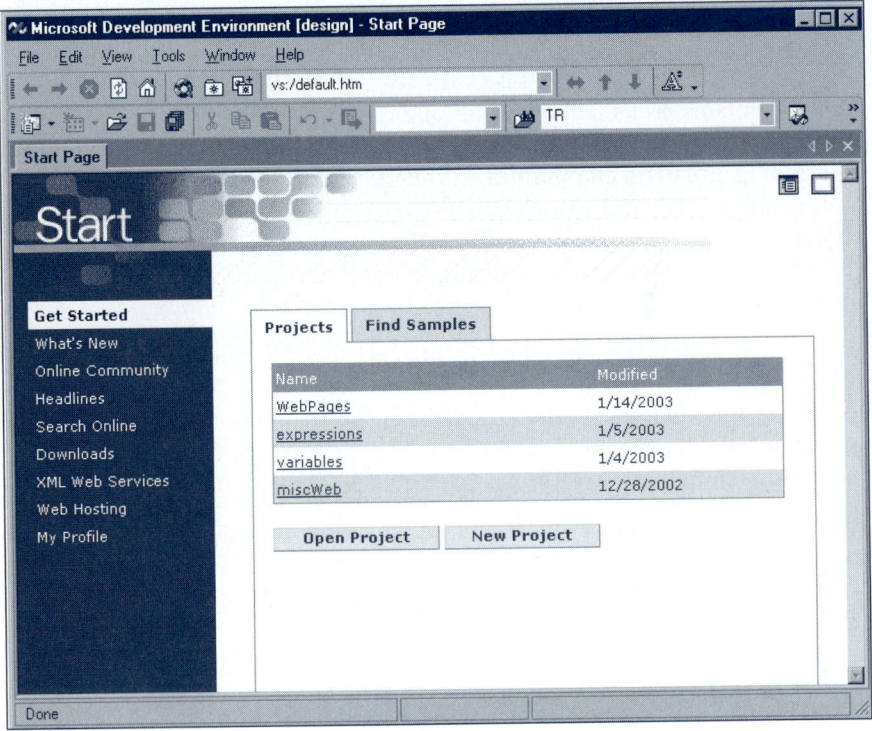

FIGURE 1.1   Visual Studio.Net with Start Page

On the menu, go to Tools|Options to open the Options dialog box. Here is where you can set many of your preferences for the way in which you interact with VS.Net (Figure 1.2). You should already be in the Environment node on

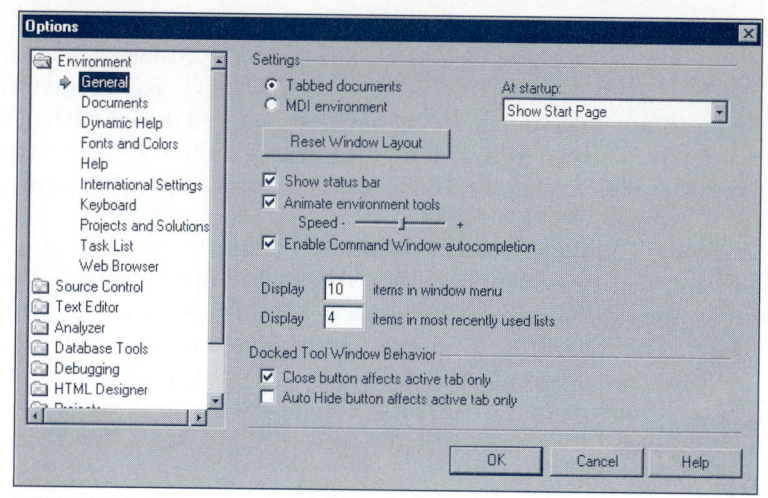

FIGURE 1.2 The Options Dialog Box

the General tab. Go to the drop-down box under "At startup" and choose "Show empty environment", then click OK. Go to the File menu and choose Exit (or click the Exit button at the top right of the application window), then open VS.Net again. You should now see VS.Net as shown in Figure 1.3.

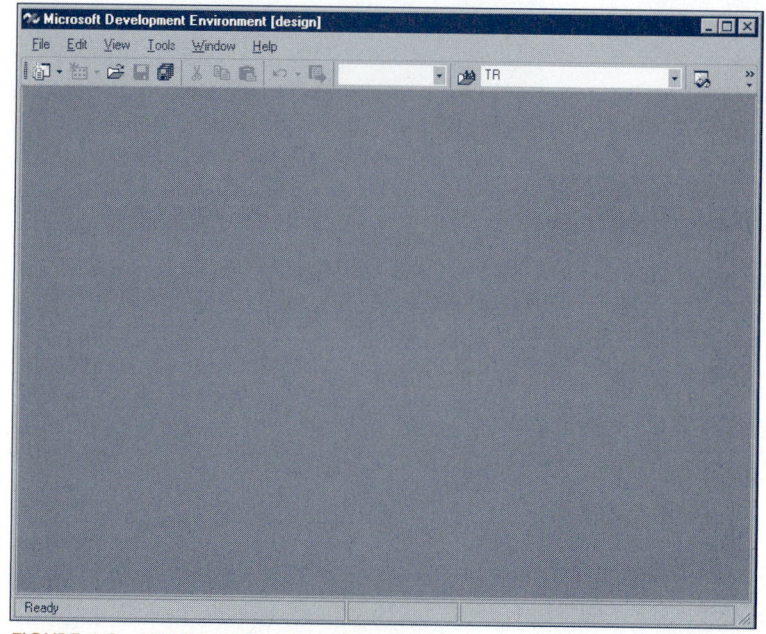

FIGURE 1.3 VS.Net without the Start Page

Menus and Toolbars

On your menu you should see choices for File, Edit, View, Tools, Windows, and Help. Each of these is a drop-down menu with more choices related to the main menu choice it falls under. In the next sections we'll discuss each of these menus and their choices, with a bit of introduction to how VS.Net works and what menu choices and tools are available under normal operating conditions.

The File Menu The File menu contains choices about creating files (and solutions and projects), opening files, saving files, and finding recently worked-on files (and projects). You also can exit VS.Net from this menu. And it has a choice for Source Control, so if you happen to have a source control program (such as Visual Source Safe) installed, you can access it here. Source control is the term used for programs that manage collaborative work on projects, as various individuals work together on the same files. Figure 1.4 shows the basic File menu choices.

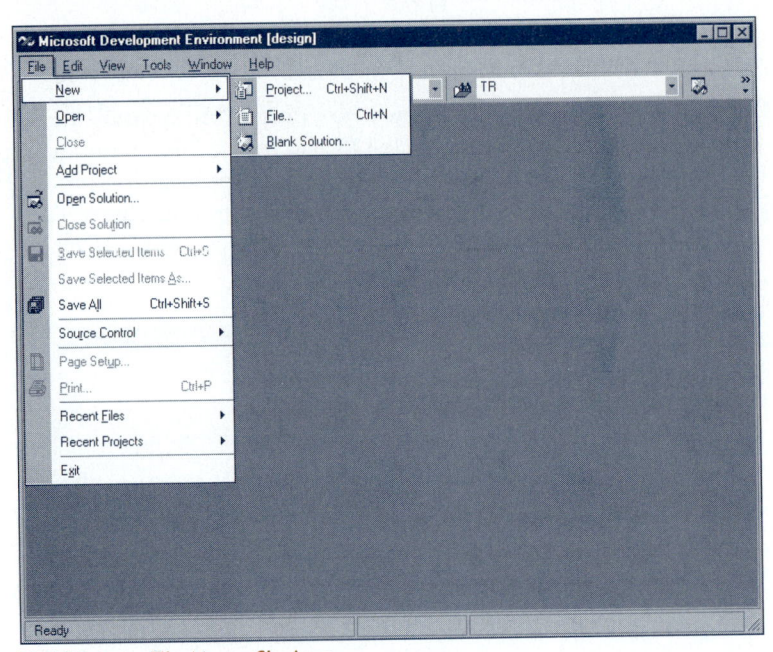

FIGURE 1.4   File Menu Choices

The Edit Menu The Edit menu contains choices about making changes to files you are working on. Typically, these choices are only active when you have a document open, because they only work on text, images, and other objects inside files. For example, if you delete a word in a text document, you can use the Undo and Redo choices on the Edit menu to undo the action, and then redo it if you like. This menu also contains the standard Cut, Copy, Paste, and Delete choices that let you put selected text or objects on the clipboard and copy or move them to other locations in a document (or in other documents).

Another valuable tool you'll find in the Edit menu is Find and Replace (Figure 1.5 shows the Edit menu and the Find and Replace menu). Find and Replace lets you find (and replace) occurrences of text within a document, and as you can see from the figure it also lets you find (and replace) occurrences of text within multiple files that are not opened. Because you can search files that are not open, the choice is active even though we don't have a document open.

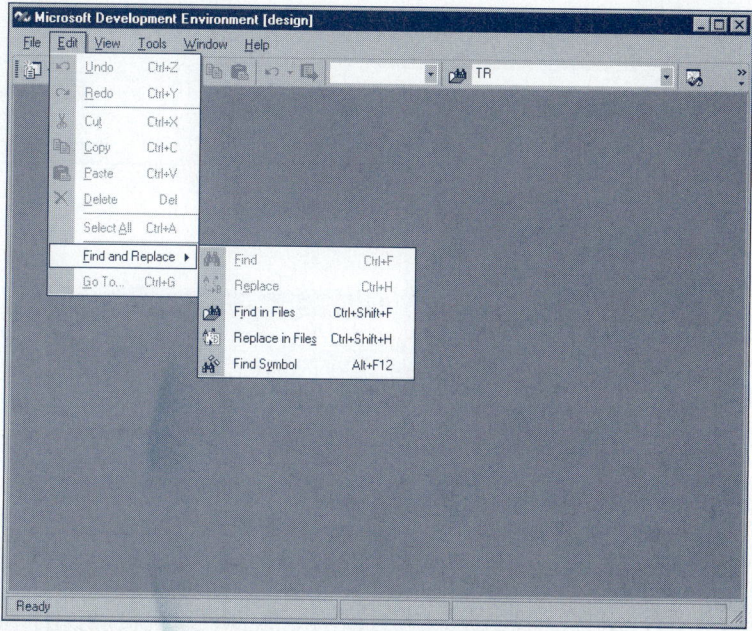

FIGURE 1.5 The Edit Menu, with the Find and Replace Menu

If you choose Edit|Find and Replace|Find in Files, you'll see the Find in Files dialog box as shown in Figure 1.6. Notice that you can tell the tool to match the case of the text you've set it to look for, as well as to match whole words. You also can use Regular expressions, a powerful method for matching similar text strings using patterns rather than exact matches.

Clicking the button with the ellipsis (three little dots) on the right of the "Look in" drop-down box will display the Look In dialog box shown in Figure 1.7. This window lets you select folders and files to examine during your search.

The View Menu The View menu contains choices for opening many of the common tools used to view your files, projects, solutions, and their various components (Figure 1.8). The View tools in this menu choice show you what you are working on from many different angles, and let you inspect the pieces that make them up in detail. Some of the tools give you the further ability to open or work with those files or components.

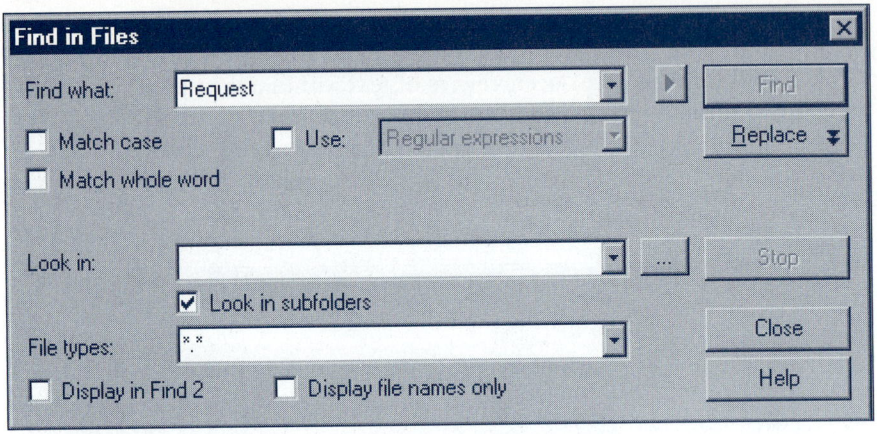

FIGURE 1.6 The Find in Files Dialog Box

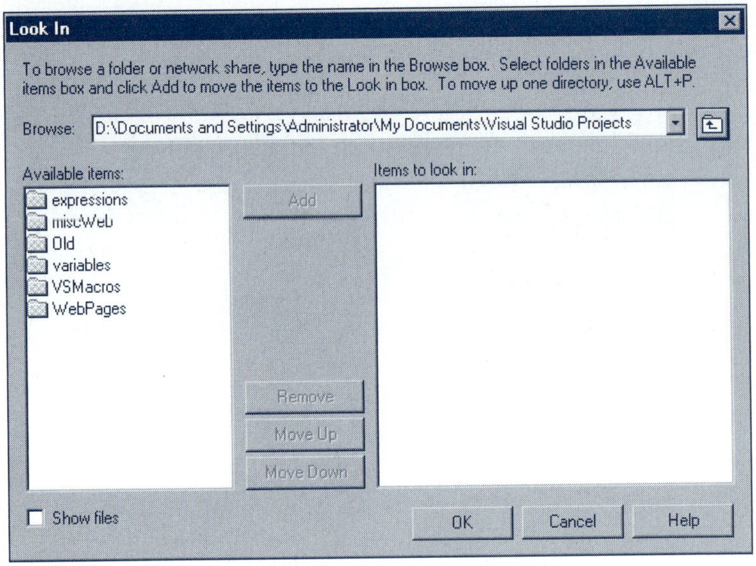

FIGURE 1.7 The Look In Dialog Box

The **Solution Explorer** will open if you click it, but will be a small blank window, as we have no **Solution** open for exploration. If we had a Solution open, we would be able to see the projects, folders, and files in the Solution in a tree-like view similar to the one in Windows Explorer.

The Class View menu displays icons representing symbols of various types, such as namespaces, classes, methods, properties, variables, and events. It provides an easy visual reference to the objects in your projects and their scope (how they can be addressed).

The Visual Studio.Net IDE

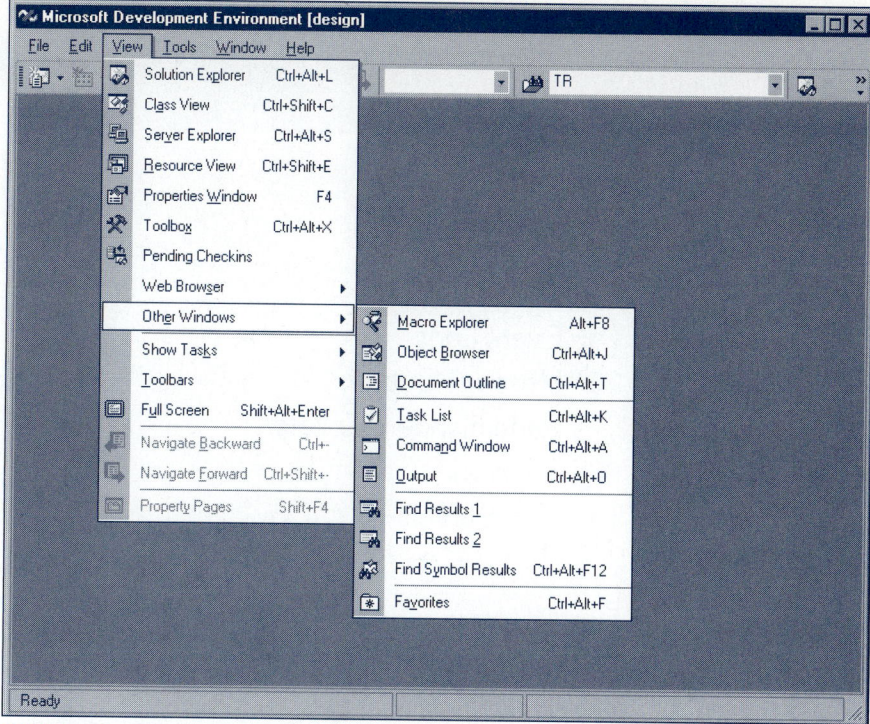

FIGURE 1.8 The View and Other Windows Menus

The Server Explorer gives you a view of the available servers, and allows you to add new ones or make connections to existing ones, including databases. Figure 1.9 shows some of the servers available, as well as the buttons for making connections and refreshing the view.

The Resource View gives you a window to look at all the resource files in your project. Resource files are nonexecutable data that go along with your application, such as error messages. It's important to put these kinds of resources in a separate place so that they can be easily changed without having to reconstruct critical parts of your application, and so that they can be changed just once to affect the appearance of the entire application.

The Properties window, if you open it, also will appear to be a blank window, as we have no file or control open and selected. If something that has properties were open, you'd see a list of all the properties for the item currently selected (the names would be in a column on the left) and corresponding spaces in a column on the right for entering values for each property. For example, if we were working on an HTML file, the **DOCUMENT** (the body of the Web page as it is displayed in a browser) would have a property named "bgcolor" (for background color) and the acceptable values would be a hexadecimal number preceded by the "#" sign (such as #FFFFFF for white) or a named color (such as "white").

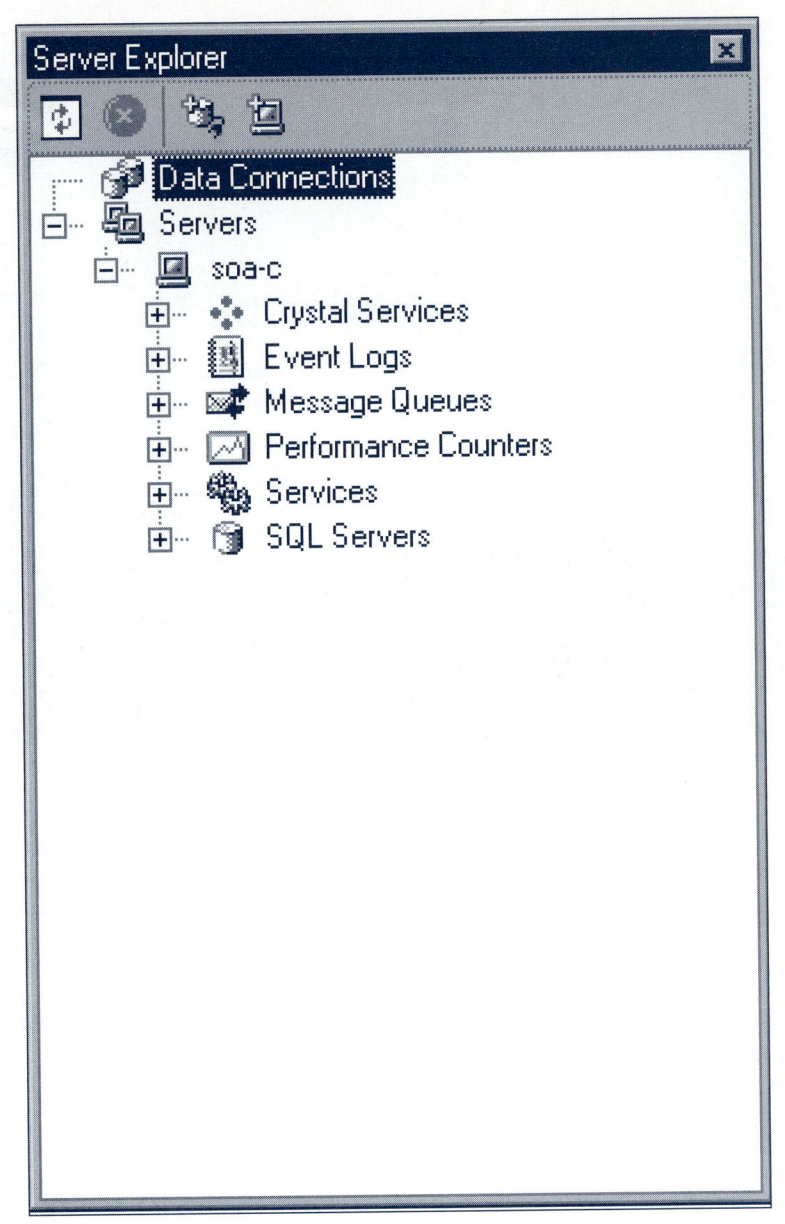

FIGURE 1.9 The Server Explorer

The Toolbox is a container for controls that may be added to your Web application forms (and objects applicable to other applications and file types as well). If you open the Toolbox when you are working on a Web application form, you'll see lists of HTML and server controls that you can drag and drop onto the form. Once you drag a control onto the form, it will be selected, so you can view and set its properties in the Properties window, and you can also modify it visually with your mouse. As you modify the control visually, VS.Net will write the appropriate changes into the properties or into the HTML of the form for you.

Pending Checkins is useful if you are using Source Control, to view files and work with files that have been checked out.

The Web Browser menu choice gives you a menu-driven tool for working with the browser, something you'll commonly do when building ASP.Net Web applications. However, we'll often use the Build and Browse menu choice that appears on the File menu (but only when working on a Web application). Note that you can simply open the browser and keep it ready for working with your application as well.

On the Other Windows menu choice you'll find choices such as Macro Explorer (for working with macros, if you choose to create them), Object Browser (for finding and viewing objects and their members), Document Outline (for viewing documents in the form of an outline showing parent and child relationships between elements in the document), Task List (for managing the assignment and completion of tasks for a project), Command Window (for executing commands and for debugging purposes), Output (for displaying the Output window, showing the output of your applications as they run in Debug mode), several Find Results choices, and Favorites (to quickly get you back to something you found recently while browsing, such as reference material for your application).

The Show Tasks menu choice gives you the Tasks window but also gives you more menu options to work with Tasks. The Toolbars menu choice lets you turn on or off any toolbar available, meaning you can display or not display that toolbar (note that even if you display a toolbar, unless you are working on something that accepts those toolbar actions, they will be inactive or "grayed out"). The Full Screen menu choice simply toggles between your current view of VS.Net and a full-screen view.

The Tools Menu The first choice on the Tools menu, Debug Processes, allows you to view the Processes dialog box and attach to any program so that you can debug it.

The next two choices, Connect to Database and Connect to Server, open the Server Explorer and Connection dialog boxes so you can make new connections to either a database or a server.

The Customize Toolbox menu choice opens the Customize Toolbox dialog box (Figure 1.10). This box lets you choose which controls you would like to have available on the Toolbox for dragging and dropping into your application forms.

The Add-in Manager menu choice opens the Add-in Manager dialog box (Figure 1.11). In this box you may activate available add-ins (utility programs) such as the Web Hosting Provider Upload Utility program shown. These programs operate separately but in conjunction with VS.Net.

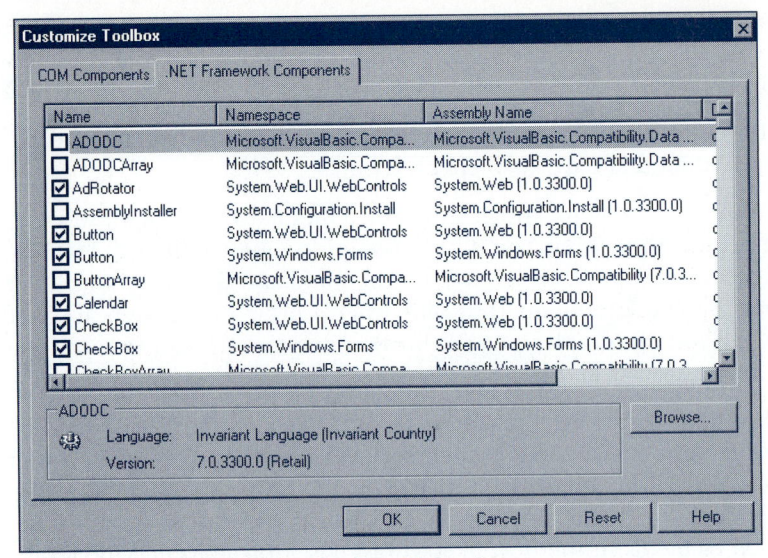

FIGURE 1.10   The Customize Toolbox Dialog Box

FIGURE 1.11   The Add-in Manager Dialog Box

The Macros menu choice gives you a number of menu choices for working with Macros. If you've created or used macros with other applications, you'll find these choices quite familiar.

The next few choices represent external programs that can be started within VS.Net, and the External Tools menu choice opens a dialog box for editing how these external tools are started, as well as adding and deleting them from the menu.

The Customize menu choice opens the Customize dialog box (Figure 1.12). This box is mainly for modifying toolbars by adding and deleting commands from them, and it also contains a button that brings you to the Keyboard customization sections of the Options dialog box, so you can set keyboard shortcuts.

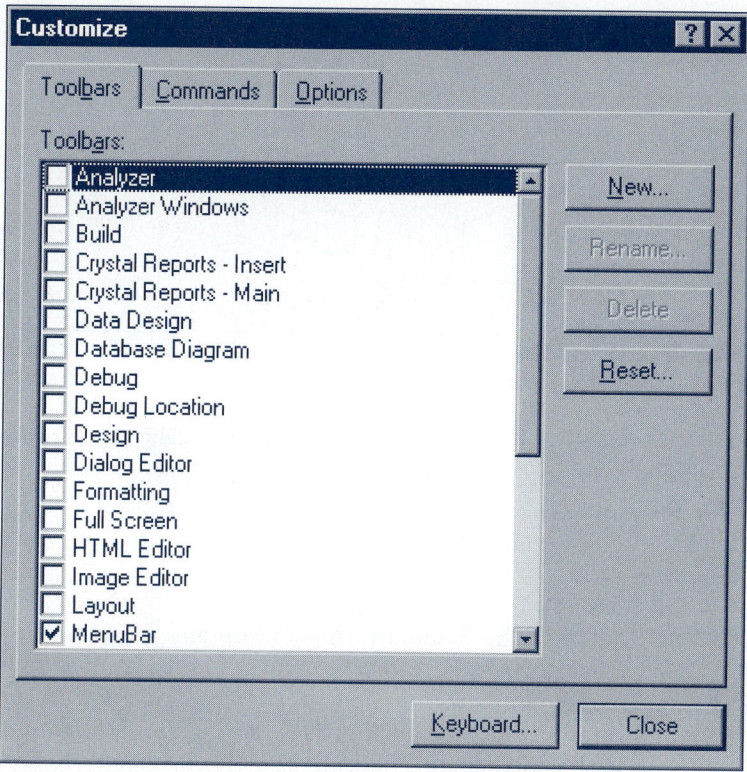

FIGURE 1.12 The Customize Dialog Box

The Options menu choice opens the Options dialog box. This box contains a number of nodes (Environment, Source Control, Text Editor, and so forth), each having subsections (the subsections appear when the node is clicked). Your settings for each subsection appear in the right side of the box when the subsection on the left side is clicked. Figure 1.13 shows the Environment node with the Projects and Solutions subsection displayed. Notice the drive and folder location for solutions can be set here, as well as whether or not the Output window opens when you start to build an application, and other pertinent options.

The Windows and Help Menus The Windows menu choice gives you several choices for working with Windows, mainly to help display your work in a more easily usable way. The Help menu gives you all the standard Help choices,

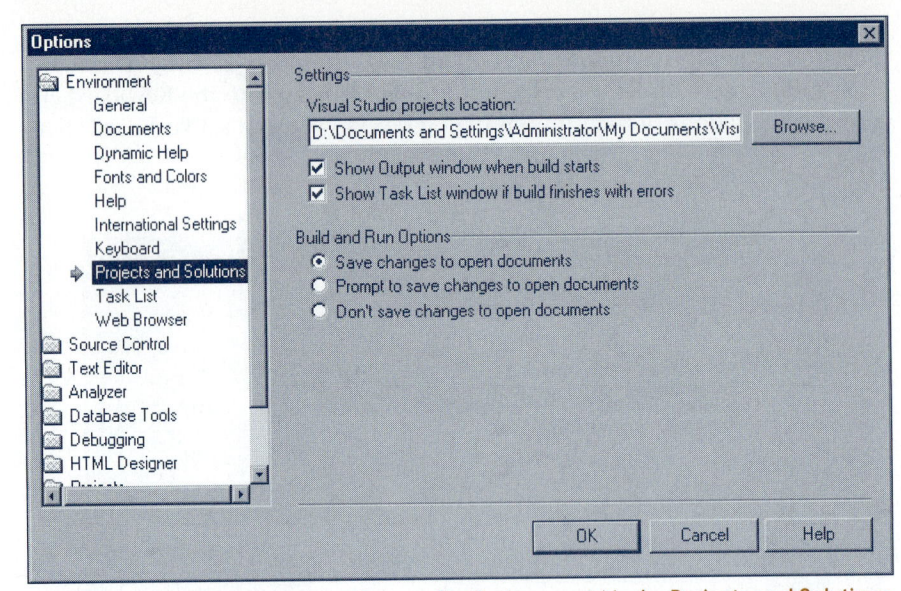

FIGURE 1.13 The Options Dialog Box on the Environment Node, Projects and Solutions

such as searching for Help using the index, dynamically, or using the contents. You also can find out the version and other information about VS.Net using the About VS.Net menu choice, and you can check for updates and get tech support as well.

The Standard Toolbar The Standard Toolbar contains many of the menu choices you can find on the File and Edit menus. The reason it's there is to give you easy access to commonly used menu choices. It just means you have one-click buttons rather than two or three clicks to get to the menu choice. You can display other toolbars by choosing View|Toolbars and then picking the toolbar you'd like to see, and you can customize what's found on toolbars with the Customize menu choice. Keep in mind that you don't have to display all toolbars all the time just to make sure they're available; many of them will open automatically when you begin to work on a particular file type.

VS.Net Editors and Other Tools

Because it is an Integrated Development Environment (IDE), Visual Studio.Net contains a number of editors and designers specifically suited for working with text, code, HTML Web pages, XML documents, and so forth.

The Text and Code Editor The Text Editor functions like a simple text editor when you are working on ordinary text documents, but if you are working with code it become the VS.Net Code Editor. The Code editor provides language-specific support to help you get your syntax right and use functions and objects correctly.

The HTML Designer The HTML Designer, like many HTML editors, gives you a graphical view of your Web page during the design process. The view is much like what you'd see in final form in a browser, thereby making it much easier to place elements on the page and arrange them in a pleasing way. You can work with text in HTML documents much like you would in a word processor, changing fonts and colors, adding tables, creating hypertext links, and so forth. All the changes are written immediately to the HTML code, which you can easily view at the click of a button (and edit as well).

The XML Designer The XML Designer helps you create well-formed and valid XML documents, and has a built-in XML schema generator to help you create XML schemas from the elements and attributes you write. While it isn't so much a visual tool like the HTML Designer, it is extremely helpful for quickly creating and validating XML documents and writing schemas in a more natural way. It also includes a visual tool for working with XML schemas that is much more natural than trying to write the code by hand.

Debugging Tools VS.Net contains a number of powerful tools for assisting with the debugging process (it's very unusual for any application under development not to require debugging). When you build an application (meaning you compile it), the Output window will display error messages if your application doesn't build properly. These errors are low level and mean something about your syntax or calls wasn't right.

Logic or semantic errors result when you've used proper syntax but the processing is not set up properly. For example, if you want to multiply two numbers but use the division operator in your code, the application will still build and run okay, but an incorrect answer will be produced. Catching and fixing these kinds of errors is assisted by setting breakpoints in code. The application will then halt execution at the breakpoint, and you can use the Watch window, the QuickWatch dialog box, and the Memory window to view what's happening inside your application at the specific point. You also can change the value of variables and perform other editing, and then set the application in motion again. These capabilities make it much easier to determine where erroneous values are coming from, and thereby make the appropriate changes to fix your application.

How Examples Are Organized in This Book

As you become more and more familiar with the way VS.Net operates, what menu choices are available, and what actions they perform, we'll spell out what to click less and less specifically. For example, in our first Hands On Project (near the end of this chapter), we indicate what to click to open

Visual Studio.Net from the desktop (Start|Programs|Microsoft Visual Studio.Net|Microsoft Visual Studio.Net). This sequence of clicks will probably never be written out again in this book, as it is so basic that after the first time we expect you to know it. While we'll always include specific buttons and choices to click, and what data to enter, when working on something for the first time (or if it's complex, the first few times) for routine things that you'll do over and over we'll gradually become more concise. For example, we'll just say "Open VS.Net" and expect that you'll have no problem getting it done.

Also, since you may or may not follow each exercise and project exactly as they are done in the book, you may or may not already have VS.Net open. We won't remind you to open the program each time, but if it needs to be open, you should open it yourself. The same goes for some of the common files you're working with. If we're working on a form in a project or exercise, you can be sure you should open it if you don't already have it open.

Finally, a few words about menu choices and code. Notice the way we write menu choices when describing the sequence you should follow. We'll separate the menu choices you'll see with a "|". When you see this, it indicates that each word or phrase is a menu choice that you should click, in that order. And the code examples written out in this book do not have the "_" character at the end of lines that are actually still part of the same line. What this means is you should always copy the code examples from the CD, rather than try to write them out from what you see in the book. On the CD, the code is exactly what we used in our applications and examples on the server, and it should run fine if your system is configured in a similar way.

Discussion—VS.Net Features

Visual Studio.Net is an application program itself, of a special type called an Integrated Development Environment (IDE). Application development, whether for Windows or Web applications, requires the use of many specialized programs because of the many resources and file types included with applications. Text editors, code editors, image editors, compilers, debugging utilities, and so on are all commonly used during application development. Integrated Development Environments such as VS.Net provide many of these tools intrinsically, and provide connections to external tools as well. The objective is to provide an efficient working environment for the developer.

Like any good IDE, VS.Net has common facilities for creating, opening, and saving your work in files; editing the file types you are working on; viewing your applications under development from many angles; opening the available tools to perform your work and debug your application; arranging windows; and finding helpful information. These facilities are all available from the menu system, and a variety of toolbars can be displayed to make accessing common functions more convenient.

Creating an ASP.Net Web Application in VS.Net

Using VS.Net to develop your ASP.Net Web Applications makes your life easier, but there are some things you should know about the way VS.Net organizes your applications.

Solutions and Projects

First off, a new application under development is contained in a Solution. A Solution is simply a file that serves as a reference point for all the folders, files, and other resources making up the entire application (or at least a major subset of it).

Inside a Solution, individual chunks of processing logic called **projects** are contained. Each project should be logically self-sufficient, but what goes into a project is up to you. Projects contain files and folders related to the functionality they possess.

When you start a new application, you can start with a blank Solution and then add projects and items to it, or you can begin with one of the prebuilt application templates that come with VS.Net. For example, there are templates for Visual Basic Projects for Windows applications, ASP.Net Web applications, ASP.Net Web Services, and so on.

Starting a project using a template will automatically create a new Solution to hold the project if no Solutions are open. VS.Net creates a Visual Studio Solutions folder in My Documents, and each solution file (the reference point for all parts of the Solution in VS.Net) will be stored in its own folder here. ASP.Net Web applications also have folders set up automatically in the appropriate folder in IIS, so IIS can run and manage them.

The ASP.Net Web Application Template

When you create a new project using the Visual Basic Projects ASP.Net Web Application template, several files and folders are created automatically. If you want to find these files on your hard drive using Windows Explorer, look in your "C:" drive (or whatever is the drive your operating system was loaded on) for a folder named "Inetpub". Inside Inetpub look for "wwwroot". Inside the wwwroot folder look for a folder named the same as the project you created. Inside that folder you'll find all these files:

- References—these are references to some classes that are frequently used in ASP.Net applications, such as System, System.Data, System.Drawing, System.Web, and System.XML. For example, the Request and Response objects are made from their **Http classes** in the System.Web namespace.

- AssemblyInfo.vb—this file contains information about the assembly (applications are programmed as assemblies, the main structural unit for .Net applications).
- Global.asax—this file is a special file that is designed for use with ASP.Net Web applications. It is used to respond to applicationwide events such as the start and end of the application. It also can respond to session events. There will be more on Global.asax in Chapter 5.
- A VSDISCO file—this file is an XML file that helps users discover Web services (if your application is or contains a Web service). More on Web services can be found in Chapter 9.
- Styles.css—this file contains default HTML style settings and can be modified to give your pages a distinctive style.
- Web.config—this file contains configuration settings for your application. More on Web.config can be found in Chapter 6.
- WebForm1.aspx—this file is the first Web form, created by default. You build your main user interface from this file (or one like it).

Quick Check Questions

1. What two objects can you find in both ASP and ASP.Net?
2. What makes Web applications different from Windows applications?
3. How does the available bandwidth affect a Web application?
4. How does the CPU performance of the server computer hosting your Web application affect it?
5. What is Visual Studio.Net?
6. What kinds of tools would you expect to find in VS.Net? List at least three.
7. What two views are available in the HTML designer in VS.Net?
8. What does the Solution Explorer show you?
9. During Web application design, why might you have to repeat the debug step?

Summary

Windows and Web applications perform much of the computer-based work that people do. Web applications, unlike Windows applications, have a distributed structure in which the user interface is on the user's computer (usually a browser), while the processing logic and data can be distributed across the Internet in multiple locations.

ASP and ASP.Net both are technologies, not programming languages, and make use of many built-in classes from which objects can be created. Objects such as the Request and Response objects facilitate many common functions of a Web application, such as accepting and understanding communications from the user and creating and sending communications to the user.

Web application development benefits from the .Net Framework and Integrated Development Environments such as Visual Studio.Net because these technologies and application development programs bring all the facilities required for efficient development and programming into one clean user interface with a solid foundation.

Using the ASP.Net Web application template for Web application development in VS.Net makes the developer's job easier because all the basic files and quite a bit of the code required for any .Net Web application is already created, and only needs to be modified or used as is.

For each of the following tasks, VS.Net is open but no solutions, projects, or files are open.
1. Set VS.Net to display the Start page when opened.
2. Display the Image Editor toolbar.
3. Display the Find in Files dialog box.
4. Display the Solution Explorer.
5. Display the Properties window.
6. Display the Toolbox.
7. Open the Options dialog box.
8. Set HTML pages to start in HTML view, then set it back.
9. Find the Options dialog box node and choice for creating keyboard shortcuts.
10. Find the Options dialog box node and choice for changing tab size in Visual Basic in the Text Editor.

Creating an ASP.Net Web Application in VS.Net

In this project you will create an ASP.Net Web application in VS.Net using the Visual Basic.Net projects template for ASP.Net Web applications. Once you've created your application from the template, you'll explore the various files and folders that have been created. Next, you'll add controls to the form. Finally, you'll add some VB.Net code to your application to make it perform some basic activities when the user interacts with it. This project is one of the few in this book that does not really function as a realistic Web application; it is only for demonstration purposes and to familiarize you with solution and project basics.

OPEN VS.NET AND CREATE A SOLUTION

Start this project by opening VS.Net and creating a Solution

1. Click Start|Programs|Microsoft Visual Studio.Net|Microsoft Visual Studio.Net. The program should open on your desktop.
2. Choose File|New|Project. The New Project dialog box should open. Make sure the Visual Basic Projects node is selected on the left side, then choose ASP.Net Web Application from the templates visible on the right side. Name your Web application ANWA01 by clicking in the Location area and changing it to "http://localhost/ANWA01" as shown in Figure 1.14.
3. Click OK to create the project. Note that when you start by creating a project without a Solution already created and open, VS.Net automatically creates a Solution to contain the project.
4. Your screen in VS.Net should now resemble Figure 1.15.

FIND THE SOLUTION FILE AND THE WEB APPLICATION FILES

Visual Studio.Net has created both a Solution file and a set of Web application files. Use Windows Explorer to find out where these files are stored. Note that if you are not allowed to browse files on the Web server (if you are working on a remote Web server, for example), you may not be able to perform all of this portion of the project, but that will not keep you from doing the work required to finish the project.

1. Click Start|Programs|Accessories|Windows Explorer to start Windows Explorer.
2. Open My Computer and find the primary drive on which your file is stored. This is often the C: drive.

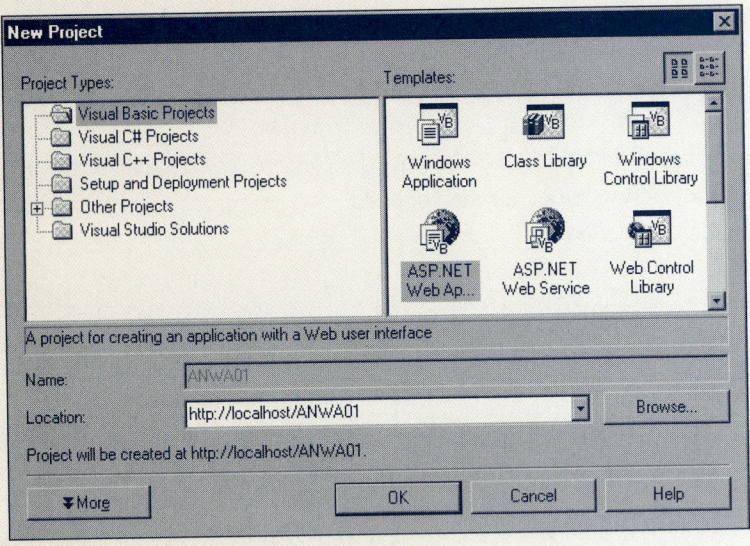

FIGURE 1.14 Naming the Web Application

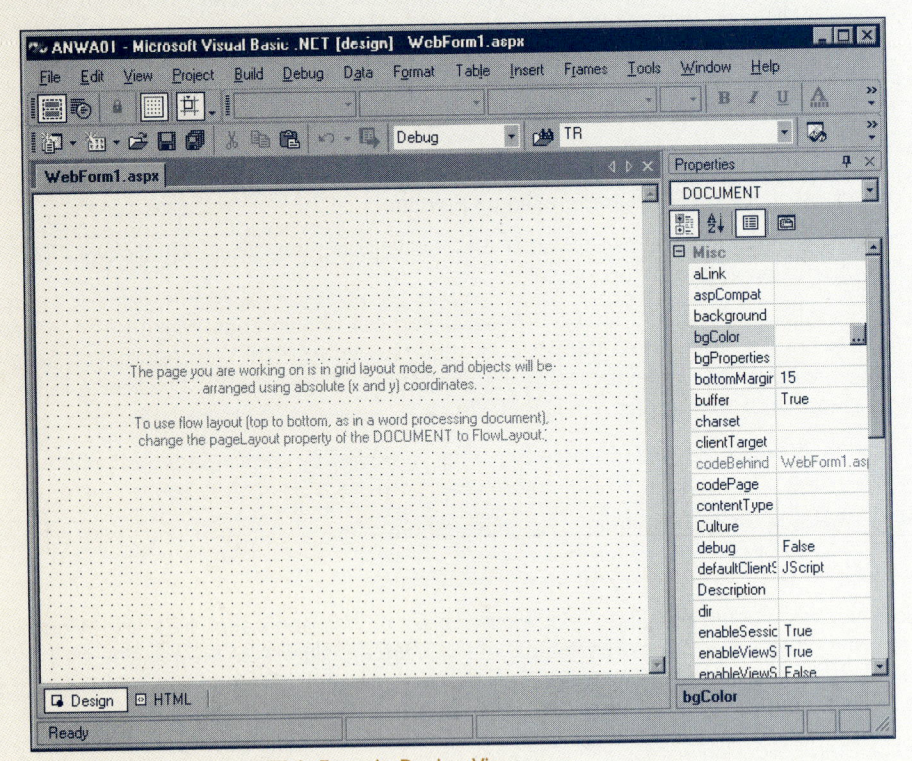

FIGURE 1.15 The New Web Form in Design View

3. Open nodes in this drive until you find the "My Documents" folder. Inside this folder should be a folder named "Visual Studio Projects", and inside this folder should be a folder named "ANWA01".

4. In the ANWA01 folder you should find a file named "ANWA01.sln". This file is the reference point for the Solution. If you come back to this Solution later, you can open it by opening this file in VS.Net.

5. Now look for the Web server folders "Inetpub" and "wwwroot". The wwwroot folder is the folder in which all Web pages and Web applications are stored for output by the Web server software, Internet Information Server (IIS).

6. Inside the wwwroot folder you should find a folder named "ANWA01". Inside this folder you'll find a folder named "bin" and the files shown in Figure 1.16. These files make up your application and perform its work. They were all created when you used the ASP.Net Web application template from the Visual Basic Projects node in VS.Net.

7. Close Windows Explorer.

Name	Size	Type
bin		File Folder
ANWA01.vbproj	6 KB	Visual Basic .NET Project
ANWA01.vbproj.webinfo	1 KB	WEBINFO File
ANWA01.vsdisco	1 KB	VS.NET Web Service Dynamic Discov...
AssemblyInfo.vb	2 KB	Visual Basic Source
Global.asax	1 KB	Active Server Application file
Global.asax.resx	2 KB	.NET XML Resource Template
Global.asax.vb	2 KB	Visual Basic Source
Styles.css	3 KB	Cascading Style Sheet Document
Web.config	4 KB	Web Configuration file
WebForm1.aspx	1 KB	Web Form
WebForm1.aspx.resx	2 KB	.NET XML Resource Template
WebForm1.aspx.vb	1 KB	Visual Basic Source

FIGURE 1.16   The Web Application Template Files

OPEN THE SOLUTION EXPLORER AND EXAMINE YOUR WEB APPLICATION FILES

The Solution Explorer is a key tool for examining what's in your Solution and for managing (adding and deleting) projects and other items in the Solution.

1. You should still have VS.Net open and your new project visible, showing the Web form and the Properties window. Click View|Solution Explorer to open the Solution Explorer, as shown in Figure 1.17.

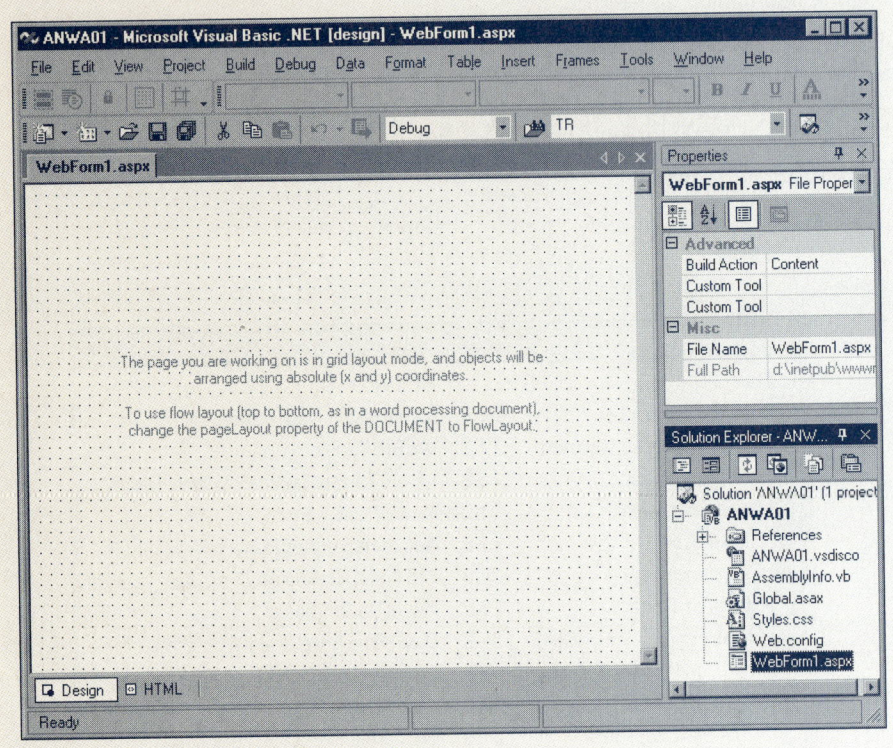

FIGURE 1.17 The Solution Explorer Open

2. There are several buttons available on the Solution Explorer. Click the fifth from the left (Show All Files). Doing this reveals the "bin" folder and some other files in the list.

3. Click the "+" next to the file named WebForm1.aspx. This should reveal the WebForm1.aspx.vb file underneath it.

4. The WebForm1.aspx.vb file is called a code-behind file. When you write VB.Net code affecting controls on WebForm1.aspx, this is where the code will go.

5. Click the "Show All Files" button again to remove the display of the extra files from the Solution Explorer.

CHANGE DOCUMENT PROPERTIES FOR WEBFORM1.ASPX

Using the Properties window, you can view and change the properties of any object in your Web application. Examine and change properties for the Web form with the Properties box and with the Document Properties dialog box.

Hands On Project

1. Click the main area of the form. In the Properties window the selected object should change from the WebForm1.aspx file to "DOCUMENT" as shown in Figure 1.18.

2. In the Properties window, click in the "bgColor" property and click the ellipsis (the button with three dots) to open the Color Picker dialog box, shown in Figure 1.19.

3. From the Web Palette choose a pleasant color (such as the light blue we've chosen; Figure 1.20) and click OK. The entire background of the Web form should turn this color.

4. You'll notice the Web form has several sentences on it, telling you about grid layout and flow layout. Scroll down the Properties window until you find the "pageLayout" property. We could change the pageLayout property here, but we're going to do that another way.

5. Instead of changing the pageLayout property in the Properties window, right-click the surface of the Web form. A shortcut menu will appear. At the bottom of the menu is the Properties choice. Click this menu choice. The DOCUMENT Property Pages dialog box should open, as shown in Figure 1.21.

6. On the General tab you'll find a drop-down box for selecting grid or flow layout. Changing the property here will also affect it in the Properties window, and vice versa. However, we're not going to change this setting, so don't change it in either place. Using grid layout makes it easier to get good alignment of controls on the form.

7. Select the Color and Margins tab. You'll see settings for Background Color, Links, and Page Margins. As you can imagine, changing these settings will affect the colors and margins of your Web form. You should see the Background Color settings you made earlier reflected here.

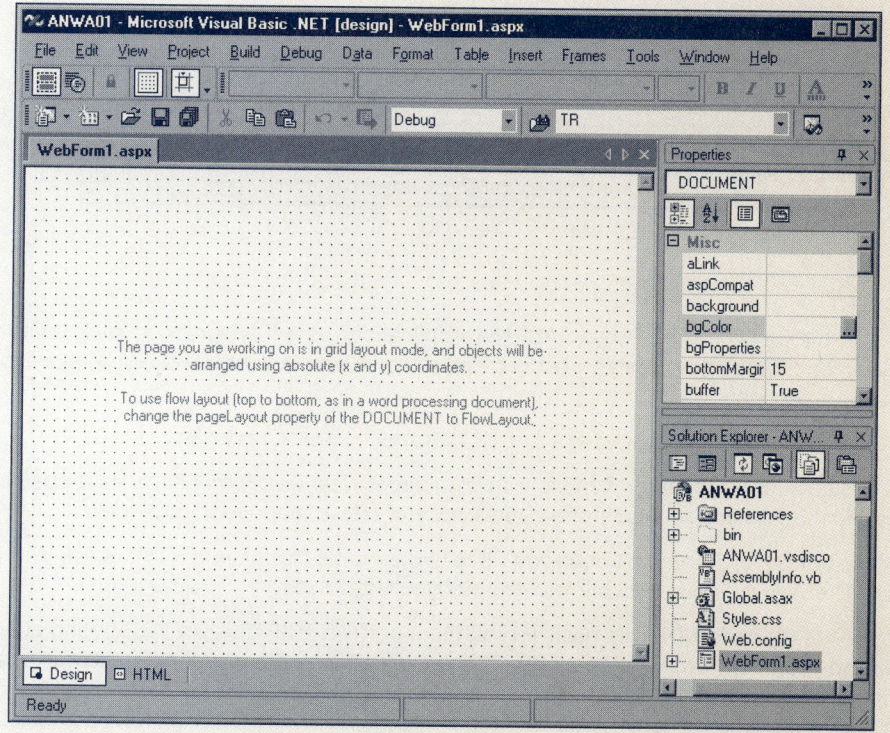

FIGURE 1.18   The DOCUMENT in the Properties Window

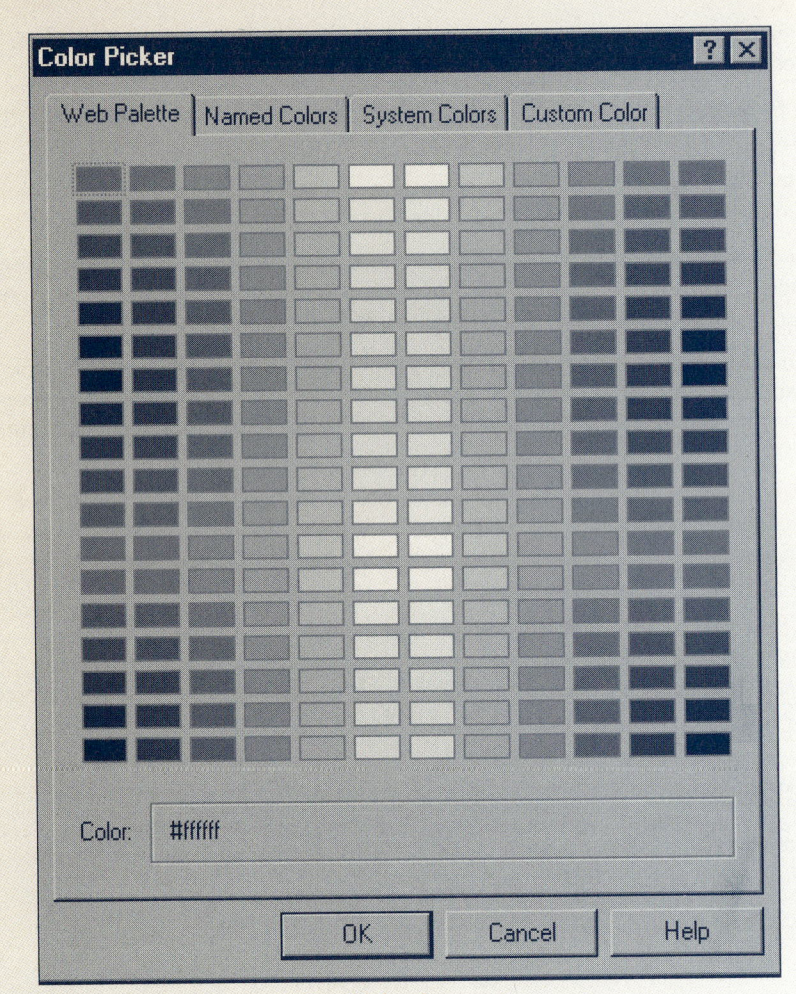

FIGURE 1.19 The Color Picker Dialog Box

8. Select the Keywords tab. Enter "ASP.Net Application" as a Keyword, and click OK to close the dialog box. Doing this creates what is called a "meta" tag in your HTML. We'll take a look at it in our next section.

EXAMINE THE HTML AND ASP.NET ELEMENTS AND ATTRIBUTES IN WEBFORM1.ASPX

The HTML Designer is the editor for working with Web pages. The WebForm1.aspx file is open in this editor and has two modes: Design mode for a visual view and HTML mode for a code view.

1. At the bottom of WebForm1.aspx you'll see two buttons: Design and HTML. Click the HTML button. The view in Figure 1.22 shows the code you should see.

2. For those of you familiar with basic HTML, the `<HTML>`, `<HEAD>`, `<TITLE>`, and other tags will remind you of any ordinary Web page. The line in yellow at the very top has special meaning and we'll discuss it in detail later in this book. There should be a list of "meta" tags, with the attributes "content" and "name", and the first one in the list should be "ASP.Net Application", named "keywords". This is the keyword we added in the previous section.

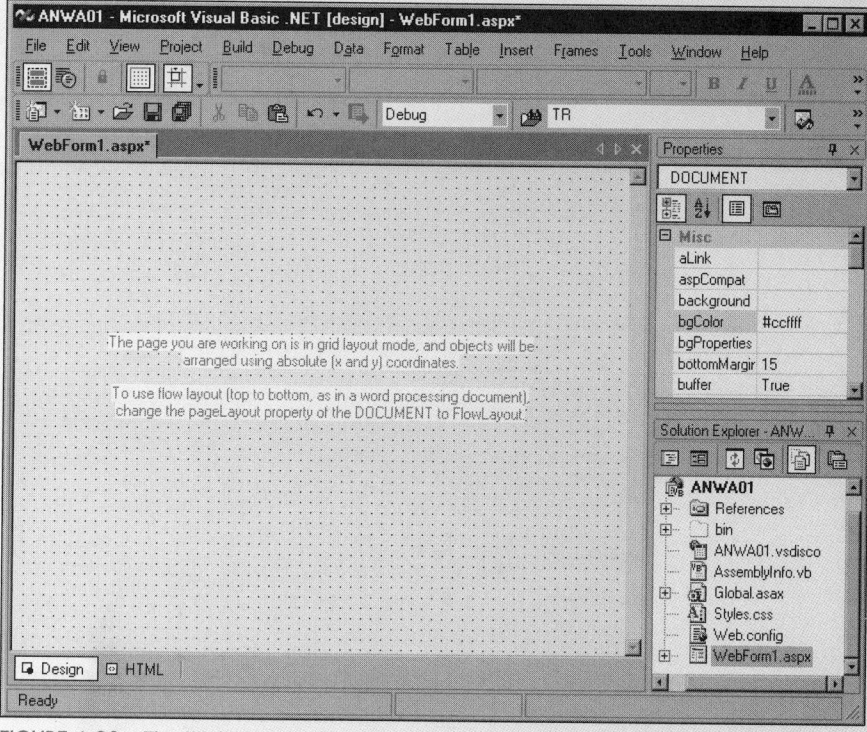

FIGURE 1.20 The Web Form with a Light Blue Background Color

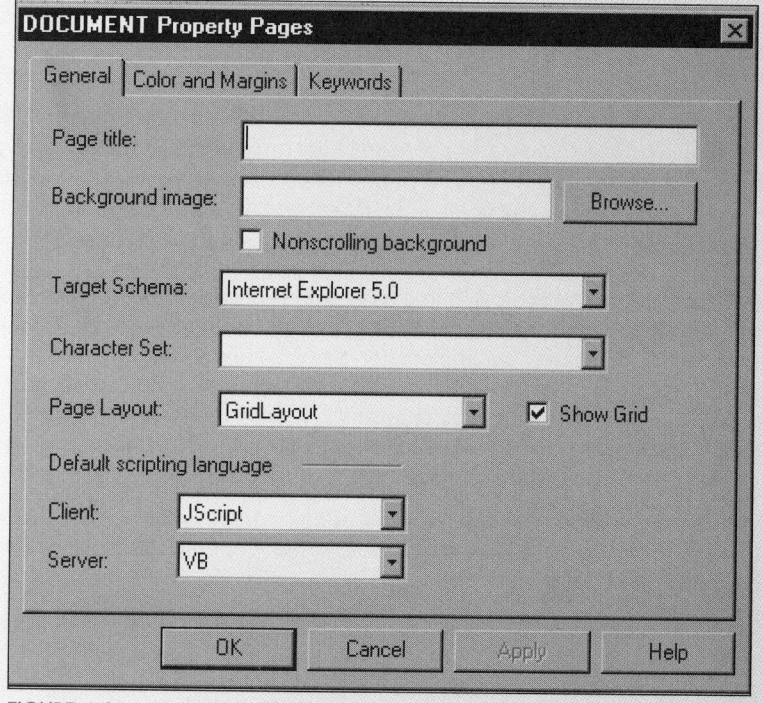

FIGURE 1.21 The DOCUMENT Property Pages Dialog Box

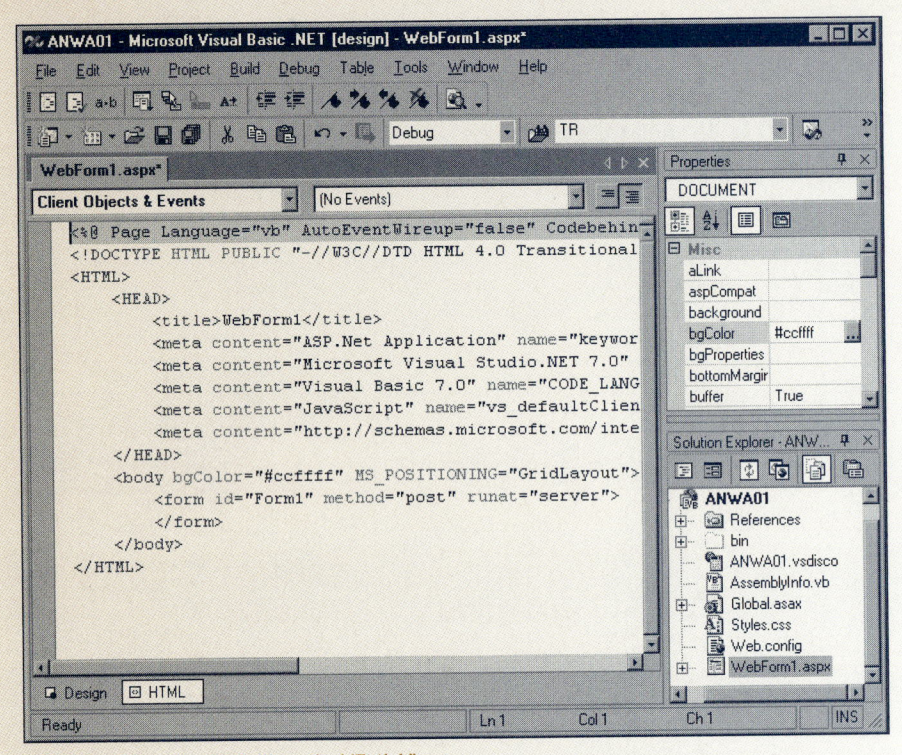

FIGURE 1.22 The Web Form in HTML View

3. In the code, change "ASP.Net Application" to "Ecommerce Application". Click the Design button at the bottom to go back to Design mode.

4. Right-click the surface of the Web form and open the DOCUMENT Property Pages dialog box again. You should now see your recent change to the meta tag reflected in the Keywords tab. The point of this little demonstration is that any changes you make to the DOCUMENT Property Pages should be reflected in one or all of the Properties window, the Design view, and the code.

OPEN THE TOOLBOX AND PUT A LABEL CONTROL ON THE FORM

The Toolbox contains controls for Web forms, and these controls provide user interface functionality. Dragging controls onto the surface of the Web form (in Design view) creates their code (in HTML). When controls are dragged onto the surface, they are immediately selected and their properties are displayed in the Properties window. They can still be manipulated visually with your mouse (in Design view) and deleted by hitting the Delete key (or by right-clicking and choosing Delete). Note that their width, height, and X-Y coordinates are affected when you move or resize them visually with your mouse, and you can see these values (in pixels) in the corresponding properties.

1. Click View|Toolbox to open the Toolbox. It will appear as shown in Figure 1.23. Your form will be a bit compressed, so if you like, adjust the sizes for the Properties window, Solution Explorer, and WebForm1.aspx until you feel comfortable.

2. Notice the tool categories available: Data, Web Forms, Components, HTML, and so forth. The Web Forms category should be displayed. Choose Label and drag it on to the surface of the Web form. A box with the word "Label" should appear on the form. Note that you can also just click the **Label control** on the Toolbox and then draw a Label control of any size onto the form surface.

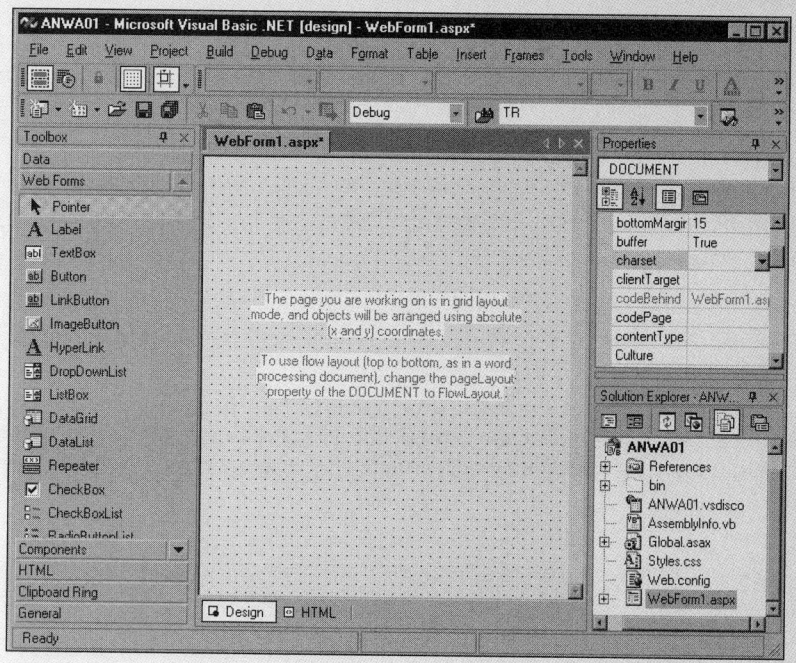

FIGURE 1.23 The Toolbox

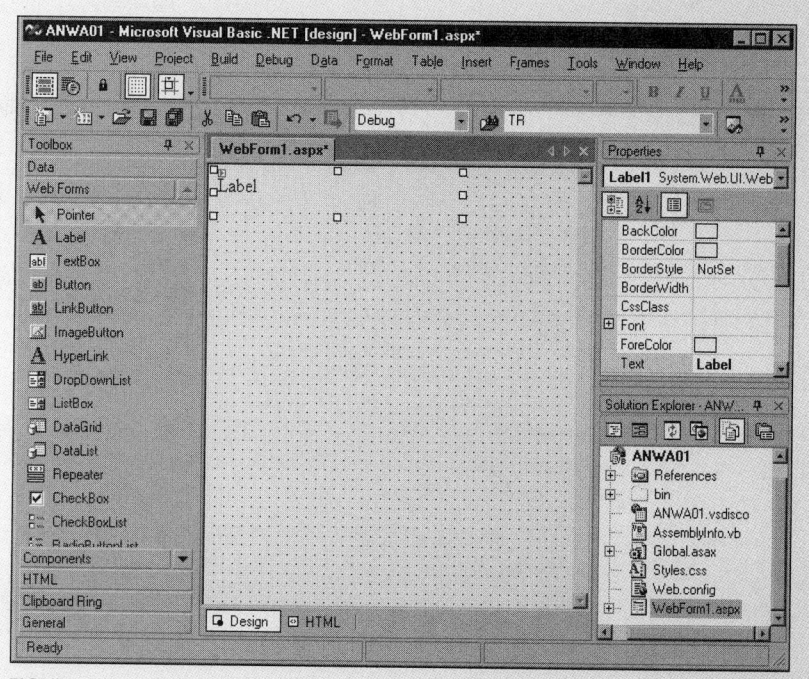

FIGURE 1.24 The Label Control on the Web Form

3. The Label control is rectangular and you can tell it is selected because it has anchors (little boxes on each corner) that can be clicked and dragged to resize the control. If you want to resize the control, click and drag one of the anchors. If you want to move the entire control to a new location, click over the control but away from the anchors, then drag. You can tell what's going to happen by looking at the cursor and seeing if it is a double arrow or crossed arrows.

4. Place the Label in the upper left corner of your form and enlarge it so that it can serve as a heading for the application. It should end up looking like Figure 1.24.

CHANGE THE LABEL CONTROL'S TEXT, FONT, AND BACKGROUND COLOR PROPERTIES

Label controls have a number of properties that affect their appearance and one that affects the wording of the text they display. All properties can be changed programmatically (in code) from their original setting (the settings you are making in the Properties window).

1. In the Properties window, in the BackColor property, click and then click the drop-down arrow. This opens a color picker. Choose the Web tab and choose a darker color to complement your form background color (we chose Aqua). The entire Label control will turn this color (Figure 1.25).

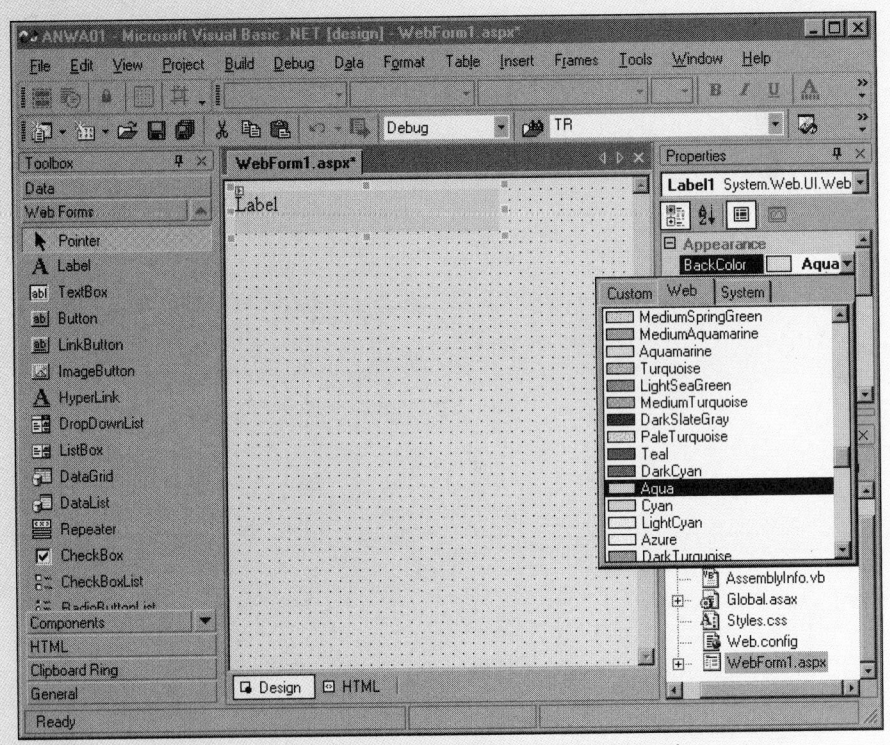

FIGURE 1.25 The BackColor Property Picker for the Label Control

2. Scroll down to the Font node in the Properties window and open it (click the + sign). You should see font properties such as Bold, Italic, Name, and Size. Change Bold to True, Size to X-Large, and Name to Arial. Your Label should now look like Figure 1.26.

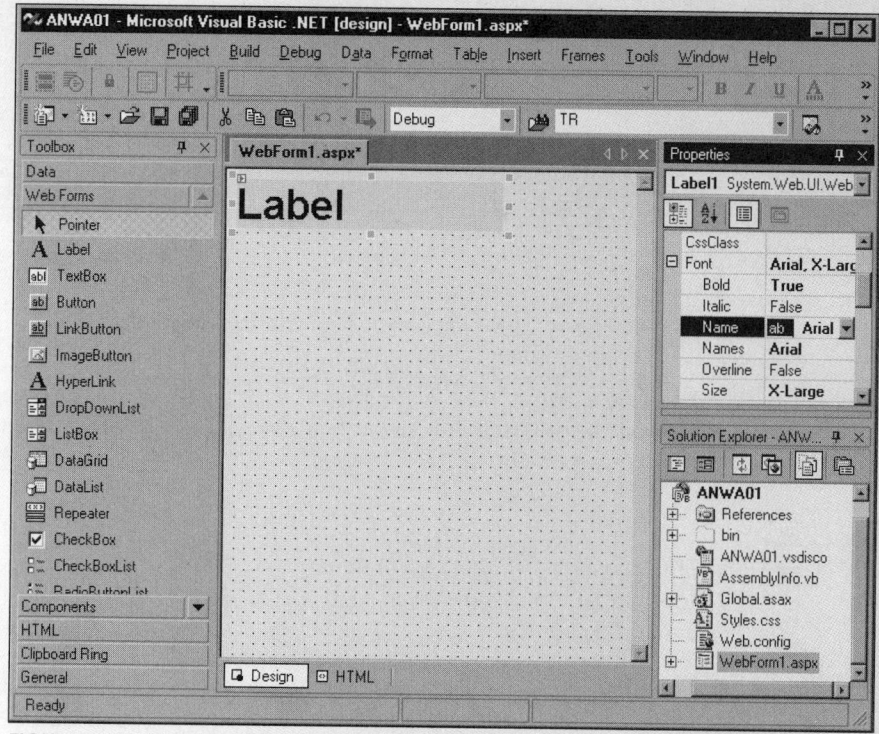

FIGURE 1.26   The Label After Changing Some Properties

3. Scroll a little farther down to the Text property. Whatever you put in here becomes the wording displayed on the label when your application is running. Note that the dots of the grid do not appear on the form when the application is running; they are there for your convenience while developing your application. Enter "Welcome" as the Text property. Click anywhere (in another property or on the form) and the word "Welcome" will show up on the label.

ADD A TEXTBOX CONTROL AND A BUTTON CONTROL

To capture data submitted by the user (an obvious requirement for most applications), form fields are required. To submit the data, a Submit button is required (hypertext links also can be used for this purpose under some circumstances). Add both to the form using the Toolbox.

1. Click and drag a **TextBox control** and a **Button control** onto the surface of the form. Select the TextBox control and then, in the Properties window, change the Text property to "Put name here". This makes it so "Put name here" appears as the default value when the form first opens in the user's browser.

2. Select the Button control and change the Text property to "Submit". This makes the button read "Submit" when the form first opens (and it will stay this way unless we change it programmatically, because the user can't change this property of the button). Your form should now look like Figure 1.27.

CHAPTER 1 ASP.NET

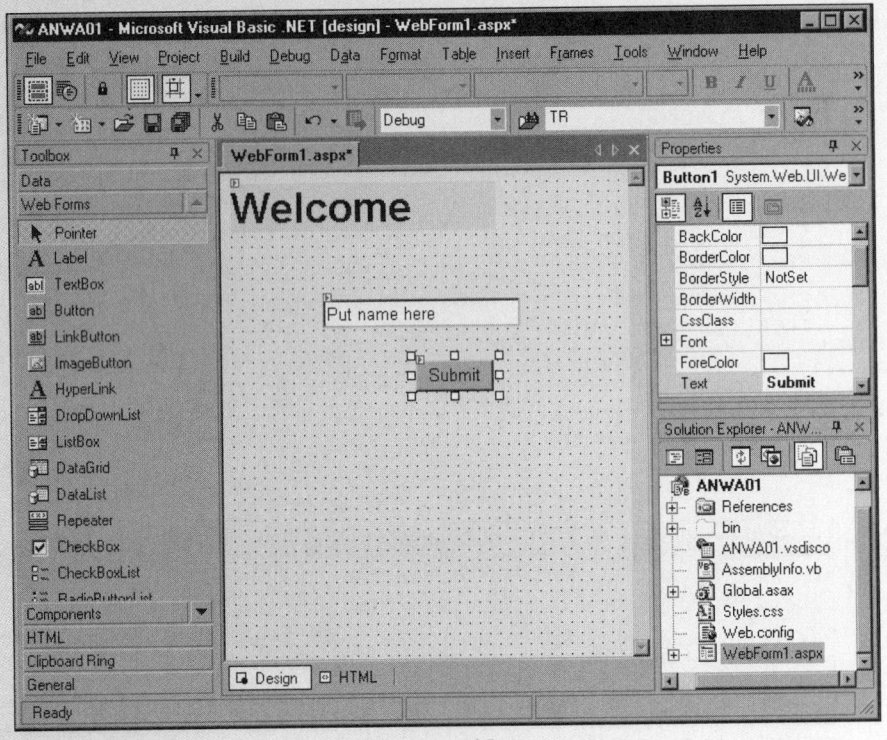

FIGURE 1.27 The Web Form with TextBox and Button

CREATE AN EVENT HANDLER FOR THE SUBMIT BUTTON AND ADD VB.NET CODE

To make your Web application respond to user inputs, you create what is called an **event handler**. The event handler is a block of code added to the code-behind page (the WebForm1.aspx.vb file). Code that you write inside it will run when the particular event it is designed for happens. For example, we'll create an event handler for the Button control's Click event. You can guess by its name that the Click event is what happens when the user clicks the button as the application is running. Once the button is clicked, any code in the Click event's event handler will run, which is just what we want.

1. Double-click the Button control. The code-behind page will open with an event handler block for the Click event created and the cursor blinking inside it. This is where your code will go. Notice that both the form file and the code file are open, and that you can go back and forth between the two easily by choosing them from their tabs at the top of the Design area. Close the Toolbox to give yourself a little more room to work on your code.

2. Enter the following code:
```
Dim strName_submitted As String
strName_submitted = TextBox1.Text
If TextBox1.Text = "" Then
    TextBox1.Text = "Please enter a name"
Else
    TextBox1.Text = "Welcome " & strName_submitted
End If
```

3. The first line of the code dimensions a variable in VB.Net and gives it a name and data type (string). The second line of the code sets the variable equal to the value entered by the user (notice how the value of this property changes in real time while the application is running, based on what the user enters). The next section is an If...Then...End If block that checks the value entered and sets the TextBox.Text property accordingly.

BUILD AND BROWSE YOUR APPLICATION, AND TEST IT

ASP.Net Web applications are easier than Windows applications to deploy, in that the application works without anything more than copying them to the Web server. In this case, we're developing on the Web server, so we can just open the application in our browser (or from within VS.Net in the browser view) to run it. The first time an ASP.Net page is opened, any code is compiled. After that, it runs much more quickly, but if you make more changes to the files, they are compiled again the next time they are opened. Once you open your application, test it out, and if it doesn't do what you want, go back and modify it until it does. If you've made code or syntax errors, it won't build properly, but you should get some pretty descriptive error messages in the browser instead.

1. Click on the WebFrom1.aspx file tab at the top of the HTML Designer, then choose File|Build and Browse from the menu. The application should compile and the Browse view should appear as a file open in the Design view, as shown in Figure 1.28.

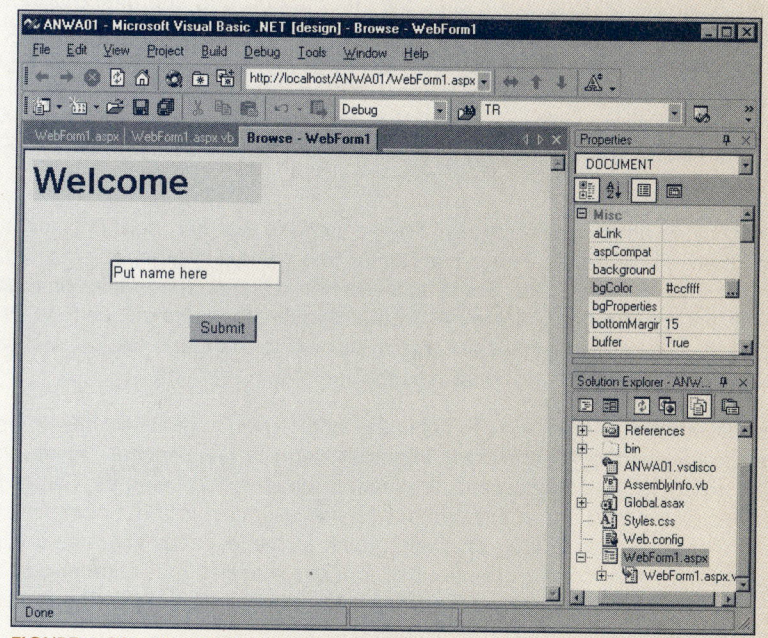

FIGURE 1.28   The Web Form in Browse View

2. Enter your name, click the Submit button, and see what happens. Your name should be displayed in the TextBox after the word "Welcome".

3. Erase everything in the TextBox and try it again. The "Please enter a name" message should be displayed.

HTML and XHTML   Although we'll cover HTML and XHTML more in Chapter 4, if you're unfamiliar with these terms, a little explanation is in order. HTML and XHTML are used to make Web pages (you can see HTML or XHTML code if you select View|Source in your browser). HTML and XHTML are markup languages, meaning they are written in plain text files as "tags" (such as `<body>`text goes here`</body>`) that form elements of a page. Your browser reads these plain text tags and constructs the page you see from them. Because all Web pages you see contain HTML or XHTML tags, you need to be familiar with HTML when developing Web applications. The main difference between HTML and XHTML is that XHTML is XML-compliant, but we'll get into that in Chapter 4.

Server-Side versus Client-Side Processing   Most of the Web applications and examples in this book all perform their processing on the server. However, you can cause the user's browser to perform some of the processing if you include Javascript, VBScript, or some other interpreted language that is specifically coded to be sent intact to the user. The advantages of doing all the processing on the server are that the user never gets to see unprocessed code and that no dependency on the user's browser is created. The advantages of doing processing on the user's browser are that it offloads some of the processing requirements from your CPU and it is also faster in some circumstances.

Interactivity in Web Applications   In Chapter 3 we discuss the way in which users (through their client applications, browsers) communicate with Web applications (hosted on servers somewhere on the Internet), but again a little discussion to get the ball rolling is a good thing at this point. Basically, you can send a request to a Web server from a Web page in your browser two ways: by clicking a link or submitting a form. Typically, clicking a link uses the Get method and submitting a form uses the Post method. If you click a link that happens to have a question mark and then some data, that generates what's called a Querystring on the server, and your Web application can parse this string and use the data it finds. If you fill out a form and hit the Submit button, that generates a collection of data on the server that happens to be named "Form" in ASP.Net, and once again your Web application can iterate through this collection and use the data it finds. Examples of creating Querystrings and Form collections are given in Chapter 3.

Hot-Keys   Menu choices often have "hot-key" key sequences that can perform their actions quickly if you've memorized them. For example, I often use Ctrl+C to copy text or other objects to the clipboard and Ctrl+V to paste text from the clipboard. Some of these hot-key sequences are common to many other applications as well (and you probably already know them) while others are unique to VS.Net and may take a little getting used to. Hot-key sequences are displayed next to the menu choice, and you can make up your own as well by customizing the keyboard (see the Tools menu section).

Namespaces   You'll encounter many new terms in this book if you're relatively new to programming and application development, and one particularly important term is *namespaces*. Although it has specific meaning in certain contexts, it also represents a concept: the idea that using the names of things in programming can be facilitated (and errors prevented) with namespaces. Without going into too much detail (this concept is further discussed in later chapters), think of namespaces like area codes for telephone numbers. If you attach an area code to the front of a phone number, that number can be reused many times across the country without confusion. The same goes for XML elements, VB.Net variable and object names, and so on. Attaching a namespace eliminates confusion.

Name/Value Pairs   The notion of name/value pairs (such as "bgcolor" and "#FFFFFF") occur frequently in programming, databases, and markup languages. In XML and HTML, name/value pairs are called attributes, in object-oriented programming they are called properties, and in databases they are called fields. The reason they are so common is that a piece of data (such as "#FFFFFF") is pretty meaningless without the context provided by a name. Note that names are often fixed and that values are often limited to a certain data type and a limited range of values.

Key Terms

- Active Server Pages (ASP)
- application programs
- ASP.Net
- Button control
- Common Language Runtime
- DOCUMENT
- event handler
- Http classes
- Integrated Development Environment (IDE)
- Label control
- .Net Framework
- objects
- projects
- Properties window
- Request and Response objects
- Server object
- Solution
- Solution Explorer
- TextBox control
- Visual Basic.Net
- Visual Studio.Net
- Web applications

Review Questions

ASP.Net and Visual Studio.Net

1. What is ASP? What is ASP.Net?
2. Web applications have some key differences from Windows applications. For one, the user interface of a Web application is often the browser. How does this make application development more difficult?
3. Describe the parts of a typical Web application, in general terms. Indicate what each part does.
4. What is the difference between the text editor and the code editor?
5. What is the difference between a project and a Solution in VS.Net?
6. Describe what attributes, properties, and database fields have in common.
7. Where is the menu choice to open the Options dialog box in VS.Net?
8. What menu choice would you choose in VS.NET to customize toolbars?
9. How do you add a project to an open Solution in VS.Net?
10. Creating a new project creates a Solution by default. Where is the Solution file located by default?
11. You need to see the files and folders in a Solution. What tool would you open, and how?

CHAPTER 2

The ASP.Net Template

LEARNING OBJECTIVES

Upon completion of this chapter, you will be able to:

1. Explain the logical difference between Web applications and Web services.
2. Use the ASP.Net template to create a VB.Net project in VS.Net.
3. Work with the Solution Explorer to navigate project files.
4. Describe the functions of ASP.Net template files.
5. Work with the Styles.css file.
6. Add and Delete files from the project.
7. Describe what ASP.Net Directives are.
8. Explain what ASP.Net Directives do.
9. Modify ASP.Net Directives in an ASP.Net file.
10. Describe how ASP.Net Server controls are coded in a Web form.

INTRODUCTION

ASP.Net is typically used to create Web applications. ASP.Net documents can be written manually in a simple text editor, but often it is best to use an Integrated Development Environment (IDE) such as Visual Studio.Net (VS.Net) to speed up the process.

One way VS.Net speeds up the process of writing ASP.Net Web applications is by providing project templates for these applications, as well as for other commonly programmed items (such as Windows applications and Web services). All the templates in VS.Net can be found by opening the New Projects dialog box and choosing the project type from the left side of the box. Applicable templates (for

VB.Net projects, for example) will be shown on the right side of the box, and when you choose and name them, a new project will be started based on that template.

ASP.Net Web application template files include the Global.asax file and the WebForm1.aspx file. The Web form file consists of an HTML-like file that indicates what will be transmitted to the user's browser and another file called the code-behind page that contains VB.Net code that is compiled and run on the server. Rendering of the page in the user's browser is the responsibility of the HTML-like code, while back-end data processing is the responsibility of the code-behind page.

In this chapter we'll cover how to create a new project from the ASP.Net Web application template for VB.Net projects, how the template files look in code and what their purpose is, and what ASP.Net Directives are. At the end of the chapter you should feel comfortable with all the files created as part of the template, and understand how they work together to make a complete ASP.Net Web application.

Differences between ASP and ASP.Net

It's not unlikely that, during your career as an application developer, you'll run into applications that have been built using ASP. Therefore, we've included a few sections here that you might find useful. We discuss the way .Net handles compilation, the differences between ASP and ASP.Net architectures, and migrating an application from ASP to ASP.Net, and offer some insight into how code is processed in ASP.Net applications. First, let's talk about how the .Net Framework is related to ASP.Net.

.NET Structures and Languages

The .Net Framework has many interfaces and classes built in, and also has the Common Language Runtime (CLR) to process applications made from the interfaces and classes. This makes the .Net Framework a technology rather than an operating system or programming language, although it can be referred to as a platform.

The CLR, supported communications protocols, built-in application objects and classes, and support for a number of popular programming languages are what make the .Net Framework an effective platform for Windows and Web applications.

The Common Language Runtime (CLR)

The Common Language Runtime (CLR) provides a managed execution environment in which multiple languages can be used to write the various parts of an application. It also provides exception handling across those languages, memory management, thread management, better security, and versioning, deployment, debugging, and profiling services. To make use of managed execution, you must use a language that has the appropriate compilers and support, such as Visual Basic.Net and C# (a managed version of C++).

Microsoft Intermediate Language Specification (MSIL)

When you use the .Net Framework and the CLR, you are using the managed execution process. The first step in using this process is to pick a compiler that will compile the various parts of your application for the CLR. As we noted above, you can use a number of programming languages for this purpose such as Visual Basic, C#, and so on.

Code compiled for the CLR is compiled into MSIL. MSIL is a set of instructions that can be efficiently turned into code native to whatever CPU it runs on. This means that MSIL is not dependent upon a particular CPU and is therefore much more portable than traditionally compiled code. Once on the machine it runs on, MSIL is turned into native code by a just-in-time compiler.

Migrating from ASP to ASP.Net

Typical ASP documents include ASP and some scripting language code (often VBScript) embedded within HTML code. Web pages are created as though a normal Web page is the intended outcome, but after the design is about finished, programmers take over and add ASP so that what the user sees in the browser varies dynamically. Many application-style actions are available, such as redirection to another page, but the user's browser receives only the finished product. Here are a few things to watch out for.

Using ASP.Net Server Controls

One of your first steps in migrating from an ASP application would be to rebuild the basic pages and separate out programming code from display (HTML or XHTML) code. Programming code would be inserted into **event handlers** in the **code-behind page**, while display code would be left in a file with an extension of .aspx rather than .asp. You also, at this point, might substitute ASP.Net Server controls for the old-fashioned HTML controls.

Using Page Directives

Another change is in the way page **directives** are handled. In ASP, you might find a few lines at the top of the page that resemble the following:

```
<% Language="VBScript" %>
<% Option="Explicit" %>
```

Change this to:

```
<% @Page Language="vb" Explicit="True" %>
```

We'll cover coding page directives in more detail later in this chapter.

VB.Net Syntax

A third area to be on the lookout for is the difference in the way certain arguments are expressed for functions and methods. For example, it is permissible to write a response in ASP as follows:

```
Response.write "This is my message"
```

In ASP.Net, the response must be written:

```
Response.write("This is my response")
```

All arguments must be properly enclosed in parentheses.

Variable Declaration and Data Types

In ASP, using VBScript, variables are not required to be declared, and if you start using them without declaring them first (as you are allowed to if the statement `Option="Explicit"` is at the top of the page), they are simply used, and no data type is required (in ASP, values are assigned a data type of "Variant", which no longer exists in ASP.Net and VB.Net). In ASP.Net, you'll need to identify all variables and specifically declare them with the appropriate data type.

There are a few other syntactical items to keep track of when porting applications to ASP.Net, but keep in mind that, because ASP.Net is so easy to use (especially with VS.Net), it will often make more sense to just convert the entire application completely to ASP.Net and use all the rich new features.

ASP.Net Web Application Files

In Chapter 1 we started a simple ASP.Net Web application and reviewed the files and **resources** contained in it. In this chapter we will examine each of the files created and look at how it is processed and used in the Web application, as well as how it is structured in code. If you happen to be creating a Web application without using VS.Net, note that you can code these files manually with a text editor.

VS.Net includes Visual Basic project **templates** for ASP.Net Web applications and ASP.Net XML Web services. The primary (logical) difference between the two is that Web applications have a user interface and Web services have a machine-to-machine interface. Otherwise, they both accept input, perform processing on the input, and produce output, like any application. Internally, some of their structures are different, and the way you make use of them is different, but how the code is written is much the same. Chapter 9 discusses Web services in detail. Illustration 2.1 shows the relationship between project types, templates types, and template files.

```
┌─────────────────────────────────────────┐
│      ┌─────────────────────────┐        │
│  ←── │     Project Types       │        │
│      │     Such As:            │        │
│      │   Visual Basic Projects │        │
│      │     C+ Projects         │        │
│      └─────────────────────────┘        │
│      ┌─────────────────────────┐        │
│  ←── │     Template Types      │ ───→   │
│      │     Such As:            │        │
│      │ ASP.Net Web Applications│        │
│      │ ASP.Net Web Services    │        │
│      └─────────────────────────┘        │
│      ┌─────────────────────────┐        │
│      │     Template Files      │ ←──    │
│      │     Such As:            │        │
│      │     Global.asax         │        │
│      │     WebForm.aspx        │        │
│      └─────────────────────────┘        │
└─────────────────────────────────────────┘
```

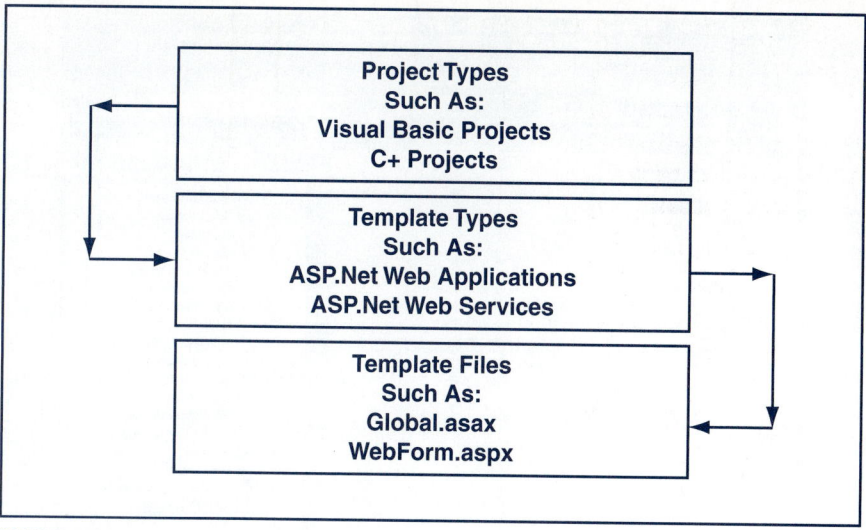

ILLUSTRATION 2.1 Projects, Templates, and Template Files

ASP.Net Web Application Structure

Like any application, ASP.Net Web applications have a structure that includes common features supporting the application as it is ordinarily designed to be built and run. When you use the **VB.Net Projects** ASP.Net Web Application template to create a new project, the template creates the files, folders, and references that have these common features. You can easily view the files created from the template by opening Solution Explorer and examining them. From that point you are free to change any aspect of the application's structure as you see fit, although changing some things would break the application. Knowing what you can change without breaking the application, why you might want to change it, and how to achieve your design objectives is the subject of the next few sections. In these sections we'll discuss each file, folder, and reference created by the template. We'll start by creating a new ASP.Net Web application from the VB.Net template. Later, in our Hands On Project, we'll demonstrate common features of an ASP.Net Web application and what effect changes have on them.

In Visual Studio.Net, create a new project using the VB.Net projects template for ASP.Net Web applications using the same method we did in Chapter 1 (click File|New Project from the menu, choose the template, and name it "WebAppStructure", then click OK). You should see a blank Web form named WebForm1.aspx on your screen. Make sure the Solution Explorer is open (you can open the Solution Explorer from the View menu). In the Solution Explorer you should see the files and folders created by the template. Click the Show All Files button to show all the files and folders created (Figure 2.1).

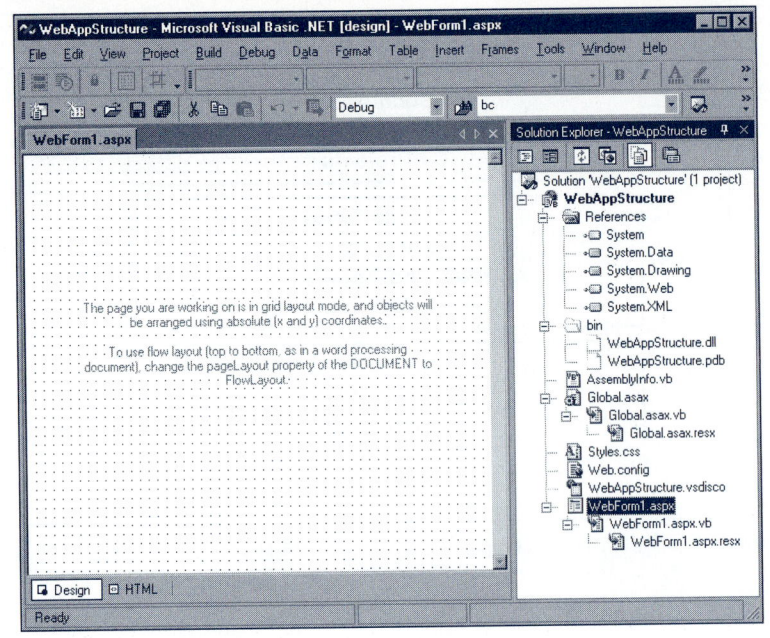

FIGURE 2.1 The WebAppStructure Project

References

The first item shown under the project (remember, creating a new project also creates the overall solution to contain the project, and other projects can now be added to the solution as well) is References. In Figure 2.1 the References node is open, and you can see the references it contains: System, System.Data, System.Drawing, System.Web, and System.XML. Each of these reference names refers to a .Net Framework namespace that contains fundamental and base classes and interfaces that support Web-based communications, events and event handlers, data and graphics processing, and XML processing.

Although from the way it's displayed you might think References is a file or folder that can be opened like any other, right-clicking on the References node in Solution Explorer only offers two choices: Add Reference and Add Web Reference. We'll discuss Web References in Chapter 9. To see how References are coded as part of an ASP.Net Web application, open Windows Explorer and go to the folder in which your WebAppStructure application is located (on this computer the application files are in the D: drive in Inetpub/wwwroot/WebAppStructure).

In this folder you will find a file named WebAppStructure.vbproj. This file can be opened with Notepad (or any simple text editor) and contains several sections related to the project, including a References section. We'll discuss the References section now and the other sections as we progress through building ASP.Net Web applications in later chapters.

The References section looks like this in code:

```
<References>
  <Reference
    Name = "System"
    AssemblyName = "System"
  />
  <Reference
    Name = "System.Data"
    AssemblyName = "System.Data"
  />
  <Reference
    Name = "System.Drawing"
    AssemblyName = "System.Drawing"
  />
  <Reference
    Name = "System.Web"
    AssemblyName = "System.Web"
  />
  <Reference
    Name = "System.XML"
    AssemblyName = "System.Xml"
  />
</References>
```

As you can see, each reference has a "Name" attribute and an "AssemblyName" attribute. These references refer to **assemblies** that are included in the global assembly cache. The global assembly cache is a machinewide code cache that stores assemblies meant to be shared by multiple applications on the computer (in this case, it would be on the server running your Web application).

To see how references are created in the WebAppStructure.vbproj file, close the file (if you have it open) and in VS.Net right-click the References node in Solution Explorer, then click the Add Reference menu choice. Choose the COM tab (for components) and scroll down to find the DHTML Edit Control for IE 5. Click the Select button and then click OK. In the Solution Explorer you'll see that the DHTMLEdLib and the MSHTML references have been added. Open the WebAppStructure.vbproj file and you'll see that the full references for these components have been added to the file, as shown in this code:

```
<Reference
  Name = "MSHTML"
  Guid = "{3050F1C5-98B5-11CF-BB82-00AA00BDCE0B}"
  VersionMajor = "4"
  VersionMinor = "0"
  Lcid = "0"
  WrapperTool = "primary"
```

```
    />
    <Reference
      Name = "DHTMLEDLib"
      Guid = "{683364A1-B37D-11D1-ADC5-006008A5848C}"
      VersionMajor = "1"
      VersionMinor = "0"
      Lcid = "0"
      WrapperTool = "tlbimp"
    />
```

You can view the properties of these references by right-clicking them and choosing Properties. The Properties window will open and display the properties of the reference. To remove the reference, click the Remove choice after right-clicking the reference. Remove both of the references you have created by right-clicking them and choosing Remove. Opening the WebAppStructure.vbproj file will verify that the references have been removed.

The bin Folder

The next item the template has created in the WebAppStructure project is the "bin" folder. This folder contains your dynamic link library (.dll) file and your Program Debug Database (.pdb) files. Notice that both of these files are automatically named the same as your project but with the appropriate extensions. The DLL file contains a library of classes created from your Web forms and controls when the project is built (or compiled). The PDB file contains debug information that is created when you build your application in debug mode. If you are using VS.Net to create your application, these files are automatically created and used (you can change your project from Debug mode to Release mode from the drop-down box on the Standard menu); if you are developing your application manually, you need to use developer tools to compile your application and create these files.

The AssemblyInfo.vb File

Assemblies are what .Net Framework applications are made from. When you create a project in a solution with Visual Studio.Net, you are creating an assembly. Assemblies form a logical unit that can include security, version, type, and other pertinent information.

The AssemblyInfo.vb file contains assembly information for your project. Open it with Notepad and you should see the contents of the file in code such as this:

```
Imports System.Reflection
Imports System.Runtime.InteropServices
' General Information about an assembly is controlled
  through the following
' set of attributes. Change these attribute values to
  modify the information
' associated with an assembly.
```

```
' Review the values of the assembly attributes

<Assembly: AssemblyTitle("")>
<Assembly: AssemblyDescription("")>
<Assembly: AssemblyCompany("")>
<Assembly: AssemblyProduct("")>
<Assembly: AssemblyCopyright("")>
<Assembly: AssemblyTrademark("")>
<Assembly: CLSCompliant(True)>

' The following GUID is for the ID of the typelib if this
  project is exposed to COM
<Assembly: Guid("3B79C0F3-E653-4C43-B274-F9A5FA0D1113")>
' Version information for an assembly consists of the
  following four values:
'
' Major Version
' Minor Version
' Build Number
' Revision
'
' You can specify all the values or you can default the
  Build and Revision Numbers
' by using the '*' as shown below:
<Assembly: AssemblyVersion("1.0.*")>
```

Assembly Attributes Assembly attributes include the following types: identity, informational, manifest, and strong name. Each one has a specific name (such as AssemblyVersion), and some of them are defined automatically (such as AssemblyName), while others can be set by the developer (such as **Assembly-Company**). In the code just shown, the AssemblyVersion attribute (on the last line of code) shows how a value (1.0) is defined for this attribute. The Imports statement on the first line allows the use of these attributes, as they are all part of the System.Reflection namespace.

Right-clicking on the AssemblyInfo.vb file gives you the option of displaying the file's properties in the Properties window, or viewing the code in the file by clicking View Code from the shortcut menu. You may want to set Company, Title, Product, Description, or other custom information in the Assembly attributes shown in the code, either from inside VS.Net or simply by opening the file in a text editor.

The Global.asax File

The **Global.asax file** is the next item shown in the project in Solution Explorer. This is an optional file, but it is highly useful in ASP.Net Web applications as it contains code for responding to application and **session events**. The term *application event* means an event that happens to the entire application.

Application events include the Application_OnStart and Application_OnEnd events, occurring when the application starts and when it ends, respectively.

Code inside the Application_OnStart event runs when the application starts and can be used to create variables that persist as long as the application is running and make their values accessible to all users of the application. For example, suppose there are 100 users using your Web application. Each user works with the application privately (in many applications, users work in individual sessions, but even this is not a requirement for Web applications). When an individual user sends a request to the application, any variables or values used in processing the request are unique to that user, and no other user can access those variables or values.

In some instances (such as Web applications that perform surveys), there must be a mechanism for making variables available to everyone using the application, since the responses of individual users are combined, averaged, and summarized and then the results are shown to all users. The Global.asax file provides this mechanism for applications and sessions (we'll discuss and demonstrate applications and sessions in more detail in Chapter 5).

Note that the Global.asax file's Application_OnStart and Application_OnEnd events provide a mechanism for maintaining variables and values across the entire application; the Session_OnStart and Session_OnEnd events provide a mechanism for maintaining variables and values across an individual user's page requests. If session variables are not used, it becomes more difficult to access variables and values that must be present even when the user goes to a different page in the application.

To open the Global.asax file for coding (the Global.asax.vb file), right-click on it and choose View Code. You'll see the code shown here:

```
Imports System.Web
Imports System.Web.SessionState

Public Class Global
    Inherits System.Web.HttpApplication

#Region " Component Designer Generated Code "

    Public Sub New()
        MyBase.New()

        'This call is required by the Component Designer.
        InitializeComponent()

        'Add any initialization after the InitializeComponent()
          call
```

```vb
    End Sub

    'Required by the Component Designer
    Private components As System.ComponentModel.IContainer

    'NOTE: The following procedure is required by the
      Component Designer
    'It can be modified using the Component Designer.
    'Do not modify it using the code editor.
    <System.Diagnostics.DebuggerStepThrough()> Private Sub
      InitializeComponent() components = New System.
      ComponentModel.Container()
    End Sub

#End Region

    Sub Application_Start(ByVal sender As Object, ByVal e As
      EventArgs)
      ' Fires when the application is started
    End Sub

    Sub Session_Start(ByVal sender As Object, ByVal e As
      EventArgs)
      ' Fires when the session is started
    End Sub

    Sub Application_BeginRequest(ByVal sender As Object,
      ByVal e As EventArgs)
      ' Fires at the beginning of each request
    End Sub

    Sub Application_AuthenticateRequest(ByVal sender As
      Object, ByVal e As EventArgs)
      ' Fires upon attempting to authenticate the use
    End Sub

    Sub Application_Error(ByVal sender As Object, ByVal e As
      EventArgs)
      ' Fires when an error occurs
    End Sub

    Sub Session_End(ByVal sender As Object, ByVal e As
      EventArgs)
      ' Fires when the session ends
    End Sub
```

```
Sub Application_End(ByVal sender As Object, ByVal e As
   EventArgs)
   ' Fires when the application ends
End Sub
```

End Class

In the Source Code Editor you'll see a region (denoted by #Region...#End Region and named Component Designer Generated Code) that is grayed out. Make sure not to change this code in the Source Code Editor. Below that you'll see several Sub and End Sub statements, starting with Application_Start. This code block is where you would place code that you want to run when the Application_OnStart event occurs. These code blocks are event handlers, and you can create variables in them, dispose of variables, perform data processing to initialize them, basically anything you want to do at these specific times in the lifetime of an application or individual user session.

The Global.asax.resx file is used to store data that do not change, such as error messages. This makes it easier to change the content of this type of data without affecting the rest of the application.

The Styles.css File

The next item shown in Solution Explorer is a file named Styles.css. This file is understood to contain data for Cascading Style Sheets styles based on the file extension of .css. **Cascading Style Sheets (CSS)** is actually a language for specifying elements (such as the HTML P or Paragraph element) and setting the properties of these elements globally or individually by defining values for them.

Elements and the property values assigned to them are specified in CSS as a **selector** (such as the HTML element BODY, which means the body of your Web page) and a **declaration** (such as BACKGROUND-COLOR: white), which sets the background color displayed in your browser's screen to white for the current page.

A single stylesheet file can be linked to all Web pages in an application. Doing this enables you to easily control and manage style settings for all pages in your Web application. This means it is much easier to convey a consistent look and feel to users, no matter what page they happen to be on, and that updates flow automatically to all pages throughout the application. You also can create custom style element names and then apply them only to selected elements within an application, so there is unlimited flexibility in the application of styles for special purposes.

You can open the stylesheet file by right-clicking it and choosing Open With, and then choosing the CSS Style Editor. A text version of the file will be displayed, and you should see code such as the following (we've left out much of the code for the sake of brevity):

```css
/* Default CSS Stylesheet for a new Web Application
   project */

BODY
{
   BACKGROUND-COLOR: white;
   FONT-FAMILY: Verdana, Helvetica, sans-serif;
   FONT-SIZE: .8em;
   FONT-WEIGHT: normal;
   LETTER-SPACING: normal;
   TEXT-TRANSFORM: none;
   WORD-SPACING: normal
}

H1, H2, H3, H4, H5, TH, THEAD, TFOOT
{
   COLOR: #003366;
}
H1   {
      font-family: Verdana, Arial, Helvetica, sans-serif;
      font-size:         2em;
      font-weight:       700;
      font-style:        normal;
      text-decoration:   none;
      word-spacing:      normal;
      letter-spacing:    normal;
      text-transform:    none;
     }

H2   {
      font-family: Verdana, Arial, Helvetica, sans-serif;
      font-size:         1.75em;
      font-weight:       700;
      font-style:        normal;
      text-decoration:   none;
      word-spacing:      normal;
      letter-spacing:    normal;
      text-transform:    none;
     }

H3   {
      font-family: Verdana, Arial, Helvetica, sans-serif;
      font-size:         1.58em;
      font-weight:       500;
      font-style:        normal;
      text-decoration:   none;
```

```
word-spacing:      normal;
letter-spacing:    normal;
text-transform:    none;
}
```

As you can see, the Styles.css file is formatted with the selector first (such as H3). This selector indicates that any H3 element found in a Web page should be rendered with the properties indicated, not with the browser or HTML default properties.

Stylesheet files are called external stylesheets because they are linked to Web pages with a LINK element. Stylesheet commands also can be embedded in a Web page document with the Style element, as well as embedded directly in HTML elements. We'll cover the use of the Styles.css file in more depth in our Hands On Project at the end of this chapter.

The Web.config File

ASP.Net Web applications can be configured with specialized configuration files that are located in the root folder of the application and in any subfolders in which you care to put them. Open the **Web.config file** by right-clicking it and choosing Open With, then choosing Source Code (Text) Editor. You'll see code such as the following (we've again left out some of the code for brevity's sake):

```
<?xml version="1.0" encoding="utf-8" ?>
<configuration>

    <system.web>

        <!-- DYNAMIC DEBUG COMPILATION
        Set compilation debug="true" to insert debugging sym-
        bols (.pdb information) into the compiled page.
        Because this creates a larger file that executes more
        slowly, you should set this value to true only when
        debugging and to false at all other times. For more
        information, refer to the documentation about debug-
        ging ASP.NET files.
        -->
        <compilation defaultLanguage="vb" debug="true" />
```

As you can see from this code, the Web.config file is formatted as an XML file. The entire DYNAMIC DEBUG COMPILATION topic is commented out with XML/HTML comment delimiters (<!-- and -->). The first element is "configuration" and all other elements in the document are contained within this element (for more information about XML document structure, see Chapter 4). Notice the "compilation" element on the last line shown in our code. It has an attribute named "defaultLanguage" set to a value of "vb". This tells the CLR what language is in use for this application. And the debug element is set to a value of "true". This tells the CLR to include debug information when the application is compiled.

In Chapter 6 we cover how configuration works for Web applications in greater detail. For now, it is sufficient that you understand what this file is and what it does. Note that if you are using VS.Net to develop your application, the Web.config file will be edited for you when you change settings (such as turning off debug mode).

The WebAppStructure.vsdisco File

Files ending in **.vsdisco** are for making discovery of Web services possible. They are formatted as XML documents and included by default in ASP.Net Web applications even though they are for discovering XML Web services. They are included because many of the Web applications you create will include Web services.

You can open the WebAppStructure.vsdisco file by right-clicking it, choosing Open With, and then choosing Source Code (Text) Editor. You'll see code such as the following (we cover these file types and XML Web Services in Chapter 9):

```
<?xml version="1.0" encoding="utf-8" ?>
<dynamicDiscovery xmlns="urn:schemas-dynamicdiscovery:
   disco.2000-03-17">
<exclude path="_vti_cnf" />
<exclude path="_vti_pvt" />
<exclude path="_vti_log" />
<exclude path="_vti_script" />
<exclude path="_vti_txt" />
<exclude path="Web References" />
</dynamicDiscovery>
```

The WebForm1.aspx, WebForm1.aspx.vb, and WebForm1.aspx.resx Files

The last items in our list are the WebForm files that the template creates. The file ending with .aspx is the file that most resembles HTML and contains HTML and XML elements making up the rendered display in the user's browser. This file is already open in VS.Net and is displayed as a blank form in Design view. If you switch to HTML view, you'll see the HTML and XML code that make up this file, as shown here:

```
<%@ Page Language="vb" AutoEventWireup="false"
   Codebehind="WebForm1.aspx.vb" Inherits=
   "WebAppStructure.WebForm1"%>
<!DOCTYPE HTML PUBLIC "-//W3C//DTD HTML 4.0
   Transitional//EN">
<html>
   <head>
```

```
        <title>WebForm1</title>
        <meta name="GENERATOR" content="Microsoft Visual
          Studio.NET 7.0">
        <meta name="CODE_LANGUAGE" content="Visual Basic 7.0">
        <meta name=vs_defaultClientScript content="JavaScript">
        <meta name=vs_targetSchema content="http://schemas.
          microsoft.com/intellisense/ie5">
    </head>
    <body MS_POSITIONING="GridLayout">
        <form id="Form1" method="post" runat="server">
        </form>
    </body>
</html>
```

Between the beginning `<html>` and ending `</html>` tags are the HTML and XML elements and attributes that make up the document that is returned to the user's browser, such as the "title", "body", and "form" elements. The first line (starting with `<% @ Page`) contains the **@ Page** directive, a Language attribute indicating what language may be used inline, a path to the code-behind file, and indication of the class inherited by the page. The second line is simply a reference to the DTD for HTML (we'll discuss DTDs in more detail in Chapter 4).

The WebForm1.aspx file can be coded manually, in much the same fashion as an ordinary HTML Web page, although visual tools such as the HTML Designer in VS.Net are much more efficient for this task. For more information about Page Directives, see the Page Directives section later in this chapter.

The WebForm1.aspx.vb file is called the code-behind file, as it contains the code that runs when controls on your form respond to events. As we demonstrated in our previous Web applications, double-clicking on controls displayed in Design view causes an event handler to be created in the code-behind page (the file ending in .vb). Once an event handler is created, you can put code in it that will run when the user clicks the button (or performs some other action) that triggers the event. Event handler code blocks are the main mechanism by which data processing takes place, although, as we've explained, code also can be placed in other locations in your Web applications (such as the Global.asax file).

You can open the .vb file directly by displaying all files in the Solution Explorer and then double-clicking it. Doing so displays code such as this:

```
Public Class WebForm1
    Inherits System.Web.UI.Page

#Region " Web Form Designer Generated Code "

    'This call is required by the Web Form Designer.
    <System.Diagnostics.DebuggerStepThrough()> Private Sub
      InitializeComponent()
```

```
    End Sub

    Private Sub Page_Init(ByVal sender As System.Object, _
      ByVal e As System.EventArgs) Handles MyBase.Init
        'CODEGEN: This method call is required by the Web Form
          Designer
        'Do not modify it using the code editor.
        InitializeComponent()
    End Sub

#End Region

    Private Sub Page_Load(ByVal sender As System.Object, _
      ByVal e As System.EventArgs) Handles MyBase.Load
        'Put user code to initialize the page here
    End Sub

End Class
```

Note once again that you shouldn't change code within the Region (denoted by #Region...#End Region) from within the Source Code Editor, although appropriate changes will be made to this code block when you make changes to the Web form in Design view. Notice also that the Page_Load event handler code block has already been created for you. This event is triggered when the page first loads and can be used for the special setting that must occur only the first time the page is loaded, not on each subsequent request.

The WebForm1.aspx.resx file is used to store resources applicable to the Web form. Resources are any data that are not compiled and do not change, such as error messages. Storing these in a resource file makes them much easier to change without affecting the rest of the application.

Coding Controls into a Web Form Manually   Although you can use Visual Studio.Net's Toolbox to drag controls such as buttons, textboxes, and labels onto a form, you can also simply type the appropriate code into any .aspx file manually. In the Exercises section at the end of this chapter there is an example, and you can create controls on forms and then view the code in HTML view to get an idea of the syntax and structure to use.

ASP.Net Page Processing

At the top, the .Net Framework provides classes from which objects can be derived for Windows and Web applications, among other programmed structures. ASP.Net is built upon the .Net Framework (like ADO.Net and other .Net-based technologies). ASP.Net provides not only classes from which objects useful for Web applications can be derived, but is also a complete Web platform for any Web application you care to develop. So long as you use a programming language that is compatible with the Common Language

Runtime (CLR), you can use any language you like, although only one language per ASP.Net page is allowed.

The ASP.Net page framework is the architecture running on the Web server that dynamically produces and manages Web forms. You can think of Web pages and Web forms as the same thing, except that Web forms use the HTML form model as the mechanism for allowing interactivity with users.

Essentially, Web forms in the ASP.Net page framework are an abstraction of the ordinary Web page, HTML-form interaction. The way ASP.Net abstracts the display code from the programming code allows you to use visual development tools to rapidly program Web applications just like you can rapidly program Windows applications, a big step forward in the development process. And although the Web is stateless (we'll discuss state in greater detail in later chapters), the ASP.Net page framework automatically maintains the state of the page and its controls, also making the development process easier.

Unlike ASP, ASP.Net pages typically use two files to contain the display code and the programming code. The file extensions for these pages are .aspx and .aspx.vb (or .aspx.cs if you're programming with C#). You can include programming code in a single file also containing display code (called in-page or single-file Web forms), but in our opinion it's best to use the two-file model.

So, for example, when you create a new Web form named by default in Visual Studio.Net as WebForm1.aspx, a new class named WebForm1 is derived from the base class (including with .Net) named System.Web.UI.Page. If you make changes to either the .aspx file or the code-behind file while the application is running, they are detected and new .dll files are compiled on the fly, but the changes are not apparent to the user until the next time the pages are requested.

The ASP.Net Compilation Process

Files containing code-behind classes (when you write code in a code-behind page, it creates a "class"; more about classes, objects, and so forth in Chapter 3) are all compiled into a dynamic link library or .dll file for the project of which they are a part (files with an extension of .dll are used in many types of applications for Windows and the Web). The first time a user requests an .aspx page in your Web application, a .Net class file is automatically generated from that page and then compiled into a second .dll file that inherits from the overall .dll file (which itself was generated from the code-behind pages). Thereafter, any call to that page is responded to by the application running as an executable program, not from static HTML like an ordinary Web application.

Page Processing

The basic class in an ASP.Net Web application is the page class, and a Web forms page goes through a series of page processing steps every time it is requested: initialize, process, and dispose. A special stage called *render* is performed toward the end of the processing cycle, and it is during this stage that the HTML output is created.

Page Life Cycle Each time a page is requested, the server initializes the page and in the rendering stage creates the appropriate output to send to the user. The server is able to detect whether or not this is the first time the form was requested, or is being requested as the result of a postback (the user clicking something that causes a roundtrip to the server). The server also is able to preserve the state of the page and controls between roundtrips, thereby enabling a truly event-driven experience. The page itself goes through a series of processing steps including page initialization (the Page_Init event), loading the page (the Page_Load event), validation (ASP.Net Server Validation controls perform validation functions), event handling (any controls on the page whose events were activated run their code), and cleanup (the page is unloaded on the server). We discuss events and event handlers in more detail in Chapter 3; this sequence of page processing steps plays an important role throughout our exercises and projects in this book.

Discussion—The VB.Net ASP.Net Template

When you create a new project using the Visual Basic Projects ASP.Net Web Application template, the template creates a number of files and folders for you. These files and folders provide all the basic features necessary to construct a Web application. The files include a Web form and a global file (with their code-behind files), a stylesheet file, a file for storing assembly information, a configuration file, a bin folder, and a file for discovering XML Web services.

Each of the files created can be viewed in the Solution Explorer, and right-clicking them provides options for working with them in various editors. Another way to open and work with the files is via Windows Explorer and Notepad, but care must be taken not to disturb code in blocks designated as Regions (unless you are sure you should edit these blocks).

ASP.Net Directives

ASP.Net Directives are settings used when a page or control is compiled, such as the "@ Page" and "@ Imports" directives. The actual page (the file ending in .aspx) browsed to by the user is compiled dynamically, and the @ Page directive contains an attribute (named Inherits) that defines the class from which the .aspx file derives (the example code below shows how the Inherits attribute works).

Although directives can be placed in any location in your file, the traditional place to locate them is at the top of the file. Illustration 2.2 describes the general layout of directives in ASP.Net files.

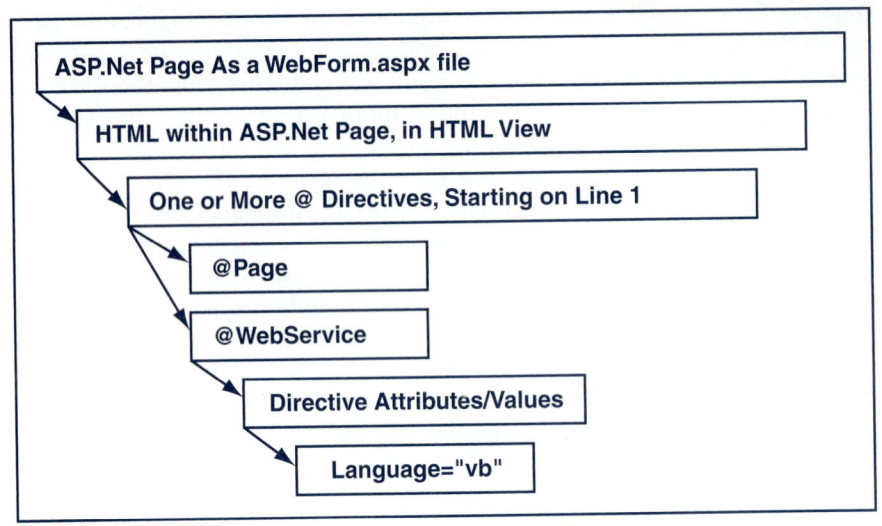

ILLUSTRATION 2.2 How Directives Appear in ASP.Net Files

Coding Directives

Let's review the first line in the WebForm1.aspx file (in the code we found in HTML mode, not the code from the code-behind page):

```
<%@ Page Language="vb" AutoEventWireup="false" Codebehind=
    "WebForm1.aspx.vb" Inherits="WebAppStructure.WebForm1"%>
```

This line begins and ends with ASP delimiters (`<%` and `%>`). Inside the delimiters is a Directive, in this case @ Page, a language attribute set to "vb", an AutoEventWireup attribute set to "false", a reference to the code-behind page, and an Inherits attribute indicating the class inherited by the page. There are a number of directives that may be used with ASP.Net applications, and each one has a number of attributes that are associated with it. We'll discuss them in the following sections.

The @ Page Directive

The @ Page directive defines attributes that are specific to pages for the ASP.Net page parser and compiler, such as Language and Buffer. This means that when a page is parsed (read and separated into its components) and compiled, these directives tell the parser and compiler how you want it done.

For example, if you specify `Language="vb"`, this tells the parser and compiler that you are specifying Visual Basic as the appropriate language when code is included inline in your ASP.Net pages. This is not the same as the language for the project or the language in the code-behind page, although if you are working with Visual Basic in the project you might want to work with Visual Basic inline as well.

The Buffer attribute determines whether page buffering is enabled. The default is "true"; what this means is any data processing on the page is completed before content is returned to the user. As we discuss in Chapter 3, you might want to use the Response.Flush method to send back a partial response to the user if you expect processing to take quite a bit of time.

Note: If the "Page" part of the directive is left out, it will be assumed to be an @ Page directive. This is for compatibility with ASP.

The @ Control Directive
This directive is for ASP.Net controls, not ASP.Net pages. It uses many of the same attributes as the @ Page directive.

The @ Import Directive
This directive is used to explicitly import namespaces (and thereby the associated classes) into a page or control. It has only the namespace attribute, and this attribute can be set to a value indicating the name of the namespace being imported. For example, the following code would import the System.Net namespace:

```
<%@ Import Namespace="System.Net" %>
```

If you need to import multiple namespaces, use multiple import directive lines.

The @ Implements Directive
This directive is used to declare that a page or control implements a specific interface. It has only one attribute (interface) and may only be used on the page or control, not in a code-behind page.

The @ Register Directive
This directive is used to register custom ASP.Net controls with their associated namespace. It has several attributes, including the prefix to be used for the namespace (tagprefix), the name of the class for the control (tagname), and the name of the namespace (namespace). Use it when you develop your own custom ASP.Net controls.

The @ Assembly Directive
This directive links an assembly to the page in which it is included. This makes all of the assembly's classes and interfaces available within the page. Note that any assemblies in the bin folder are automatically linked to pages in your Web application, and so this directive is not needed for those assemblies.

The @ Output Cache Directive
This directive can be used to set page caching, much like changing cache properties of the Response object get and set caching values. Attributes

include Duration and several that vary output options in different ways (VaryByHeader, VaryByParam, VaryByCustom). Use this directive for fine-grained caching control.

The @ Reference Directive
This directive allows you to dynamically compile a control or page and link it to this page.

Discussion—ASP.Net Directives

ASP.Net directives provide Web application developers with a means for setting compilation options for specific pages and controls within an ASP.Net Web application. Directives are typically coded first in a Web form or control file, and include @ Page, @ Control (for pages and for controls, respectively), and several other directives. Each directive has one or more attributes, and directive attributes contain specific values that tell the parser and compiler what to do. For example, the @ Page Language attribute can be set to "vb", so that the compiler expects Visual Basic to be used for any inline coding on the page.

Quick Check Questions

1. List four files that are created when the ASP.Net Web Application template in the Visual Basic projects node is used to create a new project in VS.Net.
2. How is an ASP.Net Web application project named when the template is used?
3. What effect does this name have on any of the files created?
4. What is the extension for the file that controls application and session events in an ASP.Net Web application?
5. What is the extension for the file upon which HTML and ASP elements are placed during development?
6. What are files called in which event handlers are created, when the event handlers are created by double-clicking controls on a Web form in Design view?
7. What file would you modify if you wanted to change the color of the background on your Web forms?
8. Where are ASP.Net directives usually written in a WebForm file?
9. What directive attribute sets the programming language the compiler expects to see for any code written inline in a Web form?

1. Creating a new project with the Visual Basic Projects ASP.Net Web Application template causes a number of files and folders to be created in a root application folder on an IIS Web server. These files and folders contain all the basic features and structures required to support a typical Web application.
2. Files created by the ASP.Net Web Application template include a WebForm, a Global.asax file, code-behind files formatted for Visual Basic.Net, a Styles file formatted as CSS, an AssemblyInfo file, references to several Web-related namespaces, and a Web.config file. These files can be opened and edited inside Visual Studio.Net.
3. The first line found in a WebForm file (in HTML view) contains an ASP.Net @ Page directive. Directives are used in ASP.Net to inform the parser and compiler how to process individual pages and controls.

Exercise 2.1—Coding ASP.Net Server Controls in a Web Form

The main purpose of this exercise is to demonstrate how buttons, textboxes, labels, and other Web form controls are added to a Web form and how they are coded. While we use the visual tools in VS.Net to add controls to forms, you also can write them in manually in an .aspx file if you follow the conventions you find in HTML view.

1. Open VS.Net if it is not already open, and open the WebAppStructure solution. You should have the blank Web form open and in Design view.
2. Open the Toolbox and add a Label control to the surface of the form.
3. Click the HTML button at the bottom of the designer to view the HTML code.
4. The code should look something like this:

```
<asp:Label id="Label1" style="Z-INDEX: 101; LEFT: 8px; POSITION: absolute; TOP: 8px"
    runat="server" Width="248px" Height="48px">Label</asp:Label>
```

5. In the HTML code, change the value for the "Width" attribute to "50". Click the Design button to see what effect this change has on the control.
6. Try performing several other changes in the code and see what effect they have on the label.
7. In Design view, click on the Label control and open the Properties window. In the Properties window select the BorderStyle property and set it to "Solid". What happens to the code for this control in HTML view? Why do you suppose this property didn't appear in code until you set it for the first time?
8. The elements "html", "title", and "body" are part of the HTML language, but the element "asp:Label" is not. How do you suppose ordinary browsers understand how to display the "asp:Label" control? Where do you suppose the "asp:Label" control is defined? (Hint: We'll talk more about how "asp" elements are defined for Web applications in Chapter 4.)
9. Remove the Label control by going back into Design view and clicking on it, then hitting the delete key.

Exercise 2.2—Creating a Virtual Directory in IIS

Ordinarily, your ASP.Net Web application files will be contained in project folders created within the "wwwroot" folder in "Inetpub", the default location for Web applications and Web pages running under IIS. However, you may want to create a virtual directory that is viewed by IIS as a Web directory but is located in just about any spot on the server's hard drive. The main purpose of this exercise is to demonstrate how to create a new virtual directory in IIS.

1. Click Start|Programs|Administrative Tools|Internet Services Manager from the desktop. The Internet Information Services window should open, as shown in Figure 2.2.

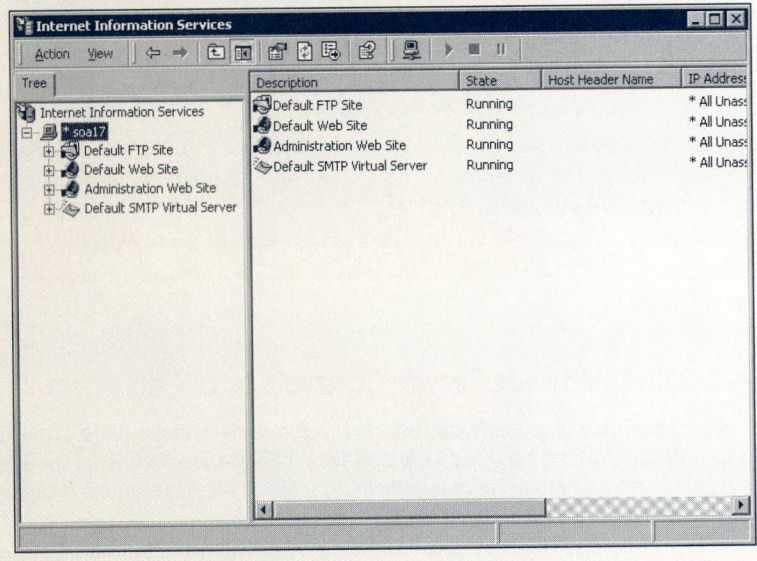

FIGURE 2.2　The IIS Window

2. Right-click the Default Web Site node to bring up the shortcut menu and choose New|Virtual Directory. The Virtual Directory Creation Wizard will open, as shown in Figure 2.3. The first screen is information only, so click Next.

FIGURE 2.3　The Virtual Directory Wizard

3. Give the virtual directory a short name, called an alias, as shown in Figure 2.4. Click Next.

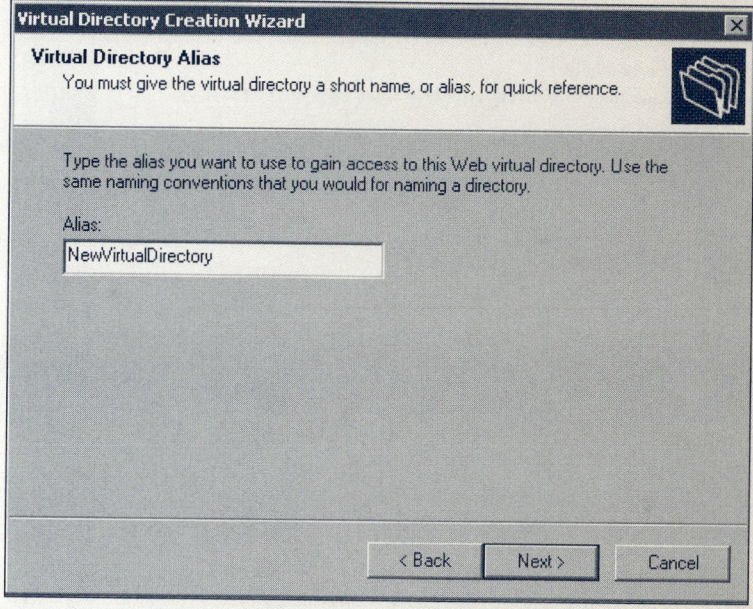

FIGURE 2.4 Giving the Directory an Alias

4. Browse to the existing folder you'd like to make into a virtual directory. In Figure 2.5, we've created a folder on the E: drive named NewDirectory and used that for our virtual directory. Click Next.

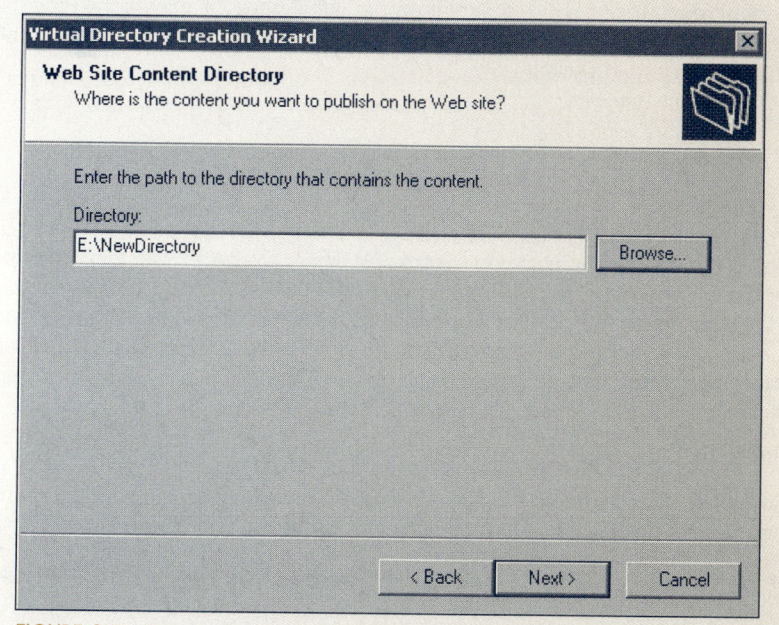

FIGURE 2.5 Browsing for the New Directory Location

5. On the next screen, select Read, Run Scripts, and Execute ISAPI, as shown in Figure 2.6. Click Next.

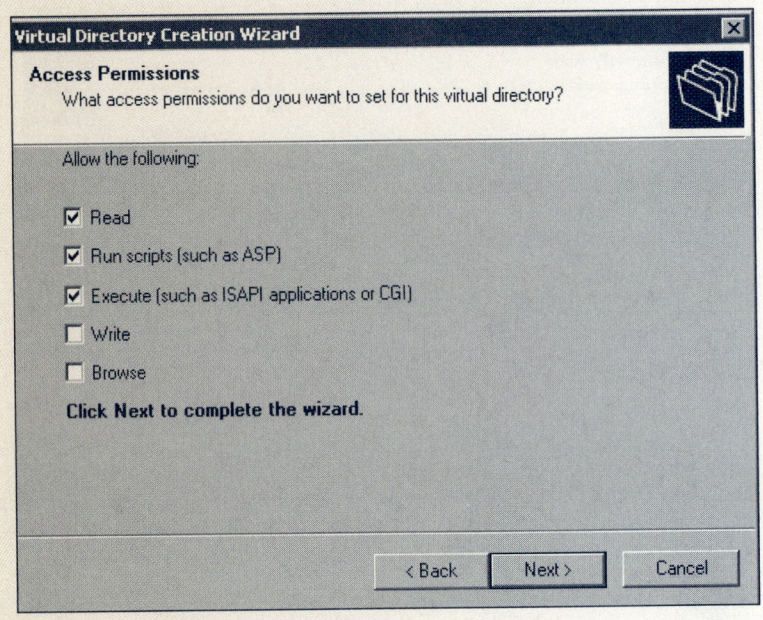

FIGURE 2.6 Setting Access Permissions

6. The last screen is also information only, so click Finish. Your new virtual directory should appear in Information Services Manager as a new node. You can right-click this node and choose Properties from the shortcut menu to set IIS Web Server properties. Figure 2.7 shows the Properties dialog box. Open VS.Net if it is not already open, and open the WebAppStructure solution. You should have the blank Web form open and in Design view.

Asp.Net Web Applications

In this project we will use the Web application we created earlier (WebAppStructure) from the ASP.Net Web Application template in the Visual Basic Projects node of the New Projects dialog box. If you haven't already created this application from the template, please do so now. You should have the blank Web form displayed on your screen in VS.Net. You also should have the Solution Explorer and the Properties window open. Close up the References node and click the Show All Files button in Solution Explorer (again) to stop the display of all files.

ADDING WEB FORMS

1. Click on the WebAppStructure project, then right-click it to open the shortcut menu. Choose Add from the menu to display the Add menu (shown in Figure 2.8 on page 74).

2. Choose Add Web Form from the menu. When the Add Item dialog box is displayed, choose Web Form from the item templates available and rename it WelcomeForm.aspx (Figure 2.9). Click Open to open the new Web form.

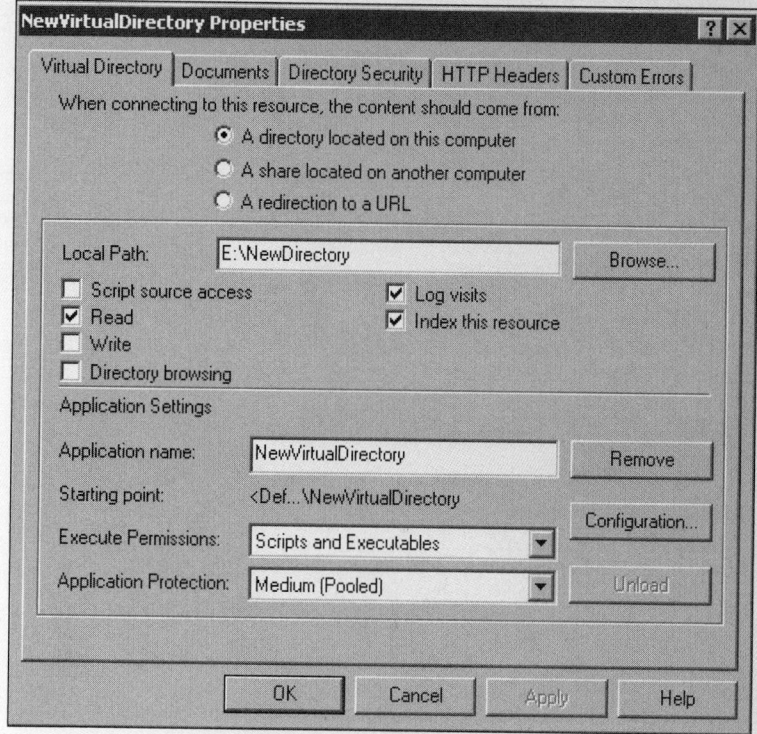

FIGURE 2.7　The Properties Dialog Box

3. Click the WelcomeForm.apsx file in Solution Explorer. Right-click it and choose Set as Start Page from the shortcut menu. Doing this sets the entire application so that this becomes the first page to appear when a user enters the URL of the application.

4. Click on the WebAppStructure project and right-click it. Choose Properties from the shortcut menu. The WebAppStructure Property Pages dialog box opens. Click on the Configuration node in the left side of the dialog box. Next to Start Project (on the far right) you'll see Page: and a drop-down list of pages, with WelcomeForm.aspx selected from the list (as shown in Figure 2.10).

5. In the Property Pages dialog box, switch to the Build node. Notice the Output Path: setting. This setting means your class library and debugging information will go into the bin folder when the application is built.

6. Close the Property Pages dialog box.

ASSEMBLYINFO.VB SETTINGS

1. Right-click on the AssemblyInfo.vb file and choose View Code from the shortcut menu. Enter the title "Welcome" and a description "Template Application" in the appropriate places in the code. Your code should resemble the following:

```
<Assembly: AssemblyTitle("Welcome")>
<Assembly: AssemblyDescription("Test Application")>
```

2. Save and close the AssemblyInfo.vb file.

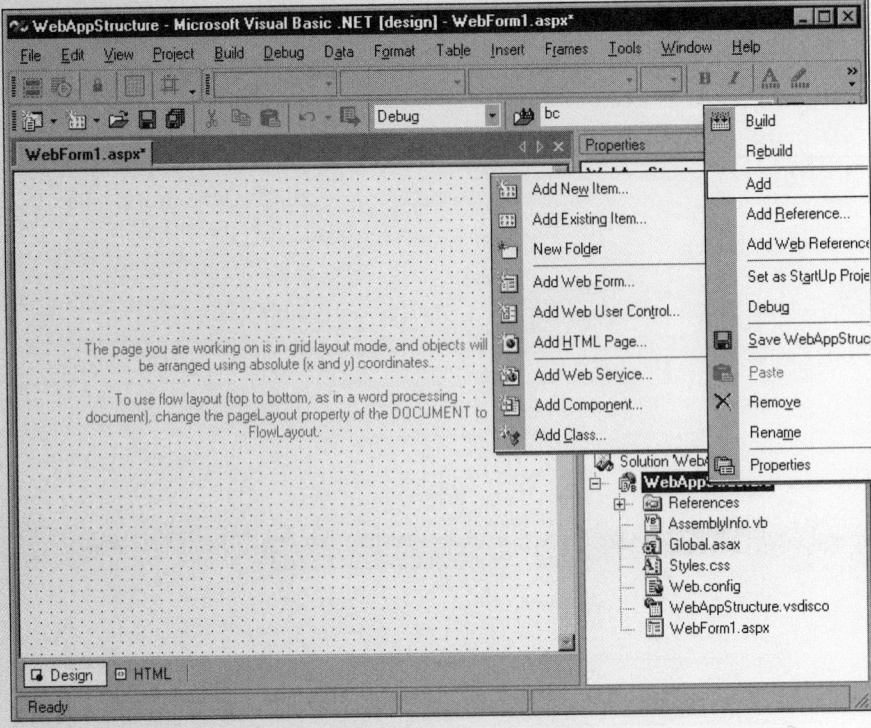

FIGURE 2.8 The Add Menu

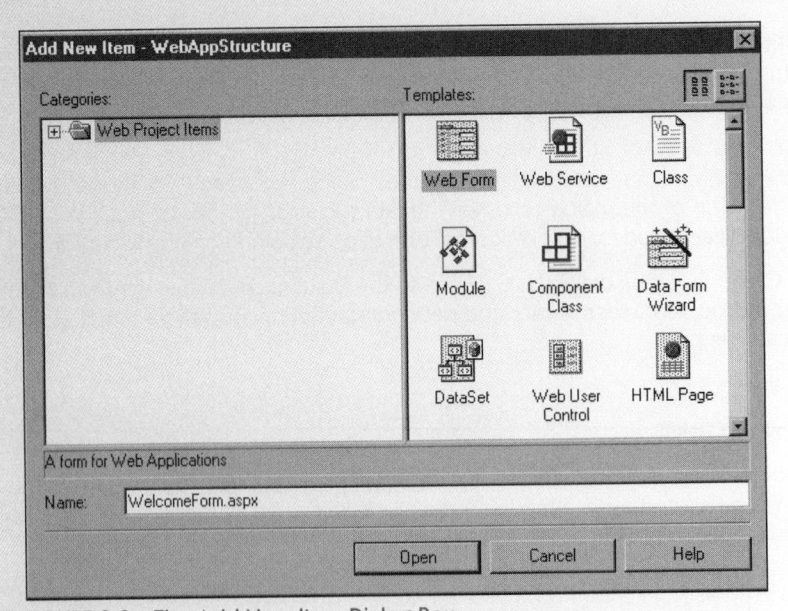

FIGURE 2.9 The Add New Item Dialog Box

Hands On Project

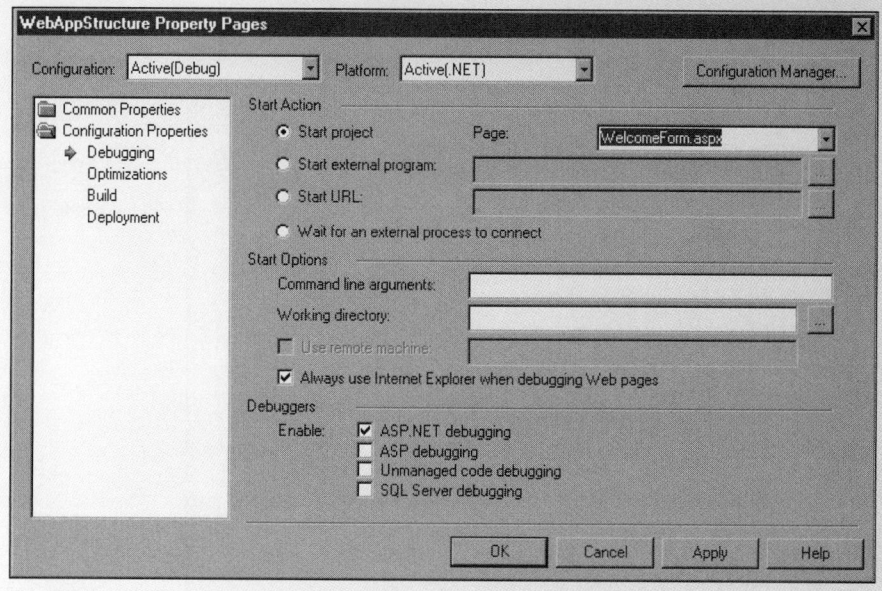

FIGURE 2.10 The WebAppStructure Property Pages Dialog Box

SETTING CSS STYLES

1. Click on the surface of the WelcomeForm.aspx file in Design view. Choose Format|Document Styles from the menu. The Document Styles dialog box will open (Figure 2.11).

2. Two buttons are activated in this dialog box: Add Style Sheet and Add Style Link. Click the Add Style Link button. The Select Style Sheet dialog box will open. Choose Styles.css in the top-right box of the dialog box, as shown in Figure 2.12.

3. Click OK. The stylesheet will be shown connected to the WelcomeForm.aspx file in the Document Styles dialog box (Figure 2.13).

4. Save the WelcomeForm.aspx file. Switch the form to HTML view. You should see the following line has been added to the HTML code in the HEAD element block:
   `<LINK href="Styles.css" type="text/css" rel="stylesheet">`

5. Right-click the Styles.css file in the Solution Explorer, then choose Open With. The Open With – Styles.css dialog box will open (Figure 2.14). Choose CSS Source Editor from the list and click OK.

6. The Styles.css file will open in the CSS Source Editor (Figure 2.15).

7. Change the value for the background color of the body to Teal, then save and close the file.

8. Click on the surface of the WelcomeForm.aspx file in Design view, then choose File|Build and Browse from the menu. Your WelcomeForm should resemble Figure 2.16 in Browse view. Close the browse view.

9. Close the solution.

FIGURE 2.11   The Document Styles Dialog Box

FIGURE 2.12   The Select Style Sheet Dialog Box

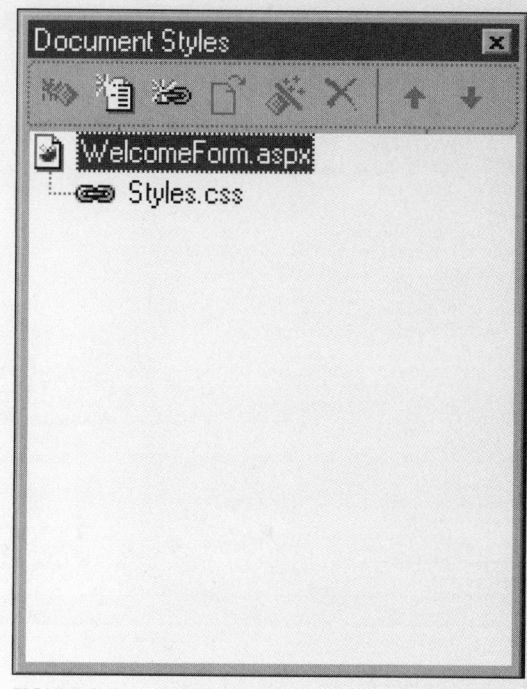

FIGURE 2.13 The Connection between the Stylesheet and the WelcomeForm.aspx File

FIGURE 2.14 The Open With Dialog Box

CHAPTER 2 The ASP.Net Template

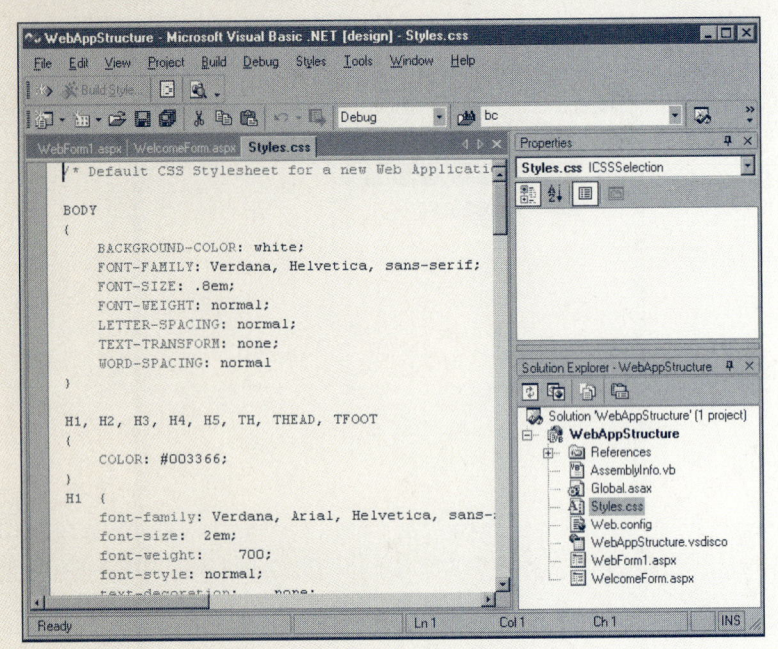

FIGURE 2.15 The CSS Source Editor

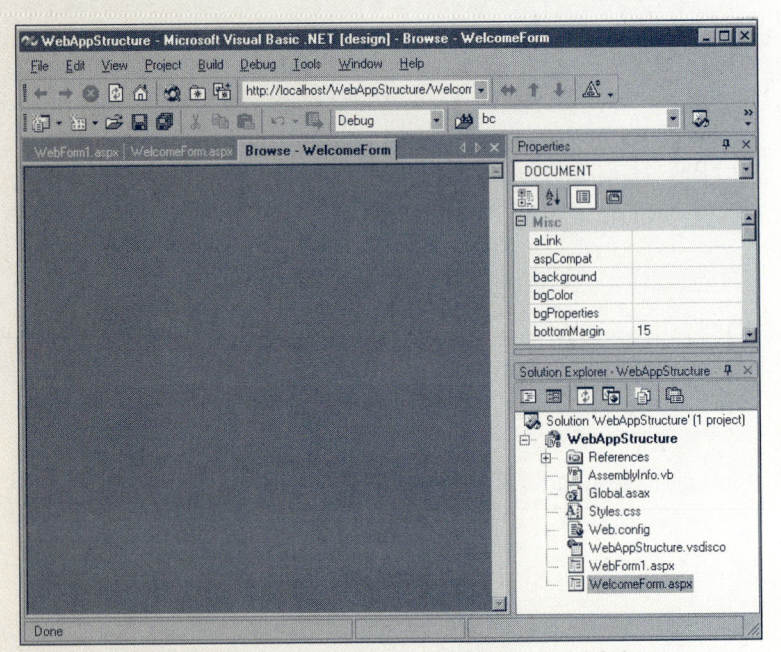

FIGURE 2.16 The WelcomeForm with a Teal Background Color

AutoEventWireup The AutoEventWireup attribute is True by default, and if it is missing from the @ Page directive, it will be considered True automatically. If left True, the page framework will call page events automatically, by their default names. In Visual Studio.Net, you may want to rename event handlers or use them for additional code, so the default when you use templates to create Web forms in VS.Net is to include the AutoEventWireup attribute but set it to false.

Key Terms

@ Page
application events
assemblies
AssemblyCompany
AssemblyTitle
Cascading Style Sheets (CSS)
code-behind page
declaration
directive
event handler
Global.asax file
resources
selector
session events
template
Visual Basic.Net Project
.vsdisco file
Web.config file

Review Questions

1. What kind of project can be used for creating ASP.Net Web applications from templates in VS.Net?
2. What is the name for the part of an ASP.Net Web application made from a template that does not show up as a file or folder in the Solution Explorer? Where can you find the file that represents this part?
3. What files are contained in the bin folder when the template is done creating a new ASP.Net Web application for Visual Basic projects?
4. What is the purpose of the file with the .pdb extension?
5. The template creates a file named WebForm1.aspx and another one named WebForm1.aspx.vb. Why does it create two files? What is the purpose of the file with the .vb extension?
6. Suppose you write a Web form page manually, using a text editor. If you intend to put Visual Basic code inline in the file, what directive must be used?
7. In what language are Web forms written?
8. What kind of code blocks are used in the code-behind page? Describe an easy way to start this type of code-block in the code-behind page.
9. What is CSS? Why is it helpful in Web applications?
10. What CSS selector would you use to modify all HTML header elements of size 6 in your Web pages?
11. Describe how to add a new Web form to a project.

CHAPTER 3

HTTP Classes

LEARNING OBJECTIVES

Upon completion of this chapter, you will be able to:

1. Describe how HTTP works.
2. Describe the stateless nature of the Web.
3. Find the HTTP classes in an Application.
4. Understand the basics of OOP and Objects in ASP.Net.
5. Describe how the Request and Response objects are used.
6. Access the Server Variables Collection with the Request object.
7. Create a QueryString variable in HTML.
8. Capture form data submitted by a user with the Form collection.
9. Work with form values in VB.Net code.

INTRODUCTION

When you use the typical desktop Windows application, it is self-contained, with all executables, files, data, and so forth on your local computer. When you are working with it, communications between the Windows that make up the user interface and the running application logic are direct, without any ambiguity about the status of the user interface or the processing logic.

Web applications are different. The user interface is often a browser, and you as the developer don't necessarily know what brand or version of the browser is running (although you can sometimes find out). And even if you know the version of browser being used, you may not have the luxury of not supporting the browser.

Likewise, the processing logic and the data stores supporting your Web application may be located on one or more servers across the Internet. Because of the stateless nature of the Web and HTTP (HyperText Transport Protocol, the protocol or format used to transmit requests from pages to your Web server and responses from your Web server back to the user), there is no intrinsic way for the processing logic to be absolutely sure about the status of the user interface, or even if it is the same user making another request.

Of course, developers have been hard at work trying to overcome these difficulties, and ASP.Net and the .Net Framework have a number of classes and design features that greatly reduce problems that arise from the stateless nature of the Web. In this chapter we examine some of the basic issues, the HTTP protocol, and the HttpRequest and HttpResponse classes and their properties, methods, and events. Note that we include many short chunks of code to indicate how the syntax works in the main part of the chapter; in the project at the end of the chapter we show how some of these code chunks might be used in an application.

Internet Communications and HTTP

There are many types of computer networks, including the Internet and your Local Area Network (LAN). The purpose of networks is to allow one computer to communicate with others. Communications from computer to computer are said to be layered, meaning several communications formats and components are used for any given network. A popular representation of the layers of a network is the OSI Reference model, which breaks the protocols used into seven layers. For example, Layer 1 is the Physical layer (the wire, fiber, or frequency upon which bits are transmitted). Layer 4 is the Transport layer, in which data packets are sent across the network. When communications take place (from your computer to a server, for example), your application program and operating system begin the process of transmitting data being sent by breaking them down and adding header information at each layer. When the data reach Layer 1, they are sent across the wire (or through the air). When the data reach their destination, the header information is stripped off and the packets are reassembled for use at the other end. Illustration 3.1 shows how this process works.

TCP/IP is a set of protocols used at Layer 4 to break data into datagrams (sets of bits) of the appropriate size from transmission and reassembly. The IP part of TCP/IP refers to the addressing scheme used to ensure that datagrams arrive at the right computer on the Internet.

Layer 7 is the Application layer, and it is at this layer that HTTP operates. HTTP is designed specifically for use with HyperText documents. Note that communications between computers use all of the layers, with additional bits being added to the front end (and the back end) of a data packet or datagram for each layer.

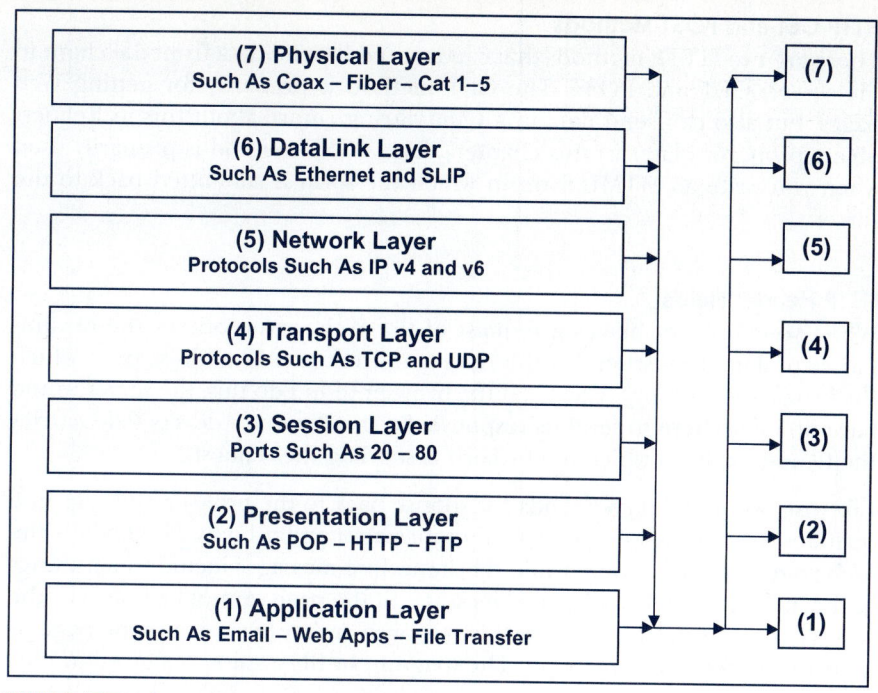

```
┌─────────────────────────────────────────────────────────┐
│         (7) Physical Layer                              │
│       Such As Coax – Fiber – Cat 1–5          →   (7)  │
│                                                          │
│         (6) DataLink Layer                              │
│       Such As Ethernet and SLIP                →  (6)  │
│                                                          │
│         (5) Network Layer                               │
│       Protocols Such As IP v4 and v6           →  (5)  │
│                                                          │
│         (4) Transport Layer                             │
│       Protocols Such As TCP and UDP            →  (4)  │
│                                                          │
│         (3) Session Layer                               │
│       Ports Such As 20 – 80                    →  (3)  │
│                                                          │
│         (2) Presentation Layer                          │
│       Such As POP – HTTP – FTP                 →  (2)  │
│                                                          │
│         (1) Application Layer                           │
│    Such As Email – Web Apps – File Transfer    →  (1)  │
└─────────────────────────────────────────────────────────┘
```

ILLUSTRATION 3.1   OSI Model of Network Layers

When your computer (through your browser) communicates with a Web server, the browser generates a request to the Web server. Protocols (such as HTTP, TCP, and IP) running on your computer break the request down into datagrams and packets, adding headers (extra bits on the front end) and footers to each little chunk of data. The headers tell the various routers, computers, and programs what to do with each packet, so that the request can be properly received and reassembled at the Web server. After processing your request, the Web server sends out a response using the same "break down and reassemble at the other end" process that your computer did.

HyperText Transport Protocol (HTTP)

HyperText Transport Protocol (HTTP) is the protocol at the top of the chain, and messages sent using HTTP contain headers and other elements as well. Your browser (and the Web server at the other end) knows what these headers and elements mean, and works with them to fulfill your browsing experience.

The most recent version of HTTP is HTTP 1.1, built and maintained by the World Wide Web Consortium (www.w3.org). It also can be found under Request For Comment (RFC) 2616. It is a stateless request/response protocol, meaning that there is no built-in way for the server to know anything about the user interface. The Web server simply responds to requests and delivers the data requested if possible.

HTTP GET and POST Methods

There are two HTTP methods that can be used to send data from the client to the server: GET and POST. The GET method is primarily for getting Web pages, but also can send data in a QueryString (more about this in Request object properties later in this chapter). The POST method is primarily used when you write an HTML form in which the form is submitted back to the server.

HTTP Header Fields

When your browser makes a request of the Web server, one of the obvious pieces of data it must send is the return address (the IP address from which the browser is sending). Clearly, if the browser didn't do this, the server would have no idea where to send its response. So the Remote Address field carries the IP address from which the browser is sending the request.

Likewise, when the server sends a response back to the browser, the response includes headers as well as status line messages and a body. The body is the Web page you are viewing, while the status line messages include such things as the infamous "404 Not Found" message (if the page cannot be found by the server). Your browser interprets this response and either displays the page or an error message of some type. The diagram in Illustration 3.2 gives an idea

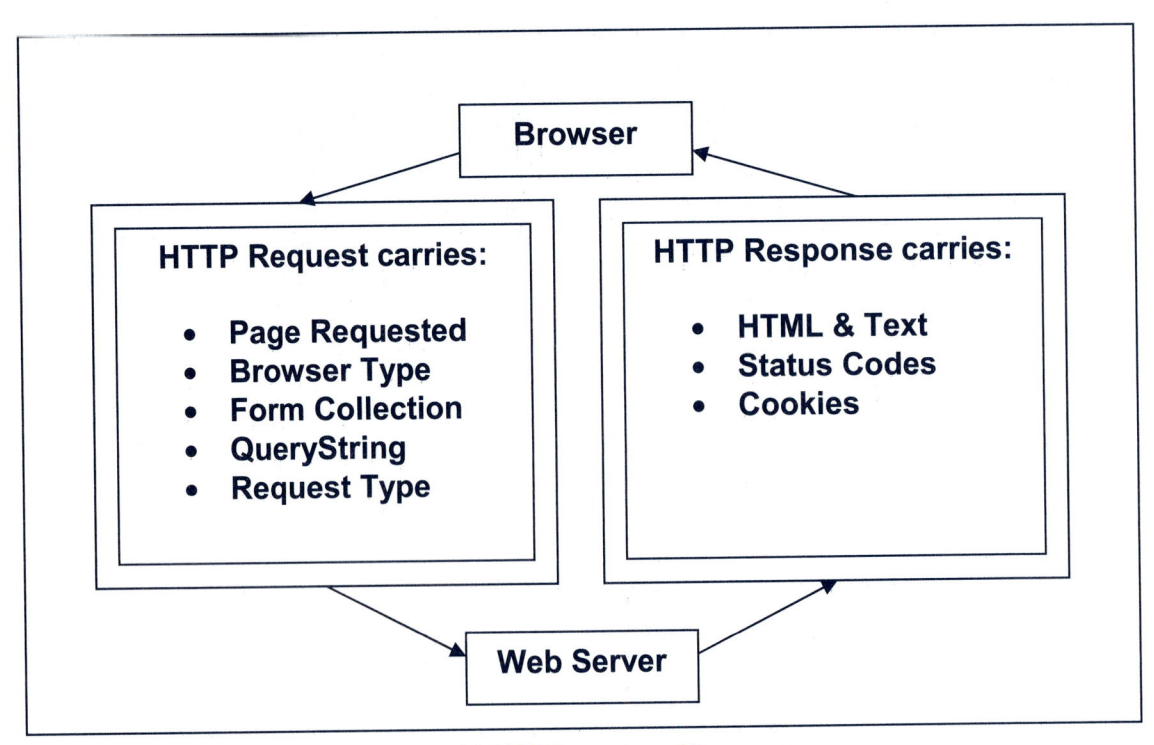

```
                    ┌──────────┐
                    │ Browser  │
                    └──────────┘
         ↗                            ↖
┌─────────────────────────┐   ┌─────────────────────────┐
│ HTTP Request carries:   │   │ HTTP Response carries:  │
│                         │   │                         │
│   • Page Requested      │   │   • HTML & Text         │
│   • Browser Type        │   │   • Status Codes        │
│   • Form Collection     │   │   • Cookies             │
│   • QueryString         │   │                         │
│   • Request Type        │   │                         │
└─────────────────────────┘   └─────────────────────────┘
              ↘                           ↗
                    ┌──────────────┐
                    │  Web Server  │
                    └──────────────┘
```

ILLUSTRATION 3.2 Web Communications with HTTP Requests and Responses

of the relationship between HTTP requests and responses during Web communications.

It's important to understand a little about how HTTP works, because the Request and Response objects work directly with HTTP messages to enable effective communications between your ASP.Net application and the user's browser.

Objects, Properties, Methods, and Events

There was a time when computer programs consisted of lines of code that would be executed sequentially. If you needed to perform some lines of code over again, you could reinsert those lines, or have the program "goto" a specific line number and perform the code again. This is a rather inefficient programming style and can be hard to debug. Writing callable functions is a little easier, because the functionality is contained in the function and can be reused from anywhere in the program.

Several decades ago, a new kind of programming style called "object-oriented programming" (OOP) emerged. The idea is to create "objects" from base classes, and to hide the details or inner workings of the object from other code. In a sense, an **object** is like a little application program; you send it input and it sends back output, but you don't need to know how it does its job in order to complete the rest of your application and be sure that it functions correctly. The diagram in Illustration 3.3 shows how classes, objects, properties, and so on work.

Object-oriented programming is now mainstream, and if you've had any programming classes, you're already familiar with it. For those who are just getting started, you're actually ahead of the game, because you'll learn how to use objects in your programming before you even really understand everything about how they work. Just think of objects like this and you'll be okay:

An object can be anything in an application (all applications, not just Web applications). An object can be a form, a button, a service, a component, anything. Some objects, if they represent interactive elements on a form, are called controls (but they are still fundamentally objects) like buttons, radio buttons, list boxes, drop-down boxes, and so on. Qualities of objects (such as color, size, position, caption text) are called **properties**. Things objects can do (such as send messages) are called **methods**. Things that happen to objects (such as a button object being clicked) are called **events**.

In the following sections we discuss these concepts further, but keep in mind that your main job as application developer is to decide and set all of your objects' initial properties and to change those properties or have your objects

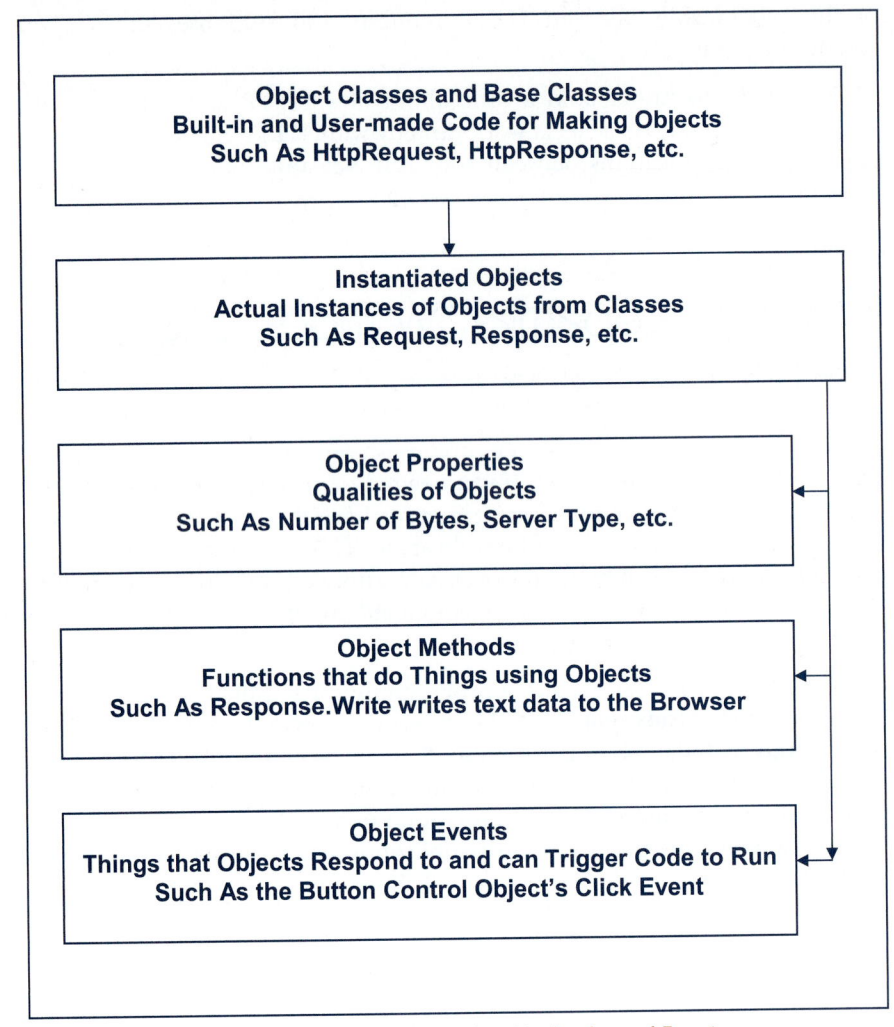

```
┌─────────────────────────────────────────────────────┐
│   ┌─────────────────────────────────────────────┐   │
│   │        Object Classes and Base Classes      │   │
│   │   Built-in and User-made Code for Making    │   │
│   │              Objects                        │   │
│   │   Such As HttpRequest, HttpResponse, etc.   │   │
│   └─────────────────────────────────────────────┘   │
│                        │                            │
│                        ▼                            │
│   ┌─────────────────────────────────────────────┐   │
│   │            Instantiated Objects             │   │
│   │   Actual Instances of Objects from Classes  │   │
│   │       Such As Request, Response, etc.       │   │
│   └─────────────────────────────────────────────┘   │
│                                                 │   │
│   ┌─────────────────────────────────────────────┐   │
│   │             Object Properties              ◄│   │
│   │             Qualities of Objects            │   │
│   │ Such As Number of Bytes, Server Type, etc.  │   │
│   └─────────────────────────────────────────────┘   │
│                                                 │   │
│   ┌─────────────────────────────────────────────┐   │
│   │              Object Methods                ◄│   │
│   │     Functions that do Things using Objects  │   │
│   │ Such As Response.Write writes text data to  │   │
│   │                the Browser                  │   │
│   └─────────────────────────────────────────────┘   │
│                                                 │   │
│   ┌─────────────────────────────────────────────┐   │
│   │              Object Events                 ◄│   │
│   │ Things that Objects Respond to and can      │   │
│   │            Trigger Code to Run              │   │
│   │ Such As the Button Control Object's Click   │   │
│   │                  Event                      │   │
│   └─────────────────────────────────────────────┘   │
└─────────────────────────────────────────────────────┘
```

ILLUSTRATION 3.3 Classes, Objects, Properties, Methods, and Events

do some work while your application is running. Typically, you will use the objects' own events (via a code block known as an "event handler") to trigger their responses to actions the user performs while running your application. The entire programming model for ASP.Net Web applications revolves around this system of manipulating objects, properties, methods, and events.

Object-Oriented Programming (OOP)

If you are unfamiliar with OOP and you begin using Visual Studio.Net, you might assume that all the objects are already resident in the .Net Framework, VB.Net, ASP.Net, and so on. But, in fact, some developer wrote the classes for all those objects, and you may wish to write your own classes from which objects can be derived, and then use those classes in your ASP.Net Web applications. The process of writing your own classes is basically:

- Define the functionality the instantiated objects must possess. This is sometimes not easy, because there is no specific rule to go by; it's more a matter of understanding what you want the program to do and then identifying those "areas" of functionality that fit well into an object.
- Write a class using the appropriate functions and endow it with properties, methods, and events. Many programming languages contain functions that enable you to create a new class and to assign property, method, and event names, although it's up to you to write the code that implements them when the application is running and objects are instantiated from your new class.

Once you've written your class, you can use it in your application. The next few sections provide some basic characteristics of classes created using OOP: encapsulation, inheritance, and polymorphism. These terms explain fundamental properties of this type of programming and provide a glimpse of the benefits.

Encapsulation

Encapsulation means that the workings of the object are encapsulated. You may not know all (or even any) of the details that make the object work the way it does, but you don't have to know them in order to work with the object and get the results you expect.

Inheritance

Inheritance means that new classes can be created from base classes. The new classes will inherit the properties and methods of the base classes and may have additional properties and methods as well.

Polymorphism

Polymorphism means that methods and properties in new classes may have the same name as those found in base classes, and although they may arrive at their results using a different methodology, we won't know the difference. We can use them in our programming in exactly the same way and still get the results we expect.

Base Classes and Objects

The .Net Framework contains many built-in base classes from which objects can be derived. Some objects, like the Request and Response objects, are automatically available when your ASP.Net Web application is running. If a user submits form data to your application, voila! A new Request object is born from the **HttpRequest class** and is available for you to call and manipulate from your code. Part of the advantage of using the .Net Framework is that it has so many (and such useful) classes built in, and that it also takes care of things like creating and destroying objects and managing memory automatically.

You can build customized classes if you like, and create your own objects from them, although that is a bit beyond the scope of this book. But many of the functions you'll commonly need are already there. Once an object is created, it is unique. It has a name and can be called by your code. It also has attributes that contain values that may be completely different than a similar object created from exactly the same class at the same time. These attributes are called properties. Objects also have methods that let you perform work on them, or make them do things. Objects also respond to events that occur while the application is running. In order to become comfortable developing ASP.Net applications, you need to become familiar with the available objects and their properties, methods, and events.

Properties

Base classes such as HttpRequest are designed so that when objects are derived from them as the application runs, they expose properties. The term *expose* means their properties can be "read" by addressing the object and the property of the object you wish to work with. In Chapter 1 we created a simple application that contained a TextBox object. The name of the object (given to it by default in VS.Net) was TextBox1. One of the properties of TextBox1 is the Text property. We read the Text property of the TextBox1 object into a string variable we created by setting the string variable equal to the TextBox1.Text property, as in the following code:

```
Dim strName_submitted As String
strName_submitted = TextBox1.Text
```

The Request object, derived from the HttpRequest class each time your application receives HTTP values from the browser, has properties as well, and they can be read using the same sort of code:

```
Dim strHttpmethod As String
strHttpmethod = Request.HttpMethod
```

Methods

Objects often have methods as well. Methods are little chunks of processing logic (like procedures or functions). By calling an object by name and including a method name (of course, the object must actually be programmed to respond to that method; you can't use any method on any object), you can make the object perform the actions of the method. For example, the Response object (derived from the **HttpResponse class**) has a method named "Write". If you call the object and this particular method, the object will write whatever string you insert back to the user's browser, like this:

```
Response.Write("This is my response to you")
```

In the user's browser, this text would appear. If you want to include some HTML as well (for example, to create a table around your text), you might use code like the following:

```
Response.Write("<table border="1"><tr><td>This is my
    response to you</td></tr></table>")
```

Events

To understand events, think of a Button control that you've added to a Web form. When the application is running and the user clicks the button, the browser takes note of that event and sends the form contents back to the server. In HTML, the button element responds to the onclick event and informs the browser that it should immediately send the contents of all fields on the form back to the server as name-value pairs (the names are identical to the names of the fields as defined in the HTML and the values are the current values entered by the user).

Back on the server, if you've written an ASP.Net application, your code also can detect that the button control has been clicked. That's the purpose of the event handler code block that was created automatically in the code-behind file (the WebForm1.aspx.vb file). Events raised for controls can be handled with the appropriate event handler, and the code included in the event handler code block will run.

Objects may be programmed to respond to more than one event. For example, a TextBox control can raise an event for its text being changed (the TextChanged event) and also the Load event (when it is loaded onto a Web form as the page is being displayed).

Control Objects and ASP.Net

ASP.Net Web applications can include HTML controls (such as textboxes, radio buttons, checkboxes, and so on), HTML server controls, and ASP.Net server controls. Ordinary HTML controls are written with plain HTML code and appear in the user's browser. When included in an HTML form element, their names and user-entered values may be sent back to your Web application via a form submission. HTML controls also function as objects in the HTML Document Object Model (DOM). This means that they are capable of responding to events (defined in the HTML DTD, which will be discussed in more detail in Chapter 4) on the client side. As a practical matter, HTML controls (and other objects in the browser) can be programmatically affected by client-side code (such as Javascript). For example, if you change the contents of a checkbox in a Web page, the textbox can raise the onchange event and Javascript in the Web page can respond to that event by doing something in that Web page. This is all independent of your Web application.

HTML server controls and ASP.Net server controls, on the other hand, are designed to react to events by running code back on the server. They maintain their state while on the user's browser and transmit any changes that have occurred (if a radio button was clicked, for example) back to the server when a roundtrip to the server is initiated. Once the data are sent back to the server, all appropriate events and code are raised and run, the new state is calculated, and the page is again built and sent to the user. In a practical sense, the user has the impression that state is being maintained in the same way it would if an ordinary Windows application were running.

ASP.Net and HTML Server Controls

ASP.Net Web server controls are defined in the "asp" schema. This is an XML schema that Microsoft has created (we take a good look at XML schemas in Chapter 4), and access to its controls is automatically included when you use ASP.Net server controls in VS.Net. Like most other things in your ASP.Net Web forms, ASP.Net Web server controls are also objects and have their own properties, as well as events they respond to. Included with ASP.Net server controls are validation controls and user controls. Validation controls are not displayed to the user, but are attached to other controls to validate user entries. We'll discuss validation controls in detail in Chapter 6, as we build a user interface (UI). User controls are built from Web and HTML controls into mini forms, and they act as custom-designed control objects in your Web application.

HTML server controls are very similar to ordinary HTML controls, except they expose an object model to the server so that your Web application can respond to their events and manipulate their properties programmatically.

ASP.Net Web Server Control Functions

There are a number of useful ASP.Net Web server controls you can use in your Web applications; we've listed their names and a short description of what they do in Table 3.1.

Dot-Notation—Syntax for Addressing Controls The syntax for addressing controls and their properties is called dot-notation. Basically, this means you can address a property of a control by writing the name of the control, a dot (period), and the name of the property. Usually you would do this in conjunction with either getting the value of the property or setting the value of the property, as shown in this code:

```
Dim strTextValue As String
strTextValue = Label1.Text
```

You also can set the value of some properties, as shown here:

```
Dim strTextValue As String
strTextValue  = "Write your string in here"
Label1.Text = strTextValue
```

Objects, Properties, Methods, and Events

TABLE 3.1 ASP.Net Web Server Controls

Name	Description
AdRotator	Cycles through a series of banner ads as your application runs. You create a list of ads and set the length of time for each ad to appear.
Button	Displays a button on the Web form. You create an event handler for code that runs when the button is clicked.
Calendar	Displays a calendar and allows the user to select dates. You can create an event handler that responds to the date, week, or month the user chose.
CheckBox CheckBoxList	Displays a checkbox or checkbox list that the user can select. Although these controls do not force a submission to the server, you can force one by changing the AutoPostBack setting, and thereby use an event handler to respond to user entries.
DataGrid	Displays a grid that can include rows and columns of data, as well as Select, Edit, Update, and Cancel buttons for which you can create event handlers.
DataList	Displays rows of data with customizable formatting for readability and allows you to display buttons for selection and editing.
DropDownList	Displays a dropdown list for making selections.
Hyperlink	Displays a programmable link on your Web form.
Image	Displays an image on your Web form and allows you to change the image displayed programmatically. You can use an event handler to respond to clicks on the image.
Label	Displays text on your Web form that can be programmatically changed.
Literal	Displays text on your Web form like the Label control, but without the span tag of the Label control. Lack of the span tag means you cannot apply styles, however.
ListBox	Displays a list of items from which the user can select.
Panel	Forms a container for other controls so you can treat them as a group.
PlaceHolder	Also forms a container for controls, but is populated at run time.
RadioButton RadioButtonList	Displays radio buttons (or a list of radio buttons). Similar to checkboxes (yes-no entries), but only one can be selected at a time.
Repeater	Displays a repeating layout defined by you. For example, you can repeat bullets, numbers, lines, and so forth, along with the data for each item.
Table TableRow TableCell	Displays a Table, with TableRow and TableCell elements for each data item.
TextBox	Displays a TextBox and can include default text. The contents can be changed programmatically or sent back to the server.

Dot-notation allows you to specify properties of objects, or run their methods, by noting the lineage (parent–child relationship) between various objects in a Web application. Forms are the parent object for controls, and controls are the child objects of a form. Controls also can contain their own child objects (also controls). This hierarchical order is called the object model, and each object in it has a name and can be addressed using dot-notation.

Focus As you tab through a form in a Web application, each control you stop at (such as textboxes, radio buttons, and submit buttons) has focus while you are stopped at it. This means that if you start typing or hit a key, the effect of your action will be on the control that has focus.

Discussion—Controls in ASP.Net Applications

ASP.Net Web applications have available to them a rich set of controls (textboxes, radio buttons, dropdown lists, and so forth) that are designed to make the user experience very similar to using a desktop Windows application. State is preserved by the ViewState property in these controls, and they are capable of responding to events by causing a roundtrip to the server, although only a few events create a roundtrip by default. Controls can be added to a Web form during development by dragging them from the Toolbox, and their properties can be set in the Properties window. Many control properties also can be set programmatically, forming the basis for an interactive Web application.

The HttpContext Class

The HttpContext class contains all HTTP-specific information about the current HTTP Request, meaning it provides just about everything you need to work with HTTP communications in your application. For example, you can address the Request, Response, and Server objects from the HttpContext class. There are also a number of other useful objects, properties, and methods available with this class.

HttpContext Properties

The properties available with this class include access to arrays of errors; the Application, Cache, and Session objects; the Request and Response objects; and the TraceContext object. In the following sections we discuss many of these objects and properties.

AllErrors
This property gets an array of errors that occurred during the current request.

Application and Session
These properties get the Application object (HttpApplicationState) or the Session object for the current request. Chapter 5 contains more detail about these objects.

Cache
This property gets the Cache object for the current request. Chapter 6 discusses the Cache object in more detail.

Request and Response
These properties get the current Request or Response object for the current request.

Trace
This property gets the TraceContext object for the current request. Chapter 6 begins a discussion of how ASP.Net Tracing works and Chapter 10 adds more detail.

The HttpRequest Class

The HttpRequest class comes with the .Net Framework, and makes an intrinsic object called Request available to ASP.Net Web applications. The Request object can be called from your code to examine several properties and collections, and also has several methods that enable you to work with it. Any time the user makes a request of the Web server with HTTP, a Request object representing the current request is generated. The properties and methods are called members (all classes have members; the term *member* includes the properties, methods, and events exposed to your code). Some properties and methods are Public, meaning they can be called from any function you write, while others are private or protected, meaning they can only be called by functions or other classes that are specifically assigned that privilege. In the following sections we discuss some of the HttpRequest class's Public properties and methods.

HttpRequest Properties

The HttpRequest class has several properties associated with it. We list them here, along with a short description and some example code showing how to call them in your code.

AcceptTypes

This property consists of a string array of MIME types that the client (the browser) accepts. MIME stands for Multipurpose Internet Mail Extensions, and MIME types refers to the name of a type (such as image) and a common extension for it (such as gif). You might retrieve these data using the following code:

```
Dim strArr() As String
strArr = Request.AcceptTypes
```

At this point all the MIME types would be available in the variable strArr, and you could review them using an index number to find each value in the array.

ApplicationPath

This property is a string value containing the ASP.Net application's virtual application root path on the server. You could retrieve these data using a string variable, like this:

```
Dim strAppPath As String
strAppPath = Request.ApplicationPath
```

Browser

This property contains information about the browser capabilities of the browser making the request, such as Type, Name, Version, Major Version, Minor Version, and so forth. It can tell your application what capabilities the current user's browser has, and your application can use this information to decide how to format Web pages it sends back. For example, if the user is using an older browser that doesn't do Dynamic HTML, then you might have your application send back Web pages that don't depend on DHTML to render properly. You could use code such as the following to retrieve this information:

```
Dim bcBrowserCap As HttpBrowserCapabilities
bcBrowserCap = Request.Browser
```

At this point all the data would be in the bcBrowserCap object (notice it is dimensioned as an object of the type HttpBrowserCapabilities) and you could write the capabilities out one by one or access any of them by name. The bcBrowserCap variable contains an object, and therefore you could address the various pieces of data as property names, like this:

```
Dim strBrowserType As String
strBrowserType  = bcBrowserCap.Type
```

ClientCertificate

This property contains data about the client's security certificate settings. Like the Browser property, it is accessed using an object whose individual properties can be accessed with a string variable, as shown here:

```
Dim ccClientCert As HttpClientCertificate
Dim strCert As String
ccClientCert = Request.ClientCertificate
strCert = ccClientCert.Certificate
```

ContentEncoding

The term *encoding* refers to the format used to represent letters, digits, punctuation, and other characters. Common encoding types are ASCII, Unicode, and so on. The browser can request certain content encoding formats, and if it does, the server will produce those formats. This property uses an object whose properties can be read with a string variable, much like the Browser and ClientCertificate properties:

```
Dim strEncodingName As String
strEncodingName = Request.ContentEncoding.EncodingName
```

ContentLength

This property contains the length in bytes of any content sent by the client. This can be useful in situations where you are expecting no more than a set amount of content from the user (such as image files of a certain size). Since the value is the number of bytes, the variable used to retrieve the length could have a data type of integer, as shown here:

```
Dim intContentBytes As Integer
intContentBytes = Request.ContentLength
```

ContentType

This property contains the MIME type of the incoming request, such as text/html. It can be read with a string variable:

```
Dim strRequestMimetype As String
strRequestMimetype = Request.ContentType
```

Cookies

This property represents a **collection** of cookies that are currently on the browser (for this application). A corresponding collection of cookies can be set on the browser using the Response object (we'll discuss this a little later).

Since Cookies is an object containing the cookies collection, and since each cookie may have subcookies attached to it, you will want to retrieve these data using Cookie objects and string arrays, like this:

```
Dim strCookieArray() As String
Dim ccCookiesCollection As HttpCookieCollection
Dim cACookie As HttpCookie
Dim strCookieName As String
```

```
ccCookiesCollection = Request.Cookies
strCookieArray = ccCookiesCollection.AllKeys
cACookie = ccCookiesCollection(strCookieArray(0))
strCookieName = cACcookie.Name
```

Note that the properties of an individual cookie have their own names, such as Name, Expires, Secure, and so forth, and that the array of cookies (or subcookies) is retrieved using the AllKeys property.

CurrentExecutionFilePath

This property contains the virtual file path of the currently executing page when you have redirected the user to another page. You can retrieve these data using a string variable:

```
Dim strCurrentPath As String
strCurrentPath = Request.CurrentExecutionFilePath
```

FilePath

This property contains the virtual file path of the current request. You can retrieve these data using a string variable:

```
Dim strFilePath As String
strFilePath = Request.FilePath
```

Files

This property contains the files uploaded by the user (if any). To retrieve these files, you should use an HttpFileCollection object, and you may need an array to access each individual file and then a string variable to access an individual file name, as shown here:

```
Dim fcUploadedFiles As HttpFileCollection
Dim strFileCollection() As String
Dim strFileName As String

fcUploadedFiles = Request.Files
strFileCollection = fcUploadedFiles.AllKeys
strFileName = strFileCollection(0)
```

Form

This property contains a collection of name-value pairs representing all the form field names and the current values entered by the user prior to the user submitting the form. You can access individual form field values by using the name of the form field (you will probably know the form field names, given that the form was created by you) or you can iterate through the entire collection to find all the form fields and their values. You might use code such as the following to obtain the value of a single form field:

```
Dim strFormAddress As String
strFormAddress = Request.Form("address")
```

Headers

This property contains a collection of HTTP header names and their values in the current request. HTTP headers include Date, Server, CacheControl, and so forth. The content for a given header can be read using code such as the following:

```
Dim nvcHeaderCollection As NameValueCollection
Dim strHeadersArr() As String
Dim strHeaderName As String

nvcHeaderCollection = Request.Headers
strHeadersArr = nvcHeaderCollection.AllKeys
strHeaderName = strHeadersArr(0)
```

HttpMethod

This property contains the method used to transmit HTTP data. Common methods include GET and POST. These data can be read with a string variable:

```
Dim strTransferMethod As String
strTransferMethod = Request.HttpMethod
```

IsAuthenticated

This property is a Boolean value telling your application whether or not the user has been authenticated with HTTP Authentication. It can be either True or False, and you can use this value directly in If...Then...End If code blocks, like this:

```
If Request.IsAuthenticated Then
    'do this
Else
    'do that
End If
```

IsSecureConnection

This property is a Boolean value telling you whether the request is secure (using the https connection). Like IsAuthenticated, it can be used directly in If...Then...End If code blocks.

```
If Request.IsSecureConnection Then
    'do this
Else
    'do that
End If
```

Params

This property contains a collection that has all QueryString, Form, Cookies, and ServerVariable name-value pairs. It can be accessed using a NameValueCollection object and arrays.

Path
This property contains the virtual path of the current request and can be accessed using a string variable.

PathInfo
This property contains additional path information, in the form of a path trailer.

PhysicalApplicationPath
This property contains the file path on the server for the currently executing server application's root directory. For example, if your application is executing from the C: drive in the InetPub/wwwroot folder, you will get all this information in a string variable:

```
Dim strCurrentActualPath As String
strCurrentActualPath = Request.PhysicalApplicationPath
```

QueryString
This property contains a collection of name-value pairs representing the names and values attached to the link just clicked by the user. QueryString fields can be accessed by name, using code such as the following:

```
Dim strQsValue As String
strQsValue = Request.QueryString("field_name01")
```

Creating a QueryString in HTML A QueryString can be created by adding names and values onto a link, in the HTML, like this:

```
<a href="Web_page.htm?field_name01=joe&field_name02=
   jim">Click Here</a>
```

In the link above, `Web_page.htm` is the name of the page the user will be taken to, and the QueryString collection consists of two fields (field_name01 and field_name02) with the values "joe" and "jim", respectively.

RawURL
This property contains the raw URL of the request, which is the part after the domain name, and can be accessed using a string variable.

RequestType
This property contains the HTTP data transfer method (like the HttpMethod property), such as GET or POST, and can be accessed using a string variable.

ServerVariables
This property contains a collection of server variables included with the request, such as SERVER_NAME and SERVER_PORT. You can use a NameValueCollection object and an array to iterate through each variable and determine its value.

TotalBytes
This property contains the total number of bytes in the request and can be accessed using an Integer variable.

Url
This property pulls information about the requested URL into a Uri object and then makes the information available through properties of the Uri object. Properties such as the Port and Scheme can be read with string variables.

UrlReferer
This property contains the URL of the page from which the browser was referred. This property is useful if you'd like to know where your users are coming from, as in the case of an affiliate program. The property can be accessed using a Uri object and reading its properties with a string variable.

UserAgent
This property contains the raw user agent string of the browser, meaning it contains the name and version numbers of the browser. This property can be accessed using a string variable.

UserHostAddress
This property contains the IP address of the browser making the request and can be accessed using a string variable.

UserHostName
This property contains the domain name of the IP address from which the browser is making the request and can be accessed using a string variable.

HttpRequest Methods

There are also methods associated with the Request object, and these methods basically work with the incoming data to produce a result. For example, MapPath takes the virtual path of the requested page and returns a physical or actual path. Methods use the syntax "Request.Method()" where "Method" is replaced with the name of the method and any arguments (required values) are placed inside the parentheses.

BinaryRead
This method performs a BinaryRead of a number of bytes from the incoming request. You provide the number of bytes to read, and the method returns these bytes in a Byte array. The following code could be used to read a specified number of bytes from the request:

```
Request.BinaryRead(1000)
```

MapImageCoordinates
This method returns an array of integers representing the x-y coordinates contained in the image-field form parameters of the incoming request. This is useful for capturing the exact location the user clicked on an image map.

MapPath
This method returns the physical path of a requested Url.

SaveAs
This method saves the request to disk, provided you include the path and file name where you want the information saved and a Boolean value (True or False) indicating whether you want the HTTP headers included.

ToString
This method returns the entire request as a string.

The HttpResponse Class

The HttpResponse class also comes with the .Net Framework and makes an intrinsic object called Response available to ASP.Net Web applications. The Response object can be called from your code to set several properties and use several methods. Any time the server sends an HTTP response back to the user, a Response object is used. As with the Request object, we discuss some of the Public properties and methods in the next few sections.

HttpResponse Properties

The HttpResponse class has several properties associated with it. We list them here, along with a short description and some example code showing how to call them in your code. Using the Response object, you can read (or get) many properties, as well as set them.

Buffer
This property can be used to get or set whether or not to buffer (save up) the output before sending it back to the user. This is useful if you don't want the user to see the result until after all processing is complete. Buffer is no longer the preferred way to do this; use BufferOutput with ASP.Net applications.

BufferOutput

This property can be set so that before the response is delivered to the user, all processing must be complete. It is a Boolean value and can be set with code such as this:

```
Response.BufferOutput = True
```

Cache

This property can be used to read caching policy parameters for the current Web page and, if you choose, write them to the current response. Caching policy parameters include expiration and cachability.

CacheControl

This property can be used to set the HTTP Cache Control header of the current response to Public or Private. You could use code such as the following to perform this action:

```
Response.CacheControl = "Public"
```

ContentType

This property can be used to read or set the HTTP MIME type for the current response. The default value is "text/html". Code such as the following can be used to set it:

```
Response.ContentType = "text/html"
```

Cookies

This property can be used to set cookies in the current response. The following code could be used to accomplish this:

```
Dim cNewCookie As New HttpCookie("c_id")
Dim intCustID As Integer

intCustID = 6
cNewCookie.Value = intCustID
Response.Cookies.Add("cNewCookie")
```

Expires and ExpiresAbsolute

These properties get or set the number of minutes before the page expires, or the date on which the page expires. They are for compatibility with ASP and should not be used.

IsClientConnected

This property is a Boolean value that tells your application if the client is still connected to the server. It is useful for determining if the client is still connected (or, more importantly, if the client is no longer connected) when processing takes an unusually long time. You can use it directly in an If...Then... End If code block.

Status, StatusCode, and StatusDescription

The Status property can be used to set the status line (such as 200 OK) of the current response. The StatusCode property sets the status code (such as 200) of the current response. The StatusDescription property sets the status description (such as OK) of the current response.

HttpResponse Methods

The HttpResponse class also has methods associated with it, and they are used for performing work with the current response. Essentially, they give you control over exactly what is sent back to the user. Methods use the syntax "Response.Method()" where "Method" is replaced with the name of the method and any arguments (required values) are placed inside the parentheses.

AddCacheItemDependency and AddCacheItemDependencies

These methods set an item so that it is cached when certain other items (the item or items it is dependent upon) are also cached.

AddFileDependency and AddFileDependencies

These methods add a file name or file names to the collection of files upon which the current response depends.

AddHeader and AppendHeader

Both of these methods add an HTTP header to the response, but AddHeader is for ASP compatibility only.

Clear, ClearContent, and ClearHeaders

These methods clear the buffered stream, but ClearContent clears only content and ClearHeaders clears only headers.

Close

This method closes the socket connection to the browser.

End and Flush

These methods send any buffered output to the browser, but End also ends execution of the processing for the page and raises the Application_EndRequest event. Code such as the following can be used to accomplish these actions:

```
Request.Flush()
```

Redirect

The **Redirect** method redirects the browser to another URL. Code such as the following can be used to perform redirects:

```
Response.Redirect("topage.htm")
```

RemoveOutputCacheItem

This method removes all cached items from the cache for the current response.

Write and WriteFile

These methods write data to the response, with Write writing text output and WriteFile writing files.

The HttpServerUtility Class

Another important HTTP class is the HttpServerUtility class. Through the intrinsic Server object the HttpServerUtility class's properties and methods are exposed. Several useful properties and methods are available through the Server object, including the ability to change the timeout period for the script, the ability to instantiate COM objects on the server, the ability to execute from another page, and so on. In the following sections we discuss some of these properties and methods.

The HttpServerUtility ScriptTimeout Property

This property can be used to get or set the script timeout, the period (in seconds) for which the Web application will wait for a response. Code such as the following can be used:

```
Server.ScriptTimeout = 600 'this equates to 10 minutes
```

HTTPServerUtility Methods

There are a number of valuable methods available via the Server object discussed in the following sections.

CreateObject

This method creates an instance of an object on the server. Code such as the following may be used:

```
Dim objObject As New Object
objObject = Server.CreateObject("name.object")
```

HTML Encode and Decode
These methods encode or decode HTML code and special characters for transmission via HTTP.

MapPath
This method returns the physical file path for the virtual path of the current request.

Transfer and Execute
These methods terminate execution at the current page and begin execution at another page (Transfer) or simply execute on another page (Execute).

URL Encode and Decode
These methods encode and decode URL for transmission via HTTP.

Discussion—HTTP Classes

The HttpContext object provides access to the Application, Session, Request, and Response objects, in addition to other properties and methods, for the current HTTP request. The Request and Response objects are intrinsic to ASP.Net and come from the HttpRequest and HttpResponse classes of ASP.Net as part of the .Net Framework. They are tools for working with the HTTP protocol. HTTP is a stateless, request-response protocol, meaning the client (the browser, in most cases) and the server (the Web server, in most cases) simply send messages back and forth to each other without any built-in way to determine the relationship between any two requests or responses.

The fact that HTTP is stateless complicates application development because under ordinary circumstances (when running a Windows application, for example), the application can make the assumption that any communications it receives are from the same user, and therefore what the user has done in previous communications may be taken into account on future communications. A good example of this is when a user must log in. In a Windows application, the user can log in once and the application may assume that, if it hasn't been closed, the same user is using it and doesn't need to log in again. A Web application cannot make this same assumption, because it doesn't know if the next request it receives, even if it happens to be from the same IP address, is from the same user. Therefore, Web applications resort to extra measures such as the use of session cookies to establish state management.

The Request and Response objects provide methods and properties to work with cookies, as well as to identify other data traveling in the HTTP Request-Response streams. For example, the Request object contains data submitted via HTML form, via query-string (tacked onto the end of the URL), and other variables such as the IP address of the sender, the type of browser the sender is using, and the page from which the sender was referred. The Response object contains methods for writing cookies, text, files, and HTTP headers into the response in the appropriate HTTP protocol format.

The Server object, which is exposed via the HttpServerUtility class, contains a property that can be used to get or set the script timeout and methods useful for creating COM objects on the server, encoding and decoding HTML and URLs, and transferring and executing code on various pages in your Web application.

Quick Check Questions

1. What is an object?
2. What is a property?
3. What is a method?
4. What is an event?
5. What is the difference between an object and a class?
6. What is HTTP?
7. How are HTTP communications different from the way ordinary desktop applications receive input and send output?
8. What is the name for the syntax for addressing objects and properties?
9. What is focus?

1. Web applications consist of separate processing and user interface, unlike typical desktop Windows applications. The user interface is rendered on a client (often a browser) that may be anywhere on the Internet or network, while processing may take place on one or more servers also anywhere on the Internet or network. The protocol used to provide communications between client and server is HyperText Transport Protocol (HTTP).
2. HTTP is stateless, meaning there is no built-in way to keep track of a usage session between client and server. Therefore, extra measures must be taken to create sessionlike characteristics while the application is running, or the application must be designed so that state is not important.
3. The HttpContext class provides access to the Application, Session, Request, and Response objects.
4. The HttpRequest and HttpResponse classes are base classes built in to ASP.Net as part of the .Net Framework. From these classes the ASP.Net Request and Response objects can be derived. These objects are derived each time an HTTP request or response occurs.
5. The Request and Response objects are designed to make working with HTTP communications in your applications smooth, comfortable, and familiar. These objects have properties that offer easy access to common HTTP components such as headers and methods for working with these HTTP components.
6. The HttpServerUtility class provides access to server capabilities, such as the ability to create COM objects on the server.

Exercise 3.1

The following exercises expand upon what we've started with the Hands On Project. Each exercise adds a bit more to this application.

1. Add a Select Case block to the application for the Request.Form collection. Add two fields to the form for username and password, and display the values entered by the user as items in the ListBox control.
2. Add a Select Case block to the application for the Request.ServerVariables collection. Display the server variables values as items in the ListBox control.
3. Create another Web form page named "WebForm2.aspx" in the RequestResponse project. On the first Web form page, add a Button control and change its Text property to read "Go to Web Form 2". Create an event handler for this button, and in it put a Response.Redirect("WebForm2.aspx") line, using the Response object's Redirect method. Text this functionality to see if you are redirected to the second Web form.

Hands On Project

Request and Response Properties and Methods

In this project we will create an ASP.Net Web application that demonstrates usage of many of the Request and Response object properties and methods. Although this application doesn't necessarily do something important in and of itself, the Request and Response objects are real workhorses, and you'll often find their properties and methods handy in working applications.

The application will be named RequestResponse and will be created with a Visual Basic Project Template for ASP.Net Web applications. If Visual Studio.Net is not already open, open it. This Web application template begins with a Web form that can contain HTML and Server controls. We will format the page to make it look acceptable and use the Toolbox to pick from the available controls. We will use the Properties window to examine and change the properties of some controls, and we use Visual Basic.Net (VB.Net) on the code-behind page to write our code and call the Request and Response objects and their properties and methods.

SETTING UP THE WEB FORM

1. Click File|New|Project to open the New Project dialog box. Ensure that Visual Basic Projects is selected on the Project Types side of the dialog box and that ASP.NET Web Application is the selected template (shown in the right side of the dialog box).
2. Enter the name "RequestResponse" as the folder specified in the Location URL (the full URL is http://localhost/RequestResponse). The New Project dialog box is shown in Figure 3.1.
3. Click OK. A blank Web form with the name WebForm1.aspx should be displayed, as shown in Figure 3.2.
4. Open the DOCUMENT Properties Page dialog box and change the background color of the page to a pleasant color such as light blue. Make the title of the page read "Http Request – Response". Leave the page in grid layout mode. Close the DOCUMENT Properties Page dialog box.
5. Open the Toolbox. Put a Label control at the top of the page and change its Text property to "Http Request – Response". Change the font properties so the text is boldfaced, the font name is Arial, and the size is "Larger".
6. Add another smaller label and make it read "Show Values for Request Object Property". Below it add a **DropDownList control**. Next to the dropdown list, on the right side, add a Button control.
7. Copy these controls once and move them to a position below the first set of controls. Change the Text property of the second label to read "Work with Request Object Method".

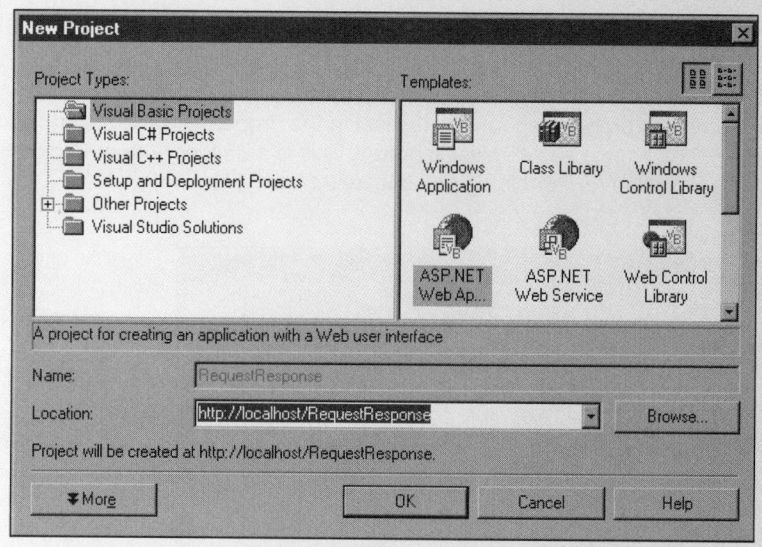

FIGURE 3.1 The New Project Dialog Box

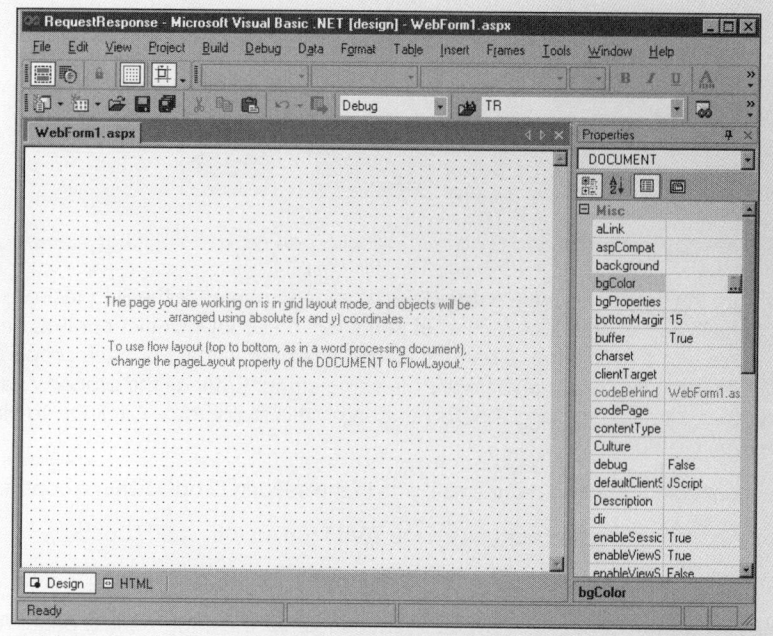

FIGURE 3.2 The Blank Web Form Named WebForm1.aspx

8. Add another label and make it read "Results Shown Here". Add a **ListBox control** below this label and resize it so it is large enough to display some results.

9. Select the first DropDownList control (it should have been named DropDownList1 by VS.Net). Find its Items property (this property should be the last in the Properties window) and click in the field for this property. You should see an ellipsis button. This is a Builder button. Click this button to open the ListItem Collection Editor dialog box (Figure 3.3).

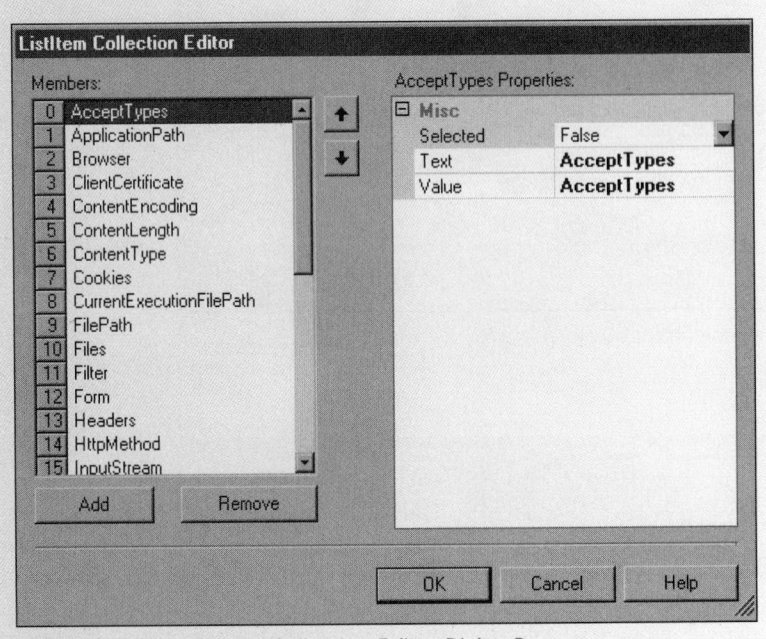

FIGURE 3.3 The ListItem Collection Editor Dialog Box

10. As you can see from the figure, we have entered each property name for the Request object. The Items property actually represents a collection of items for the DropDownList control. Each item has an index number (starting at zero), a text value, and a regular value. For each property name we've entered as an item, the text and value are the same string. Enter all the property names for the Request object as items by clicking the Add button on this dialog box. Click OK to close this dialog box when you are done.

11. Enter all the Request object method names as items in the second DropDownList control.

12. Change the Text property of the two buttons on the Web form so they read "Submit".

13. Close the Toolbox if necessary. At this point your Web form should look like Figure 3.4.

14. Double-click the first Button control to start an event handler in the code-behind page. An event handler is a code block that is triggered when the event it handles occurs. The event that is triggered in this case is the Click event of the Button control. So when the application is running and the user clicks the first Submit button, it will send an HTTP request to the server. At the server, the application will respond by running whatever code is in the event handler code block.

15. In order to demonstrate what values are contained in the Request object for some of its properties (we won't demonstrate all of them, even though we've made list items for each property

Hands-On Project

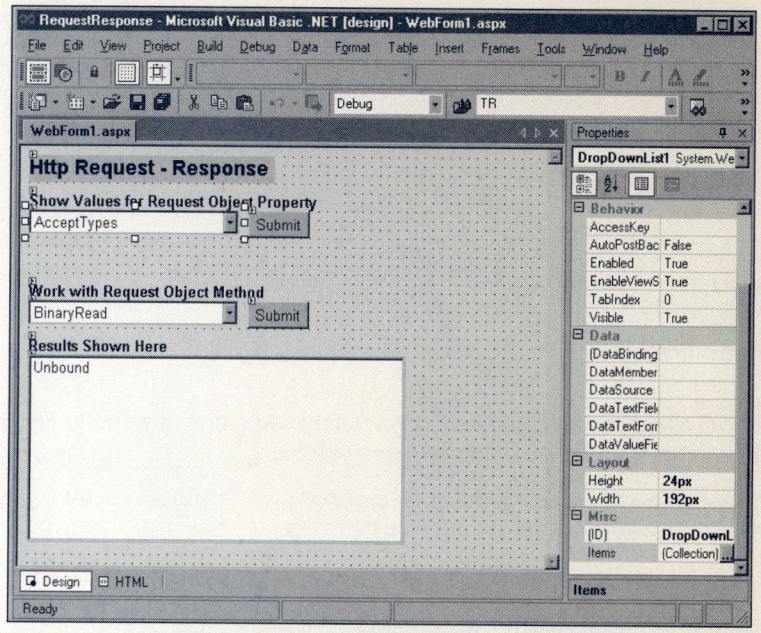

FIGURE 3.4 The Web Form, Ready for Coding

name), we need to have a means of capturing the value entered by the user and then showing the values for that property in the ListBox control we added to the form.

16. The following code shows how the event handler begins (you don't need to write in the line that starts with "Private Sub"). The Dim keyword is used to create a String variable. The next line sets the "strReqProperty" variable to the string value of the item that was selected in the DropDownList (remember, this is the value of that item). Enter the lines starting with "Dim" and "strReqProperty" in the event handler code block.

    ```
    Private Sub Button1_Click(ByVal sender As System.Object, ByVal e As System.EventArgs) Handles Button1.Click
        Dim strReqProperty As String
        strReqProperty = DropDownList1.SelectedItem.Value
    ```

17. To run different lines of code depending upon what the user has chosen, a **Select Case code block** will be used. Select Case, as its name implies, selects among different cases and runs the code applicable to each case. Enter the following code in the event handler code block:

    ```
    Select Case strReqProperty
        Case "AcceptTypes"
    ```

18. For the Case in which "strReqProperty" equals "AcceptTypes", we'll add code that creates another String variable named "strAType", and another one named "intI" that has a data type of Integer:

    ```
    Dim strAType As String
    Dim intI As Integer
    ```

19. Next, our code will set the "intI" variable to zero. Then our code will establish a **For Next loop** that runs for each value found in the Request object's AcceptTypes array (remember, the AcceptTypes property actually consists of an array of string values). This For Next loop will have one line of code in it that adds a list item to the ListBox control (the line starting with "Me").

```
            intI = 0
       For Each strAType In Request.AcceptTypes
           Me.ListBox1.Items.Add(New ListItem(strReqProperty & " - " & Request.
              AcceptTypes(intI), strReqProperty))
           intI = intI + 1
       Next
    End Select
End Sub
```

20. Each time through the For Next loop, we'll increment "intI", so we can use it to run through the index numbers for the String array of Request.AcceptTypes (notice "intI" is used at the end of Request.AcceptTypes(intI)).

21. The last three lines of the code block end the For loop, end the Select block, and close the Sub procedure.

22. To run your application and see what happens, click on the Web form, then go to File|Build and Browse on the menu. The Web form will appear in browser view.

23. Choose "AcceptTypes" from the top dropdown list and then click the Submit button. The ListBox control should fill up with all the Accept Types in the current request, such as image/gif, as shown in Figure 3.5.

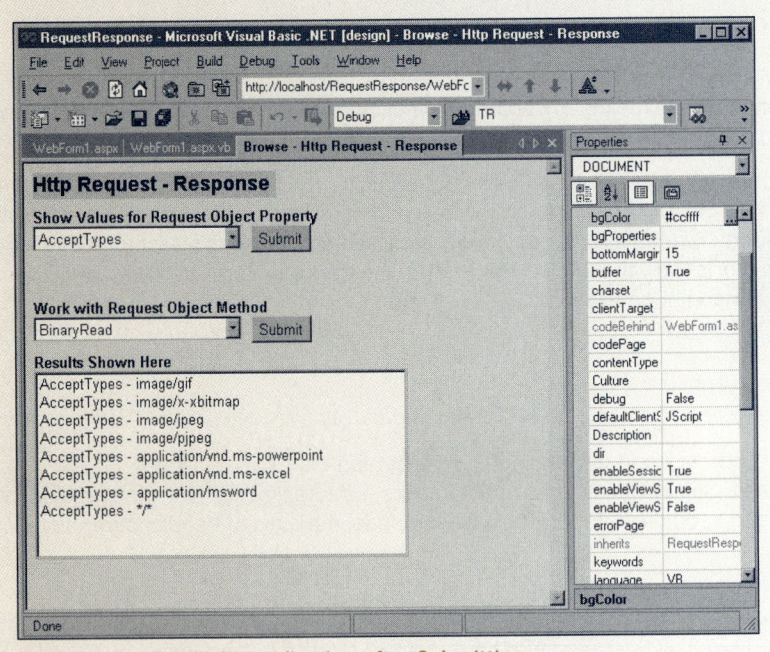

FIGURE 3.5 The Web Application after Submitting

DEMONSTRATING MORE REQUEST OBJECT PROPERTIES

1. Now we'll add the code to display the Browser properties. Make another "Case" statement in your code (before the ending End Select line, of course).

2. In this new Case block, dimension a variable named "bcaps" with a data type of HttpBrowser Capabilities.

Hands-On Project

3. Next, add lines of code for each browser capability and make them into items added to the ListBox control, as shown in the following code:

```
Dim bcBcaps As HttpBrowserCapabilities
bcBcaps = Request.Browser
Me.ListBox1.Items.Add(New ListItem("Type = " & bcBcaps.Type))
Me.ListBox1.Items.Add(New ListItem("Name = " & bcBcaps.Browser))
Me.ListBox1.Items.Add(New ListItem("Version = " & bcBcaps.Version))
Me.ListBox1.Items.Add(New ListItem("Major Version = " & bcBcaps.MajorVersion))
Me.ListBox1.Items.Add(New ListItem("Minor Version = " & bcBcaps.MinorVersion))
Me.ListBox1.Items.Add(New ListItem("Platform = " & bcBcaps.Platform))
Me.ListBox1.Items.Add(New ListItem("Is Beta = " & bcBcaps.Beta))
Me.ListBox1.Items.Add(New ListItem("Is Crawler = " & bcBcaps.Crawler))
Me.ListBox1.Items.Add(New ListItem("Is AOL = " & bcBcaps.AOL))
Me.ListBox1.Items.Add(New ListItem("Is Win16 = " & bcBcaps.Win16))
Me.ListBox1.Items.Add(New ListItem("Is Win32 = " & bcBcaps.Win32))
Me.ListBox1.Items.Add(New ListItem("Supports Frames = " & bcBcaps.Frames))
Me.ListBox1.Items.Add(New ListItem("Supports Tables = " & bcBcaps.Tables))
Me.ListBox1.Items.Add(New ListItem("Supports Cookies = " & bcBcaps.Cookies))
Me.ListBox1.Items.Add(New ListItem("Supports VB Script = " & bcBcaps.VBScript))
Me.ListBox1.Items.Add(New ListItem("Supports JavaScript = " & bcBcaps.JavaScript))
Me.ListBox1.Items.Add(New ListItem("Supports Java Applets = " & bcBcaps.JavaApplets))
Me.ListBox1.Items.Add(New ListItem("Supports ActiveX Controls = " & bcBcaps.ActiveXControls))
Me.ListBox1.Items.Add(New ListItem("CDF = " & bcBcaps.CDF))
```

4. Click on the Web form file, and then go to File|Build and Browse on the menu to run your Web application. Choose Browser from the dropdown list and click the Submit button. You should see the results shown in Figure 3.6.

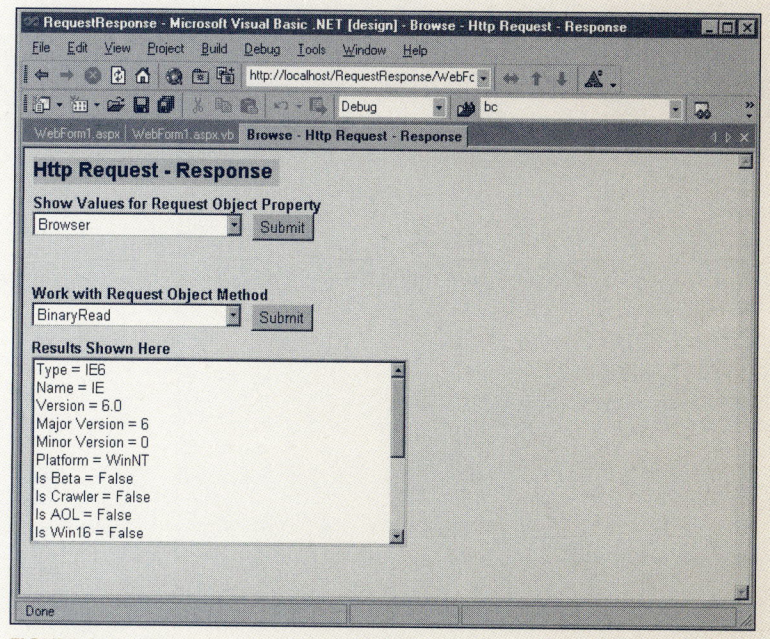

FIGURE 3.6   The Browser Capabilities

CHAPTER 3 HTTP Classes

REQUEST OBJECT METHODS

1. Close the Web application Browser view. On the Web form in Design view, double-click the second Submit button to start another event handler code block in the code-behind page.

2. In the event handler block, enter the following code (note that we're not showing the event handler code itself this time):
```
Dim strReqMethod As String
strReqMethod = DropDownList2.SelectedItem.Value
Select Case strReqMethod
   Case "MapPath"
      Dim strReqPath As String
      strReqPath = Request.MapPath(Request.FilePath).ToString
      Me.ListBox1.Items.Add(New ListItem(strReqPath, "Value"))
End Select
```

3. The code above dimensions the variable strReqMethod as a String data type, sets it to the selected item value (in this case we're using "MapPath"), and then sets up a Select Case block for MapPath.

4. The code then dimensions another variable named strReqPath and sets this variable equal to the value returned by the Request object's MapPath method. Notice that we must include the virtual path as an argument for the MapPath method, so we've used the Request object's FilePath property to provide this information to the MapPath method.

5. The last line in the MapPath Case block creates a new item in the ListBox control, so we can see what value we obtained.

6. Run your application and choose "MapPath" from the second dropdown box, then click the second Submit button. You should see a result such as shown in Figure 3.7.

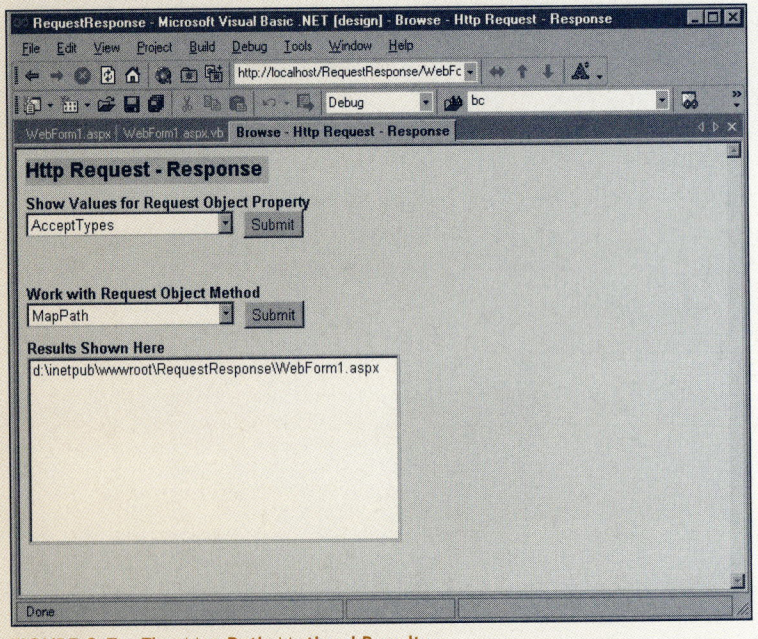

FIGURE 3.7 The MapPath Method Results

Programming Practices Notes One thing you'll often do as a programmer is declare variables, and variable declaration involves giving the variable a name (according to the appropriate naming rules and restrictions) and deciding what data type the variable is going to be. One good programming practice that unfortunately is not followed often enough is to prefix a three-letter string to the beginning of your variable names, representing the data type of the variable (for example, strFirstName for a string variable holding a person's first name). We always try to use this practice in this book; in real life you'll find many examples of code not using this practice. Please follow your instructor's guidelines when naming variables.

Collections Many of the code examples show the use of string variables to store the values, and so we don't repeat the examples in every case. Some of these properties come in the form of collections. In our code examples, we put the collections into arrays, a special type of variable that has keys (a numerical index or the name of that particular field in the array) and values. If you know the index number or field name for a particular value in an array, you can access it directly by calling it by name. If you don't know the index number or field name, you can iterate through the entire array using a For...Next loop, and then work with each value as it comes up. Note that these indexes always start with zero (0), not one (1). And note that some of the collections have subcollections. Cookies are an example of a collection that may have subcollections, as cookies can have subcookies.

MIME Types Multipurpose Internet Mail Extensions (MIME) types are data that inform the browser or server what format a file or part of a message is. MIMEs are represented as type/subtype, so a text file formatted as HTML would be a MIME type of "text/html", while an image file would be "image/gif" or "image/jpg".

Key Terms

- Browser Capabilities property collection
- DropDownList control
- event
- For Next loop
- Form property
- HTTP protocol
- HttpRequest class
- HttpResponse class
- HyperText Transport Protocol (HTTP)
- ListBox control
- method
- object
- property
- Redirect
- Select Case code block
- Server Variables property

Review Questions

1. What is a protocol, and why do we need them for computer communications?
2. What does it mean that HTTP is stateless?
3. What is an object in OOP? What characteristics make it useful?
4. Suppose you have an object that represents a button on a form. What would you call (in OOP terms) a feature of the button that can be read, such as the x-y coordinates of the button on the form?
5. Keeping with our button example, what would you call (in OOP terms) a function that forces the button to change color when called?
6. Again with our button example, what would you call a feature that works when something happens to the button (when the button is clicked, for example)?
7. Suppose a user has filled out a form and submitted the form to your server. What object would you use to retrieve the data he/she submitted? What property of this object contains the submitted values?
8. When retrieving submitted form data, how are the data formatted, and what would you have to do to extract them?

9. Suppose you want to send the user text data with HTML included. What object would you use, and what method of that object?
10. Suppose you are sending the user a page that includes a text message telling him/her that processing is underway and that it might take a minute, so please wait. What method of the Response object can you use to send the text message before processing is complete and the remainder of the page is sent?
11. What method would you use to redirect the user to another page automatically? How does this method work?
12. What object and property tells you things about the browser being used by the user? Is this information always accurate?

CHAPTER 4

ASP.Net and Languages

LEARNING OBJECTIVES

Upon completion of this chapter, you will be able to:

1. Describe the difference between markup, interpreted, and compiled languages.
2. Understand how HTML, XHTML, and XML are related.
3. Understand the relationship between XML and ASP.Net Web services.
4. Write HTML elements in ASP.Net Web forms.
5. Write ASP.Net Server controls in ASP.Net Web forms.
6. Explain how Visual Basic.Net (VB.Net) works.
7. Use common VB.Net language structures with ASP.Net objects.

INTRODUCTION

ASP.Net objects and their properties, methods, and events are instantiated, called, and worked with from within code. In code-behind pages, the programming language may be C#, Jscript, or Visual Basic.Net (among the variety of compiled programming languages that are compliant with the .Net Framework).

In Web forms pages, ASP.Net objects also may be used directly, and while the programming language might be Visual Basic.Net or one of the others just mentioned, the programming code would be interspersed with HTML, Javascript, XHTML, and so forth.

ASP.Net Web services, covered in more detail in Chapter 9, are written in XML-based documents using one of the many XML languages that have been created in the past few years. XHTML is an example of an XML-based language that mimics HTML and is gradually coming into more common use.

Structured Query Language (SQL) is the standard query language for working with databases of all types. We cover SQL basics in Chapters 7 and 8.

The point of these observations is that, while learning about ASP.Net objects is clearly desirable in a textbook about ASP.Net, you also must be familiar with several other compiled, interpreted, and markup languages in order to really learn how to use ASP.Net.

In this chapter we cover the basics of Visual Basic.Net, HTML, and XML. We also go over interpreted languages, both server side and client side (server side means the processing is done on the server and client side means the processing is done at the browser). More importantly, we show numerous examples of incorporating ASP.Net objects within these languages.

Web Sites and Web Applications

ASP.Net Web applications consist of Web pages, text, image, and other media content; back-end programming for data processing; and often include data stored in databases or other data storage structures. The Web server provides access to Web pages and their content to any browser (client software) capable of making an HTTP request.

When Web sites and Web pages first became common, they consisted mainly of just Web pages with text and image content. Rather quickly, features were added that made Web sites function more like applications, and the Web application became common. Of course, the average user doesn't care how Web sites work, just that they do. But developers need to be aware of how traditional and current Web sites and Web applications work, because Web applications use many features of traditional Web sites along with more advanced features only recently available.

How Traditional Web Sites Work

Traditional Web sites are made from HTML documents (and possibly some Javascript and Flash) that display text content (and images) when rendered in a browser. Javascript is an interpreted, mainly client-side programming language that gives Web pages the ability to do data processing (HTML is a display language only and does no data processing). Flash is a proprietary but standard language/technology for creating smoothly animated graphics and incorporating audio and video into Web pages. We discuss interpreted languages a bit later in this chapter.

A key feature of HTML is the ability to specify HyperText links, and another key feature is the ability to accept data from the user via query strings or form submissions. Text structures such as tables, paragraphs, headings, and so forth add to the usability and functionality of Web pages. Web pages form the user interface for the Web site, and typically the closest the site comes to processing is to accept form submissions from the user and perhaps send out an email in response (using back-end scripting).

In traditional Web site design, each "page" is a separate HTML file, and pages are connected by links, so the site can be traversed or navigated. The content of the pages is static, meaning it only changes if the developer rebuilds the page. Single Web sites sometimes have thousands of static pages, a maintenance nightmare to say the least.

The Web pages are stored on a server computer and transmitted to users by Web server software. In the Web server software, the "first" page is designated (by tradition the page named "index"), so that a user who simply types the URL (http://www.whatever.com) is automatically served the first page upon arrival at the site. The DNS server stores the connection between the domain name (whatever.com) and the IP address (the numerical value unique to this particular node on the Internet) so that the domain name, rather than the IP address, can be used to find the Web site.

How Web Applications Work

In a Web application, some of the content and user interface are stored as static Web pages, although using HTML, XHTML, and other XML-based elements and attributes is becoming more common (some elements and attributes included in ASP.Net Web applications are defined in a special XML schema for ASP objects rather than either HTML or XHTML).

In addition, content may appear only as a result of data processing, not because it was statically written as in traditional HTML Web pages. And content is often retrieved by the application programming from data stores such as Access and SQL Server databases.

In practice, what this means is that, rather than thousands of pages of static content, Web applications may have just a few (or only one) pages of static content and all the rest of the pages seen by the user are generated dynamically from programming and data retrieved from data stores.

Because they still use the traditional Web site client-server method of interaction with users, Web applications still deliver results to users as Web pages written in HTML or XHTML, with perhaps some text, images, hyperlinks, Javascript, and other traditional media. So users may not know the difference, but the back-end programming techniques are very similar to normal application programming.

And Web applications still require a Web server to serve up their pages (the pages are still stored in a folder that is typically connected to a domain name) as well as perform management and configuration functions for the application. Although the Web application is developed like and functions like a Windows application in many ways, the legacy of traditional Web sites still drives basic Web site requirements.

Programming Language Basics

There are similarities in most computer languages that are present in just about every language, although like anything else there are always exceptions to the rule. In the following sections we'll categorize languages by a few salient characteristics, and then describe the things that make them similar. We'll also give some coverage to what makes one language popular for a particular use in comparison with other languages.

Markup, Interpreted, and Compiled Languages

Computers can perform data processing because they have a central processing unit (CPU) that reads programmed instructions, accepts data as input, and produces processed data as output. Of course, there are many little devices (such as a keyboard, mouse, monitor, and speakers) in between you and the CPU that help out, but the CPU does the bulk of the data processing work.

The CPU reads strings of bits (the familiar 0 and 1 or on and off). Strings of seven or eight bits are called bytes, and bytes represent characters (letters, digits, punctuation marks, and so forth). At the machine level, bytes are formed into machine code or assembly language. Assembly language can be programmed manually, but it is a very-low-level language, meaning that the instructions are processed almost literally. For example, in assembly language, your program might tell the CPU to move a string of bits from one register location in memory to another. Languages that compress the meaning of many assembly language instructions into a single statement are called high-level languages. High-level languages are often **compiled** for a range of CPUs and OSs, but some types of high-level languages are **interpreted**, not compiled. There are also some languages that are not for programming in the traditional sense, called **markup languages**. The next sections discuss these three types of languages.

Markup Languages

Markup languages such as HTML, WML, XHTML, and so on are not programming languages; they are languages whose main feature is the ability to format and display content on a variety of client devices. For example, when you see a Web page in your browser, your browser is actually reading the

HTML elements and deciding how to format the text and image (and other media types) of content inside the HTML tags. You can verify this by clicking View|Source in Internet Explorer. You'll see the HTML, and in between some of the HTML tags you'll be able to read the text content. HTML is not compiled and it is not interpreted in the same sense that Javascript is interpreted.

Interpreted Languages

Interpreted languages include VBScript, Php, Javascript, and so on. Interpreted languages are compiled in real time as they are used. For example, if you write a Web page with Javascript in it, the Javascript is actually sent as source code (uncompiled code) along with the Web page to the user's browser. When the browser receives the page, the Javascript is interpreted and compiled as it is read. This is fine for small programs such as the ones that make fancy Web page effects, but would slow down normal programs too much. Therefore, interpreted languages tend to be used where the functions they perform are smaller and less complex. Interpreted languages used in Web pages also tend to be much more limited in the range of functions they can perform, so they will not easily transmit viruses.

Compiled Languages

High-level languages such as Visual Basic and C++ allow you to write statements that are much less verbose, such as "if the value in variable A equals the value in variable B, then display a message box to the user." With high-level languages, you can write much more compact statements and expect the CPU to work with the operating system to take care of memory issues and so forth.

However, high-level languages are still translated into machine code or assembly language before they are run as programs. They are compiled before being released, and although they run quickly in this state, they must be compiled for use on a particular operating system/CPU combination.

Markup Languages and Specifications

Markup languages are used for defining and rendering content. Content includes text, images, and many other types and formats of data. **HTML** is a markup language with which we should all be familiar, and examining its structure and syntax provides important clues about markup languages in general.

HTML and SGML

HyperText Markup Language (HTML) is the language used to create most Web pages. If you click View|Source in Internet Explorer, you can see HTML source code in a Notepad file. HTML was created and is maintained by the

World Wide Web Consortium (W3C at www.w3.org), but it has been superseded by **XHTML**, an XML-compliant version of HTML. The following example code shows a basic HTML document in the old style:

```
<HTML>
<HEAD>
<TITLE>Your Title Here</TITLE>
</HEAD>
<BODY>All Body content (text and images) goes here</BODY>
</HTML>
```

HTML is not really a programming language because there are many characteristics of programming languages that are absent in HTML. However, it was easy to read and create HyperText documents with it for use over the Internet, and as such gained wide acceptance.

HTML's strength rested on its ability to properly render text, images, forms, tables, and so on. Since it is not compiled, anyone could write a Web page in HTML and it will run on any computer, so long as that computer has the appropriate browser to render the HTML.

HTML, XHTML, and other markup languages are derived from Standard Generalized Markup Language (SGML). **SGML** is really a comprehensive specification for creating markup languages, called applications. It is complex and very powerful, and application languages made from SGML have found uses in many industry and government documents. Illustration 4.1 shows the relationship between SGML, HTML, XML, and XHTML.

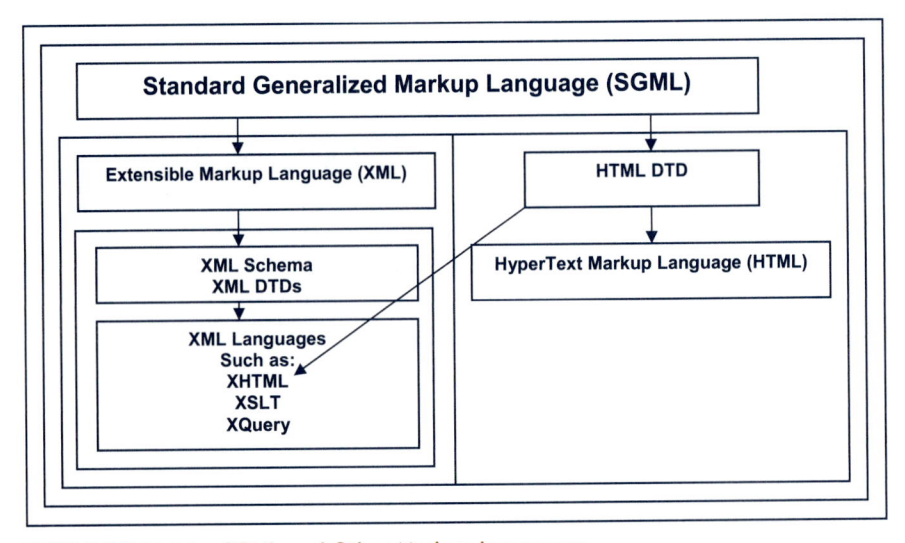

ILLUSTRATION 4.1   SGML and Other Markup Languages

Document Type Definitions (DTDs)

Like other SGML-based markup languages, the components of HTML are defined in what is called a **Document Type Definition (DTD)**. The HTML DTD is a specification defining the allowable **elements** and **attributes** (and their values) for HTML. The DTD for HTML is written in Backus Naur format, and defines each element and attribute of HTML in a format similar to the following (the HTML element IMG):

```
<!ELEMENT IMG - O EMPTY    - Embedded image ->
<!ATTLIST IMG %attrs;      - %coreattrs, %i18n, %events -
src    %URI;    #REQUIRED  - URI of image to embed -
alt    %Text;   #REQUIRED  - short description -
```

Note that IMG is the identifying part of the HTML <IMG> tag. Most HTML elements consist of a starting and ending tag enclosed in angle brackets, but the IMG element is allowed to have just a starting tag to produce its effect on a Web page (it causes an image to be included in the Web page).

The source attribute (src in the DTD segment above) is the name of the attribute that specifies to your browser where to find the image file to render in the Web page. Note that the value it contains is specified as a URI% in the DTD. Note also that attributes consist of a name-value pair in most cases.

HTML elements and attributes are the primary components making up HTML source code in Web pages, and they are also some of the most important and most used components of many other markup languages.

XML and XHTML

As we mentioned, XHTML is an XML-compliant version of HTML. The elements and attributes that make up HTML are the same in XHTML, but with a few added rules to make them XML compliant. Before we discuss XHTML and what makes it XML compliant, let's talk about what XML is.

XML is not a markup language; in fact, it is not a language at all. XML is a specification for creating markup languages, in the same way that SGML is a specification for making markup languages, but XML is a subset of SGML that is easier to use.

XML documents must be **well-formed**, meaning they follow the rules of XML syntax and structure. XML documents also may be **valid**, meaning they conform to the specifications of a DTD (or XML schema, written using the XML Schema Language) made within the guidelines of the XML specification. Note that XML documents are not required to be valid, but they can be. However, all XML documents must be well-formed. The following example shows a well-formed XML document:

```
<customers>
    <customer id="1">
```

```xml
        <orders>
          <order id="1">
        </orders>
      </customer>
      <customer id="2">
        <orders>
          <order id="1">
        </orders>
      </customer>
    </customers>
```

Note that in the example above, it is not necessary to include the XML version (even though it would be good practice), and because there is no reference to an XML schema or DTD, the document is not valid. However, it is still a perfectly good XML document and can be parsed by applications that read XML.

Data-Oriented versus Document-Oriented XML

One of the qualities of XML documents is that they impose a hierarchical nature on their elements, from the rule that no elements may overlap. There is only a single element allowed to contain all the other elements in an XML document (the root element), and all other elements have a parent-child relationship to this root element and each other. Therefore, it is easy to create data-oriented XML documents mimicking the hierarchical structure of relational databases, and a number of tools have been developed that translate database data into XML and vice versa.

Human beings would rather view data in a more intuitive way, so XML-based languages for transforming XML documents into something easy to read also have been developed. For example, eXtensible Stylesheet Language (XSL) is available for transforming XML documents from data-oriented into document-oriented for a wide variety of target platforms. XSL actually consists of XSLT (the part that does the transformation), X-Path (the part that filters for specific parts of the document), and XSL Formatting Objects (the part that specifies how the transformation is performed for a given platform).

XML DTDs and XML Schema Language

XML DTDs are written in Extended Backus Naur Format (EBNF) and define elements, attributes, and a number of other components that can be included in any XML documents based on the DTD. XML documents that use the elements defined in a DTD are said to be valid for that DTD.

XML Schema Language is another, richer way of defining the elements, attributes, and other components that may be included in an XML document, and if the document uses those defined components, it is said to be valid for that XML schema. The advantage of using XML Schema Language is that the schema itself is an XML document and is therefore easier to use than a DTD written in EBNF. Additionally, XML Schema Language contains much richer tools for defining data types, an important consideration for XML Web services and other applications of XML. We cover ASP.Net XML Web services in greater detail in Chapter 9.

Namespaces in XML   With XML schemas, the concept of namespaces is relevant, because you can incorporate defined elements and attributes from several XML schemas into a single XML document. For example, consider an industry in which there are different definitions for product specifications, depending upon which company you buy from, such as the clothing industry (a European size 5 is not the same as an American size 5). If companies in this industry build XML schema definitions of the terms they use to define their products, they both may define an element named "size" but mean something totally different (inches versus centimeters, perhaps). If you were to create an XML document listing products from both American and European companies, you'd want a means of differentiating between the European "size" and the American "size."

To include elements from both XML schemas in your XML document, you'd include an "xmlns" (XML Namespace) attribute in your document, and you would use it to define aliases (such as "euro" and "amer") that would prefix the "size" elements from each. Then you could use "euro:size" and "amer:size" to identify these elements in your XML document, thus avoiding any confusion.

You can see an example of the use of namespaces for defining elements when you look at ASP.Net Web Server controls in an ASP.Net Web form. In HTML code view, you'll see "asp:label" used to denote an ASP.Net Web Server Label control. This means that Microsoft has defined a set of controls under the namespace "asp" and uses that namespace to include access to these controls in ASP.Net Web forms.

XHTML

HTML and XHTML are almost identical, but XHTML is compliant with the XML specification, so certain rules must be followed when writing XHTML documents. These rules give some insight into what it means to write well-formed XML documents, as you'll see in the following sections.

Making XHTML Documents XML-Compliant   XHTML documents must be XML-compliant. The following rules ensure they are. Once you get used to writing Web page documents with these rules, you'll find that it's easy, and not much different from writing ordinary HTML documents.

1. All XHTML documents must have a DOCTYPE declaration before the root element in the document, such as

```
<!DOCTYPE html PUBLIC "-//W3C//DTD XHTML 1.0
Transitional//EN" "http://www.w3.org/TR/xhtml1/
DTD/transitional.dtd">
```

2. The root element of the document must be `<html>`. There may be only one element at this level, and no other elements may come before the starting `<html>` tag or after the ending `</html>` tag.

3. XHTML elements and attributes must be written lowercase. XML is case-sensitive, and the accepted convention is to write all XHTML elements and attributes lowercase (only `<html>` is acceptable).

4. Attribute values must be encased in quotes. Attributes are inserted inside the tags that make up elements (in the starting tag only) and normally are written as the name of the attribute, an equals sign, and then the value of the attribute. For example, to set the width of an image to 120 pixels, you would write the following: `<img src="image.jpg" width=120>`. In XHTML, putting quotes around attribute values is required, as shown in the following: `<img src="image.jpg" width="120">`.

5. Attribute values may not be minimized. In XHTML all attributes must include a value.

6. Leading and trailing spaces in attribute values will be stripped. This means any blank spaces before or after the value part of an attribute (a name-value pair) will be removed.

7. Only the id attribute can be used to identify an element uniquely.

8. Nonempty elements must be terminated (they must have an ending tag, or be terminated with a slash, like this: `<br/>`).

9. Elements must be properly nested, not overlapping, if they are contained within another element.

10. SCRIPT and STYLE elements must be marked as CDATA areas, as shown in the following code example:

```
<script language="Javascript">
<![CDATA[
function buttonalert() {
alert("You clicked a button")
}
  ]]>
</script>
```

Following the rules above makes your XHTML documents compliant with XML, and you'll find that many of the rules above apply to any language that intends to be XML-compliant (languages created using XML DTDs or XML schemas).

Scripting (Interpreted) Languages

Interpreted languages are programming languages with many of the same capabilities as compiled programming languages, but they are written as source code and then, instead of being compiled at that point, they are interpreted (which is like real-time compiling) when they are used.

Php and VBScript

There are some differences in how interpreted languages are interpreted. For example, Php and VBScript are both interpreted **scripting languages** (Php is an open-source project, while VBScript is a lower-level version of Microsoft's Visual Basic programming language), meaning they are sent to an interpreter (called a scripting engine) when a Web page is requested, so that before the HTML is gathered and sent back to the user, the Php or VBScript mixed in with the page is processed. All the user sees is HTML code; the Php or VBScript is processed and removed (except for the results). Here is an example of Php code:

```
<? if (isset($posted) {
   echo "Your name is $first_name";
} else {
   echo "Don't know your name";
}
?>
```

Here is an example of similar functionality using VBScript:

```
<% If posted="True" Then
Response.Write "Your name is " & FirstName
Else
Response.Write "Don't know your name"
End If
%>
```

Javascript

Javascript, on the other hand, is sent to the user along with HTML making up a Web page, and is interpreted by the user's browser. Javascript can perform many programming language functions but is restricted from accessing the hard drive and reading or writing files, to protect users from malicious Web page designers.

The two major differences between interpreted and compiled programming languages are, in addition to how they are processed, interpreted languages generally run much more slowly than compiled languages and interpreted languages run on many more platforms (CPU/OS combinations) than compiled languages. Running more slowly is not really a problem in many cases as most interpreted language programs are much smaller and more function-specific than compiled language programs.

VB.Net and Other Compiled Languages

Visual Basic.Net is based on Microsoft's Visual Basic but has some important differences and improvements. Support for VB.Net is included with VS.Net, as well as support for C# and J#. Many of the features of VB.Net are found in C# and J# as well, so choosing a language to use may depend more on what you are used to than which one is technically best for any particular application.

Programming languages, VB.Net included, typically have the ability to define variables and set their data types, perform data processing conditionally or with loops, and perform common arithmetical and alphabetical operations, and come with built-in functions for working with data and creating expressions. Illustration 4.2 shows how variables, operators, and expressions make up data processing in most languages.

Variables, Properties, Attributes, Fields
- Are Name/Value Pairs
- Have Data Types
- Are Data-Containing Structures

Operators Are Used to Perform Data Processing
- On Name/Value Pair Data Values
- Arithmetic, Alphabetic, Date, and Other Operations

Expressions Contain Values and Operators
- Are Formed Much Like Equations
- Can be Embedded in Functions
- Are Resolved (Calculated For Results) When Code Runs

ILLUSTRATION 4.2   Variables, Operators, and Expressions

Compiled Language Features

In the following sections, we discuss many of these features in VB.Net. We use VB.Net for our ASP.Net applications throughout this book, and a basic understanding of how the language works is required. In-depth coverage of VB.Net is beyond the scope of this book, but these sections will assist in your programming efforts with ASP.Net.

Defining Variables

One thing programming languages have in common is the ability to define variables. **Variables** are storage spots for data. For example, if the user enters his/her name, and your application needs to use the user's name to look something up in a database, storing the name in a variable helps, because then you can use the variable name in code for lookups and any other purpose you might have in mind. Any user can enter his/her name and you will be able to use the same variable as a container in your code for the name.

In VB.Net, you can define variables with the **Dim** keyword, as well as a few other **keywords** that denote variables with values that don't change (such as Const, for constant), and variables whose lifetimes and value persist beyond the current Sub procedure (such as Public). When you create a new variable in VB.Net, you also must set the **data type** of the variable, such as string, integer, datetime, and so on. We'll offer more coverage of data types in the section entitled Data Types.

Variables are declared with a statement such as Dim, then the name, and then the data type. Variable names should be descriptive, and some programmers like to prefix their variable names with the data type so they can easily remember later what they are working with. Variable names cannot be just anything (they cannot duplicate a keyword, for example); they must follow a few broad rules in VB.Net:

- Begin with an alphabetic character.
- Contain no more than 255 characters.
- Use no special characters or punctuation symbols.

A Dim statement might look like this, where strFirstName is the name of the variable:

```
Dim strFirstName As String
```

Comments in Code

Another feature of programming languages is the ability to write comments into your code. Comments are notes that are not compiled or executed. They help you write good code by allowing you to document in plain English what your code is supposed to do, and they also help you debug and maintain it later. Comments in VB.Net are any line that starts with an apostrophe. A comment might look like this:

```
"Check to see if they've entered a name in the text field
If strFirstName = "" Then
   'give warning to user
Else
   'do normal processing
End If
```

Note that the comments actually inside the If...Then...Else block are placeholders indicating other code that will be added later.

Data Types

Computers store values differently according to what data type they are. For example, a value assigned a data type of **Integer** is allocated less storage space in memory than a value assigned a data type of Long (a long integer). Computers also process values differently depending upon the data type they are assigned. A value assigned a data type of **String** can be sorted alphabetically, but you cannot add String values even if the values contain numerical digits (unless you convert the values to numerical data types).

Programming languages, databases, and many other languages and technologies used by developers have the ability to define and work with values of various data types. Some data types are common across many languages while others are pretty specific to a limited number of languages or technologies. Another feature of many languages and technologies is the ability for users or developers to define their own special data types, usually by combining primitive data types into more complex data types.

The Common Type System in .Net The .Net Framework includes the Common Type System. This system organizes and defines how types are used in .Net-related languages and applications. It defines two broad categories of types: values and references. Values and references are further categorized into run-time, user-defined, and enumeration types (for values) and self-describing, pointer, and interface types (for references). Types in the Common Type System correspond to their related types in .Net programming languages, applications, and so forth, and are converted back and forth during development and the compilation process. For example, in the CTS a 32-bit floating-point number is called "Single", in VB.Net it is called "Single", and in C# it is called "float". In each of these, the names represent the same data type.

VB.Net has built-in and user-defined data types, and these data types have a corresponding type in the CLR (remember, the CLR works with more than one programming language, so it contains common data types for more than just VB.Net, as shown in Table 4.1). The following sections discuss these data types and the VB.Net tools used to work with them.

Strings Values that are Strings are simply characters (letters, digits, punctuation marks, and so forth). They can be sorted and compared, connected together (concatenated), divided apart, searched, and so on. You can use the CStr function to convert other data types into strings.

Numerical Data Types Numerical data types are used when you want to perform arithmetic (and other) calculations on values. Numerical data types

TABLE 4.1 VB.NET and CLR Data Types

VB.NET Type	CLR Type	Size
Boolean	System.Boolean	2 bytes
Byte	System.Byte	1 byte
Char	System.Char	2 bytes
Date	System.DateTime	8 bytes
Decimal	System.Decimal	16 bytes
Double	System.Double	8 bytes
Integer	System.Int32	4 bytes
Long	System.Int64	8 bytes
Object	System.Object	4 bytes
Short	System.Int16	2 bytes
Single	System.Single	4 bytes
String	System.String	Constrained by OS
User-defined	System.ValueType	Sum of sizes

include several sizes of integer and several sizes of floating-point (numbers with decimal points) numbers, plus the Decimal data type, which is suitable for calculating values that represent currency. You can use the Cint, CDbl, and other functions to convert to numerical data types.

Dates   Dates and times are often-used values in programming, and have their own data type because working with them requires special calculations. For example, if you add one month to a date, are you adding 28, 30, or 31 days? Getting the right answer depends on the starting date, and the system must understand how dates are different from ordinary numbers. Using the **Date** and time data types means the system will properly calculate results, taking into account the differences.

Bit and Byte Types   A bit is the smallest unit of storage, the 1 or 0 (on/off, yes/no) Boolean data type. It is quite useful in many situations where a simple true or false is all that is required.

The Object Data Type   It is often useful to store whole objects in variables, and the Object data type makes this possible. Quite a few languages have an Object data type for this purpose.

User-Defined Data Types User-defined data types are possible in many programming languages and other technologies, and typically user-defined types are built from the combination of several more primitive data types. For example, if you want to store the combination of a person's last name with his/her SSN, you might make a data type with two strings, one for the last name and one for the SSN.

Operators

Operators are the processing instructions used on variable values. They are denoted by common arithmetical signs (such as plus +, minus −, equals =) and can be used to perform arithmetic, alphabetical, and other operations on variable values. In the following sections we discuss each type. Note that some operators are used in more than one context, and you may get different results depending upon the context in which you use them and the data type of the values being operated upon.

Arithmetical Operators If you have two variables, each with a data type of Integer, you can add them together using the plus sign (+), as shown in this code:

```
Dim varA As Integer = 6
Dim varB As Integer = 12
Dim varC As Integer
varC = varA + varB "The value in varC should now be 18
```

Notice how we set up the expression with two variables to hold the initial values and an additional one to hold the answer. We also could have changed the initial value of one of the variables to the answer value, like so:

```
Dim varA As Integer = 6
Dim varB As Integer = 12
varA = varA + varB 'The value in varA should now be 18
```

Arithmetical operators include addition (+), subtraction (−), multiplication (*), and division (/). If you suspect your data processing might result in numerical values that have a decimal place, make sure to use floating-point data types for your values, such as Single or Double.

Comparison Operators Comparison operators include relational and logical operators. These operators can help your program determine whether one value is equal to another, greater than another, true when the other value is also true, and so forth. The symbols used for these operators include

- Equality (=)
- Inequality (<>)
- Less than and less than or equal to (< and <=)
- Greater than and greater than or equal to (> and >=)

- And: True if both values or expressions are true
- Or: True if either value or expression is true
- Not: True if the first value or expression is true but the second is not

Concatenation Operators Concatenation is typically used with strings to join them. The plus (+) sign can be used to accomplish this action, but it is best to use the ampersand (&) in order to avoid confusion with addition of numbers.

Keywords

Keywords (also called reserved words in many programming languages) are words that represent statements that perform a function in the language and may not be used as variable names. For example, the keyword "Dim" is used to create (or dimension) variables in Visual Basic.Net. Quite a few other keywords exist in VB.Net, and it is important to know what they are. Look in the documentation to find a list of them.

Expressions

The number 4 can be represented as "4", or as "2+2". Both of these representations mean the same value, but the difference is that "2+2" must be processed to get the final answer. In the same way, a variable value can be represented by a final answer (a number such as "4") or by an expression ("2+2").

Expressions are not just equations; they can be the result of processing a function, such as the following:

```
varA = CStr(varB)
```

This code sets the variable "varA" equal to the result of the expression "CStr(varB)". This implies that varB contains some value that can be converted to a String value. The expression is processed and the result is placed in varA. This method is used to perform many of the common data processing tasks found in applications. In fact, capturing data from direct entry (or from object properties), putting them in variables, processing variable values with expressions, and then outputting them back to users is almost a complete definition of the most important things an application does.

Control Flow Structures

Processing data in applications is rarely as simple as adding two numbers. Your application must often make decisions about how to process data, and frequently must choose one or more different courses of action based on data that were entered or are the result of processing. In addition, it is often useful to process data items repeatedly, using the same processing instructions over and over until processing is complete for all data items. **Control flow structures** are used for these purposes.

If…Then…End If and Select Case structures allow your application to select different courses of action depending upon data values entered or processed. For, Do, and While loops perform processing over and over until a set number of or all data items are processed. These two kinds of control flow structures are found in VB.Net and many other programming languages (in fact, the ability to perform this kind of processing is a hallmark of programming languages, and one of the things that separate most markup languages from programming languages). Here is a description of VB.Net control flow structures:

- **Do…Loop**   *Do [{While | Until} condition] [statements] [Exit Do] [statements] Loop.* This structure performs a set of program statements until a condition is true or while a condition is true, depending on how it is set up.
- **For…Next**   *For counter = start To end [Step] [statements] [Exit For] [statements] Next.* This structure performs a set of program statements until the counter runs out (the counter is set up as a variable that takes on a new value each time through the loop). You can set the value the counter must reach, as well as the step size for each time around. The step can be either positive or negative.
- **For Each…Next**   *For Each element In group [statements] [Exit For] [statements] Next [element].* This structure performs a set of program statements for each item (element) in an array or collection.
- **Select Case**   *Select Case testexpression [Case expressionlist-n [statements-n]] … [Case Else expressionlist-n [elsestatements-n]] End Select.* This structure checks the value of a variable (set as the "Case") and performs the set of program statements matching the value for that case. It is set up as blocks of statements with a different "Case" value for each block.
- **While…Wend**   *While condition Version [statements] Wend.* This structure performs in a manner similar to the Do While loop, and most programmers use the Do While loop instead.
- **With**   *With object statements End With.* This structure allows you to create a reference to an object once and then execute multiple statements against that object, without having to reference the object again for each statement.

Discussion—Markup, Interpreted, and Compiled Programming Languages

Web applications are built with languages such as HTML, XML, VBScript, and Visual Basic.Net. ASP.Net objects and features are manipulated using programming languages, and the user interface is built with HTML and XML-based languages. Knowledge of language fundamentals is a key ingredient in successful Web application development.

HTML is a markup language whose elements and attributes are specified in the HTML Document Type Definition (DTD). The HTML DTD was written according to the SGML specification, a widely used set of rules for building markup languages. XML is a subset of SGML, and markup languages may be built from the XML specification as well. XHTML is an XML-based version of HTML, and many of the general XML rules about making well-formed documents apply to XHTML (and are what differentiate XHTML from HTML). HTML and XHTML are used to render text and image content in the browser (and other client devices), but lack common programming language features and so are not used for data processing.

VBScript is an example of an interpreted language that is mainly processed on the server, and Javascript is an example of an interpreted language that is mainly processed on the client. In either case, programs written with interpreted languages are not compiled in the traditional sense and are more portable than traditional programming languages. Javascript also lacks some common programming language features, to make it safer for users downloading Web pages from anonymous sites.

Visual Basic.Net (VB.Net) is an example of a full-featured programming language. It is compiled and must run on a particular range of CPU/OS combinations. However, since it works with the .Net Framework and applications using it can be written in Visual Studio.Net, it helps make application development very easy.

VB.Net allows developers to create variables, set and convert data types, write objects (or work with built-in objects), use keywords for built-in functions, write and process expressions, and run control flow structures, as any good programming language does. Many developers across the world are familiar with Visual Basic, so creating applications using VB.Net functions, keywords, and syntax is often quickly learned.

The Concept of Scope

When a variable is declared in Visual Basic.Net (or any programming language, for that matter), it means a space in memory is reserved. Computers have only so much memory available (we're talking random access memory (RAM); hard drive space is different), and so memory is considered a resource that must be managed. When you declare a variable to be of a particular data type, you not only set how the data are processed, you set the amount of memory reserved.

Because memory is reserved when variables are declared, good programming languages/technologies include facilities for disposing of variables and their values when they are no longer required. Therefore, variables are said to have a lifetime.

The concept of scope extends from the lowest level code blocks to your projects, applications, your computer, your local network, and the Internet as well. For example, there are addressing methods that make every domain, folder, and file on the Internet unique. While a single filename (such as "logo.gif") has undoubtedly been used millions of times at different Web sites, the IP address (or domain name) and folder path, in combination with the filename, differentiate that file in question from all others of the same name across the Internet.

A good analogy to scope is the concept of local and long-distance dialing on the phone system. If you can call someone without adding an area code to the number you dial, he/she is in the same "scope" as you are. If you have to add an area code, he/she is outside your scope, but you can still reach that individual because you added additional data to the basic number (equivalent to a variable's name) to uniquely identify him/her.

The point is, names for files, variables, and other objects may not be unique, but in many cases adding the parent object's name (or domain name and folder path) allows you to access the object across normal scope boundaries. Calling a variable, object, or file directly by name is possible when the calling code resides in the same scope, but additional data must be added to call objects outside the calling code's scope. Adding names to the call is referred to as "qualifying" the name. There are numerous qualifying or addressing schemes, but they all boil down to providing enough information to uniquely identify the object in question.

Scope in VB.Net

In VB.Net variables are declared by using the Dim statement, a valid variable name, the As statement, and the data type. The variable can then be accessed by name in your code. Accessing the variable means setting its value or using it in an expression. Variables are a convenient way of referring to values that may vary as the program runs, hence the name variable. Values that don't change are called constants, but they use the same type of mechanism to carry their values and can be called or accessed in the same way in code.

The concept of scope refers to how variables can be called and how long they live (their lifetime). For example, if a variable is created within a control flow or loop block (such as For...Next), the variable is accessible by name from any expressions also inside the control flow or loop code block, but once the block is done, the variable cannot be accessed by other code in the Sub procedure (although it remains in memory until the procedure finishes). The scope of the variable is said to be the For loop.

There are a number of levels of scope in VB.Net, and you can set them by the location of your declaration statements, with variable declaration keywords such as Dim, Private, Public, and so on. These levels may be applied to variables, Sub procedures, and other structures in VB.Net. On a higher level, within VS.Net applications, while variables may have scope only within the project in which they reside, it is also possible to expand their scope so that other projects in the same VS.Net application may access them. Note that if you add qualifiers or use an Imports statement, your code can gain access to a variable that would otherwise be hidden from it.

Levels of Scope in VB.Net
Some variables in VB.Net are only accessible directly by name within their scope. Other variables can be called from outside their scope by adding qualifiers to their names. Scope is set by a combination of location (inside a flow-control code block, in a procedure, in a module) and the declaration keyword used to create them (Dim, Private, Public, and so on). Scope levels in VB.Net are block, procedure, module, and namespace.

Block Scope   A variable has block scope when it is declared within a loop or flow-control block such as If...Then or For...Next. After the block is done processing, the variable cannot be accessed by other code in the procedure. Variables with block scope cannot be addressed outside the block by qualifying their names.

Procedure Scope   In a Sub procedure, you might write code blocks, and variables declared in these code blocks have scope of the code block. But if you want a variable to be accessible from any code block in the procedure, declare the variable outside any blocks in the procedure. Variables with procedure scope cannot be addressed outside the procedure by qualifying their names.

Module Scope   A module can contain multiple procedures, and variables declared outside any procedure in a module have module scope. Any procedure in the module can access these variables. You also can use special keywords to declare these variables, and the keyword you use will affect how the variable can be accessed. For example, while the Dim keyword is the only one available for use in procedures, you can use the Private and Public keywords. Using the Private keyword means the variable is only accessible within that module, while using the Public keyword means the variable is accessible from anywhere in the same projects, from other projects, and from an assembly built from the project.

Namespace Scope   A project is considered a namespace if it contains no other explicit namespace statements. A variable declared at the module level with the Public or Friend keyword has namespace scope. If you want to use variables declared in another project or namespace in your current project, you can use the Imports statement to bring them in, and then you can call them directly, without any qualifiers, as long as their names are unique. If their names are not unique, you must qualify them with the name (or the alias) of the namespace from which they are imported.

Discussion—Scope

Scope is a property of variables, objects, procedures, files, and so forth, but it is not set using a property sheet. The scope of a variable or object is based on how it is declared (the keywords used) and what it is contained in (the code block, procedure, module, or other structure). For example, variables declared with the keyword Public (at the module level) are accessible by code in other projects.

If your code must call a variable in the same scope, it can do so using the variable's name; if your code must call a variable outside the code's scope, it can do so in some cases by adding qualifiers (names of parent objects) to the name of the variable. Some variables cannot be accessed outside their scope, even by adding qualifiers.

Quick Check Questions

1. What is a DTD? What does a DTD do?
2. Where are the elements and attributes found in HTML defined?
3. What is the image element in HTML?
4. How is an image element written in HTML?
5. How is an element in HTML terminated?
6. What is the main difference between HTML and XHTML?
7. What is the difference between well-formed and valid XML documents?
8. List three rules that help make an XML document well-formed.
9. What is a data type?
10. What keyword in VB.Net is commonly used to create variables?
11. Can a variable name in VB.Net start with an underscore?
12. What is an operator?
13. What is a control-flow structure?
14. What control flow structure would be used to loop through processing statements exactly 5 times?

Summary

1. Traditional Web sites are stored on a computer running Web server software as static HTML files. When a user browses to the Web site, the Web server software sends a copy of the Web page to the user's browser, which then renders the Web page by reading the HTML code. The first page in a Web site is set on the server and is often named "index".
2. HTML and XHTML are markup languages and SGML and XML are specifications for creating markup languages. HTML was made from the SGML specification, and XHTML was made from the HTML DTD and the XML specification. A DTD is a Document Type Definition for a markup

language, essentially the rules and element/attribute definitions that completely define what is allowed in that particular language.
3. HTML documents are used to render text and image content in browsers. XHTML is very similar except that it conforms to the rules that make XML documents well-formed. Well-formed means an XML document follows certain rules (such as always terminating elements properly and always enclosing attribute values in quotes) but it does not specify the elements and attributes that are allowable.
4. A valid XML document is one that is not only well-formed but also conforms to a DTD or XML schema. XML schemas are similar to DTDs in that they define the allowable elements and attributes for a particular XML-based markup language (or vocabulary), but they have more flexibility for specifying data types. In addition, XML schemas are XML documents themselves, and this makes them easier to process and manipulate.
5. Programming languages can be broadly categorized by how they are compiled. Ordinary programming languages are compiled for a particular range of CPU/OS combinations and, while they run faster, are not very portable. Interpreted languages, on the other hand, are not compiled (until they are being run) and are therefore slower running but much more portable, as the compilers reside on the machine on which they run.
6. Programming languages have some features in common, such as the ability to create variables and process data with control flow structures.

Exercise 4.1

1. Open Internet Explorer. What page comes up? Why does this page come up? Change the page that comes up when you open the browser. Describe the process you used to change the opening page.
2. In IE, browse over to Microsoft's Web site. What did you enter in the Address field of the browser to get to Microsoft's Web site?
3. What is the name of the page that first came up on Microsoft's Web site? How does the Web site developer ensure that this page comes up first, instead of one of the other pages on the site?
4. On the top menu in IE, choose View|Source. What happens?
5. In the HTML file, find the starting and ending BODY tags. What makes one the starting tag and the other the ending tag?
6. What do the starting and ending tags make, in HTML?
7. List two attributes of the BODY element in HTML.
8. Where is the content contained within the BODY tags rendered in your browser? How about the content inside the HEAD tags?

Exercise 4.2

1. The XML specification allows you to write XML documents with any tags you please, so long as the finished document is well-formed. Write an XML document with elements for "parent" and "child" so that the document is well-formed.
2. Add a "name" attribute for your parent element and make the name "Joe".

3. Add an "age" attribute to the parent element and set it to "35".
4. Give Joe three children in this document.
5. Add name attributes to each child element and make up names for them.
6. Give the first child a pet. Make the pet a dog and name it "Rex".

Exercise 4.3

1. Using comments instead of real code, write a program that captures user input from the Request object in the form of a username and password and, if the username and password are valid, allows the user to see page content. If the username and password are not valid, the code should display a warning to the user.

Creating HTML Documents

1. Open VS.Net. Start a new ASP.Net Web application from the Visual Basic projects template, and name it WebAppUI. Open the Properties window and the Solution Explorer if they are not open.
2. Close WebForm1.aspx. In the Solution Explorer, right-click the WebAppUI project and choose Add|Add HTML Page from the shortcut menu. Leave the name HTMLPage1.htm.
3. Right-click the surface of the HTML document and choose Properties from the shortcut menu. In the DOCUMENT Properties Page dialog box, change from Grid to Flow layout.
4. Enter the words "Here is some HTML content". Your HTML form should now resemble Figure 4.1.

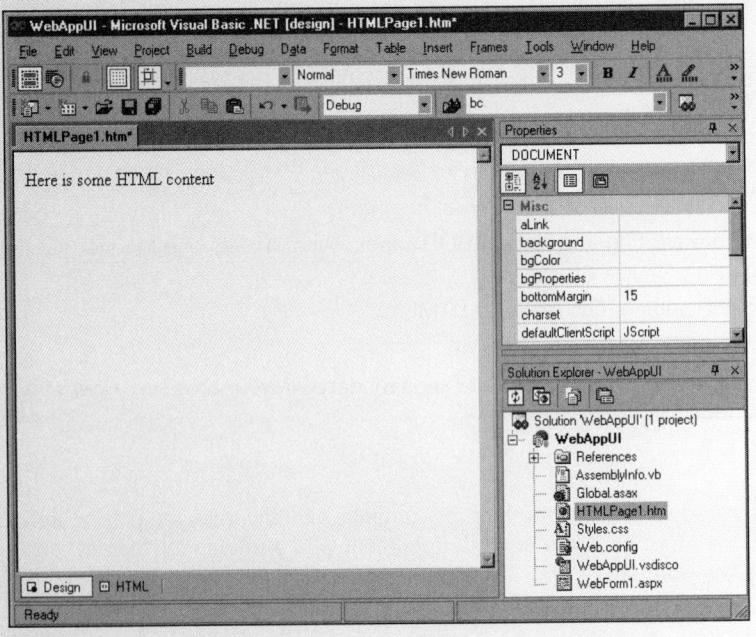

FIGURE 4.1 An HTML Web Page in Flow Layout

5. Click the HTML button at the bottom of the Designer. You should see the following code (also shown in Figure 4.2):

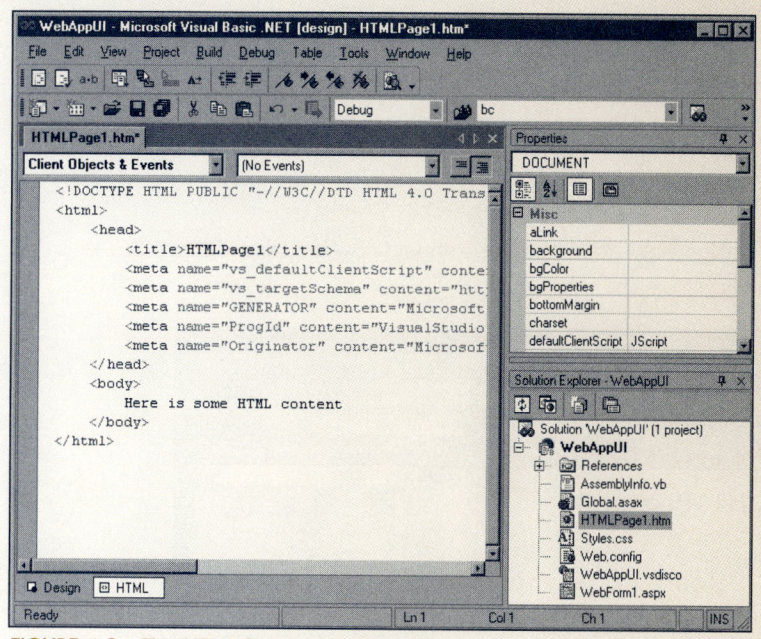

FIGURE 4.2 The HTML Source Code

```
<!DOCTYPE HTML PUBLIC "-//W3C//DTD HTML 4.0 Transitional//EN">
<html>
  <head>
    <title>HTMLPage1</title>
    <meta name="vs_defaultClientScript" content="JavaScript">
    <meta name="vs_targetSchema" content="http://schemas.microsoft.
      com/intellisense/ie5">
    <meta name="GENERATOR" content="Microsoft Visual Studio.NET 7.0">
    <meta name="ProgId" content="VisualStudio.HTML">
    <meta name="Originator" content="Microsoft Visual Studio.NET 7.0">
  </head>
  <body>
    Here is some HTML content
  </body>
</html>
```

6. The first line of code is a reference to the HTML "Transitional" DTD and is optional for most browsers.

7. The text content you just added to the page is contained between the starting and ending body tags. Add the following code to the text content:

```
<h2>Here is some HTML content</h2> And another line of content
```

8. Switch back to Design view. What has happened to the text as it is displayed in the Design view? Will this be reflected in the browser? Choose File|Build and Browse to find out.

ADDING HTML HYPERLINKS

1. In Design view, click at the end of the line of text (now a heading of size 2) and hit Enter. This makes a new line on your page.

2. Enter "Link to Page 2" as text on the page. Switch to HTML view and enter the following HTML code around the text you just entered:

   ```
   <a href="HTMLPage2.htm">Link to Page 2</a>
   ```

3. Switch back to Design view. Your Web page should now look like Figure 4.3.

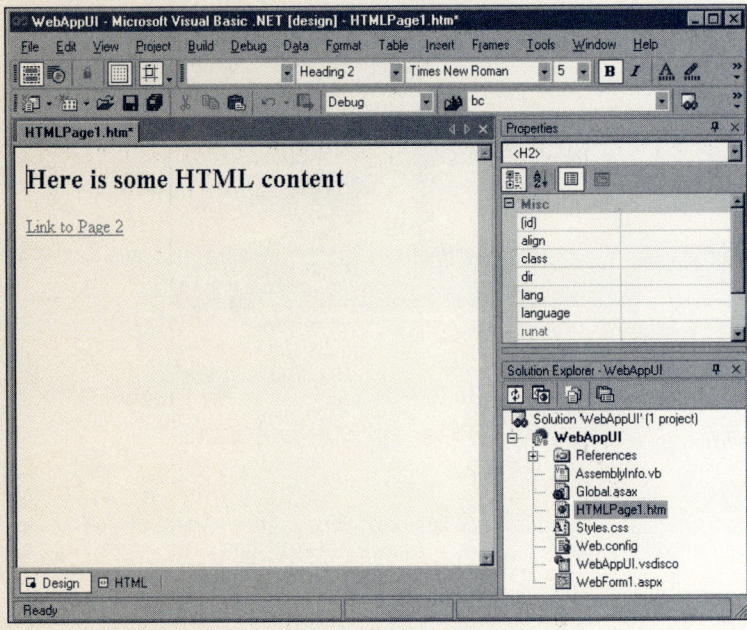

FIGURE 4.3 The Web Page with a Heading and a Link

4. If you build and browse this page, will the link to Page 2 work? Why not? Try it. What response do you get from the Web server?

5. Add another HTML Web page to your project. Change its page layout property to Flow layout, and then switch to HTML view. Set the bgcolor attribute of the body element to purple by changing the HTML code for the body elements as shown here:

   ```
   <body bgcolor="#8899FF">
   ```

6. Switch back to Design view and enter "Page 2" as text at the top of the page. Save the page.

7. Click back over to HTMLPage1.htm in Design view (you should still have this page open). Choose File|Build and Browse from the menu and try the link. Does it work now?

ADDING HTML TABLES AND IMAGES

1. In Design view in HTMLPage1.htm, click at the end of the line of text that is the link and hit Enter twice.
2. From the menu choose Table|Insert Table. The Insert Table dialog box will open (Figure 4.4).

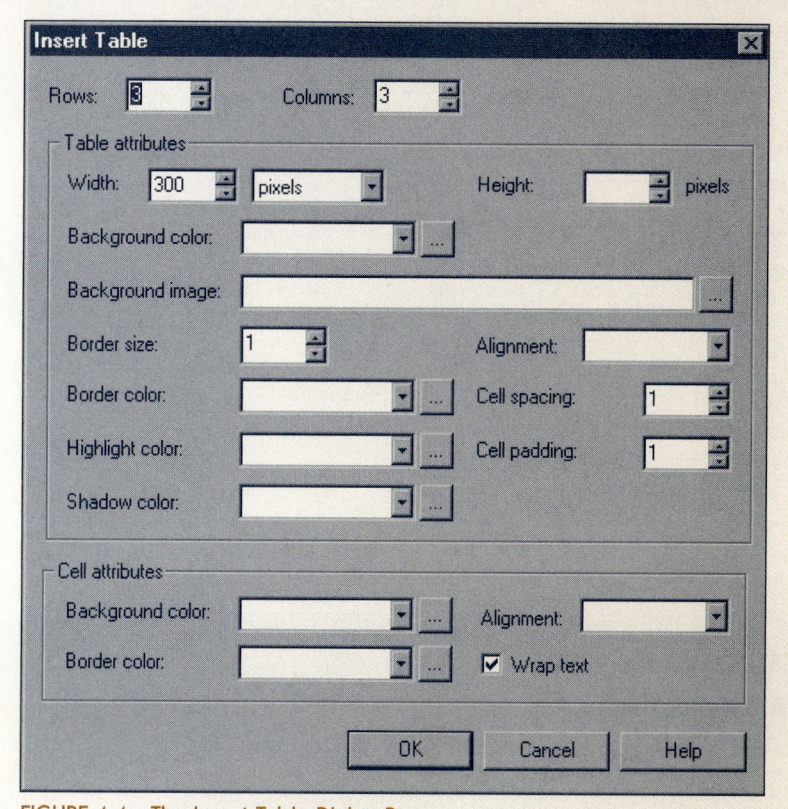

FIGURE 4.4 The Insert Table Dialog Box

3. Set Rows to 2, Columns to 2, Background color to #ccffff, Border size to 5, and click OK. A new table should appear on the Web page, as shown in Figure 4.5.
4. In the first cell of the table, type "Cell 1". Make the text boldfaced using the B button on the Formatting toolbar in VS.Net.
5. Switch to HTML view and examine the HTML code. What HTML element starts the table? What attribute sets the table's Border size to 5? What do you suppose the number 5 stands for in this attribute?
6. Select the table in Design view and then drag the right anchor to your left. This resizes the table. Your table should now resemble Figure 4.6.
7. Find a small GIF, JPEG, or PNG image file you like and copy it into the folder for WebAppUI. Name it myimage with the appropriate filename extension for the image file type it is.

CHAPTER 4 ASP.Net and Languages

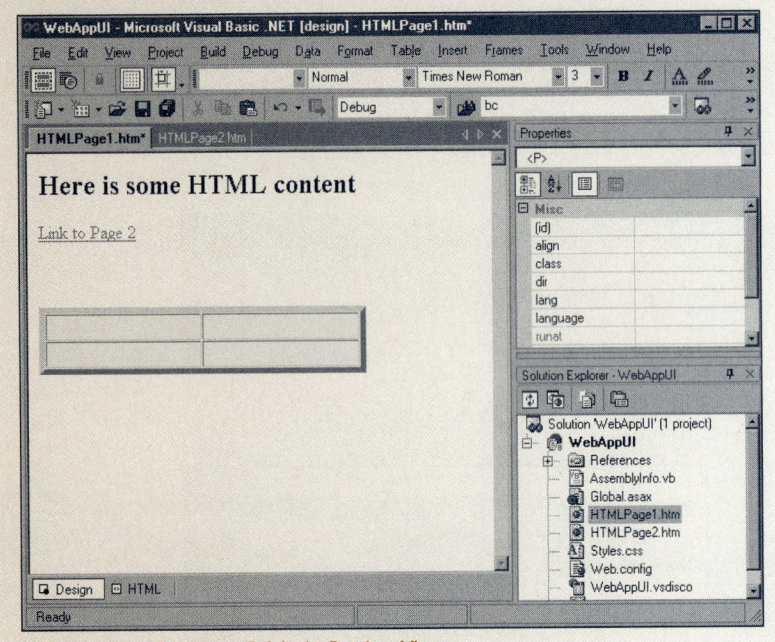

FIGURE 4.5 The New Table in Design View

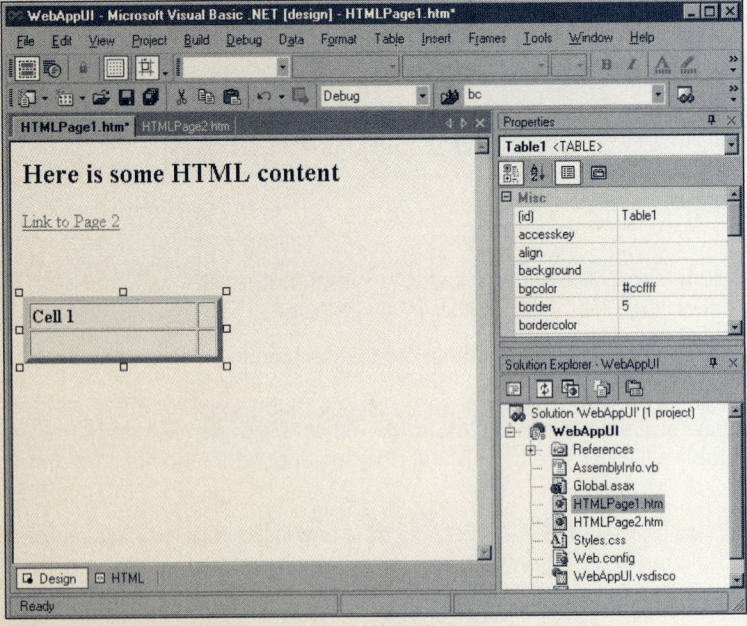

FIGURE 4.6 The Selected Table, Resized Smaller

Hands On Project

8. Right-click the project in Solution Explorer and choose Add Existing Item. Browse to the file you just copied into the WebAppUI folder and add it to the project.

9. Click in the cell under Cell 1. Choose Insert|Image from the menu. The Insert Image dialog box will open as shown in Figure 4.7.

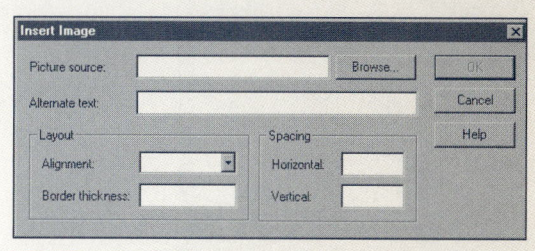

FIGURE 4.7 The Insert Image Dialog Box

10. Browse to the image you just copied to the WebAppUI folder by clicking the Browse button. The Create URL dialog box will open, as shown in Figure 4.8.

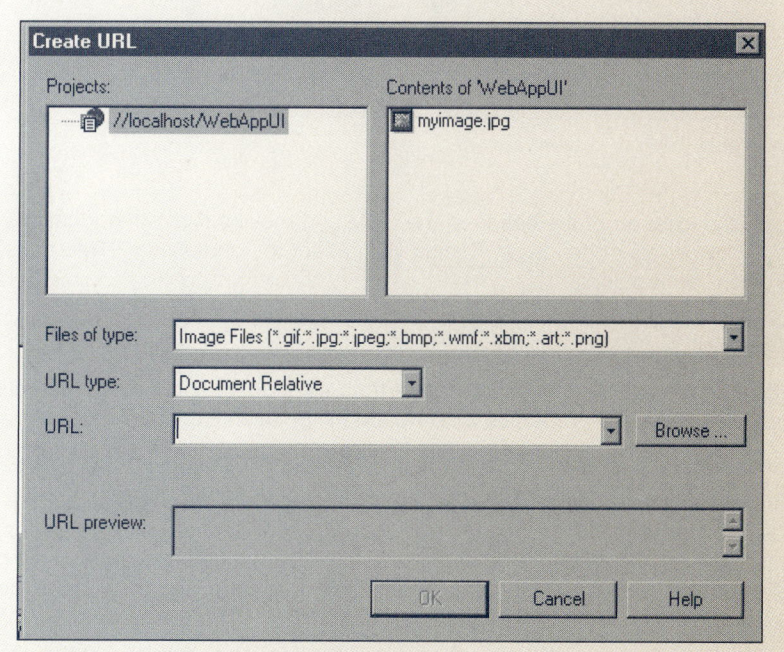

FIGURE 4.8 The Create URL Dialog Box

11. Select myimage.jpg from the Contents pane and click OK. The filename will be added to the Picture Source field in the Insert Image dialog box.

12. Enter the text "My Image" in the Alternate text field, and set the horizontal and vertical spacing to 4 for each field (this gives a margin of 4 pixels on all sides of the image).

13. Click OK. Your Web page should now resemble Figure 4.9.

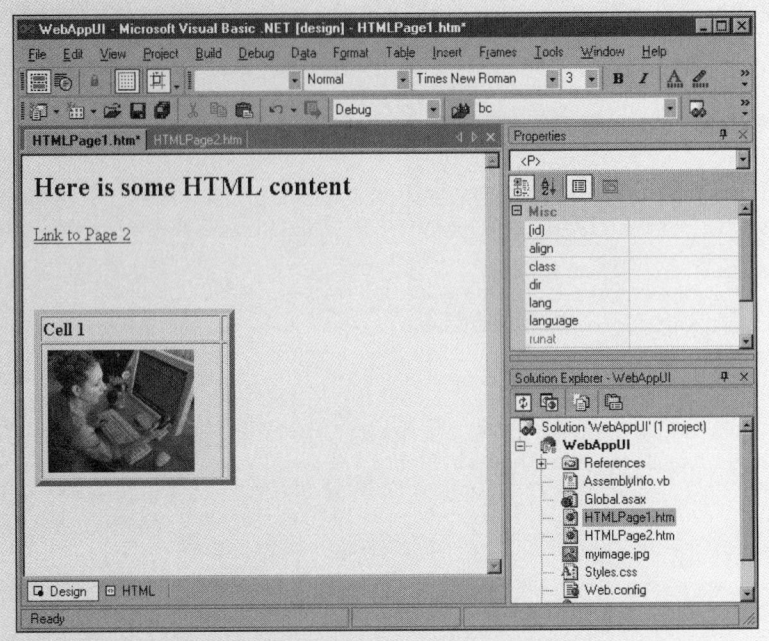

FIGURE 4.9 The Image inside the Table

14. Practice changing the location of the image in the table and moving it to other locations on the page as well. Check how your changes in Design view affect the underlying HTML code. Close the application when you are done.

Working with Dates in VB.Net

1. Open VS.Net. Start a new ASP.Net Web application from the Visual Basic projects template and name it WebAppDates. Open the Properties window and the Solution Explorer if they are not open.

2. In WebForm1.aspx open the Toolbox and add the following controls to the form:
   - A Label control named TopLabel at the top of the form (use the ID property to set the name). This label tells the user what the application is supposed to do. Set the Text property to "Working With Dates", and set the Background color to #C0FFFF. Set the Font property so the text is Arial and Bold. Set the Border color to Aqua, the Forecolor to Blue, and the Border width to 1 pixel.
   - A Label control named TheCurrentDate to the right of the TopLabel control. Set the color, border, forecolor, and Font properties of this control similar to those of the TopLabel, but set the Size property to "XX-Small". Leave the Text property blank.
   - A Label control named Note01 below the TopLabel control. Set the Font properties the same as for TheCurrentDate control, but do not change the color, border, or forecolor properties. Set the Text property to "Add or Subtract This Many Days, Weeks, or Months From the Current Date".
   - A Label control named Note02 several lines of space below the Note01 control. Set the Font properties the same as for Note01. Set the Text property to "Display the Result in This Format".

- A Label control named Note03 several lines of space below the Note02 control. Set the Font properties the same as for Note02. Set the Text property to "Display the Day of Week or Year".
- Two Radio Button controls named RB_Add and RB_Subtract between Note01 and Note02. Change their Text properties to "Add" and "Subtract" and change their GroupName to "Add_Subtract" to make them a group together (mutually exclusive). Set the Selected property of RB_Add to True.
- A TextBox control named TB_Number to the right of the two radio buttons. Set the Text property to "0".
- A DropDownList control named DDL_DayWeekMonth to the right of the TB_Number control. Click in the Items property and create three items with Text and Value properties set to Days, Weeks, and Months, respectively.
- Two Radio Button controls named RB_Short and RB_Long between Note02 and Note03. Change their Text properties to "Short Date" and "Long Date" and change their GroupName to "Short_Long". Set the Selected property of RB_Short to True.
- Two Radio Button controls named RB_Week and RB_Year below Note03. Change their Text properties to "Day of Week" and "Day of Year" and change their GroupName to "Week_Year". Set the Selected property of RB_Week to True.
- A Button control named Button1 (the default) with color, border, forecolor, and Font properties similar to TheCurrentDate. Change the Text property to "Get Results".
- Two Label controls named AnswerLabel01 and AnswerLabel02, with color, border, forecolor, and Font properties similar to TheCurrentDate. Change the Text property of AnswerLabel01 to "Date:" and the Text property of AnswerLabel02 to "Day of Week or Year:".

3. Close the Toolbox. Your WebForm should now resemble Figure 4.10.

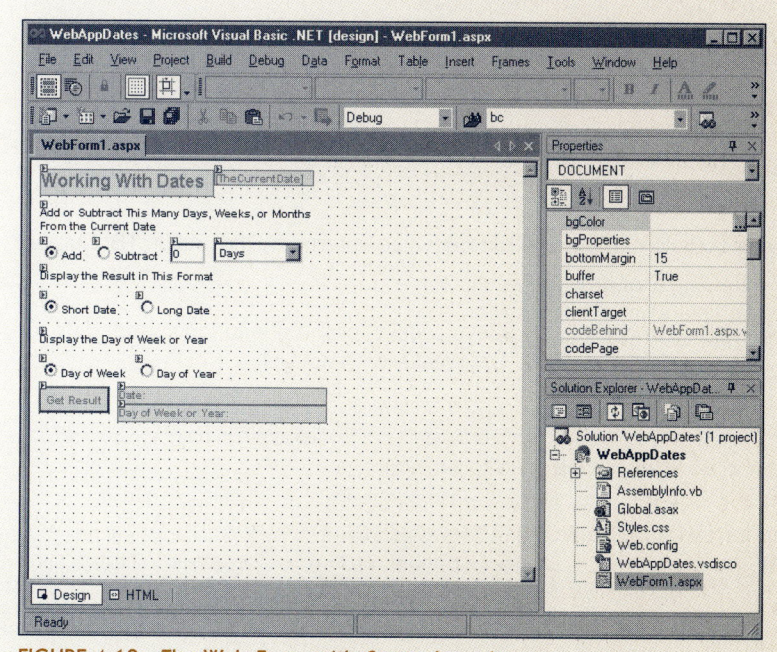

FIGURE 4.10 The Web Form with Controls on It

4. Double-click the surface of the form (but not any of the controls) to go into Code view. Enter the following code in the Page_Load event handler:

    ```
    TheCurrentDate.Text = Now().ToShortDateString
    ```

5. This code sets the Text property of TheCurrentDate Label control to display the current date. Note that the current date is retrieved using the Now() function, and its ToShortDateString property is used to supply the appropriate string value to the Text property. Since this code appears in the Page_Load event handler, this value will appear each time the form is requested and the page is loaded in the user's browser.

6. Click back over to the Web form in Design view and double-click the Button1 control. This starts an event handler for the Click event of the button. Code in this event handler will run when the button is clicked.

7. Enter the following variable declarations in the Click event handler for the button:

    ```
    Dim UserNumber As Integer
    Dim ResultDate As Date
    Dim DayOfWeekName(7) As String
    Dim DayOfWeekOrYear As Integer
    ```

8. The UserNumber variable will hold the number of days, weeks, or months entered by the user to add to or subtract from the current date. The ResultDate variable will carry the calculated date value through our code. The DayOfWeekName variable is an array with seven places in it (0 through 6) to convert the numerical values generated by the DayOfWeek function into the correct names for the days of the week. The DayOfWeekOrYear variable is an integer that will hold the numerical value generated by the DayOfWeek or DayOfYear functions.

9. Enter the following lines of code to initialize the array variable values:

    ```
    DayOfWeekName(0) = "Sunday"
    DayOfWeekName(1) = "Monday"
    DayOfWeekName(2) = "Tuesday"
    DayOfWeekName(3) = "Wednesday"
    DayOfWeekName(4) = "Thursday"
    DayOfWeekName(5) = "Friday"
    DayOfWeekName(6) = "Saturday"
    ```

10. Enter the following code to capture the number value entered by the user in TB_Number:

    ```
    UserNumber = CInt(TB_Number.Text)
    ```

11. Enter the following block of code to add days, weeks, or months to the current date, depending upon what the user selected in the DDL_DayWeekMonth control:

    ```
    If RB_Add.Checked Then
       If DDL_DayWeekMonth.SelectedItem.Value = "Days" Then
          ResultDate = Now().AddDays(UserNumber)
       ElseIf DDL_DayWeekMonth.SelectedItem.Value = "Weeks" Then
          ResultDate = Now().AddDays(UserNumber * 7)
       ElseIf DDL_DayWeekMonth.SelectedItem.Value = "Months" Then
          ResultDate = Now().AddMonths(UserNumber)
       End If
    End If
    ```

12. Notice in the previous code that we use the AddDays function to add days to the current date (retrieved with the Now( ) function), and that we simply change it to AddDays * 7 to add weeks. (For months we use the AddMonths function).

13. Enter the following block of code to subtract days, weeks, or months from the current date, depending upon what the user selected in the DDL_DayWeekMonth control:

```
If RB_Add.Checked Then
   If DDL_DayWeekMonth.SelectedItem.Value = "Days" Then
      ResultDate = Now().AddDays(UserNumber * -1)
   ElseIf DDL_DayWeekMonth.SelectedItem.Value = "Weeks" Then
      ResultDate = Now().AddDays(UserNumber * 7 * -1)
   ElseIf DDL_DayWeekMonth.SelectedItem.Value = "Months" Then
      ResultDate = Now().AddMonths(UserNumber * -1)
   End If
End If
```

14. Notice in the previous code that we use still use the AddDays function to subtract days, but we multiply by negative one (-1) in the expression so the result is actually subtracted rather than added. There is no SubtractDays function, so we multiply by negative one to get our answer instead.

15. Enter the following code to check and set the date format for the result and place it in the Text property of the Answer01 Label control:

```
If RB_Short.Checked Then
   AnswerLabel01.Text = ResultDate.ToShortDateString()
End If
If RB_Long.Checked Then
   AnswerLabel01.Text = ResultDate.ToLongDateString()
End If
```

16. Enter the following code to check and set the day of the week and day of the year answers in the AnswerLabel02.Text property:

```
If RB_Week.Checked Then
   DayOfWeekOrYear = ResultDate.DayOfWeek()
   AnswerLabel02.Text = "Day of Week = " & DayOfWeekName
      (DayOfWeekOrYear)
End If
If RB_Year.Checked Then
   DayOfWeekOrYear = CStr(ResultDate.DayOfYear())
   AnswerLabel02.Text = "Day of Year = " & DayOfWeekOrYear
End If
```

17. Notice in the previous code that we use the DayOfWeekName array to specify the name for the day of the week depending upon the result we get from the DayOfWeek function. This function produces a numerical value (such as 1 for Monday), and our array is indexed with week name values that correspond to these numerical values. When the DayOfWeekOrYear variable is set to the numerical value resulting from the DayOfWeek function, we can then use that variable value as the array variable index to retrieve the correct day of the week.

18. Once you've entered this code, click back over to the Web form in Design view and choose File|Build and Browse from the menu. Your application should correctly display results, as shown in Figure 4.11.

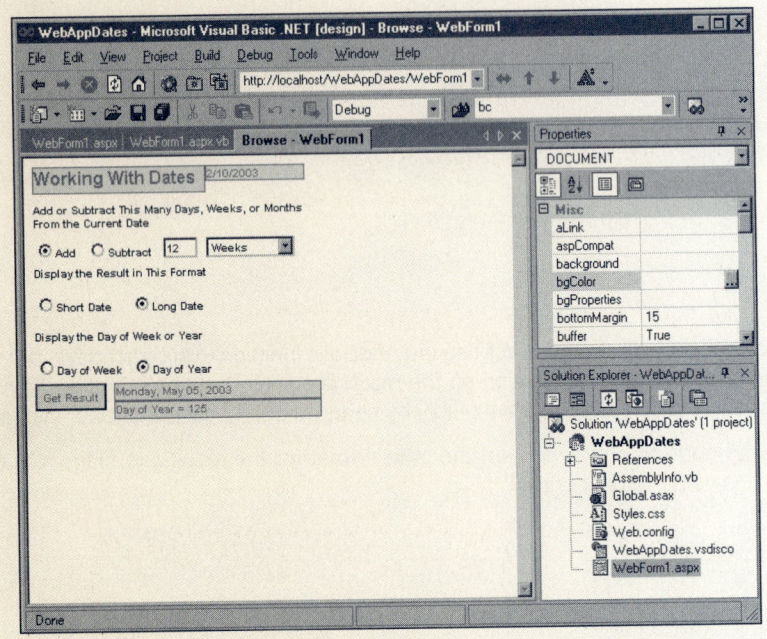

FIGURE 4.11 The Web Application in Action

19. Close the Solution and VS.Net.

Creating XML Documents and XML Schemas

The purpose of this project is to demonstrate how to create an XML document in VS.Net, and how to create a schema and DataSet from the document. VS.Net has many tools that help you create XML documents, XML schemas, and DataSets, as well as tools that check to see if your XML documents are well-formed and valid. However, you should know that VS.Net cannot validate XML documents that are linked to XML DTDs, and also that not all well-formed XML documents can be converted logically into an XML schema and DataSet.

1. In VS.Net, create a new project from the Visual Basic projects node using the ASP.Net Web Applications Project template. Name the project "XMLDemo". Close the default WebForm1.aspx that appears.

2. Open Solution Explorer (if not already open) and right-click the project. Choose Add|Add New Item from the shortcut menu. You should see the Add New Item dialog box shown in Figure 4.12. Leave the name as is, and click Open.

3. A new XML document should appear in the screen, as shown in Figure 4.13.

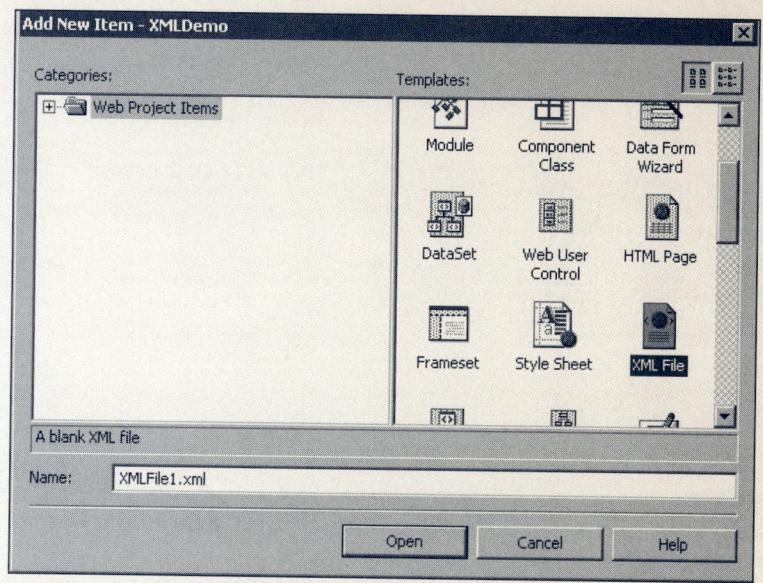

FIGURE 4.12   The Add New Item Dialog Box

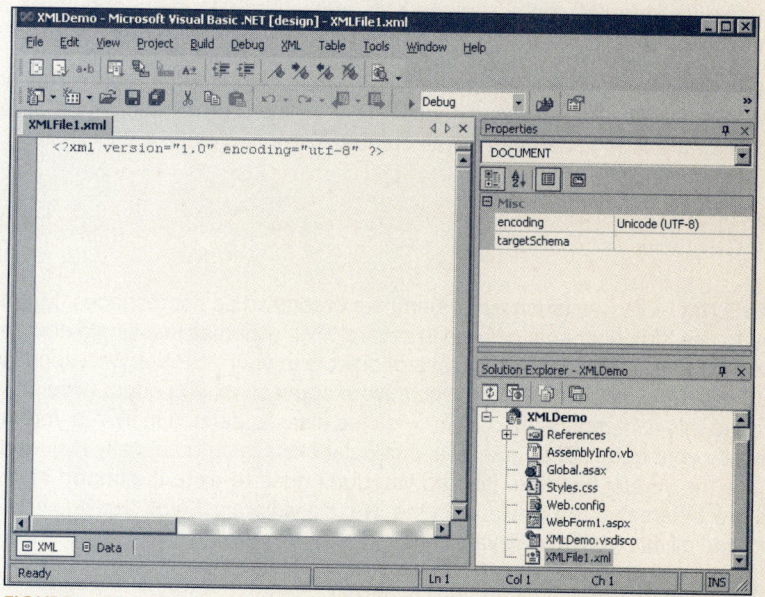

FIGURE 4.13   The New XML Document

4. Add the following XML code to your new XML document:

```xml
<customers>
    <customer cid="1" name="John">
        <orders>
            <order oid="1" amount="27.50"></order>
            <order oid="2" amount="77.50"></order>
        </orders>
    </customer>
    <customer cid="2" name="Jack">
        <orders>
            <order oid="3" amount="37.20"></order>
        </orders>
    </customer>
</customers>
```

5. From the XML menu, choose Create Schema. An XML schema file (named XMLFile1.xsd) should be created and added to the Solution, and the following should be added to the first element (customers) in the XML document:

```xml
<customers xmlns="http://tempuri.org/XMLFile1.xsd">
```

6. The "tempuri.org" is just a temporary marker for the location of the schema you've just created. Now choose Validate XML data from the XML menu. The document should be validated with no problems (the status bar will reveal that "no validation errors were found").

7. In Solution Explorer, double-click on the XMLFile1.xsd file. It will appear in the screen showing a visual representation of the dataset (Figure 4.14). At the bottom, click the XML button to see the XML code for the XML schema that was created. Save and close the project.

Alerts and Advice

Namespaces in VB.Net Classes (such as System) are organized as namespaces. Much like XML namespaces allow you to use XML elements defined in several XML schemas in a single document, .Net Framework namespaces allow you to use many classes of objects in your ASP.Net Web applications. For example, if you want to use the classes in System.Web in your application, you could write an Import statement in your code to bring this namespace (and thereby all the classes defined in it) into your application, available for direct use by your code. Of course, this particular class is automatically included in Web applications when you use the VS.Net template (and so you don't need to write the Import statement again), but there are quite a few others that are available in the .Net class library. If you see one you like, just write an Import statement and all its classes are available.

HTML Colors Colors are set in HTML using the hexadecimal numbers for 0–255 for each of the colors Red, Green, and Blue, preceded by a pound sign (#). A zero value for all three colors (#000000, with two characters for each color) renders as black, while a value of 255 (FF in hexadecimal) for all three colors (#FFFFFF) renders as white. Colors in between are created using a combination of these three colors. You also can set the bgcolor attribute with the names of common colors, as the browsers recognize these names as well as hexadecimal color values.

Key Terms

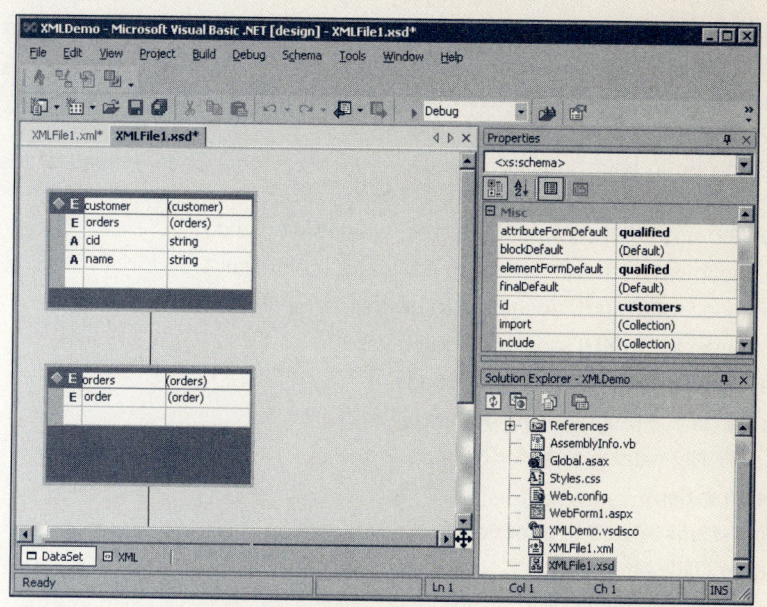

FIGURE 4.14 The XML Schema File

HyperText Links in HTML Links are created using the A element. The A element stands for Anchor, and the href attribute contains the URL, path, and filename of the Web page to open when the link is clicked. The content between the starting A tag and the ending A tag is displayed as a clickable link on the Web page.

The file to be opened when the link is clicked can be designated using an absolute URL (the full URL, path, and filename) or a relative URL (just enough information to tell the server where the file is relative to the current file). In our example, we can use just the filename to reference Page 2, because Page 2 is in the same folder on the same Web server as the Web page containing the link.

- attributes
- compiled
- control flow structure
- data type
- Date data type
- Dim
- Document Type Declaration (DTD)
- Document Type Definition (DTD)
- element
- expression
- HTML
- Integer data type
- interpreted
- keyword
- markup language
- operator
- scripting language
- SGML
- String data type
- valid
- variable
- well-formed
- XHTML
- XML DTD
- XML Schema Language

Review Questions

1. HTML documents can be written using HTML code in a plain text editor. Give an example of a text editor that is suitable for this purpose.
2. When you write an HTML document, it is written in HTML source code. To render it in a browser, what would you do with the file, and how would you name it?
3. What would you do in your browser to view the HTML source code instead of the rendered Web page?
4. To publish a Web page to the World Wide Web, what must you do?
5. Is an HTML document written in standard HTML XML-compliant?
6. What does it mean for an XML document to be well-formed?
7. What does it mean for an XML document to be valid?
8. What are keywords in a programming language?
9. What are variables in a programming language?
10. What are the VB.Net naming rules for variables?
11. What is an expression?
12. How are expressions related to operators?
13. What is a control flow structure?
14. What does the Dim statement do?
15. Why do variables have data types?
16. What data type is appropriate to hold the value "1998"? Why?

CHAPTER 5

Applications & Sessions

LEARNING OBJECTIVES

Upon completion of this chapter, you will be able to:

1. Explain how an application or session affects an ASP.Net Web application.
2. List the events associated with applications and sessions.
3. List the properties, methods, and events of the HttpApplication class.
4. List the properties, methods, and events of the HttpSession class.
5. Describe how the Global.asax file works.
6. Build code in application event handlers.
7. Build code in session event handlers.
8. Explain why to add code to application and session events.

INTRODUCTION

When you create an ASP.Net Web application, you are building a collection of files that reside on a Web server in a virtual root folder. For many applications, this is how your Web application is stored, although for some uses you may decide to use multiple servers or multiple processes on a single server to support your application. If you run the application from a single Web server in one process on that server, you can take advantage of the HttpApplication and the HttpApplicationState classes.

We began our discussion of applications and sessions in Chapter 2 when we talked about the Global.asax file. Unlike Windows applications that can maintain state information intrinsically, ASP.Net Web applications need a separate file to perform this function. The Global.asax file is a key component for any ASP.Net Web application that needs to track state.

Note that an ASP.Net Web application is still an application, even if you don't make use of its application or session properties, so please don't let the two uses of the term *application* get confusing. A good definition of "Web application" is "any set of Web pages that allows user interaction," while a good definition of "application" in the context of "applications and sessions" is "a container for the state of a Web application while it is running."

By now you've guessed that "state" is the current condition of a Web application and that applications and sessions are used to monitor the state of your Web application and work with it. In this chapter, we'll discuss what state is in technical terms; the HttpApplication, HttpApplicationState, and HttpSessionState classes; and their properties, methods, and events. We'll also work with them in an application through the Global.asax file.

State

State is a concept that applies to ASP.Net applications, but it also applies to other programming constructs as well as many other things found in the world. In general, it means the condition of something that can change over time. If you ask, "What is the state of the economy" or "What is the state of your health," you'd be interested in knowing whether either of these is doing well or poorly (as measured by some criteria or another). State is important, both to things like the economy and to things like computer programs and databases, because changes in state can affect how we interact with them.

For database applications, the state of the application can be valid or not. For example, in a database, there is a condition (actually, a constraint imposed upon how the database can work) called referential integrity. Referential integrity means that if a record in one table is required to refer to a record in another table, then the record being referred to cannot be removed without also removing all records referring to it. So if referential integrity is imposed on tables in a database, and then a parent record is removed without first removing its child records, the result is an invalid state and an exception is generated. Databases are just one example of computer-related data structures that depend on the concept of state.

ASP.Net Web Application State

For ASP.Net Web applications, Microsoft defines them (in the context of a discussion about state) as "the sum of all files, pages, handlers, modules, and code that reside in a given virtual directory and its subdirectories and that users can request through that virtual directory hierarchy." Therefore, the state of the application at any given time can be defined as the current condition of all those files (and so on) plus the changes that have been made by users of the application. Note that if you, as a developer, make design changes, even while the application is running, you are redefining the application (making a new one) and setting state back to its original values for a new application. Illustration 5.1 depicts state and its relationship to applications and sessions.

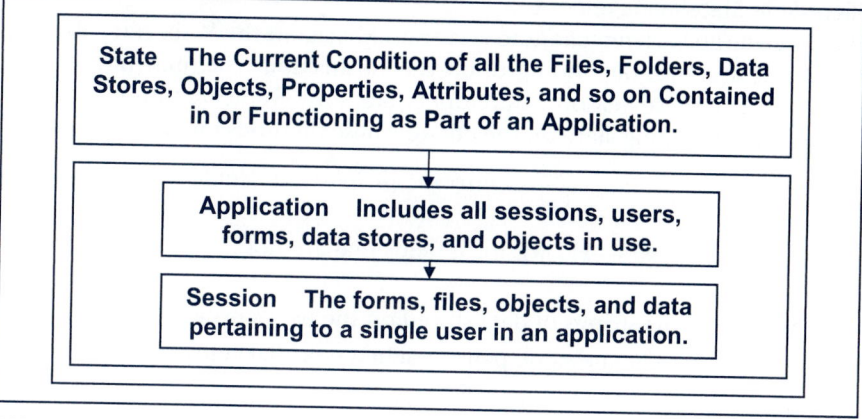

ILLUSTRATION 5.1   State, Applications, and Sessions

In ASP.Net Web applications, code that runs in the event handler for a button can create variables, capture user-entered values, and then process those data (and do database lookups and so forth), and then pass that output back to the user. But once that's done, the data (the variables and values) are lost. They're not available to the user anymore, and they're not available for any other parts of the application to work with either. In most cases this is good, as there's no need to store or use transitory data later. But in some cases data must be maintained across processing occurring on a single page or across many page requests from a single user, or across all the pages and requests of all the users working with the application. Applications and sessions provide this mechanism for maintaining state across your Web application, and the Global.asax file is the developer's access point.

The Stateless Nature of the Web

As we indicated in the introduction to Chapter 3, communications on the Web are stateless, meaning there is no mechanism intrinsic to HTTP for managing state on the Web. ASP.Net's application and session classes provide such a mechanism for the server, but there are also methods for using the client to provide state information. Client-side methods are important because the user can make multiple changes to controls rendered on the browser without in any way notifying the server.

The only opportunity for the server (and the server-side code in your Web application) to capture what has happened on the browser is when the user clicks a link or submits a form (each of these actions makes a request to the server). Think of these requests as "roundtrips" to the server. We think nothing of this type of action when using a desktop application; in fact, we expect that the code doing the processing is constantly aware of what the user is doing within the user interface forms.

Client-Side State Management

Making roundtrips from client to server and back, on the Web, can cause significant delays and, depending upon the connection type, may not work as expected. For these reasons, developers employ several methods for maintaining and managing state on the client. These methods include

- The **ViewState property**—an intrinsic property of .Net forms and controls.
- **Hidden form fields**—HTML form fields that are not displayed on the page.
- **Cookies**—short strings of data stored on the user's browser.
- **Query strings**—name-value pairs attached to a clickable URL.

The ViewState Property An ASP.Net Web Forms page and each of the controls on it has a ViewState property. When the page is processed and sent to the user, the current state of all its controls is turned into a string and stored on the page in a hidden form field (this is done automatically, not as an explicit action you have to code into your application, as is done in the next section about hidden form fields).

When the user submits the form, the value of the hidden form field is automatically sent as well, and the server (and therefore your code) can retrieve this value. Notice that in this scenario, you will know the difference between the state of the page and its controls as it was sent and the current state. But you won't know anything about what the user might have done in between those states.

For example, suppose you send a form with a DropDownList control. The user might have opened the list and checked out all the choices, but ultimately decided not to choose any of them. Upon submission, you would not know this. Even though it's unlikely that doing this would be significant, it is an important difference from Windows applications, in which you can detect (and react to) just about everything the user does.

ViewState data reside in a hidden form field on the page sent to the user but are hashed into a form unrecognizable by the user, as shown in this example:

```
<input type="hidden" name="__VIEWSTATE"
    value="dDwxMDQ5NjEwMDE2Ozs+" />
```

Hidden Form Fields Hidden form fields are created when you add `<input type="hidden" name="whatever" value="true">` to an HTML form. The name and value you give your hidden form field can be retrieved when the user submits the form. You can maintain state (as name-value pairs) across multiple page submissions this way, but note that it is easy for sophisticated users to see these values (by checking View|Source in their browser) and they don't work for clicking links or query strings (unless you add them to the URL). For example, the following hidden form field data would be pretty easy for the user to figure out:

```
<input type="hidden" name="CustomerID" value="2634">
```

Cookies Cookies (small strings of data stored on the user's computer) also can be used to maintain state data, and they give you more flexibility because they can be set to expire immediately or after a very long life. However, not all users allow cookies to be set, and the value of cookies also can be retrieved and modified by sophisticated users.

Query Strings Query strings carry name-value pairs in which state data can be maintained (much like hidden form fields), but their limitations are roughly equal to the limitations of hidden form fields, except that they work for clicking links but not for form submissions.

Applications and Sessions

The choices made by the user while interacting with the user interface can be detected using client-side state management features such as the ViewState property, hidden form fields, cookies, and querystrings. These mechanisms all maintain state data across multiple page requests for the same page. But for state data to be maintained across page requests for different pages, or across multiple users of the application, additional mechanisms are required. These additional mechanisms are referred to as server-side state management mechanisms, and they include the concepts of applications (for multiple users) and sessions (for different page requests by the same user). Note that it is also possible to store state data from page request to page request using the ViewState property, but this is accomplished by storing the data in a hidden field within the Web form and may increase the size of page downloads.

Application and Session Events

When the first user requests the first page of your Web application, the application starts (more on this in the section entitled Intrinsic Application and Session Objects). Each user that requests a page from the application also starts a session. The start of the application and the start of each session trigger the Application and Session Start events. These events have event handlers (see the next section about Global.asax) in which code can be placed. There are also events that are triggered while requests are being processed, when each session ends, and when the entire application ends. Sessions end when they time out, when a user has disconnected, or when the sessions are explicitly abandoned (using the Abandon method in your code, for example). Applications end when the Application_End event occurs, and this happens when the last user's session times out or is ended. Before we approach using applications and sessions in an application, we're going to examine in detail the Global.asax file.

The Global.asax File

When you make an ASP.Net Web application using the Visual Basic projects template, a Global.asax file is created automatically. While it is not mandatory that you use this file in your Web application, it comes in handy for responding to events that occur for the application as a whole, or for the session as a whole. For example, the entire application starts the first time the first user makes a request for any page in the application, and it continues until after the last user has made the last request. As you might expect, the lifetime of the application as a whole may be many days, months, or years. Note that data in application variables can be lost accidentally (if the server crashes, for example), but they also can be lost by deliberate actions, such as when the application developer makes code updates or changes.

Although the Global.asax file may exist in the same folder as the rest of the pages in an application, it is not accessible to users, so it is safe for holding sensitive information. And if you make changes to Global.asax, ASP.Net will detect them and complete all existing requests before closing and restarting the application.

Event Handlers in Global.asax

As with other pages in your ASP.Net Web application, the Global.asax file contains event handlers in which you may place code for initializing your application and for initializing individual sessions. Illustration 5.2 shows the relationship between the Global.asax file and the event handlers it contains.

You can see these event handlers in the code of a Global.asax file created by default as part of a template:

```
Sub Application_Start(ByVal sender As Object, ByVal e As
  EventArgs)
  ' Fires when the application is started
End Sub
Sub Session_Start(ByVal sender As Object, ByVal e As
  EventArgs)
  ' Fires when the session is started
End Sub
Sub Application_BeginRequest(ByVal sender As Object,
  ByVal e As EventArgs)
  ' Fires at the beginning of each request
End Sub
```

Applications and Sessions

```
┌─────────────────────────────────────────────────────────────┐
│  ┌───────────────────────────────────────────────────────┐  │
│  │  Global.asax – The file in an ASP.Net Web application │  │
│  │  used to hold code for application and session event  │  │
│  │  handlers and application and session variables.      │  │
│  └───────────────────────────┬───────────────────────────┘  │
│                              ▼                              │
│  ┌───────────────────────────────────────────────────────┐  │
│  │  Application Event Handlers                           │  │
│  │  • Includes Start and End events                      │  │
│  │  • Processed when application starts or ends          │  │
│  │  • Can be used to create or destroy Application       │  │
│  │    variables                                          │  │
│  └───────────────────────────────────────────────────────┘  │
│                                                             │
│  ┌───────────────────────────────────────────────────────┐  │
│  │  Session Event Handlers                               │  │
│  │  • Includes Start and End events                      │  │
│  │  • Processed when individual sessions start or end    │  │
│  │  • Session Start only occurs after Application Start  │  │
│  │  • Session End only occurs before Application End     │  │
│  │  • Can be used to create or destroy Session variables │  │
│  └───────────────────────────────────────────────────────┘  │
└─────────────────────────────────────────────────────────────┘
```

ILLUSTRATION 5.2   The Global.asax File and Event Handlers

```
Sub Application_AuthenticateRequest(ByVal sender As
    Object, ByVal e As EventArgs)
  ' Fires upon attempting to authenticate the user
End Sub
Sub Application_Error(ByVal sender As Object, ByVal e As
    EventArgs)
  ' Fires when an error occurs
End Sub
Sub Session_End(ByVal sender As Object, ByVal e As
    EventArgs)
  ' Fires when the session ends
End Sub
Sub Application_End(ByVal sender As Object, ByVal e As
    EventArgs)
  ' Fires when the application ends
End Sub
```

Each comment (beginning with 'Fires when...) indicates where to put code that you would like to have run when that particular event occurs. For example, when a new user first makes a request of the application, you may want to check to see if he/she has any cookies, and if so use the cookie to personalize his/her experience at your site (assuming the cookie contains data for this purpose). You could put the code that begins this personalization process in the Session_Start event handler. This event fires every time a new session is started.

In addition to the Start and End events for applications and sessions, there are other event handlers in the Global.asax file to which code can be added. These include Application_BeginRequest, Application_AuthenticateRequest, and Application_Error. The BeginRequest event is the first event to happen when a request is made. AuthenticateRequest occurs next, followed by a series of other events related to the processing of a page. The Error event occurs when there is an unhandled exception (an error) and provides the opportunity to respond gracefully to errors. We will demonstrate usage of some of these events in the ASP.Net Web applications we develop later in this chapter. First, let's take a close look at the intrinsic Application and Session objects exposed as properties of the **HttpApplication class**.

The Intrinsic Application and Session Objects

An instance of the **HttpApplicationState class** is created when an application starts, defined as "the first time a client (browser) requests any URL resource from within an ASP.Net application virtual directory." This instance is exposed as a property of the HttpApplication class named "Application". This class also exposes a property named "Session" that gets the **HttpSessionState** for the current request. These objects are similar in nature to the ASP Application and Session objects and can be worked with in a very similar fashion. For example, you can store variable values in a session simply by calling the session and a variable associated with it and then setting the value of the variable. The variable is then accessible from any page or request so long as the user remains connected to the application. Following are some descriptions of the accessibility of variables with or without Applications and Sessions, and some cautions about using them:

1. When an ordinary ASP.Net application is running and Application or Session variables are not used (and no other method of maintaining state is used either), all variables and their values live only during the execution of the page in which they are created.

2. If you create variables and values in the Application or Session either via the Global.asax file's event handlers or directly from the page by calling these objects and creating variables in them, then these variables and their values live until the session or application is terminated (or you get rid of them).

3. Variable values in the Session object can be changed in code at any point during a session. For example, if a user's preference for hotels is stored in a session (think of some travel ordering system) and the user changes his/her preference on a form and submits it, your code can change this value in the Session object. If a summary value for response from all users of an application is stored in the Application

object, this value could be changed each time a new user submits his/her response (think of an online survey or poll-taking system). However, note that because each user could make changes to the summary value, you need to use the Lock and Unlock methods when changing application variable values while the application is running. This prevents multiple users from accessing the same variable and changing it at the same time.

User login, shopping carts, and many other common Web application needs can be fulfilled using Applications and Sessions, and in the following sections we discuss both of these objects and the properties, methods, and events available for working with them.

Adding Variables to an Application or Session

One of the most common uses for Application and Session objects is to contain values in variables across the entire application or an individual session. You can create and initialize application and session variables in the Global.asax file by placing code in the appropriate event handler, as shown in the following code example (in the Application_Start event handler):

```
Sub Application_Start(ByVal sender As Object, ByVal e As
    EventArgs)
    Dim AppVar As String
    Application("AppVar") = "Starting Application Variable
        Value"
End Sub
```

A variable is dimensioned in the ordinary fashion as a string, and then set to a value by calling the Application object and putting the variable name inside parentheses and using the equals (=) operator. The variable and its value can now be accessed and changed from any page or request in the application. For example, if you have a page with a TextBox control named "UserValue" and a Button control, you can place the following code in the event handler for the button to modify the value of the AppVar variable:

```
Application("AppVar") = "New Application Variable Value"
UserValue.Text = Application("AppVar")
```

This code first changes the string value in the AppVar variable, and then sets the Text property of the UserValue TextBox control equal to the value now contained in AppVar. Of course, if there is a possibility that other users might be trying to change the value at the same time, it would be appropriate to use the Lock and Unlock methods of the Application object, as shown here:

```
Application.Lock()
Application("AppVar") = "New Application Variable Value"
Application.Unlock()
UserValue.Text = Application("AppVar")
```

Note that if another user happened to change the value of AppVar while your code is running, it's possible that you might not get the value you were expecting, so you could save the Application.Unlock() statement until after you've set the value of UserValue.Text.

Adding variables to sessions works in much the same way, as shown in this code:

```
Sub Session_Start(ByVal sender As Object, ByVal e As
    EventArgs)
    Dim SesVar As String
    Session("SesVar") = "Starting String Variable Value"
End Sub
```

Changing the value is as simple as this:

```
Session("SesVar") = "New Session Variable Value"
```

There is no need to lock the session, because there is only one user for a session, so there is no Lock method available for the Session object. However, there are a number of other properties and methods for sessions that are useful.

ASP.Net Sessions

When a new user makes a request for a page in your application, a 120-bit SessionID is generated. This ID is unique and allows your application to identify and maintain state for a user while he/she is connected to the application, so long as he/she continues to make requests without exceeding the timeout period between requests. The SessionID is stored as a cookie, or is automatically included on every link in the URL, depending upon how you configure your application.

Session variables and values (created by you and loaded with data by the user) as well as any objects are stored in a dictionary-based, in-memory cache. You can use out-of-proc mode to store session state in memory, or SQL mode to store session state in a SQL Server database. A State Server for each processor or Web form supports processes requiring session state, and this separation makes your Web application more stable and robust. The SessionStateModule is responsible for getting SessionIDs and for storing and retrieving session state data from the State Server.

The Session object has a Contents and a StaticObjects collection that can be accessed as properties. The Contents collection contains all items that have been added to the session via code, and the StaticObjects collection contains all objects that have been added using the `<object runat="server">` tag, with session scope. These collections provide convenient access points to add, edit, and delete variables and objects. The Session object also has a number of properties and methods for working with sessions and for manipulating data and objects you store in sessions.

Session Properties

The Session object exposes the following Public properties.

- **CodePage.** This property can be used to get or set the code page value, normally ANSI 1252.
- **Contents.** This property gets a reference to the current session-state object. You can set new values using code such as the following:

  ```
  Session("myvariable") = "myvalue"
  Session.Contents("myvariable") = "myvalue")
  ```

- **Count.** This property provides a count of the items in the session-state collection. You can put the number of items in a session, **Session.Count**, into an appropriately dimensioned variable using code such as this:

  ```
  NumItems = Session.Count()
  ```

- **IsCookieless.** This property allows you to determine whether the session ID is being stored in a cookie or in the URL (as a query string).
- **IsNewSession.** This property allows you to tell if the session was created during this request or previously. This value is Boolean, and you can therefore use it as a test in an If...Then...Else code block.
- **IsReadOnly.** This property tells you if the session is read-only.
- **IsSynchronized.** This property tells you if the session is synchronized.
- **Item.** This property can be used to get or set the values for session items.
- **Keys.** This property returns a collection containing all the keys (names) for the items in the session.
- **LCID.** This property gets or sets the Locale Identifier for the current session.
- **Mode.** This property gets the current session-state mode. Modes include InProc (the default), Off (session state is disabled), SQL Server, and StateServer.
- **SessionID.** This property retrieves the session ID value from **Session.SessionID**. You can use code such as the following to retrieve this value:

  ```
  MySessionID = Session.SessionID
  ```

- **StaticObjects.** This property gets a collection of any objects declared with the object tag (`<object runat="Server" Scope="Session">`) in the Global.asax file.
- **SyncRoot.** This property gets an object that can be used to synchronize access to the collection of session-state values.
- **Timeout.** This property gets or sets, in minutes, the timeout period for requests in the current session: **Session.Timeout**.

Session Methods

The Session object has the following Public methods:

- **Abandon.** Using this method will cancel the current session. You can call this method using code such as:

```
Session.Abandon()
```
- **Add.** Using this method will add a new item to a session. You can add items using code such as this:

```
Session.Add("myvariable","myvalue")
```
- **Clear.** Using this method clears all the values from session state.
- **CopyTo.** Using this method copies the collection of session-state values to an array, beginning with the index specified.
- **Equals.** Using this method you can determine whether two object instances are the same.
- **GetEnumerator.** Using this method gets an enumerator of all session-state values in the current session.
- **GetHashCode.** Using this method produces a hash code for a particular type.
- **GetType.** Using this method gets the Type of the current instance.
- **Remove.** Using this method deletes an individual item from the session-state collection. You can call this method using code such as this:

```
Session.Remove("myvariable")
```
- **RemoveAll.** Using this method removes all items from the session-state collection.
- **RemoveAt.** Using this method removes an item from the session-state collection by index number.
- **ToString.** Using this method produces a string value representing the current object.

Discussion—Applications and Sessions

Because ASP.Net applications run on the Internet, they are subject to the limitations of the HTTP protocol, and therefore have no built-in mechanism for maintaining state. Instead, features of ASP.Net can be used to maintain and manage state information.

State is the current condition of all variables, values, files, and so forth contained in an application. When the application first starts, it is in its initial state, and all the interactions and processing occurring while the application runs change its state. State can be very important to an application and to individual users. For example, when a user logs in with his/her username and password, the application should know (while the user is using the application) that the user is properly logged in, so he/she doesn't have to relog in each time he/she goes to another page or uses another feature.

ASP.Net uses the HttpApplicationState and HttpSessionState classes to provide a means for managing state. The classes expose the Application and Session objects, which in turn provide the developer with a rich set of tools for managing state. In addition, the Global.asax file provides a place to access and code actions that will be triggered when application and session events occur (such as the start or end of an application or session).

Variables and values can be added to both applications and sessions; these values are then accessible across page requests (for session variables) or across the entire application (for application variables). The Session object also offers fairly fine-grained control of variables and objects, plus the ability to get the number of objects in the session and the ability to change the timeout period between session requests.

Quick Check Questions

1. What .Net classes enable the use of the Application and Session objects in ASP.Net Web applications?
2. Why is it harder to work with state when an application runs over the HTTP protocol?
3. What mechanisms can be used in an ASP.Net Web application to maintain state data?
4. Where in an ASP.Net Web application would you write code that runs when the application starts?
5. What is the name of the code block in which you would place code that runs when an application starts?
6. How would you address a variable that is stored as part of session state in order to place the value it contains in another variable?
7. What happens if a user doesn't make a request within the timeout period for a session?
8. What session property is used to set the timeout period, and in what units?
9. Can a user in a session access application variables?
10. Can one user access another user's session variables?

Summary

1. The concept of state is important when designing applications, especially Web applications. In Windows applications the current state of the application is always available to your code, but in Web applications, due to the stateless nature of the HTTP protocol, you must work a little harder to maintain and manage state.
2. ASP.Net and the .Net Framework provide several classes (HttpApplication, HttpApplicationState, and HttpSessionState) that allow you to store state information across page requests and across an entire application. You can store variables in the intrinsic

Application and Session objects, and these objects also give you access to a number of other important properties and methods as well.

3. You can maintain a session in a number of ways, including by using the ViewState property, as hidden form fields, as cookies, and in query strings. Each of these methods has its advantages and drawbacks.

Exercise 5.1

In this exercise, you will write the code that creates and initializes an integer variable in the application for counting the current number of application users at any given time. You will use a text editor rather than an actual VS.Net project, but you can copy the default code found in any of your Global.asax files in order to use the event handler code blocks found in them.

1. Open a blank file in any text editor and copy into it the default code from a Global.asax file.
2. To create and initialize to zero an integer variable named "UserCount", put the following code into the Application_Start event handler code block:

```
Sub Application_Start(ByVal sender As Object, ByVal e As EventArgs)
    Dim UserCount As Integer = 0
End Sub
```

3. To increment the UserCount variable by one each time a new user enters the application, put the following line of code in the Session_Start event handler. Notice the use of the Lock() and Unlock() methods:

```
Sub Session_Start(ByVal sender As Object, ByVal e As EventArgs)
    Application.Lock()
    Application("UserCount") = Application("UserCount") + 1
    Application.Unlock()
End Sub
```

4. To keep the count of users valid when users leave the application, put the following code into the Session_End event handler code block:

```
Sub Session_End(ByVal sender As Object, ByVal e As EventArgs)
    Application.Lock()
    Application("UserCount") = Application("UserCount") - 1
    Application.Unlock()
End Sub
```

Exercise 5.2

In this exercise, you will write the code to call and display the UserCount variable created in the Global.asax file from an ASP.Net Web application page. Normally, you would use the PageLoad event handler code block to contain the code, but we'll write it out in a blank text file for the purpose of this exercise.

1. Open a blank file in any text editor. Write the following code:

```
Response.Write("Current users = " & Application("UserCount"))
```

Using Applications and Sessions

In this project, we will create a new ASP.Net Web application that utilizes the Application and Session objects, as well as the events handled within the Global.asax file. The application will be an online version of the game Tic Tac Toe. State (in the form of variables created when the application and the session start) is important to this game because each time a user makes a choice, it causes a roundtrip to the server. If we didn't keep track of things in an application and session, the game couldn't be played properly.

We'll use this game because most people know the rules by heart (and the rules are very simple) and also because it provides a good opportunity to sharpen our programming skills while learning about ASP.Net and Visual Basic.Net.

THE RULES OF TIC TAC TOE

Before we start programming the game, let's talk about how it might work and how we could put the rules of the game into effect. Tic Tac Toe can be played by one person (you can play yourself) or by two people at most. Players can either use "X" or "O" as markers for their play. If one person is playing, the person can play both sides, playing against him/herself. For this application, we will construct it so that a person can play him/herself. We'll use this application as the basis for other, more complex online games in later chapters.

Tic Tac Toe is played on a grid of nine squares arranged as a square with three boxes on each side. Each box can have one of three conditions: Unchosen, X, and O. Once a box is chosen, it cannot be changed. Turns are taken strictly in sequence, one after the other. We'll use X as the default starting choice, so the first box chosen will always be "X", the second choice will always be "O", and so forth until the game is won. The first player forming a row, column, or diagonal of three of their markers wins. There are a total of eight ways to win at Tic Tac Toe: three rows, three columns, and two diagonals.

PROGRAMMING TIC TAC TOE ONLINE

We'll need to create a form with a Start button to start (or restart) the game. Once the player clicks the Start button, the variables and controls we're using to run the game will be reset, since the Start button also restarts the game. We'll use the Application object to hold variables that tell whether or not the user has won the game, so that in future editions we can make the game multi-user. We'll use the Session object to track variable values across page requests, so the current status of the game can be maintained.

We'll use eight variables to hold the values for winning, and each time the user selects (or marks) a box, we'll update these variables. Then we'll check the contents of all the win variables to see if a win has occurred. If so, we'll notify the user and halt the game. The user can then restart the game using the Start button. We'll also use nine variables to track the current condition of each of the boxes on screen, from which to derive the winning condition. Each box variable will be set to "U", "X", or "O" depending upon the choices made, and a win will be represented by a combination of three Xs or three Os.

In order to keep track of whose turn it is, we'll use a variable called TurnManager. We'll set this variable at the start of the game to "X", and each time a box is chosen, we'll set it to "O" or "X", depending upon what it currently is (if X, then change to O, and if O, then change to X). We'll also use a session variable named IWon to track whether a win has occurred.

SETTING UP THE WEB FORM

To display the boxes on our Web form, we'll use a table with three rows and three columns, with an ASP.Net Server control named ImageButton. This control displays as an image that can be set in the ImageURL property. We'll make three images (blank, X, and O) using any simple image-editing program, and each image button will display one of these three images at any given time. By default, at the start of the game, all the image buttons will display the "blank" image. As the user chooses, the TurnManager will be checked and the ImageURL property will be programmatically changed to reflect the X or the O image depending upon which is current.

This description of the rules of the game and programming it online may seem a bit complex, but as we step through programming each part of the game, it will become much easier to see how the pieces fit together. Note that you should create three graphic images with any image-editing program and name them blank30_30gif, X_30_30.gif, and O_30_30.gif. The 30_30 stands for 30 pixels by 30 pixels. Make the background white and the foreground (text color) black and use an Arial font about size 16. Save them to your desktop so you can import them into your application. Have fun!

SETTING UP THE APPLICATIONSESSION ASP.NET WEB APPLICATION

1. Open VS.Net. Start a new ASP.Net Web application from the Visual Basic projects template, and name it ApplicationSession. You should see a blank ASP.Net Web form named WebForm1.aspx appear on your screen. If they are not open, open the Properties window and the Solution Explorer.

2. Right-click on the ApplicationSession project in Solution Explorer and choose Add Existing Item from the shortcut menu. Find your three graphic images and bring them into the application.

3. Open the Toolbox and place a Label control at the top of the form and change its Text property to "Online Tic Tac Toe". Change its font properties so that it is Bold, uses Arial for the font face, and the text is X-Large. Change its Border, BorderWidth, BorderColor, and BackColor properties for a pleasing effect (we've used yellow colors and a 4-pixel border width).

4. Place a Label control right below the first one and set its Text property to "Welcome to Online Tic Tac Toe. Please click Start". Use Arial and Smaller for the font properties.

5. Place a Button control to the right of the second label and change its Text property to "START". Change its ID to "StartButton".

6. Choose Table|Insert|Table from the menu. In the Insert Table dialog box choose three rows, three columns, and 200 pixels width, then click OK. Select the table and move it to a central position below the second label.

7. To each cell in the table add an ImageButton control. Name these nine controls IBA1 (for Image Button in row A column 1), IBA2, IBA3, IBB1, IBB2, and so forth. Put the name in the ID property of each control.

8. In the ImageURL property of each ImageButton control, place the URL "blank30_30.gif". Note that the images must have been imported into the same folder as the WebForm1.aspx file or these URLs will not work.

9. Place another Label control below the table and change its Text property to "Game Started – Please Take a Turn". Change its ID property to "BottomLabel", and set its Visible property to "False". Your form should now resemble Figure 5.1.

SETTING UP THE GLOBAL.ASAX FILE

1. We're going to build some variables into the Global.asax file to be initialized at the start of the application and each time a session starts, so open the Global.asax file by double-clicking it in Solution Explorer. You'll see the blank Global.asax file open, and then you'll need to click the link on its surface to get into the code view.

2. In the Application_Start event handler, create an array variable named "WinBoxesArr" with a size of eight (meaning there are nine spaces to hold data in this variable) and a data type of String. This variable will hold the current values representing the condition of the nine ImageButtons on

Hands On Project

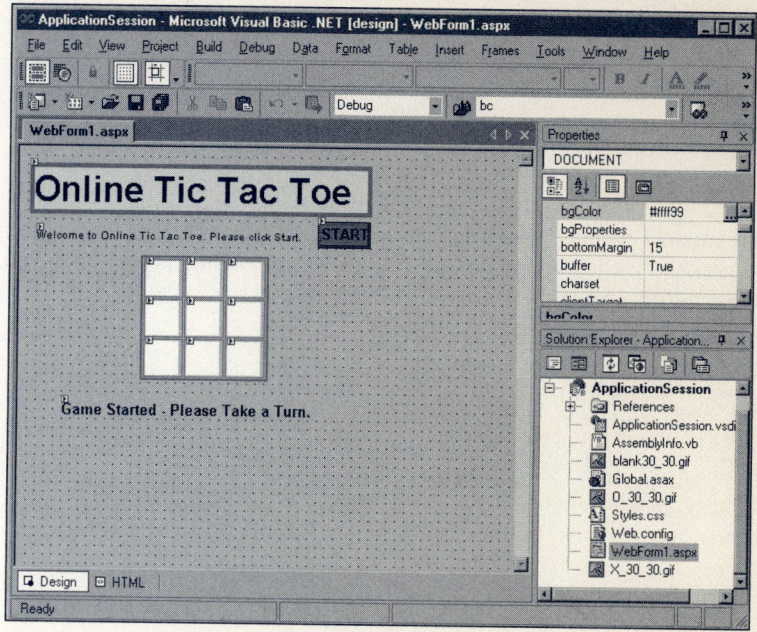

FIGURE 5.1 The ApplicationSession Web Form

the Web form. The values may be "U", "X", and "O". These values will correspond to the images displayed by the ImageButtons. Use code such as this to dimension the variable:

```
Dim WinBoxesArr(8) As String
```

3. Create an array variable named "WinArr" with a size of 7 and a data type of String. This variable will hold the current values corresponding to each possible win condition. The values may be any combination of three "Us", "Xs", and "Os", but only "XXX" and "OOO" are winners. Use code such as this to dimension the variable:

```
Dim WinArr(7) As String
```

4. Create a variable named "i" to function as a counter for the two For loops we'll perform next. Use code such as this to create this variable:

```
Dim i As Integer
```

5. Create two For loops to initialize the WinBoxesArr and WinArr variables to "U" and "UUU", respectively. Don't forget to reset the "i" variable back to zero in between loops. Use code such as this:

```
For i = 0 To 8
   WinBoxesArr(i) = "U"
Next
i = 0
For i = 0 To 7
   WinArr(i) = "UUU"
Next
```

6. In the Session_Start event handler, create a String variable named "TurnManager" with code such as this:

   ```
   Dim TurnManager As String
   ```

7. Create an Integer variable named "TurnsTaken" with code such as this:

   ```
   Dim TurnsTaken As Integer
   ```

8. Create a Boolean variable named "IWon" to indicate whether a win has occurred. This is a bit redundant but is easier to work with than checking all the win conditions each time you need to know if a win has occurred. Use code such as this to dimension this variable:

   ```
   Dim IWon As Boolean
   ```

9. Initialize these three variables with code such as this:

   ```
   'Start Turn Manager with default X
   Session("TurnManager") = "X"
   'Start TurnsTaken with zero
   Session("TurnsTaken") = 0
   'Set IWon to No
   Session("IWon") = False
   ```

10. Save and close the Global.asax file.

PROGRAMMING THE STARTBUTTON CONTROL IN WEBFORM1.ASPX

1. Click back over to your WebForm1.aspx file to display the Web form again. When the Web form is first displayed to the user, the application and session variables you've created and initialized will be available. However, we're using the Start button to restart games after the first game is played, so we'll need to reinitialize the variables at that point. There are a couple other things we must do when the Start button is clicked as well, so double-click the Start button in Design view to create an event handler in the code-behind page for the StartButton_Click event. The code-behind page should open, and the cursor should be in the event handler code block ready for you to enter code.

2. Use the following code to reinitialize these variables in the StartButton_Click event handler:

   ```
   'reset WinArr, WinBoxesArr, Session("IWon") and Session("TurnManager")
      in case second time played
   Dim i As Integer
   For i = 0 To 7
      Application.Set("WinArr(" & i & ")", "UUU")
   Next
   i = 0
   For i = 0 To 8
      Application.Set("WinBoxesArr(" & i & ")", "U")
   Next
   Session("IWon") = False
   Session("TurnManager") = "X"
   ```

3. The ImageURL property of each ImageButton control will change as the game is played, so to get the game ready to be played again, we'll need to reset these properties. Use the following code to do this:

```
'reset image buttons
IBA1.ImageUrl = "blank30_30.gif"
IBA2.ImageUrl = "blank30_30.gif"
IBA3.ImageUrl = "blank30_30.gif"
IBB1.ImageUrl = "blank30_30.gif"
IBB2.ImageUrl = "blank30_30.gif"
IBB3.ImageUrl = "blank30_30.gif"
IBC1.ImageUrl = "blank30_30.gif"
IBC2.ImageUrl = "blank30_30.gif"
IBC3.ImageUrl = "blank30_30.gif"
```

4. The Session("TurnsTaken") variable also needs to be reset back to 0. Use this code to perform this action:

```
'reset TurnsTaken
Session("TurnsTaken") = 0
```

5. The last action performed by the Start button is to notify the user that the game is running. Use this code to set the BottomLabel control's Text property and make it visible to the user:

```
BottomLabel.Text = "Game Started - Please Take a Turn."
BottomLabel.Visible = True
```

PROGRAMMING THE IMAGEBUTTON CONTROLS IN WEBFORM1.ASPX

Each ImageButton control exposes a Click event that can be handled in the code-behind page, so we can use this mechanism to change the image being displayed, update the TurnsTaken variable, update the TurnManager variable, and check for winning conditions. If a win or draw occurs, we also can notify the user within the event handler.

1. When the user clicks an ImageButton control, no matter which one it is, we want to update the TurnsTaken variable. Use code such as this for the update:

```
'update TurnsTaken
Session("TurnsTaken") = Session("TurnsTaken") + 1
```

2. The next actions we want to perform are a change to the image displayed, an update of the TurnManager value, and an update of the WinBoxesArr variable in the appropriate index. Note that each of the nine indexes in the WinBoxesArr variable corresponds exactly to one of the ImageButton controls. Therefore, if we are coding in the IBA1_Click event handler, we must change the value of the WinBoxesArr variable at the 0 index. For this application, IBA1 corresponds to WinBoxesArr(0), IBA2 corresponds to WinBoxesArr(1), IBA3 corresponds to WinBoxesArr(3), IBB1 corresponds to WinBoxesArr(4), and so on.

3. Since we need to change values according to the current value of the Session("TurnManager") variable, we need to test for the current value. If it is "X", we'll change it to "O" and vice versa. We can do this with an If...Then...End If code block, as shown here:

```
'change image appropriately and update Turn Manager
If Session("TurnManager") = "X" Then
   IBA1.ImageUrl = "X_30_30.gif"
   Session("TurnManager") = "O"
   Application("WinBoxesArr(0)") = "X"
Else
```

```
        IBA1.ImageUrl = "O_30_30.gif"
        Session("TurnManager") = "X"
        Application("WinBoxesArr(0)") = "O"
End If
```

4. Now that we've updated the WinBoxesArr variables, we can update the WinArr variable indexes, and then check to see if a win has occurred on this turn. Since the code to update the WinArr variable indexes is the same for every ImageButton Click event, we can write a single procedure that is accessible from all ImageButton Click event handlers to do this. We'll name it UpdateWinVars( ) and locate it just above the Private Sub PageLoad event handler in our code-behind page. Use this code to update these indexes:

```
Public Sub UpdateWinVars()
    Application("WinArr(0)") = Application("WinBoxesArr(0)") &
        Application("WinBoxesArr(1)") & Application("WinBoxesArr(2)")
    Application("WinArr(1)") = Application("WinBoxesArr(3)") &
        Application("WinBoxesArr(4)") & Application("WinBoxesArr(5)")
    Application("WinArr(2)") = Application("WinBoxesArr(6)") &
        Application("WinBoxesArr(7)") & Application("WinBoxesArr(8)")
    Application("WinArr(3)") = Application("WinBoxesArr(0)") &
        Application("WinBoxesArr(3)") & Application("WinBoxesArr(6)")
    Application("WinArr(4)") = Application("WinBoxesArr(1)") &
        Application("WinBoxesArr(4)") & Application("WinBoxesArr(7)")
    Application("WinArr(5)") = Application("WinBoxesArr(2)") &
        Application("WinBoxesArr(5)") & Application("WinBoxesArr(8)")
    Application("WinArr(6)") = Application("WinBoxesArr(0)") &
        Application("WinBoxesArr(4)") & Application("WinBoxesArr(8)")
    Application("WinArr(7)") = Application("WinBoxesArr(2)") &
        Application("WinBoxesArr(4)") & Application("WinBoxesArr(6)")
End Sub
```

5. We can now call UpdateWinVars( ) from each ImageButton event handler to update the WinArr variable indexes appropriately. Use code such as this to call the procedure:

```
'update Application win variables
UpdateWinVars()
```

6. Next we want to check to see whether a win has occurred. To do this we must check each value in the eight WinArr array variable indexes, stored in the Application object. We can use a For loop (shown in the following code) to do this. If any of the indexes has a value of "XXX" or "OOO", then we declare a winner by setting the Session("IWon") variable to True:

```
Dim i As Integer
For i = 0 To 7
    If Application("WinArr(" & i & ")") = "XXX" Or Application _
        ("WinArr(" & i & ")") = "OOO" Then
        Session("IWon") = True
    End If
Next
```

7. Note that in the code above, the name for the Application array variable WinArr includes an index number. For example, the name Application("WinArr(2)") specifies the third index in this array variable. But since the name is specified as a string, we cannot just use the "i" variable (which in the For loop stands for an iterating integer from 0 to 7) and expect it to be properly resolved (turned into the current integer value). Instead, we must stop the string value of the name "WinArr" at the first parentheses, use the ampersand operator to connect it to the i variable, and then use another ampersand to connect all this to the remainder of the array variable's name. It looks a bit clunky, but it works fine.

8. The only thing left to do at this point is to notify the user if a win has occurred, and we can do that with the following code:

```
If Session("IWon") = True Then
   'if Win display win message
   BottomLabel.Text = "Congratulations, you won!"
End If
```

9. Add the same code to an event handler (create it by double-clicking the ImageButton in Design view) for each ImageButton but make sure to set the name of the ImageButton and its corresponding WinBoxesArr variable index properly. For example, the code to change the ImageURL property and the WinBoxesArr index for ImageButton IBB3 should look like this:

```
'change image appropriately and update TurnManager
If Session("TurnManager") = "X" Then
   IBB3.ImageUrl = "X_30_30.gif"
   Session("TurnManager") = "O"
   Application("WinBoxesArr(5)") = "X"
Else
   IBB3.ImageUrl = "O_30_30.gif"
   Session("TurnManager") = "X"
   Application("WinBoxesArr(5)") = "O"
End If
```

10. The game is in a rough state at this point but can be tested. Click out of the code-behind page and into the WebForm1.aspx file in Design view, choose File|Build and Browse from the menu, and play a few games. Try some variations, and try using the Start button to restart the game. You'll notice some deficiencies, and we'll code them out in the next section.

ADDING CODE TO CORRECT DEFICIENCIES

The game in this stage plays, but you might notice that you can keep causing the images to change after a win has occurred. You might also note that nothing happens if a draw occurs. Both of these are logical bugs in the game. While the wrong answer is not a problem in this application, the game does not do what a normal player would expect, and so we'll have to add some code to get rid of these deficiencies.

1. To keep the user from continuing to cause images to change in the ImageButton controls after the game has been won, we need a way to freeze the game. We can do this by disabling the ImageButton controls (by setting the Enabled property to False in our code). Since this action is going to be the same for every ImageButton Click event, we'll make this into a Public procedure as well (put it just below the Public Sub UpdateWinVars( ) procedure), and name it FreezeGame( ), as shown in the following code:

```
Public Sub FreezeGame()
    IBA1.Enabled = False
    IBA2.Enabled = False
    IBA3.Enabled = False
    IBB1.Enabled = False
    IBB2.Enabled = False
    IBB3.Enabled = False
    IBC1.Enabled = False
    IBC2.Enabled = False
    IBC3.Enabled = False
End Sub
```

2. Of course, once we freeze the game, it will stay that way until we unfreeze it. So we'll need to make another function to unfreeze the game, named UnfreezeGame( ). Put it just below the Public Sub FreezeGame( ) procedure:

```
Public Sub UnfreezeGame()
    IBA1.Enabled = True
    IBA2.Enabled = True
    IBA3.Enabled = True
    IBB1.Enabled = True
    IBB2.Enabled = True
    IBB3.Enabled = True
    IBC1.Enabled = True
    IBC2.Enabled = True
    IBC3.Enabled = True
End Sub
```

3. The first place we need to call the FreezeGame( ) procedure is when the game has been won, no matter which ImageButton control is clicked. Place the call to the FreezeGame( ) procedure in the following code block for each ImageButton Click event handler, as shown here:

```
If Session("IWon") = True Then
    'if Win freeze game and display win message
    FreezeGame()
    BottomLabel.Text = "Congratulations, you won!"
End If
```

4. Next we need to place the UnfreezeGame( ) procedure call in the StartButton's Click event handler, so the game will unfreeze if the user starts a new game. Place the call in the StartButton's Click event handler after the update for the TurnsTaken variable, like this:

```
'unfreeze the game
UnfreezeGame()
```

5. Now, when the game is won, the game will freeze, and when the game is restarted, it will unfreeze.

6. At this point, the game can be won, but what about when all the turns have been taken and the game is still not won (a draw)? As it stands, the game could be played indefinitely, until there is a

win. To cope with this, we need to insert code that checks for running out of turns and freezes the game when all turns have been used, whether or not a win has occurred. The code should also alert the user of this fact.

7. At the beginning of each ImageButton event handler procedure, place the following code to check for the number of turns taken:

```
'check turns taken
If Session("TurnsTaken") < 9 Then
```

8. The code above checks to see if the number of turns taken so far (remember, this variable is stored in the Session object for this user and is incremented by one each time a turn is taken). If the number is still less than nine, the code proceeds as normal. If the number is already at nine, we can write an Else condition to run (although in practice, due to some other code we'll write next, the game will not continue to run if the number becomes nine). The Else condition will freeze the game and tell the user there was no win but the game is over, as shown in this code (placed at the end of code in all ImageButton Click event handler procedures):

```
Else
    'if no win, freeze game and display no win message
    BottomLabel.Text = "Game Over - No Winner."
    FreezeGame()
End If
```

9. Although it is possible now to reach a value for TurnsTaken of nine while still playing the game, we actually want the game to terminate on this turn if nine TurnsTaken is reached or if the game is won. Therefore, we need to reconstruct the section of code for each ImageButton Click event handler procedure that checks to see if the game has been won to test to see if TurnsTaken now equals nine, as shown in this code:

```
If Session("TurnsTaken") = 9 Then
    If Session("IWon") = True Then
        'if Win, freeze game and display win message
        FreezeGame()
        BottomLabel.Text = "Congratulations, you won!"
    Else
        'if no win, freeze game and display no win message
        BottomLabel.Text = "Game Over - No Winner."
        FreezeGame()
    End If
Else
    If Session("IWon") = True Then
        'if Win, freeze game and display win message
        FreezeGame()
        BottomLabel.Text = "Congratulations, you won!"
    End If
End If
```

10. The code above checks to see if TurnsTaken has reached nine. If so, it checks to see if the Session("IWon") variable is True. If True, the code freezes the game and declares a winner. If there is no winner but still TurnsTaken is nine, then it freezes the game and declares no winner. If TurnsTaken has not reached nine, this code checks to see if a win has occurred anyway and, if so, freezes the game and declares a winner. If none of the conditions above has been met, the game continues without interruption.

11. There is only one condition to add to the game, and that is freezing the game (making it so none of the ImageButtons may be clicked) when it first opens. At this stage, the labels, table, button, and image buttons are visible, but the image buttons should not be clickable until the user first clicks the Start button. To enforce this, use the Page_Load event and IsPostBack property of the page. The Page_Load event runs whenever the page is loaded, and the Page.IsPostBack property can be used to determine if this is the first time the page has been loaded or a subsequent Page_Load event. The following code runs the FreezeGame( ) procedure if this is the first time the page has been loaded:

```
If Not Page.IsPostBack Then
    FreezeGame()
End If
```

12. Click over to the WebForm1.aspx file in Design view and choose File|Build and Browse. You should be able to play the game through each time, and it should work as you would expect. Figure 5.2 shows the game when a win has occurred, and Figure 5.3 shows the game when a draw has occurred.

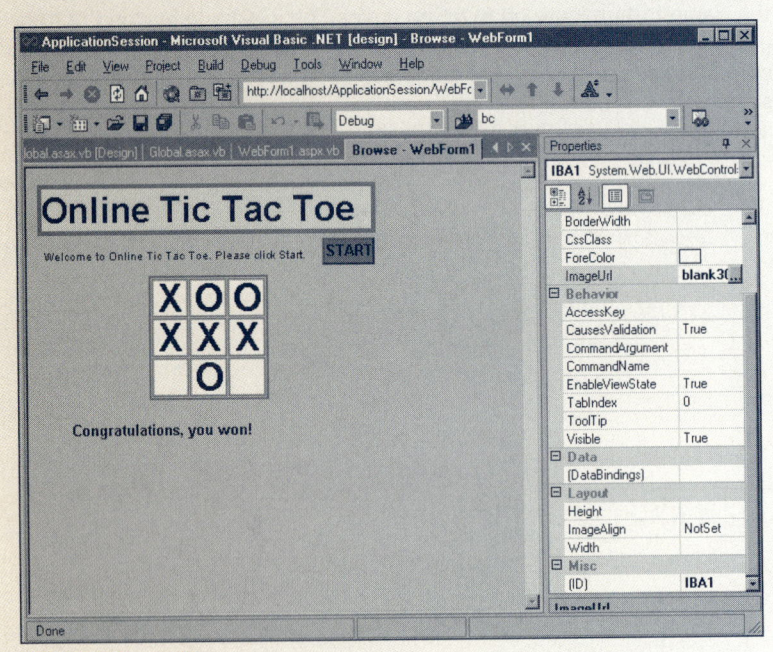

FIGURE 5.2 A Win

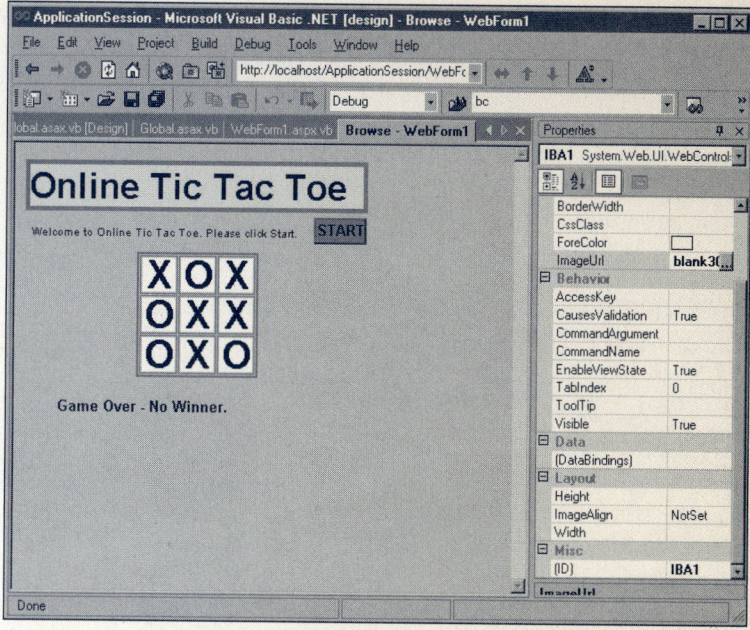

FIGURE 5.3 A Draw

Tracking User Numbers

The purpose of this application is to demonstrate tracking unique visitors to a Web site. Although log files track hits (requests for files), a unique visitor is defined by a session, so no matter which pages or other files are requested by the user, so long as the user remains connected and doesn't time out, he/she will only be counted once. Sessions are a great way to determine if a request is still from the same user, since they only remain active as long as the user is connected and doesn't time out. Tracking unique visitors as a measure of Web site traffic is particularly relevant for business Web sites, because advertising revenue and overall sales are often related to the number of unique visitors.

1. In VS.Net close any open solutions and start a new project from the ASP.Net Web Application template of the Visual Basic projects node. Name the project TrackVisitors. A blank Web form should open.

2. In Solution Explorer, double-click the Global.asax file to open it and then double-click the design surface to reveal the event handlers in its code.

3. In the Application_Start event handler, we'll create a variable to hold the number of visitors and initialize it to zero. Add the following code:

```
Dim intVisitors As Integer
intVisitors = 0
Application("intVisitors") = intVisitors
```

4. In the Session_Start event handler, we'll increment the application variable each time a session starts. Add the following code:

   ```
   Application("intVisitors") = Application("intVisitors") + 1
   ```

5. The Global.asax file should look like Figure 5.4. Close and save the Global.asax file.

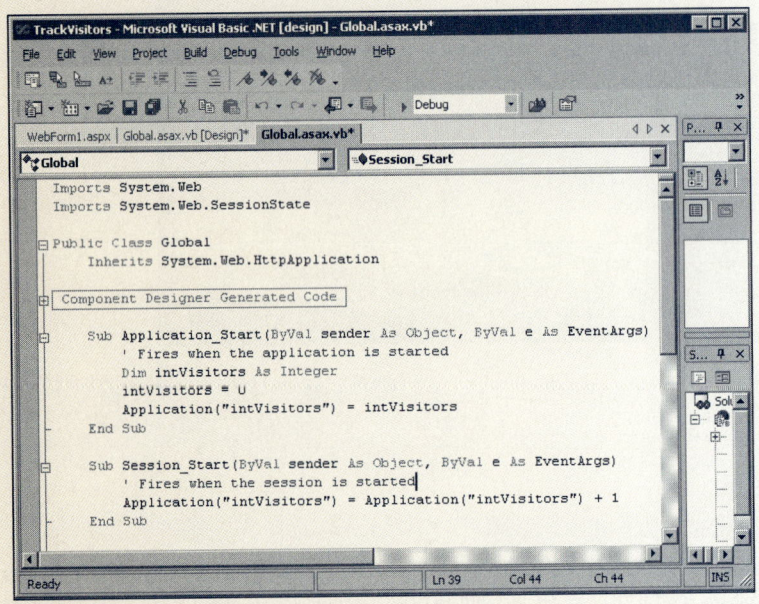

FIGURE 5.4 The Global.asax File with the New Code

6. In the Web form, add a Label control and change its Text property so that it is blank. Change its Font properties so that it uses Arial with a larger size and is Bold.

7. Double-click on the form's surface. The Page_Load event handler should appear in code view.

8. Enter the following code:

   ```
   Label1.Text = "Welcome. You are visitor " & _
     CStr(Application("intVisitors"))
   ```

9. Save the page, then choose File|Build and Browse from the menu. You should see something similar to Figure 5.5.

10. Once the page has opened, open Internet Explorer separately and browse to the correct page on the Local machine. You should see the same Web page, but incremented to the number 2 as shown in Figure 5.6.

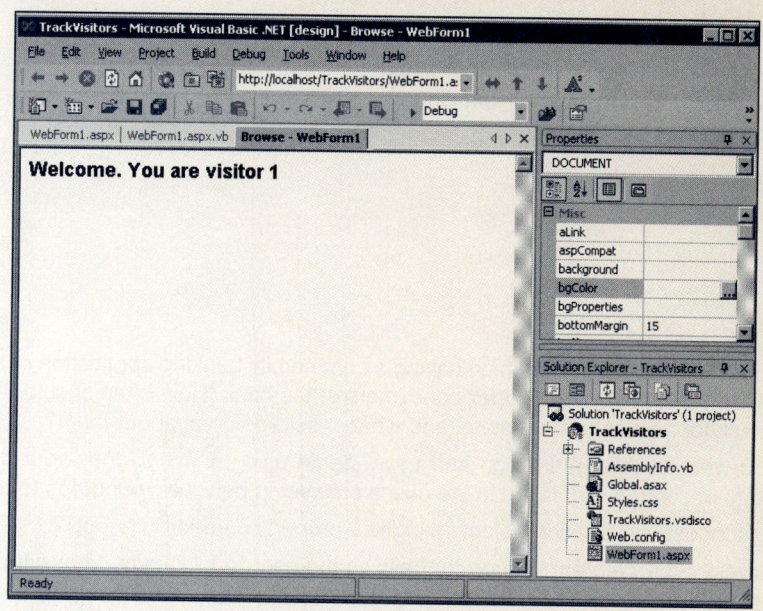

FIGURE 5.5   The Number of Visitors Displayed on the Page

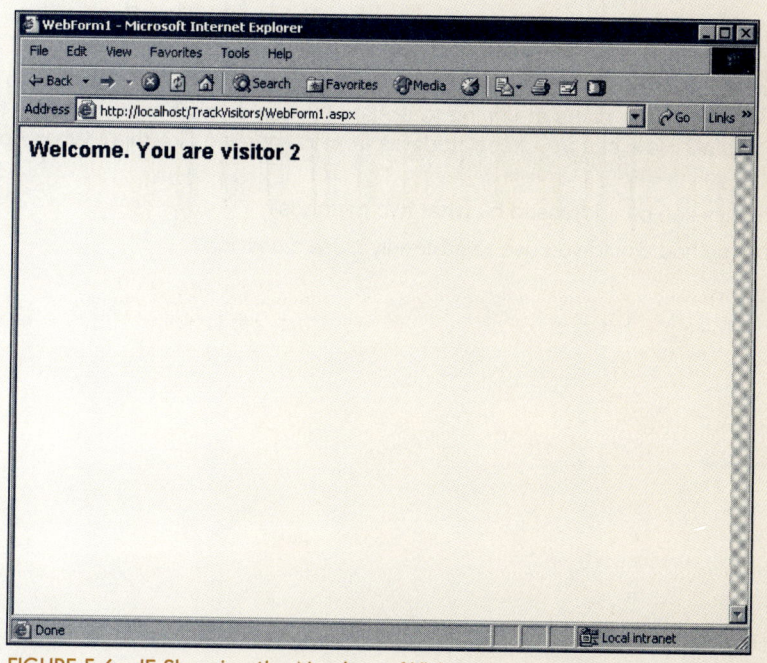

FIGURE 5.6   IE Showing the Number of Visitors Incremented

Key Terms

cookies
hidden form fields
HttpApplication class
HttpApplicationState class
HttpSessionState class
query strings
Session.Count
Session.SessionID
Session.Timeout
state
ViewState property

Review Questions

1. Describe at least two scenarios in which having a commercial banking application or a database in an inconsistent state could be very bad for consumers at the bank. How often should the application or database check for an inconsistent state, and what should be done about them?
2. Suppose you write a Web application and users begin using it. What does your application know about the state of controls displayed in the user's browser in between roundtrips to the server?
3. Why do you suppose the Session object includes a property named "Timeout"?
4. You have developed a Web application that allows the user to buy items from different pages in an online catalog. Why would you use Session object variables to hold these items in memory rather than Application object variables? If you used Application object variables for this purpose, what problems would you run into and how might you solve them?
5. You've written a Web application that needs application-level variables to persist even if the application is restarted. What might you use to store these variables beyond the life of the application?
6. How are sessions uniquely identified? How can you retrieve this value?
7. Can you run an ASP.Net Web application without a Global.asax file? Can you use the Session or Application objects from your code without a Global.asax file?
8. You have written a Web application that includes Application variables available to all users of the application. Suppose two users are trying to update the same variable at the same time. Which one will be successful? How can you keep updates from competing like this? What Application object method would you use?
9. Session variables can be addressed by what two methods?
10. What session method would you use to arbitrarily close a session?

CHAPTER 6

The User Interface (UI)

LEARNING OBJECTIVES

Upon completion of this chapter, you will be able to:

1. Explain the purpose and common features of the user interface (UI).
2. Explain how a UI integrates with a business process.
3. Design a UI for an ASP.Net Web application.
4. Use the Page_Load event with Web forms.
5. Use common ASP.Net Server controls on Web forms.
6. Manage caching on ASP.Net pages.
7. Explain how ASP.Net Web applications are configured.
8. Find Web application configuration files.
9. Describe functions of configuration file sections.
10. Make configuration file changes.

INTRODUCTION

Programming the logic in an ASP.Net Web application is sometimes the easier part of designing and developing the application; making the application easy enough to understand and use for the target market can be more difficult because how the application is used often depends on the business process employed by the organization sponsoring development of the application. If users can't quickly figure out how to make the application do what they expect it to, you'll be back at the drawing boards.

Note that the users want the application to do what they *expect* it to, not necessarily what *you* think it should do, even though you may have a fairly clear specification in hand. For this reason, it almost goes without saying that you should get the users involved as early as possible, and show them mockups of the screens so they can indicate what they expect at each point in their usage of the application. An added bonus is that this process also will give you an opportunity to educate the users about the intended function of the application, and if there is a significant difference between what they expect and what management has tasked you to do, you'll have a chance to raise this concern before getting too much of your time invested.

Along with the development of a user interface, this chapter covers some basics about how caching is performed in ASP.Net Web applications and how configuration files help configure ASP.Net Web applications. Caching is an important subject for Web applications, because caching can speed up your applications and may make them run more efficiently. Configuration is also important, because many Web applications rely on the configuration capabilities in ASP.Net Web.config files for handling default operating characteristics (such as setting application/folderwide properties such as security and custom error messages). Our discussion should make these concepts clear for the applications we develop in this and later chapters.

In this chapter, we start by demonstrating UI design principles and move on to programming concepts that affect how the user perceives the application, such as caching and configuration. At the conclusion of the chapter, you should be familiar with most of the features of a good ASP.Net Web application.

The User Interface (UI)

Some programs operate without any direct human interaction. For example, the computer chips in modern cars control many aspects of engine operation without requiring any direct manipulation by you. Although your foot on the gas pedal may have some indirect influence on some engine functions, you are probably completely unaware of what the chips are really doing to your car under most circumstances (thankfully). You don't tell the chip how much gas to inject into each cylinder, and it doesn't tell you what it did. It just works.

Other programs, such as Microsoft Word, have a **user interface (UI)**. In the old days (yes, it was just a few years ago), people interacted with computer programs using what's called a command line interface. This is still available and can be used by those who know how, but it's not very intuitive. The Windows interface was a big step forward. While most applications today have a Windows-based UI, there are a few that use speech, tactile feedback, and our other senses as components of the UI.

In either of these interfaces (or any other user interface, for that matter), the main objective is to allow people to send input to the program, and for the program to then communicate back. Note that not all programs with interfaces allow two-way communication; your watch is probably run by a computer chip, but it doesn't need you to send it input before it tells you what time it is.

Programs that have interfaces have them because there is a need for them to communicate with people, either one way or both ways. Computer programs usually perform some function, and often the function is related to work. Programs that perform work-related or task-related functions in which there is human involvement are considered good if the user interface is user-friendly. In fact, two programs that perform exactly the same processing but use different user interfaces might be perceived as excellent and abysmal, respectively. Note that there is no hard and fast objective determination of how good a user interface is; it's all up to the perception of the users.

Basic UI Requirements

For Windows-based applications (and this includes Web applications because they typically use the browser, a Windows-type program, as their UI display), the UI consists of a series of screens on which buttons, text fields, dropdown lists, images, and so forth appear. The screens are called windows, and there may be multiple windows open at any given time. The windows can be maximized, minimized, resized, relocated, and so on. They usually include scrollbars if the content exceeds the size of the window, and menus and toolbars for navigating functions and areas of the application.

The two main things people do in applications are make choices and perform work. For example, in an online tax preparation application, you might make choices about the type of return you want to prepare, and when you enter your tax data, you are performing work. Making choices includes navigating (often via the menu or links) and performing work often means data entry of some kind or another. The easier you (as the developer) make it for people to make choices and perform work (without having to open a manual), the more they will probably like your application.

User Interface Design

Many marketing studies have been done to measure how users respond to graphics, icons, the font and colors used for text and backgrounds, and so forth. Having the graphics and page layout designed by marketing professionals often will give your Web application a slick, professional look, and this by itself can set users at ease. However, there are a number of other factors that come into play in the design of a successful user interface, and we'll cover these in the following few sections. Illustration 6.1 gives a quick rundown of these considerations in checklist format.

User Demographics

Different users expect and are comfortable with (or at least familiar with) different things in Web applications. Breaking users down into groups that can be identified (such as by age, geographic location, education, and so on) may

> **User Interface Design Considerations**
> - **Who is the Target Market?**
>   - **Demographics**
>   - Education
>   - Income
>   - Age
>   - Background
> - **What is the Size of the Target Market?**
>   - How Many Hits Expected? – Over Time?
>   - How Much Bandwidth Available?
> - **What Image Must the Web Application Project?**
>   - Graphics
>   - Logos
>   - Bars
>   - Buttons
>   - Color Scheme
>   - Fonts
> - **What Information Must Be Displayed on Each Page/Form?**
>   - Splash Page
>   - Company Information Pages
>   - Forms
> - **What Menu Choices/Navigation Links Must Be Available?**
> - **Are There Any Special Needs?**
>   - Multimedia
>   - Accessibility

ILLUSTRATION 6.1   UI Design Considerations

guide you in making decisions about what to present on each screen and how to lay it out, as well as how much to present.

Security Considerations

If parts of your application must be restricted, you'll need to build in security measures and probably administrative functions for assigning and managing users and groups (unless the restrictions are very basic).

Control and Menu Layout

Most people are familiar with links, especially when they appear to be part of a menu, but some of the more complex controls may not work well for unsophisticated users. For example, there are still quite a few people who don't know how to make multiple selections from a dropdown list. Using clickable images and image maps also can be confusing for some users.

Business Process

As we mentioned, whatever controls, menu choices, links, and information are available throughout the site, the main things that should be on the screen at any given time are those that help the user understand what the present task is and help him/her accomplish that task. Unnecessary items can cause confusion, but since you do not always know what the user will choose to do next, you often must find ways to include common functions in a familiar way. For example, most Web sites include a set of text links at the bottom of all pages, so the user can navigate to any other part of the site, even if in the middle of ordering a product in a shopping cart system.

Essentially, the series of screens you present to the user must follow the **business process** the user is presently engaged in, while giving the user enough flexibility to break out of the current task and perform other tasks if he/she chooses to.

User Interface Development

In practice, you'll get the information required to make decisions about design as you progress through development. Of course, it's a good idea to get as much information as you can prior to starting development, but don't expect to build your application in complete isolation. First of all, it rarely works out that you can isolate yourself from input once development is underway, and in any case it's not a good idea even if you could. Feedback from users is perhaps the most important component of successful UI development. A more realistic development process might follow a pattern such as this:

1. Gather all the information you can about the specifications for the application, including what the application is supposed to do, who the users will be, and what browsers (clients) will most likely be used to interact with the application.

2. Interview actual users to find out how they actually perform the business process (get management's take on the business process as well, but don't assume that the official business process is identical to the actual business process).

3. Mockup some screens that contain the necessary information, forms and controls, and navigation elements to perform the business process as you understand it, and present these to management and users to verify that the application and UI will support the intended business process. Warn them that these are very rough and don't represent the finished user interface.

4. Build a rough application, with canned responses if necessary, and walk one user (or a small group of users) through the application, taking notes about their suggestions for additional information that should be displayed on each screen (or removed) and controls to

use for particular functions. Eliminate ad hoc user input as much as possible. For example, rather than let users enter their state manually, provide them with a dropdown box from which they can choose their state. Changes of this type make it easier for users to input the correct value without errors.

5. Once you have a satisfactory set of screens that support the application, go to your graphic design group and have them build representative screen mockups for each type of screen your application will display. There's no need to have them build all the screens, as some of them will be exact duplicates of others. Once they are finished, your job will be to incorporate the graphic design into all the screens.

6. Create a finished version of the application (finished graphics but not necessarily finished data processing) that allows users to walk through the entire application. Walk users through the application and make any final changes required.

7. Produce a completely finished version of the application and test it under real-life circumstances. Make any more changes requested.

As you can see from this description of the design and development of a Web application and UI, constant feedback from management and users is essential to success. Also, graphic design, logos, colors, fonts, and that type of thing should wait until you at least have a good idea of what must be included in the screens. But be careful to warn users that they are seeing a very rough application and should focus on the elements of each screen (the data presented, controls, and so forth). Otherwise, users may form a bad impression and adopt a negative bias toward the project before it really gets underway.

UI Design Hints

While there are no hard and fast rules about how pages should be designed in a Web application, there are some commonsense guidelines that will increase your chances of success. These guidelines are based on the nature of the Web and what people are currently used to.

- Even now, the majority of the population using the Web have fairly slow connections, around 40Kbps. This means pages shouldn't be more than 20 to 50KB in size, or they will probably load too slowly for most users. The size of a page is a combination of the file size of the HTML and the image and other media files loaded with it. Note that loading speed is also dependent upon the speed of your server under load. The loading time of the first page should be about five to six seconds max, but loading time of other pages can be more if users are made aware of it.

- The type of browser people are using makes a difference. While the majority of users use Internet Explorer, there is a significant population using other browsers, and mobile devices such as cell phones are also

- becoming more capable of browsing the Web (with completely different types of browsers). You may find yourself in the position of having to develop multiple versions of your Web applications, depending upon the type of browsers you expect your target audience to be using.
- Users are pretty familiar with the typical layout of Web pages in which the company logo and perhaps a menu of links appear at the top of the page, another menu appears down the left side, the main content is in the middle, and a text menu of links and the copyright information appear at the bottom of the page.
- Users dislike scrolling from right to left to see the full content of a page, and dislike scrolling down for more than three or four pages of content. Use multiple pages linked together for large documents, and consider using in-page anchors to help users navigate large documents.
- Some localities place content requirements on Web sites, such as a defined privacy policy or commercial information, and users are coming to expect to see privacy policy pages. Ignoring these requirements could be illegal, and depriving users of documentation they expect can make the site less successful.
- While media and entertainment sites may make more use of flashy, off-beat graphics, business sites generally perform better when their content is laid out sparingly on a white background, much like what you'd expect to see in most magazines. High-end business sites also are making more use of the exceptional graphics capabilities of Macromedia's Flash, although development of sites with Flash is considerably more expensive than ordinary Web development.
- Most users understand how to use common controls such as buttons, links, text fields, radio buttons and checkboxes, and dropdown lists, but more exotic controls can confuse users. Using links and simple forms will often meet the demands of a very wide market.
- Users are becoming more familiar with the "lock" that appears when a site is encrypted with SSL in IE or Netscape, so make sure to use SSL when you are trying to get the user to submit sensitive information.
- For some transactions, you can use a simple form to collect the data you need, but for others the user must submit more extensive data. Break your data collection forms into logical pieces (personal or mailing info, shipping info, and billing info, for example) and put each part on a separate page. The user will perceive that it is easier to fill out and submit this way, even though it is the same as one long form.
- Always give the users feedback, negative or positive, when they complete a step in a process that required specific action on their part. For example, if they submit a request for more information, thank them and tell them what will happen next (we'll send you an email, you'll get a phone call from us, and so on). Otherwise, they may become confused and possibly even irritated, and they may keep resubmitting the same information.

The Page Object and Control Objects

When you create Web forms in an ASP.Net Web application, you are actually creating a new Page class that will be instantiated as individual Page objects at run time. Each **Page object** represents an actual Web page, but when you request a page (a file having an extension of .aspx) from an ASP.Net Web application, you are not downloading copies of HTML Web pages as you would if you were making a request from an ordinary Web site. You are interacting with an application that is simulating ordinary Web pages but is actually using programmed Page objects and Control objects. Page objects and Control objects are all inherited from the System.Web.UI base classes (including System.Web.UI.WebControls and System.Web.UI.HTMLControls), which makes sense because they form the user interface of your application.

Page Events and the Control Execution Lifecycle

Like any object, Page objects have events, and some of these events come in handy for managing user interactions with your Web application. When a page is requested, the page and its controls are loaded, and after they have been loaded, they are unloaded. This sequence is called the **Control Execution Lifecycle**. There are a number of intermediate phases associated with this lifecycle:

- **Initialize.** Controls are initialized.
- **Load ViewState.** State information is maintained across requests for each control and is restored to controls during this phase.
- **Process postback data.** Form data (whatever default or user values are present) are processed and properties for affected controls are updated.
- **Load.** During this phase, actions such as setting up a database query are taken.
- **Send postback change notifications.** Differences between current state and previous state cause change events to be raised, for any controls that are allowed to raise them.
- **Handle postback events.** Any event that causes the postback is handled. For example, if the user clicked a button, the button's Click event is handled.
- **Prerender.** Perform updates prior to rendering.
- **Save state.** Save state information as a string and send it to the client in a hidden form field.
- **Render.** Create HTML to send to the user that will display the page and its controls in the browser.
- **Dispose.** Tear down the objects
- **Unload.** This is essentially the same as dispose.

Saving State for Controls

In Chapter 5, we discussed state and how it can be maintained. As you can see from the list, there are several phases during the Control Execution Lifecycle in which state information is either restored to controls or saved. In these phases, state information for each control is kept in a property called ViewState. When a page is sent to the user, ViewState information is sent as a string encoded in a hidden field, so that it is always returned to the server when a roundtrip to the server occurs. When state information is received, it is used to load the ViewState property. Once any processing has been completed (and any appropriate changes to state have occurred on the server), the state information is saved and sent to the user again, and the process repeats.

The Page_Load Event

When a user first requests a page in your Web application, the server processes the page in preparation for sending it to the client. This is called page loading. At this point, all the controls on the page can be initialized. In your code-behind page, you will find an event handler (called Page_Load, naturally) in which you can place code that will run when the page is loaded.

The IsPostBack Property Sometimes you want code to run within the **Page_Load event** handler only when the page is not reloaded in response to a Postback. For example, suppose you set up validation controls (a special Web server control that is not visible but performs a validation function on other controls) on your Web form. You may want responses validated in all cases except the initial loading of the page. Therefore, you might disable all validation controls in a code block within the Page_Load event handler that tests whether the request is a PostBack, as shown here:

```
If Not Page.IsPostBack Then
    ValControl1.Enable = True
End If
```

The **IsPostBack property** of the page indicates whether the page is being processed in response to a post from the user. If the IsPostBack property is true, a postback has occurred, and false if not. Since it is a Boolean value, it can be used directly in the If...Then...End If structure.

Validation

One of the central features of a Web application is that it allows users to provide input. Of course, not every Web application needs to get specific input from users; some may simply provide data when the user requests the page. But many do accept input from users, and users are notorious for entering whatever they choose, rather than what you would expect. In addition, malicious users may attempt to break or hack your application via input especially designed for this purpose. To prevent malicious entries and ensure valid data for processing, ASP.Net validation controls are available.

ASP.Net Validation Controls

ASP.Net Server controls include a number of **validation controls** for verifying that entered data are acceptable for your Web application. When a requested page is loaded, validation automatically occurs for all controls on the page that are linked to a validation control. If any data are found to be invalid, the validation control displays its error message to the user.

For example, suppose you have placed a TextField control named "txtPhone" on your form, and placed a validation control on the form that checks "txtPhone" to make sure the value in it is consistent with a phone number. You can enter an error message (such as "Please enter a phone number") in the ErrorMessage property of the validation control, and this message will be displayed if the data entered by the user violate the data pattern (called a regular expression) you set in the ValidationExpression property.

The Summary Validation Control

Error messages can be displayed as inline text (near where the validation control is on the form), and also as a summary of error messages that appears when the user submits the form. To display a summary of validation messages, use the Summary Validation Control.

Server-Side and Client-Side Validation

For Internet Explorer 4.0 and above (and other browsers that support DHTML), client-side validation is automatically enabled, but you can disable it if you want to perform validation only on the server.

Enabling Validation

Validation controls are automatically activated each time the page is loaded, so if you want to make sure they only work after the user causes a submission to the server, set their Enabled properties to False at design time, but set their Enabled properties to True in the Page_Load event when a PostBack occurs.

Available Validation Controls

The Validation controls available are

- **RequiredFieldValidator.** Makes sure the user has entered some data in a field.
- **CompareValidator.** Compares the data in a field to a hard-coded value, the value in another field, or a value from a database.

- **RangeValidator.** Compares the data in a field to a range of possible values.
- **RegularExpressionValidator.** Matches the data in a field to the data pattern in a regular expression.
- **CustomValidator.** Uses validation logic you create.

Regular Expressions

Whether or not a field requires a value, or is greater than or less than a minimum and maximum, or is equal to the value of another field; these types of validation are fairly self-explanatory. But the regular expression validator deserves a little explanation.

The term **regular expression** means a pattern constructed from a pattern matching set of symbols and operators, and for Regular Expression controls this pattern is entered into the ValidationExpression property of the control. There is a built-in wizard in VS.Net that helps you generate the appropriate pattern to match phone numbers, Social Security numbers, dates, email addresses, and so on. You also can write your own custom regular expressions to validate against.

Although a complete discussion of regular expressions is beyond the scope of this book, you can find all the symbols and operators for regular expressions in the VS.Net documentation, and online in many places. Basically, your pattern tells the matching algorithm what characters (letters, numbers, and symbols, including spaces) should be found in what places in whatever value is being checked. For example, the pattern "\w+([-+.]\w+)*@\w+([-.]\w+)*\.\w+([-.]\w+)*" tells the matching algorithm to look for characters and possibly periods, then the @ symbol, and then more characters and possibly periods. This particular pattern is useful for matching valid email addresses.

Discussion—User Interfaces

Any program that interacts with people is said to have a user interface (UI). There are quite a few types of user interface, but one of the most common and familiar is the Windows UI. Most applications have more than one "screen" or window in which controls, menus, and links allow user interaction with the application, and most Web applications (notable exceptions are email and FTP programs) use the browser as a client to render the contents of the window.

The elements displayed on screens as an application is used should be driven by the expectations of the intended users as much as by the requirements of the application. Whether an application's user interface is considered "good" or "bad" is subjective, and your best bet for designing a good UI is to have lots of feedback from users, an understanding of the main factors affecting your UI design, and a clear idea of the actual business process the UI must support.

The Page_Load event is one of several events that occur when a Page object is requested from your Web application. Page objects are instantiated from the Page class you create for each .aspx page in your Web application, and Control objects make up each of the controls on the page. Controls are loaded onto the page, populated with state, processed, and rendered during the Control Execution Lifecycle. When the contents of the page are returned to the user, state is saved as a string in a hidden form field, so it can be retrieved during the next roundtrip to the server.

Validation controls are available in ASP.Net to provide client-side and server-side validation to your Web application. Validation is important for security and for ensuring clean, valid data to process. Validation controls include the RequiredFieldValidator, the RegularExpressionValidator, the RangeValidator, and the ValidationSummary control. You also can write custom validation controls.

Caching ASP.Net Applications

The term **caching** refers to the practice of saving pages, objects, and so on after they are instantiated for the first time, so that subsequent calls for the same page or object can be answered more quickly because the object does not need to be created from scratch again. Caching is very useful when identical pages or objects are reused. As you can imagine, a Web application serving many users should be optimized as much as possible to make best use of the hardware available. Properly setting up caching is an important part of optimizing your ASP.Net Web applications.

You can perform **output caching**, in which pages are cached so they can be more easily sent to the user, and **data caching**, in which application data are cached in the **Cache object**, using the Add or Insert methods. Simply storing an item in the Application object is not the same as storing an item of application data in the Cache object; items stored in the Cache object allow you quite a bit more flexibility to update or remove them from the Cache object, based on expiration date or other parameters.

Output Caching

Output caching is the term used for storing entire pages in cache. You can set output caching for pages by using the @ OutputCache directive in your ASP.Net pages, or by manipulating output caching with the HttpCachePolicy class.

If you include the @ OutputCache directive in your pages, you also must include the Duration and VaryByParam attributes, as shown here:

```
<% @ OutputCache Duration=" 90" VaryByParam="None" %>
```

The Duration setting in this code specifies that the cached page will be used for a period of 90 seconds. From a developer's standpoint, this means that the code in your page will be run once and then exactly the same page will be delivered to users for the next 90 seconds. This is fine if you are sure all users (at least for the next 90 seconds) should get exactly the same page. If you're not sure, don't cache the page.

The VaryByParam setting in the code is set to "None", meaning there is no variation in the page. But if your users are able to specify parameters in a query string or in a form, you can set the VaryByParam to the name of the parameter to be used (or even multiple parameter names separated by semicolons). Different versions of the page will be cached for each parameter received. For example, if you have a form field named ZipCode, and your users will receive a slightly different page depending upon the ZipCode they choose, you can set VaryByParam to "ZipCode" and each time a different ZipCode is chosen, that version of the page will be saved to cache. Then all subsequent requests for the different versions of the page will be retrieved from cache, until the Duration expires.

You can use the Response object's cache property to achieve a similar result, if you like. For example, if you include the following code in your response, the page will be cached only on the server, and different versions will be cached when different ZipCodes are chosen. Expiration can be set using the Response.Cache.SetExpires method.

```
Response.Cache.SetCacheability(HttpCacheability.Server)
Response.Cache.VaryByParam("ZipCode") = true
```

Data Caching

When you start an ASP.Net Web application, a single Cache object is created automatically when your ASP.Net Web application starts, and it remains available for the life of the application. Data-related functions in your application (such as making a query on a database) consume a large amount of resources on your server. Caching the results of a query is a good way to improve performance of your ASP.Net Web applications, and the Cache object is available for this purpose. You can cache data using three different techniques: adding the name of the data item and its value, using the Add method, and using the Insert method. In each case, you put data into the Cache object and can retrieve it later.

To put an item in the Cache object directly, use code such as the following:

```
Cache("first_name") = "John"
```

To put an item in the Cache object with the Insert method, use code such as the following:

```
Cache.Insert("first_name", "John")
```

To put an item in the Cache object with the Add method (the Add method returns an object representing the item), use code such as the following:

```
Cache.Add("first_name", "John")
```

Note that if an item is already in the Cache object, using the Insert method will overwrite the item, but using the Add method will fail. You might use the Add method in the Application_Start event handler of the Global.asax file to retrieve and store data values that don't change much in the cache object, while the Insert method might be more useful for retrieving and storing more frequently changing values in your Web application pages.

Discussion—Caching

The term *caching* refers to the act of storing frequently used pages, parts of pages, and data items in memory. This technique is useful because often many pages and data items are used over and over again without change, and retrieving pages and data from cache memory is typically much faster and less processor intensive than rebuilding pages and requerying data items from scratch.

Because caching is so helpful in improving application performance, ASP.Net contains a number of methods to store items in cache, and even allows storage of dynamic pages and data by making it possible for you to set cache expiration (dynamic content may sometimes change on a regular basis) and for you to force storage of multiple versions of the same page depending upon parameters passed by the user.

Caching of pages (and parts of pages) is called output caching, while caching of data is called data caching. Output caching can be accomplished by adding the @ OutputCache directive to your ASP.Net pages, or by using the Response.Cache properties and methods in your code. Caching of data is accomplished by adding data items as name-value pairs to the Cache object.

Configuring ASP.Net Web Applications

Many types of software application can be configured. For most applications, configuration has a direct effect on how the program runs. ASP.Net Web applications are configured by the developer with configuration files. These configuration files are text files written with specific XML elements and attributes, and they reside in a number of places for any particular ASP.Net Web application. Changes to these files cause your ASP.Net Web applications to run differently. For example, if you turn Custom Errors on in the configuration file, your application will attempt to respond to error conditions with a custom error file.

You can set parameters for security, compilation, browser capabilities, and so forth in ASP.Net Web application configuration files. For any application, there is always a machine configuration file, named **machine.config**, in the Microsoft.Net\Framework\version\CONFIG folder and a Web configuration file, named **Web.config**, in the root folder of the application. You also can place an additional Web.config file in each subfolder of your application. Subfolder additional configuration files affect the contents of the folder in which they reside, but any settings in higher-level Web.config files that are not in conflict also affect these pages. So if you need special configuration settings just for a subset of the pages in your Web application, place all the pages in their own folder and put an additional Web.config file in that folder. You can use the Web.config file that is created by default when you start your application from the Visual Basic Projects ASP.Net Web application template as the model for additional Web.config files.

ASP.Net Web.config Configuration Files

The following is an example of the XML elements and attributes found in the Web.config file for the ApplicationSession Web application we created in the last chapter. We've made no modifications to it, so what you're seeing is the default Web.config file created for all Web applications when you use the Visual Basic Projects Web application template:

```
<?xml version="1.0" encoding="utf-8" ?>
<configuration>

  <system.web>
    <!-- DYNAMIC DEBUG COMPILATION
       Set compilation debug="true" to insert debugging
          symbols (.pdb information) into the compiled
          page. Because this creates a larger file that
          executes more slowly, you should set this value
          to true only when debugging and to false at all
          other times. For more information, refer to
          the documentation about debugging ASP.NET
          files.
```

```
      -->
      <compilation defaultLanguage="vb" debug="true" />
      <!--  CUSTOM ERROR MESSAGES
        Set customErrors mode="On" or "RemoteOnly" to enable
          custom error messages, "Off" to disable.
        Add <error> tags for each of the errors you want to
          handle.
      -->
      <customErrors mode="RemoteOnly" />
      <!-- AUTHENTICATION
        This section sets the authentication policies of the
          application. Possible modes are "Windows", "Forms",
          "Passport", and "None"
      -->
      <authentication mode="Windows" />

      <!--  AUTHORIZATION
        This section sets the authorization policies of the
          application. You can allow or deny access to
          application resources by user or role. Wildcards:
          "*" mean everyone, "?" means anonymous
          (unauthenticated) users.
      -->
      <authorization>
        <allow users="*" /> <!-- Allow all users -->
        <!--  <allow users="[comma separated list of
            users]"
            roles="[comma separated list of roles]"/>
              <deny users="[comma separated list of users]"
            roles="[comma separated list of roles]"/>
        -->
      </authorization>
      <!--  APPLICATION-LEVEL TRACE LOGGING
        Application-level tracing enables trace log output
          for every page within an application. Set trace
          enabled="true" to enable application trace
          logging. If pageOutput="true", the trace
          information will be displayed at the bottom of
          each page. Otherwise, you can view the application
          trace log by browsing the "trace.axd" page from
          your web application root.
      -->
      <trace enabled="false" requestLimit="10"
pageOutput="false" traceMode="SortByTime" localOnly="true"
/>
```

```
        <!-- SESSION STATE SETTINGS
          By default ASP.NET uses cookies to identify which
          requests belong to a particular session. If
          cookies are not available, a session can be
          tracked by adding a session identifier to the
          URL. To disable cookies, set sessionState
          cookieless="true".
        -->
        <sessionState
          mode="InProc"
          stateConnectionString="tcpip=127.0.0.1:42424"
          sqlConnectionString="data source=127.0.0.1;user
            id=sa;password="
          cookieless="false"
          timeout="20"
        />
        <!-- GLOBALIZATION
          This section sets the globalization settings of the
            application.
        -->
        <globalization requestEncoding="utf-8"
            responseEncoding="utf-8" />

    </system.web>
</configuration>
```

Web.config Sections

The Web.config file starts out with a "Compilation" element, with the language set to "vb" and debug set to "true". This just means that the language is Visual Basic and that we do want debug information to be generated (remember how to set debug mode?). Notice that the section contains a good volume of comments describing what it is.

The next section is for setting custom error messages, and the two sections after that (Authentication and Authorization) are for managing security settings in your application (although you have other means of working with security, in addition to these settings).

The next section, Application-Level Trace Logging, is a debugging tool that can display trace data at the bottom of pages, if you choose. Following that section is another that lets you set SessionState mode and timeout (among other things), and following that is another section for setting Globalization settings.

You can change the settings in any of the sections you find, but you must change them only to allowed values such as True and False, or the units they will accept (such as integers for the Timeout attribute of the SessionState section). But if you need custom sections, you can make those on your own and add them as necessary. Custom sections added in this manner are available to your code for dynamic management and modification.

Discussion—Application Configuration

Web application configuration files are named Web.config. A Web.config file is automatically created for you, in the root folder of your application when you start your application from the Visual Basic Projects template in VS.Net. Web.config files are text files written in XML, with configuration settings in sections headed by an XML element such as `<sessionstate>`. Allowable elements, attributes, and attribute values are part of the XML schema for Web configuration files that comes with VS.Net and the .Net Framework.

You can modify configuration settings manually by opening the appropriate configuration file and editing attribute values. For Web applications there can be a Web.config file in the root folder of the application, as well as Web.config files in any lower-level folder. Settings are inherited from the Web.config file in the root folder, on down through any Web.config files found in lower-level folders. Settings inherited from Web.config files above a particular resource apply to that resource unless they are overridden by settings in a Web.config file at the same level (or somewhere between the resource folder level and the root folder level).

Quick Check Questions

1. Computer programs that people work with usually have what kind of interface? What style of interface used to be common?
2. What quality do developers strive for when creating a user interface for their Web applications?
3. List two other types of user interface.
4. When does the Page_Load event occur in an ASP.Net Web application?
5. What happens to the Page object and Control objects during the Dispose phase of the Control Execution Lifecycle?
6. Why is caching a good thing, in general?
7. What is the name of configuration files in ASP.Net Web applications?
8. What files does a configuration file affect if it is in the root folder of an ASP.Net Web application?

1. The user interface (UI) is the part of an application with which users interact. Not all computer programs require a user interface; some programs communicate directly with other programs and not people, and so they use only a machine-to-machine interface. Most modern applications with a UI use a Windows-based UI, but examples of other types of user interface include speech and tactile feedback.
2. The Windows-based UI uses hypertext links, forms, and controls for user interaction, but the format, layout, and design elements of the UI are important as well, because without good design and layout, a UI may not be user-friendly, and therefore unsuccessful. Because UIs are to be used by people, good UI design is quite subjective.
3. The scope of a variable or object is comprised of the domain of all other objects that may access the variable without qualifying its name. Qualifying the name of a variable or object means including the name of containing objects when addressing it. Some variables cannot be accessed outside their scope by any means.
4. Variables declared inside a code block (such as a For loop) can be accessed only by code within the same set of statements. A variable declared within a procedure can be accessed only by code within that procedure. A variable declared within a module can be accessed by code within that module, or (if declared with the Public keyword) by code within the entire project.
5. Many of the parameters you can set (as the application developer) for ASP.Net Web applications reside in files called configuration files. These files are always named Web.config, except for the machinewide configuration file named "machine.config". When you create an ASP.Net Web application using the Visual Basic Projects ASP.Net Web Application template found in Visual Studio.Net, a Web.config file is automatically created and placed in the root folder. This file has settings that affect the files in the same folder as it, as well as files found in folders below it. Placing another Web.config file in lower folders overrides those same settings in Web.config files in higher folders, so creating new, lower-level Web.config files with specific configuration settings is a way of customizing configuration settings for specific files within a Web application.

Exercise 6.1

1. Your manager has assigned you to design a user interface for an ASP.Net Web application. You will decide what content must be placed on each page, although not the colors, fonts, and specific layout for the page elements. Describe the pages, content, and some of the links, forms, and controls you might use to satisfy the following business process requirements:

    The application will be part of a larger application that performs customer service tasks. The application will invite customers to take part in a survey, will present survey questions for them to answer, and will provide an option to see the current results of the survey in real time. Users must be made aware that their personal information will not be used in the survey or released, but that their summarized answers may be sold to third parties later, although the primary focus of the survey is to improve customer service.

Exercise 6.2

1. You have been assigned to develop an ASP.Net Web application in which certain files will have a very short timeout period for their session. Describe the method you could use to accomplish this functionality with configuration files.

Practicing UI and Configuration Techniques

In this project, we'll create a new application in which we can practice our skills at building a user-friendly interface, with some practice using configuration files. Our goal is to define a simple business process and then create a user interface that logically integrates with the business process. The first part of our process will be to start a new project and then define the business process it will support.

PART 1—STARTING THE NEW PROJECT

1. Open VS.Net and start a new project using the Visual Basic Projects template for ASP.Net Web Applications. Name the project WebUserInterface.

2. Next define the business process to support. We'll do this by writing a short statement declaring what the business process is, and then a list of steps the application must perform to support the process.

Business Process: This project will support the process by which a user logs in and picks the color, font, layout, and other parameters of a customized news page. The first Web form the user sees (Step 1) will welcome him/her to the site and request that he/she log in (Step 2). Once the user is logged in, we'll ask the user to set his/her preferences for using the application (Step 3).

PART 2—CREATING THE LOGIN FORM

1. You should have a blank Web form open in VS.Net right now. Open the Properties window and the Toolbox. Add a Web Forms Label control to the top of the form and set its Text property to "Welcome to Your Customized News". Set the background color of the form to light blue, and the color of the text in the Label to dark blue. Make the text in the label larger, Arial, and bold.

2. Add another small label to the form and set its Text property to "Please Login". Set its other properties the same as the Welcome label, but make the size of the font XX-Small. Place it in the middle of the form under the Welcome label. Name it "PleaseLogin".

3. Add two TextBox controls under the PleaseLogin label. Name the first TextBox "Username" and the second TextBox "Password". These will be the entry fields for the username and password. Set their Text properties to "username" and "password", respectively, so users will immediately understand what they must enter to log in.

4. Place a Button control named LoginButton underneath the TextBox controls and set its font properties similar to those of the PleaseLogin label. Your form should now resemble Figure 6.1.

PART 3—CODING THE LOGIN FUNCTION

There are a number of ways you can log in users. One of the most common is to use a database with the usernames and passwords of registered users. For this application, we'll hard-code the acceptable username and password into the form; when we discuss databases in the next few chapters, we'll switch to database lookup for subsequent applications that require login. In this application, we'll use a simple If...Then...Else...End If condition code block to determine if the user has entered the appropriate username/password combination.

1. Double-click the LoginButton to start an event handler in the code-behind page. In this event handler, enter the following code:

```
If Username.Text = "Jim" Then
    If Password.Text = "J2" Then
        Session("logged_in") = "Yes"
        Response.Redirect("WebForm2.aspx")
```

Hands On Project

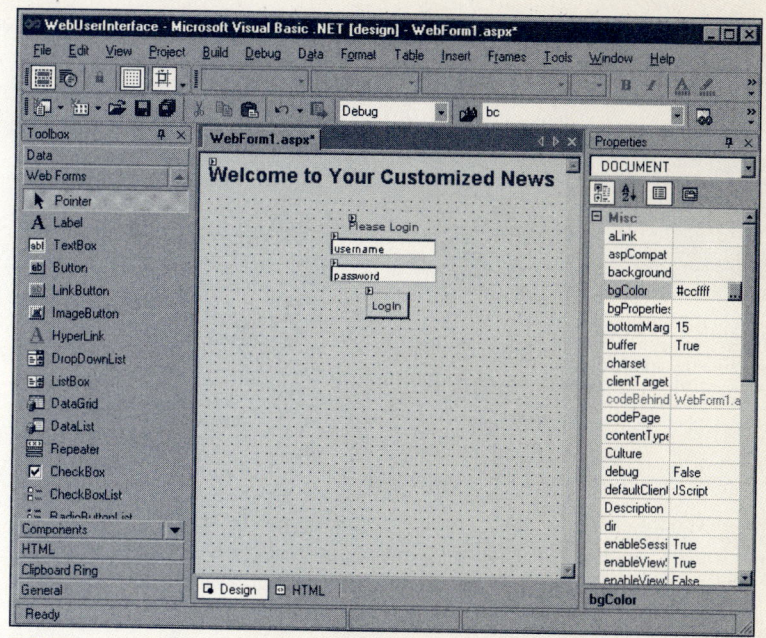

FIGURE 6.1 The Login Web Form in Design View

```
    Else
       PleaseLogin.Text = "Try Again"
    End If
Else
    PleaseLogin.Text = "Try Again"
End If
```

2. The code checks to see if the user has entered the correct username first (Jim), and if not tells the user to try again via the Text property of the PleaseLogin label. If the user enters the correct username then the code block checks to see if the password is correct. If the password is correct, the code redirects the user to another page (WebForm2.aspx).

3. Open the Solution Explorer and right-click the project, then choose Add|Add Web Form from the shortcut menu. Click OK in the dialog box to immediately add the new Web form. The new Web form will open in Design view.

4. Click back over to WebForm1.aspx and choose File|Build and Browse from the menu. Try your Login function with an incorrect username and password, and with the correct ones to verify that it works properly.

PART 4—SETTING APPLICATION TRACING IN WEB.CONFIG

Web.config files contain a section called Application-Level Trace Logging. By default this section is disabled, but if you enable it, you can retrieve highly detailed information about what is occurring in your Web application while it runs. You can enable it by making changes to the Web.config file.

1. Open Solution Explorer if it is not already open and double-click the Web.config file. The Web.config file in your project should open. Scroll down to find the Application-Level Trace Logging section.

CHAPTER 6   The User Interface (UI)

2. Change the "enabled" and "pageOutput" attributes from "false" to "true". The Web.config file should now look like Figure 6.2.

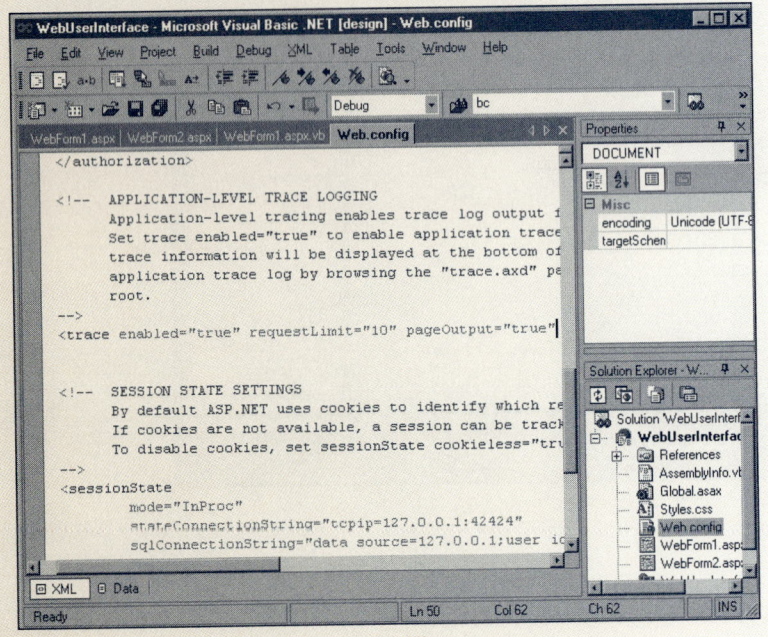

FIGURE 6.2   The Modified Web.config File

3. Click back over to WebForm1.aspx and choose File|Build and Browse from the menu. You'll see your form appear with the Trace Log information jumbled with it. Log in properly, and you should be redirected to WebForm2.aspx. Since this page is blank, it will be easier to read the Trace information.

4. Included with the Trace information is much data about the request, cookies, session state, and server variables from the HTTP headers. WebForm2.aspx should resemble Figure 6.3.

5. To prevent the Trace data from showing up on the page, change the pageOutput attribute to "false" in the Web.config file.

6. Choose View|Toolbars|Web from the menu. This opens a toolbar that gives you the same controls you would find in your browser, including the Address field for browsing pages. You'll need this toolbar for browsing to Trace Log data.

7. Build and Browse your application again. Log in, and when you get to WebForm2.aspx, enter "trace.axd" in the Address field of your Web toolbar. You should see Trace data appear on your screen, as shown in Figure 6.4.

8. Notice that this page gives you the option of clearing the existing Trace data, as well as viewing detailed Trace data for each page gotten or posted.

Hands On Project

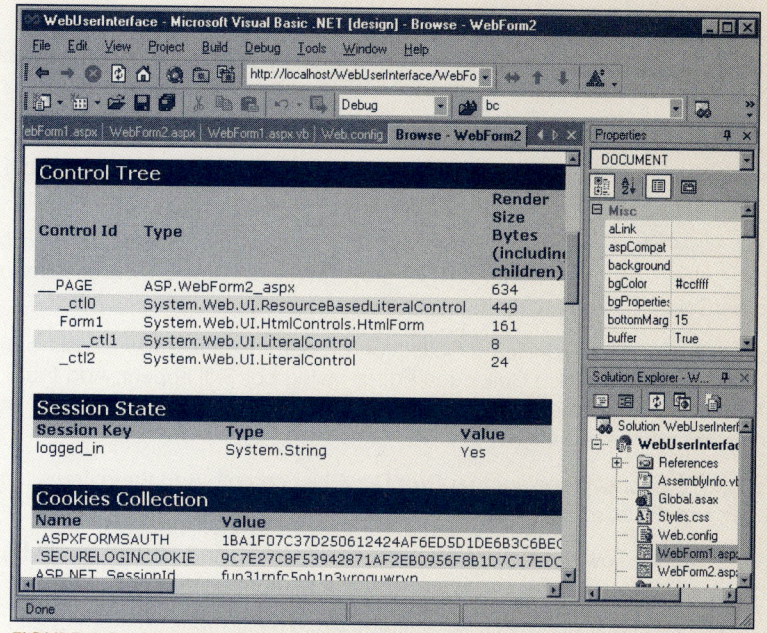

FIGURE 6.3 WebForm2.aspx with Trace Log Data

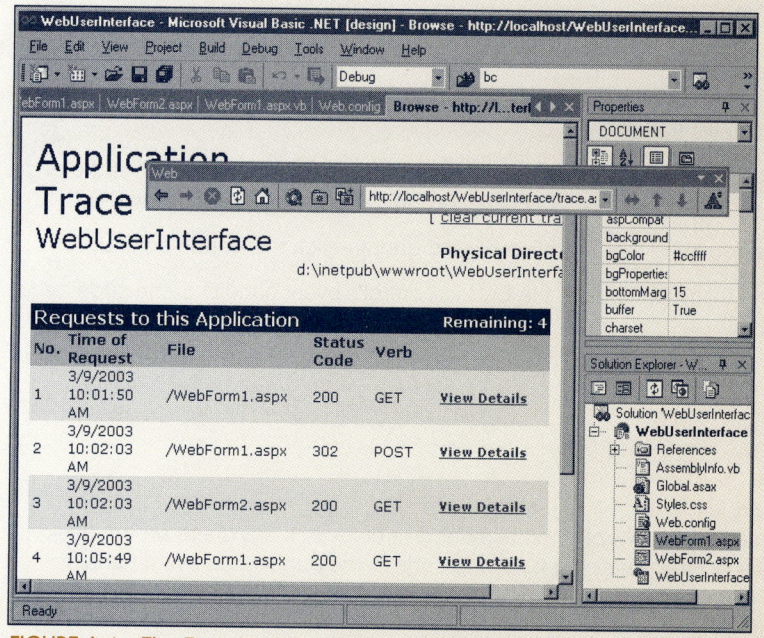

FIGURE 6.4 The Trace.axd File in Browse View

PART 5—CUSTOMIZING THE USER INTERFACE

In this section, we will build an interface that allows the users to customize certain aspects of their news page. They will have easy-to-understand options for setting color, font, size, and other common elements of their news page.

1. Close all files except WebForm2.aspx. On the surface of the form, place a Label control and set its Text property to "News Page Customization".

2. Below the label place a Label control and change the text property of this label to "Border and Box Colors". To the right of this label place a DropDownList control and name it "DDLBorderColor".

3. Click in the DDLBorderColor Items Collection property to make the ellipsis button appear, and click the ellipsis. The ListItem Collection Editor dialog box will appear. Add four List Items: Goldenrod, LightBlue, LightGreen, and Light Salmon. Both the Text and Value of each item should contain the string for the item.

4. To the right of this label place another DropDownList control. Add three items to its Items Collection: Beige, LightBlue, and LightGreen.

5. Add another label below the Border and Box Colors label, and change its Text property to "Font Face and Size".

6. To the right of this label place two more DropDownList controls. Name the first "DDLFontFace" and add to its Items Collection "Arial", "Georgia", and "Times New Roman". Name the second "DDLFontSize" and add to its Items Collection "Smaller" and "Larger".

7. Place a Button control below these controls and change its Text property to "Display Customized News Page".

8. Click on the project in Solution Explorer and add another Web form to the project.

9. On the new Web form, add a Label control to the top and change its Text property to "Customized News Page".

10. Below the label add another Label control and size it so it fits most of the page. Change its Text property so it has some placeholder text in it. Name it "CustomNewsBox".

11. Click back over to WebForm2.aspx and double-click the Button control.

12. Place the following code in the Button control's event handler in the code behind page:

```
Session("BorderColor") = DDLBorderColor.SelectedItem.Value
Session("BoxColor") = DDLBoxColor.SelectedItem.Value
Session("FontFace") = DDLFontFace.SelectedItem.Value
Session("FontSize") = DDLFontSize.SelectedItem.Value
Response.Redirect("WebForm3.aspx")
```

13. Click back over to WebForm3.aspx and double-click anywhere on the design surface not occupied by a control. Enter the following code in the Page_Load event handler:

```
CustomNewsBox.BorderColor = Color.FromName(Session("BorderColor"))
CustomNewsBox.BackColor = Color.FromName(Session("BoxColor"))
CustomNewsBox.Font.Name = Session("FontFace")
CustomNewsBox.Font.Size = FontUnit.Parse(Session("FontSize"))
```

14. Right-click WebForm2.aspx in Solution Explorer and choose "Set as Start Page" from the shortcut menu. This will enable you to start your application from this page, without having to go through the Login page each time you check it.

15. From WebForm2.aspx in Design view, choose File|Build and Browse from the menu. WebForm2.aspx in the browser should resemble Figure 6.5. Make some selections in the dropdown box and click the "Display Customized News Page" button. Your customized news page should resemble Figure 6.6.

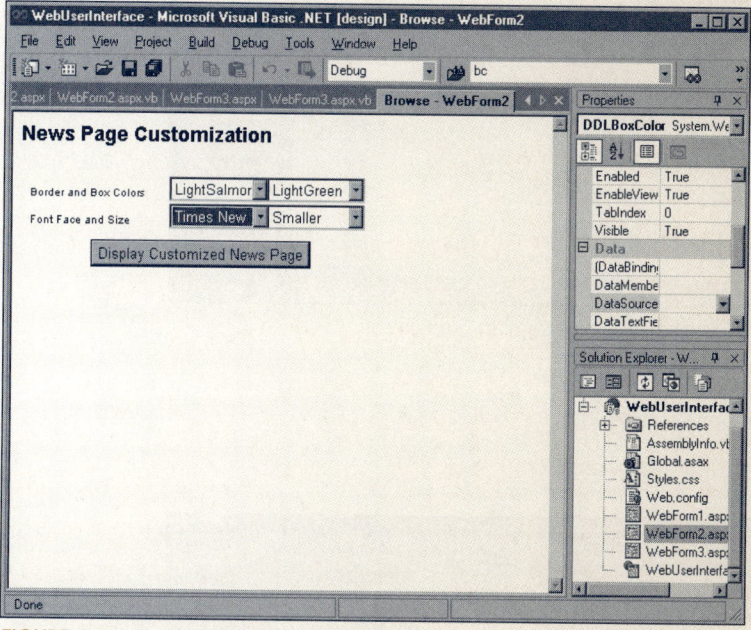

FIGURE 6.5 The News Page Customization Page in the Browser

Using Validation Controls

The purpose of this project is to demonstrate the use of validation in a business setting. This project presents users with a form they can use to enter data for real estate searches. Although no search is performed, the application demonstrates validating user-entered data in preparation for a search.

1. Open VS.Net (if not already open) and create a new ASP.Net Web application project named "ValidateSearch" from the Visual Basic Projects template. A blank Web form should open.

2. Add a Label control to the form and make it read "Please enter your search parameters". Change the Label's font properties to Arial and Bold.

3. Add TextBox controls for the following data, and set their IDs the same as their names, but with no spaces and starting with "txt": "txtFullName", "txtEmail", "txtCity", "txtZipCode", "txtPrice". Place Label controls next to these fields to identify them to the user and place a Button control at the bottom of the form, as shown in Figure 6.7.

CHAPTER 6 The User Interface (UI)

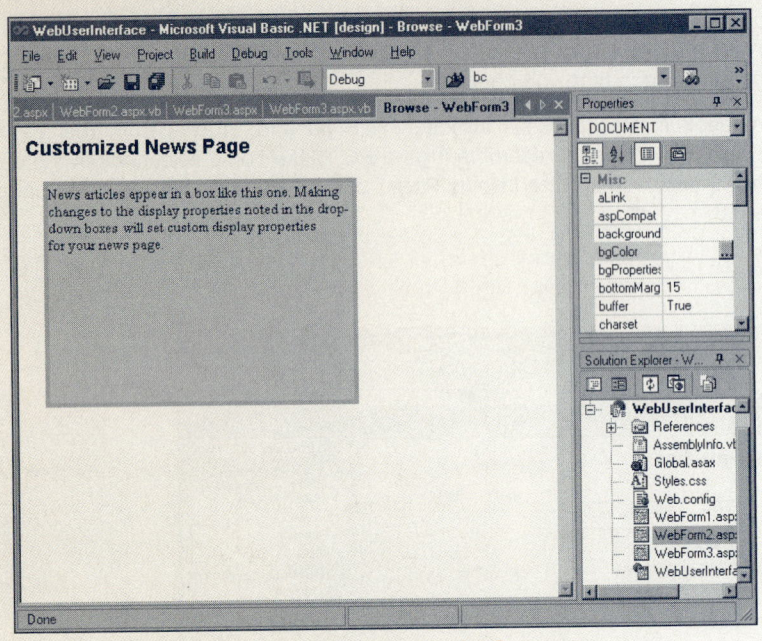

FIGURE 6.6 The Customized News Page in the Browser

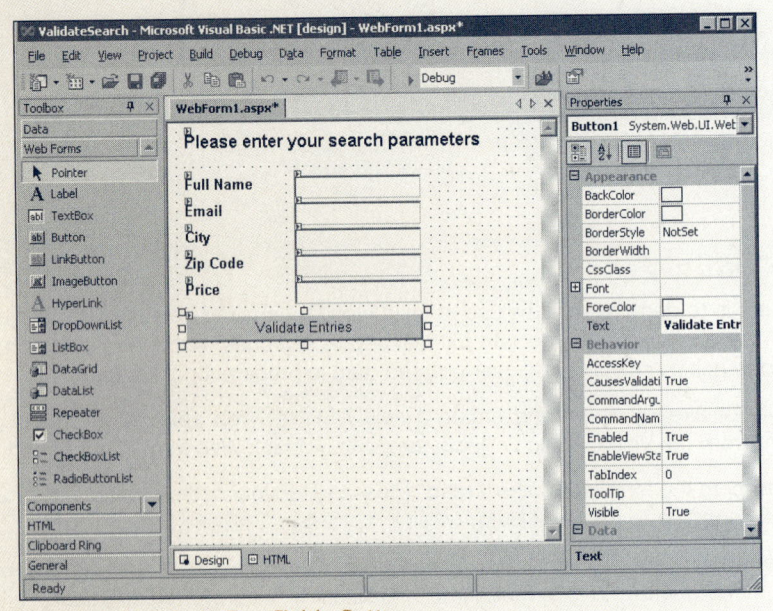

FIGURE 6.7 Labels, Text Fields, Button

4. Add Validation controls for each TextBox control and a Summary Validation Control for displaying the error messages. Add a RequiredFieldValidator for each of the fields (named "rfv" and the primary name of the field, such as FullName). Set the ControlToValidate property to the name of the TextBox associated with the Validation control, and set the Text and ErrorMessage properties appropriately (for example, set the ErrorMessage property for the rfvFullName validator to "Please enter your full name"). Set the Enabled property to False and set the Display property to "None" (this makes the error message display only on the Summary Control).

5. Add a RegularExpressionValidator for the txtEmail and txtZipCode fields and set the ValidationExpression property of these controls using the RegularExpression wizard (there are prebuilt regular expressions for Internet Email Address and U.S. Zip codes in the wizard). Set the ControlToValdiate, Display, and Enabled properties for these controls as well.

6. Add a Range Validator control for the txtPrice field and set the MinimumValue property to 100,000 and the MaximumValue property to 1,000,000. Set the Type property to Integer, the ControlToValidate property to "txtPrice", the Enabled property to False, and the Display property to "None".

7. Add a ValidationSummary control to the form and name it "vasError". Leave the default property settings for this control. Your form should now resemble Figure 6.8.

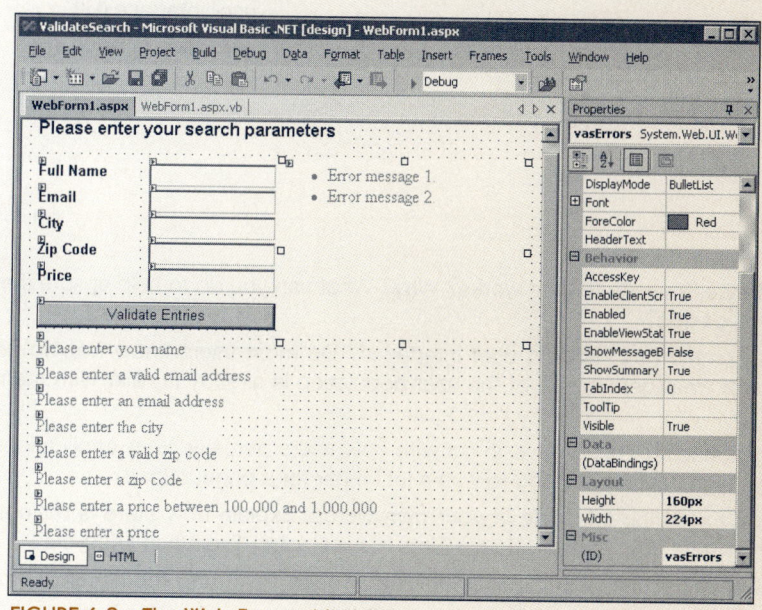

FIGURE 6.8 The Web Form with Validation Controls

8. Double-click the design surface of the form to start a Page_Load event handler and enter the following code in it:

```
If IsPostBack Then
  rfvFullName.Enabled = True
  revEmail.Enabled = True
  rfvEmail.Enabled = True
```

```
       rfvCity.Enabled = True
       revZipCode.Enabled = True
       rfvZipCode.Enabled = True
       rnvPrice.Enabled = True
       rfvPrice.Enabled = True
End If
```

9. Since all the Validation controls (except the Summary) are set to false when the page is first loaded, no validation takes place at that time. When the user submits the form, however, IsPostBack becomes true and all the Validation controls' Enabled properties become True as well, thereby allowing validation to take place.

10. Click back over to WebForm1.aspx and choose File|Build and Browse from the menu. Try submitting the form with no values entered as well as incorrect values for email, Zip code, and price to test that validation is working properly.

Key Terms

business process
Cache object
caching
Control Execution Lifecycle
data caching
IsPostBack property
machine.config
output caching
Page object
Page_Load event
regular expression
user interface (UI)
validation control
Web.config

Review Questions

1. Who determines whether a user interface works? Why? What can you do to help ensure the success of user interfaces you design?
2. What elements are common for modern user interfaces? Do most users know how to use them? Rank them in terms of what percentage of the user population is already familiar with them, in your estimation.
3. What difference does loading speed have to do with how users perceive Web applications? Under what circumstances might users be willing to wait a lot longer for a page to load?
4. Describe the Control Execution Lifecycle in your own words. Explain how state is maintained and what happens to ViewState data at the various points in the Control Execution Lifecycle.
5. Describe the concept of caching and explain why it is a good thing and the circumstances under which you might put it to work.
6. Describe at least one procedure you can use to find the machine.config file, if it exists.
7. List three configuration sections in a Web.config file.
8. How can you make additional Web.config files for specifying configuration settings on lower-level files in your Web application?
9. In what format are Web.config files written?
10. How are the settings in Web.config files changed?

CHAPTER 7

Databases and SQL

LEARNING OBJECTIVES

Upon completion of this chapter, you will be able to:

1. Explain what a database is.
2. List the main components of a database.
3. Describe key features of relational databases.
4. Explain what a primary key is.
5. Explain the common relationships found in relational databases.
6. Write Structured Query Language (SQL) statements.
7. Use SELECT, INSERT, UPDATE, and DELETE statements in ASP.Net.

INTRODUCTION

Web applications, like any other kind of application, often require access to data that are stored in a structured way and change dynamically. For example, suppose you write an application that is intended to display today's news on a Web page named "news_today.htm". In order to keep the news current, you'd have to use an HTML or Web page editor to essentially rewrite the page each day and convert the existing page into an archive page. And if you wanted to give your readers the ability to search the archives efficiently, you might have to use a special application attached to your Web site.

In contrast, databases are quite efficient at storing regularly used data, and at searching them. Databases have a long history of use in popular applications, and it's no surprise that Web developers have adopted databases as the primary means for working with structured data in Web applications. Many standards, languages, and tools have been developed to make integrating databases with Web applications efficient.

While there are a large number of database types, as well as quite a few specialized languages for retrieving data from them, the most commonly used today are relational databases, and the most common language for accessing databases is Structured Query Language (SQL). The many objects available to ASP.Net for working with databases are quite useful, but you must still be familiar with SQL in order to comfortably retrieve the data your application requires.

Programmatically, in order to retrieve and manipulate records in a database, you must make a connection from your application to a database file. Connection strings are used, and Microsoft's Active Data Objects.Net (ADO.Net) technology works hand-in-hand with ASP.Net and VB.Net to establish connections and provide access to the records. ADO.Net also provides a host of other convenient objects for working with records.

In this chapter we'll cover the basics of database structure and design, so that you'll be familiar with what you are retrieving, and we'll cover the basics of SQL and the four SQL statements you'll use throughout your ASP.Net Web applications.

Databases

The term *database* is often used in news stories and entertainment to refer to any conglomeration of data. In actuality, databases are just one form of structured data or data store. To understand the concept of data store and data structures, you must first understand what data are. Data are simply bits and bytes, or any observable differentiation from surroundings. However, to have any meaning, data must be associated with a context. For example, suppose you write the number 1995 on a whiteboard. Does this mean a price, a year, or the temperature on the planet Mercury (or the temperature inside the cylinders of your Mercury)?

When a context is applied, data take on meaning, and become information. Structured data refer to data with context. Consider an email. While the body of an email may be relatively unstructured, you can assign some meaning to it based on the To and From headers and the date it was sent, and even by making inferences about the meaning of data items in the body (Bob is talking about the contract, and he disapproves of the terms, so we probably won't get the contract in its current form).

Databases are highly structured forms of data. Each field in a record of a table has a name that implies what the field contains (or should, if the field has a descriptive name), and the data in each field of a record have a one-to-one relationship with the data in other fields of the same record. This means you can assume that the first name and the last name in a single record of the Customers table belong to the same customer.

Relational databases have even more structure because tables of data within them are also related. And because relational databases are so highly structured and so many tools have been developed to utilize their structure, databases are very efficient for a wide range of common application requirements. Databases are also long-term storage facilities for dynamic data, another common application requirement.

Using databases with your applications is relatively straightforward these days, but in order to make the most of them you need to understand the basics of how they are constructed and why they are constructed that way, the relationships they form, and the language (SQL) used to manipulate them.

Databases in Ecommerce Applications

Databases are the most common form of data storage for business and ecommerce applications. For example, when you register online with a company, you can be sure that your personal, contact, and billing information are stored in a database. When you make a payment by mail, the payment is stored in a database, and all the payment records are connected (or related) to the record storing your personal information. And when you call up the company to find out if they received your payment, you can bet the person you are talking to is looking up your information from a database.

The primary difference between storing data in an application or session variable and storing it in a database is that the database information will persist even if the server is turned off. Backups are made frequently to stored database files, so there's a good chance critical business data will be available for years to come. And database records often fill many business needs beyond simply recording current transactions. Summarized data from sales transactions are used to answer many questions about how the business is doing, whether sales are growing or falling, which customers do the most business, and so on. The bottom line is, having an understanding of how databases work to record and regurgitate data, and help to slice and dice the data to answer short-term and long-term business questions, is going to be critical to the development of many of your ASP.Net Web applications.

Designing a Database

Database design starts with an understanding of the requirements of your application. Suppose your application is going to support multi-user online gaming. It's pretty clear that the database must support individual users, so you would have a table for user data. If the application should allow users to save games to show who won or to resume at a later date, the database would have a table for games. The tables would be related, so you could match users with their games.

The Users table might contain Name, Email Address, Preferences, and so on, while the Games table might record User IDs, Game Type/Name, Start and End Date, Game Status, and so on. The idea is that the records in the tables need to capture enough data about users and games to support the application's intended functions. For example, if the users will not have the capability to extend the game play beyond a single day, there's no need to have an End Date field in the Games table.

For simpler Web applications, it is often sufficient to design a database with tables and their fields. Retrieving records and manipulating them may be done completely outside the database, in your code (and using ADO.Net). For more complex Web applications, you may find it more efficient to define relationships and perform some record manipulation tasks within the database program itself. For our projects we'll use Microsoft's **SQL Server** as the database program, and we'll conduct record operations in our code.

Defining Fields

A **field** is a named data container in a **table**, and the data values in a series of fields in a table form a **record**. You create a table by defining the names and data types of the table's fields, and you populate the table by filling it with records. While you can create fields that have coded names (such as AB01, act_year, and so on), it is really best to use descriptive names. One good naming scheme is to use lowercase names with underscores separating the words in the name, like "first_name". Don't use special characters or spaces; these can make programming or querying harder later.

One of the rules of thumb for creating fields is to group data logically, in units that can be easily searched. For example, don't create a single field called "name" or "address". Break "name" into "first_name" and "last_name", and break "address" into "street_address", "city", "state", "country", and "postal_code".

Another rule of thumb is to assign the correct data type to the field. If the field will contain dates, use a date data type. Note that the data types you assign to fields are those allowed by the database program you are using, and are not necessarily the same as the data types allowed by your application programming language. While data types are often quite similar or the same, don't assume they are.

Defining Tables

As we mentioned, the act of creating tables is essentially the act of naming its fields and setting their data types. Tables in relational databases also should have a *primary key*. A **primary key** is a special field that is always unique, and a good way to ensure this is to set the data type of the primary key field as an integer that (by a constraint enforced within the database itself) must always be unique and increments itself automatically. Although you can make primary keys from many field types, as well as from a set of fields in a table, we will use the single field, auto-incrementing type in our applications.

Having a primary key in your tables ensures that there will always be at least one unique field value per record, and this allows you to relate tables to each other. For example, if you have a Users table and a Games table, you would use a primary key filed in the Users table (perhaps named UserID), and you would relate each user to the games he/she has played by having a field named UserID in the Games table. Then, when a user plays a game, his/her own UserID value also would be entered in each Game record in the Games table for the games he/she has played. Because this is so common, it is a good rule of thumb to build in a primary key field for all the tables you define, whether or not you know in advance you'll need them. Many times you'll find out you need them later, and be glad you have them.

One-to-One, One-to-Many, and Many-to-Many Relationships When two tables have one record each that matches on the primary key value, they are said to have a **one-to-one** relationship. Essentially, this means that they are like one large table. When one table has a single record whose primary key value matches one or more primary key values in another table (in the other table, the primary key value from the first table is called the **foreign key**), the tables are said to have a **one-to-many** relationship. When the primary key values from two tables both appear in a third table (which may or may not have its own primary key and fields, and is often called a junction table), the two tables are said to have a **many-to-many** relationship. Relationships between tables are the foundation of **relational database** structure, and these relationships appear often in the real world. Illustration 7.1 shows one-to-many and many-to-many relationships.

Parents have children, customers have orders, people have pets, doctors have patients, and so on. All these are examples of one-to-many relationships. For many-to-many relationships, employees may work on several teams and teams may have several employees; doctors may prescribe many medications and medications may be prescribed by many doctors; and so on. Your job as database developer is to ensure that the tables you define can properly support the relationships involved in your application.

Adding Records
Adding records to a table in a database is done by entering data in the table's fields. Typically, manual data entry is done in forms (or, for Web applications, with Web forms), but if there are already data available in another database, you can import the records to fill the table. Depending upon how you've structured your table, some of the fields may be required, so importing data with empty fields may not work. In addition, you may have to massage the data so that the field data types match (or match closely enough). Sometimes you'll spend more effort performing data imports than in actually building the database or application that goes with the data.

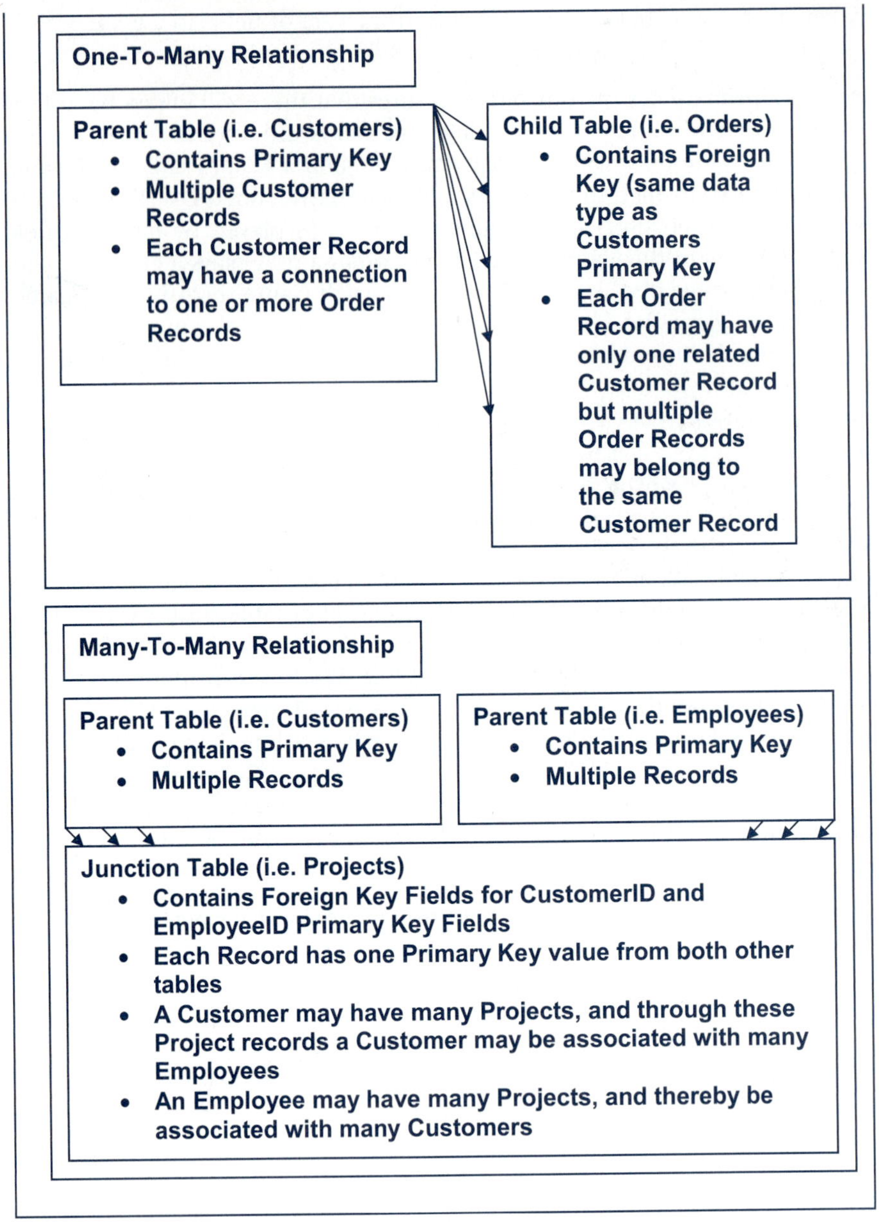

CHAPTER 7 Databases and SQL

One-To-Many Relationship

Parent Table (i.e. Customers)
- Contains Primary Key
- Multiple Customer Records
- Each Customer Record may have a connection to one or more Order Records

Child Table (i.e. Orders)
- Contains Foreign Key (same data type as Customers Primary Key
- Each Order Record may have only one related Customer Record but multiple Order Records may belong to the same Customer Record

Many-To-Many Relationship

Parent Table (i.e. Customers)
- Contains Primary Key
- Multiple Records

Parent Table (i.e. Employees)
- Contains Primary Key
- Multiple Records

Junction Table (i.e. Projects)
- Contains Foreign Key Fields for CustomerID and EmployeeID Primary Key Fields
- Each Record has one Primary Key value from both other tables
- A Customer may have many Projects, and through these Project records a Customer may be associated with many Employees
- An Employee may have many Projects, and thereby be associated with many Customers

ILLUSTRATION 7.1   Database Relationships

Discussion—Designing Databases

The first step in designing a relational database is to decide what needs to be tracked and how the tracked things relate to each other. For example, it's pretty obvious that an application meant to conduct surveys will probably need to have a table for surveys, a table for survey questions, and another table for survey answers. The surveys table will have a one-to-many relationship with the survey questions table (because one survey may have one or more questions), and the survey questions table will have a one-to-many relationship with the survey answers table (because one question may have one or more answers). Deciding what tables should be in the database and how they are related is a logical process, but there are a number of "right" answers, and some understanding of how databases work is required to arrive at an optimal solution.

The next step is to create the tables and decide what data items should be collected (what fields and data types to use in each table). For example, if your application requirements include the capability to determine when a survey was initiated, then it would be logical to include a field named "start_date" or "creation_date" to hold the date a particular survey was first built or run. Since the field is meant to hold a date, using the Date data type would also be logical. And because the tables often have to form relationships, a good rule of thumb is to always include a primary key field in your database tables.

For ASP.Net Web applications, building the tables and fields is often enough to support the application. However, for more complex applications you might want to add more features (such as stored procedures) to your database.

Structured Query Language (SQL)

Structured Query Language (SQL) is a common, English-like language that can be used to access and manipulate databases. Although there are numerous minor variations that apply to specific versions of popular relational database management system (RDBMS) applications (such as SQL Server, Access, Oracle, and so on), SQL commands are similar enough that you can easily transfer what you've learned from one application to the next.

SQL contains commands that let you create and modify tables, but for our purposes it will be enough to familiarize ourselves with the commands used to retrieve and modify records. These commands are called SQL queries.

SQL Database Queries

The term *query* implies a question, and performing a query implies getting an answer. To query a database means asking for data in the form of records (that's really the main data we're concerned with in a database, although there might be additional information about the structure of the database that is useful in our applications from time to time). But SQL queries also can be used to add, delete, or change records, so a more useful definition of query is "a means of selecting or grouping records for database operations."

SQL queries can select records from more than one table by using "joins," and can use expressions and pattern-matching techniques to select records in very specific ways. Of course, in order for queries to work properly, the underlying data in your records must be "clean." Clean data contain no deviations from what you would expect in each field. Importing data for a new database often means cleaning it up first, and keeping data clean is assisted by validation techniques during the entry process.

In addition to selecting records, SQL queries can create new fields (both field names and the data in them) during the selection process. For example, if you are selecting all customer records in which the last name is Devon, you also can have the query create a new field named full_name that contains the data from the first_name and last_name fields. Your query will then contain a field that is nowhere else to be found in the database. This capability is very useful when you don't need to store the data permanently but wish to calculate or create it for specific purposes in your application.

Sometimes your application will require values calculated or derived from a group of records, rather than data from individual records. In these cases, you can use aggregate functions to summarize data from records. For example, you may want a count or total amount of orders by customer. To get a count or a total, you could use the Count function on the OrderID field (because the OrderID field would be unique) or the Sum function on the OrderTotal field, and group your records by the CustomerID field.

The main SQL queries we'll use are shown in Illustration 7.2 and include

- **SELECT**—for retrieving all or some records based on selection criteria.
- **INSERT**—for adding records to a table.
- **UPDATE**—for editing records, singly, in groups, or all.
- **DELETE**—for deleting records, singly, in groups, or all.

Writing SELECT Queries

SQL queries can be written uppercase or lowercase, but tradition is to write them uppercase. SELECT queries start with the word SELECT. Next you write the names of the fields you wish to have in the query, or the asterisk (*) to indicate all fields. Then you use the FROM keyword and the name of the table. If you write nothing else in your query, you will get all records from the table. For example, to select all fields from the customers table, you could write

```
SELECT * FROM customers
```

If you wanted to select only the first_name and last_name fields, you would write

```
SELECT first_name, last_name FROM customers
```

SQL Query Statements

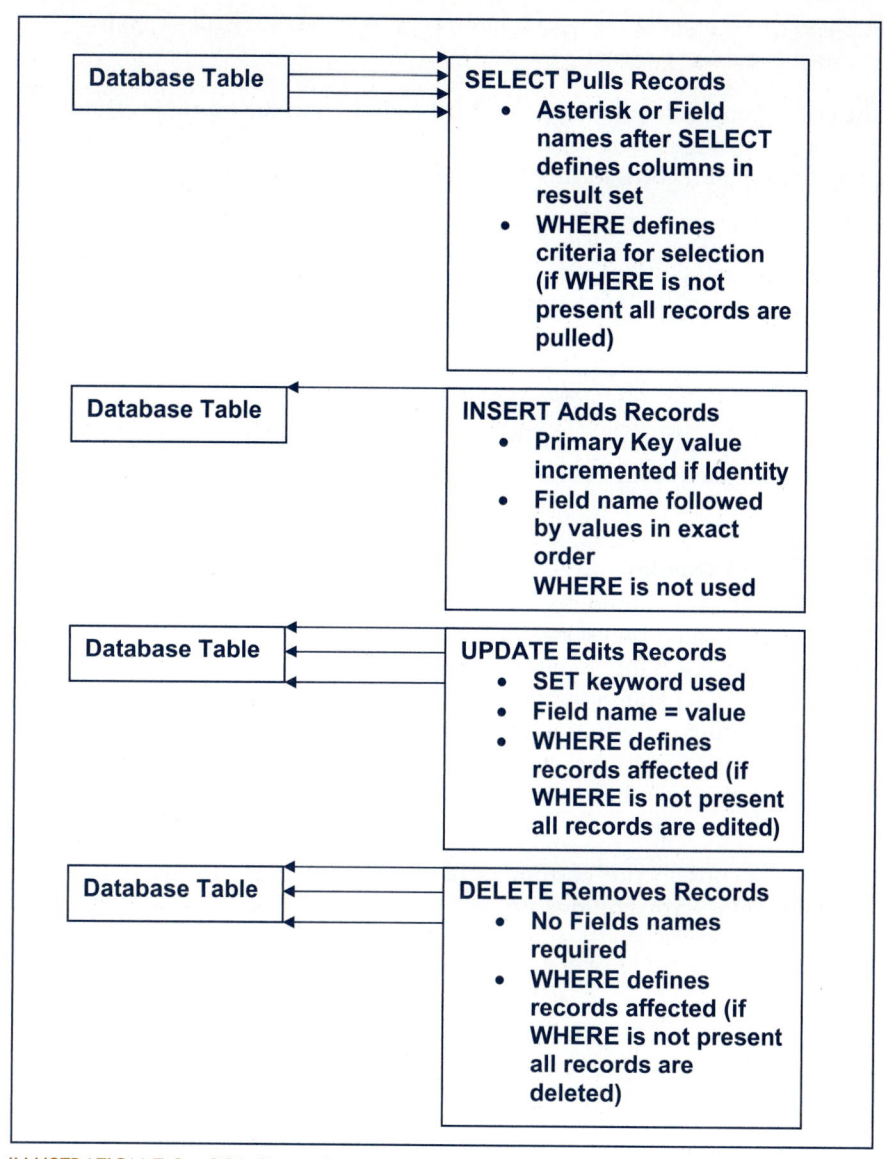

Database Table → SELECT Pulls Records
- Asterisk or Field names after SELECT defines columns in result set
- WHERE defines criteria for selection (if WHERE is not present all records are pulled)

Database Table → INSERT Adds Records
- Primary Key value incremented if Identity
- Field name followed by values in exact order
- WHERE is not used

Database Table ← UPDATE Edits Records
- SET keyword used
- Field name = value
- WHERE defines records affected (if WHERE is not present all records are edited)

Database Table ← DELETE Removes Records
- No Fields names required
- WHERE defines records affected (if WHERE is not present all records are deleted)

ILLUSTRATION 7.2   SQL Query Statements

WHERE Clauses   If you wanted to select all fields but only those records in which the last_name is Devon, you would write

```
SELECT * FROM customers WHERE last_name = 'Devon'
```

The `WHERE` keyword is used to start a **WHERE clause**. WHERE clauses are the means by which SQL queries are selective. WHERE clauses are defined by the field names used and the criteria they must meet. For example, the following WHERE clause specifies criteria for two fields:

```
SELECT * FROM customers WHERE last_name = 'Devon' AND
zip_code = '20020'
```

The criteria applied to fields can be hard-coded (as in the examples above) or can use pattern-matching. For example, the following criteria will cause the query to find all records in which the last_name begins with "D":

```
SELECT * FROM customers WHERE last_name = 'D%'
```

The percent sign is a wildcard character representing any characters after the "D". The underscore (_) is used to specify a single character, as shown in the following code:

```
SELECT * FROM customers WHERE last_name = 'D____'
```

The code above will select only records in which the last name begins with a "D" and has exactly four characters after the "D".

Writing INSERT Queries

INSERT queries are used to add records to a table. They begin with the `INSERT` keyword and then the `INTO` keyword with the table name to specify which table to insert the record into. Following that are parentheses containing field names separated by commas, the `values` keyword, and more parentheses containing the values to insert in each field. Note that the field names and values must be written (in the query) in the same order, although the query order does not have to match the order in which the field names are specified in the table.

To add a record to the customers table that only has the first_name and last_name values, you could write

```
INSERT INTO customers (first_name, last_name)
values('Henry', 'Devon')
```

Since inserting a record affects no other records, there are no clauses associated with the INSERT query, but there are a few considerations:

- There is no need to specify a value for the primary key field if you are using an auto-incrementing primary key field. The database program will take care of determining and inserting the proper value, based on a sequence. For example, in SQL Server, if you designate the primary key field as "identity", SQL Server will automatically generate the next value (the value in the primary key field for the last record, plus 1) and insert that value into the field for the new record.
- If you fail to insert required or appropriate values into fields with these constraints on them, an error will be generated.
- Fields for which no value is specified will contain a NULL value. NULL values can affect summary operations adversely (such as the Sum of numeric fields), so it's best to use a default value in most cases (the

Structured Query Language (SQL)

default value for a field can be specified during table construction, so you don't have to include it with every INSERT query).

Writing UPDATE Queries

UPDATE queries are used for editing records, much like you might make changes to an existing record from a form. But since they can be used with WHERE clauses, they can quickly make identical changes to vast numbers of records. Use them carefully though, as it can be difficult to roll back the changes once they are done.

UPDATE queries start with the `UPDATE` keyword, then the name of the table, the keyword `set`, and then field names and updated values separated by commas. For example, the following query sets all prices higher by five dollars for products in the "shirts" category:

```
UPDATE products set price = price + 5.00 WHERE category = 'shirts'
```

Writing DELETE Queries

DELETE queries are fairly simple by nature, because all they do is delete records. However, they are also very powerful because they can be used with WHERE clauses, and can be dangerous because their actions are so final. It's not a bad idea to test your DELETE queries using SELECT queries with the same WHERE clause first, to make sure you're selecting the correct records. Note that using no WHERE clause can be even more dangerous, because the default action is to delete all records in the table.

DELETE queries start with the `DELETE` keyword, then the table name, then the WHERE clause. Only entire records are deleted, so there's no need to specify fields. The WHERE clause can use all the same tools (pattern-matching, criteria, and so forth) as any other type of query to specify which fields to select for deletion, as shown in the following example:

```
DELETE customers WHERE last_name='D%'
```

Joining Tables in SQL Queries

Creating a relational database means separating what you are tracking into individual tables and establishing relationships between those tables by means of primary and foreign key fields. In fact, there is a mechanism in modern RDBMS applications that let's you enforce what is called *referential integrity*. Referential integrity acts as a constraint on the database: you'll be unable to create a "child" record without first having a parent record available, or to delete a parent record without first deleting all its "child" records.

But you are not forced to use these relationships when querying the database for records. You can use them, but you don't have to. In addition, you can form relationships between tables based on any fields you like, so long as the data types are compatible.

Typically, however, you would use the key fields to form relationships in queries because that's what you made them for. Making relationships in queries in this manner is called making *joins*. An example of this would be the situation in which you want to see all order records for a particular customer. In the query you would include a few fields from the customers table, a join with the orders table, and the fields you want from the orders table. In the list below, we discuss the types of joins that are available and the results you can expect to get:

- Equi-join. The **equi-join** is used when the joining field values are equal (like customer_id in the customers table joined to customer_id in the orders table). The result would be a record for each instance in which the values found in customers.customer_id and orders.cutomer_id match. Equi-joins also are called inner joins.
- Outer join. The **outer join** is used when you need to retrieve all records in both tables.
- Left and right outer joins. These joins are used when you want to retrieve all records from one table but only the records from the other table where the join field values match.

An example of an equi-join is shown here:

```
SELECT * FROM customers INNER JOIN orders ON customer.customer_id = orders.customer_id
```

The statement above specifies both tables (separated by the `INNER JOIN` keywords) and the field they are joined on (using the `ON` keyword). The result of this would be a record for each record in orders matching a record in customers on the customer_id field. Note that if there were two customers with 6 records each, the result would be 12 records, with the customers table field values repeated six times each.

Aggregate Queries

Aggregate queries are used whenever you need to group records together and produce a result based on the grouping. For example, if you have multiple customers and each customer has one or more orders, you may want to find out what the total amount of orders is for each customer. So you would group all order records according to their customer_id, and then perform a Sum operation on the individual order total amounts. There are a variety of summary operations you can perform in SQL, such as SUM, COUNT, AVG, and so on. The trick to performing aggregate or summary operations is to include only those fields necessary to produce the desired grouping.

An example of an aggregate query is shown here:

```
SELECT SUM(orders.amount) AS TotalOrderAmount
FROM customers INNER JOIN orders
ON customers.customer_id = orders_customer_id
```

The statement above would produce a single field named "TotalOrder Amount" for each customer record. The sum would be the total of all "amount" field values in each record for each customer. If you were to summarize the values in the amount field across the entire orders table without any reference to the customers table, you'd get the total of all order amounts contained in the orders table.

Stored Procedures

In Chapter 8, we'll discuss how you can put SQL statements (SELECT, INSERT, and other queries) in ADO.Net objects and cause those objects to run the SQL statements from your ASP.Net Web applications. For example, we'll create a Web form that allows users to register. After filling out the registration form, the user will click the Register button, which will in turn activate an event handler for the button. In the event handler, code will run that makes a connection to our database and inserts the user's registration data via an INSERT statement. The INSERT statement is loaded into a property of the ADO.Net SQLDataAdapter object we include in our Web application, and the statement runs from our Web application.

This is an acceptable way to process and store registration data. But we could also simply pass the registration information to SQL Server as parameters and cause the SQL INSERT statement to run from inside SQL Server rather than from our ASP.Net Web application. Running SQL statements from inside the database application rather than from inside our Web application can be much more efficient, because inside the database application SQL statements are compiled, in a sense, and therefore are highly optimized. It's similar to the difference between interpreted scripting languages and compiled programming languages. SQL Statements that run from inside a database application are called **stored procedures**.

Discussion—SQL

Most relational databases in use today can be accessed and managed using the appropriate database driver and Structured Query Language (SQL). SQL is written as plain text commands using statements that are similar to an English sentence, making it a little easier to write and remember. It is important to be familiar with SQL, because you will often need to compose SQL statements in order to make the database components of your ASP.Net Web application work. ASP.Net Web applications often use records in a database to persist data for use across sessions, even if the application is shut down.

The SQL SELECT, INSERT, UPDATE, and DELETE queries are used to retrieve records, add records, edit records, and delete records. Adding a WHERE clause to a SQL query allows you to narrow the selection of records by including specific criteria that a record must meet in order to be selected. SQL queries also can be used to retrieve records from multiple tables via joins and can summarize values across groups of records with aggregate functions such as SUM, COUNT, AVG, and so on.

Practical Database Design

Having an understanding of how databases store data and how records can be retrieved and manipulated is a good beginning, but there's nothing like going through the process of building a real database to reinforce what you've learned. In this section we'll build a database to support an online multiplayer game application. We'll dub our application "OMPGame."

Basic OMPGame Application Requirements

Our application will support users who play games together and individually, although we won't get quite so complex as to program artificial intelligence (AI) into it. If a player wishes to play individually, the player can play against him/herself. In this chapter and Chapter 8, we'll make our game work for individual players playing against the house; in Chapter 10, we'll set up the multiplayer portion of our game.

Players will need to register and obtain a username and password to log in before they play. They'll be able to pick a unique screen name during the registration process, and once they're logged in, they'll be able to pick a game to play and then start a new game against themselves or against another available user. Once the game is won, it is over, and the status of the game and other statistics will be recorded.

To simplify things, we won't request billing information during registration, although it would be pretty straightforward to connect billing information and payments (and later invoicing) to the registration process. We also won't allow users to put games on hold or continue them later, or check up on their game statistics. And we won't make administrative functions or screens that would allow employees of the online gaming company to manage users and games due to the added complexity. These would make good features to add in the future though, so we'll keep them in mind as we go.

Database Tables for OMPGame Application

To track players, we'll create a table named players (Table 7.1), and to track available games, we'll create a table named games (Table 7.2). To track games being played by users, we'll use a junction table called games_played (Table

7.3) (because many players may play many games, there is a many-to-many relationship). Tables 7.1 through 7.3 list the fields and data types that would be appropriate.

TABLE 7.1   The Players Table

players

Field Name	Data Type	Size	Allow Null?	Primary Key
player_id	Int4		No	Yes
first_name	VarChar	100	Yes	No
last_name	VarChar	100	Yes	No
address	VarChar	100	Yes	No
city	VarChar	100	Yes	No
state	VarChar	2	Yes	No
postal_code	VarChar	10	Yes	No
country	VarChar	100	Yes	No
home_phone	VarChar	20	Yes	No
mobile_phone	VarChar	20	Yes	No
fax	VarChar	20	Yes	No
email	VarChar	100	Yes	No
screen_name	VarChar	20	Yes	No
username	VarChar	20	Yes	No
password	VarChar	20	Yes	No

TABLE 7.2   The Games Table

games

Field Name	Data Type	Size	Allow Null?	Primary Key
game_id	Int4		No	Yes
g_name	VarChar	50	Yes	No
g_desc	VarChar	100	Yes	No
max_players	Int	4	Yes	No
active	Bit	1	Yes	No

TABLE 7.3 The Games_Played Table

games_played

Field Name	Data Type	Size	Allow Null?	Primary Key
games_played_id	Int4		No	Yes
player_id	Int4		Yes	No
game_id	Int4		Yes	No
game_date	Date	8	Yes	No
game_status	VarChar	20	Yes	No
winning_player_id	Int4		Yes	No
losing_player_id	Int4		Yes	No
winning_score	Int4		Yes	No
losing_score	Int4		Yes	No

Database Engines

The term *database* is often used to refer to a relational database management system (RDBMS, such as Oracle, SQL Server, or Microsoft Access), a database file (such as one that might be created with Microsoft Access, having a filename with the .mdb extension), or the set of stored data used with a Web application, regardless of how it is stored. Actually, there are several terms that differentiate between database files (where the data are stored) and the tools used to access the data. A database engine is the application that is used to manipulate data in a database file. For example, Access databases use the Microsoft Jet database engine. Microsoft is also now providing the Microsoft Data Engine (MSDE) that can be used with Access and SQL Server databases.

Selecting a Database Engine

In Microsoft Access and Visual Studio.Net, you have the option of selecting the database you would like to use or create, and the databases available depend on what engines you have installed or can connect to remotely. In the following sections, we discuss using Microsoft Access and SQL Server as database engines.

Microsoft Access

Microsoft Access has long been a favorite of database developers for small-scale databases that must nevertheless include sophisticated relational features. It is easy to use and has many tools and wizards built in for rapid database development. Access is very compatible with SQL and can be used as the basis for smaller commercial applications. However, it does not scale well, and database applications intended for use in high-volume situations should be migrated to SQL Server or some other enterprise-scale RDBMS.

We can use Access to create the tables and structures for our OMPGame application, and the result is stored as a file with the .mdb extension.

Microsoft SQL Server

Using Microsoft SQL Server, we can build a robust database to support our OMPGame Web application. We can first create a database and then create the tables to hold the data that support the application. Note that to perform the projects in this chapter, you must either have SQL Server installed on your development machine or have access to it across a network or the Internet, and you must have the Enterprise Manager installed.

SQL Server Enterprise Manager

SQL Server comes with a client called Enterprise Manager that allows you to work with SQL Server in a visual way. With Enterprise Manager you can configure SQL Server (or several SQL servers) options, create and manage all databases in each server, set permissions for tables and other objects you create in databases, and use a number of wizards and visual aids as you develop your databases. Think of SQL Server as the database engine and Enterprise Manager as the front end to that engine.

Opening SQL Server Enterprise Manager If Enterprise Manager is installed, you can open it by going to Start|Programs|Microsoft SQL Server|Enterprise Manager. When it opens, it should resemble Figure 7.1.

Notice that the series of nodes on the left side can be opened by clicking the plus sign to the left of the node names. As you open each node, you'll see more nodes inside until you get to the lowest level. At each level, you also can right-click the node name to find out what actions are available for you to take. In the Hands On Projects, we'll use Enterprise Manager to create a new SQL Server database and the objects needed inside it, and we'll also use it later in this book as we continue to build our application.

Discussion—SQL Server

Microsoft SQL Server is a high-performance, enterprise-scale RDBMS application that contains all the facilities needed to build databases supporting Web applications. The Enterprise Manager is a console-based client that allows easy

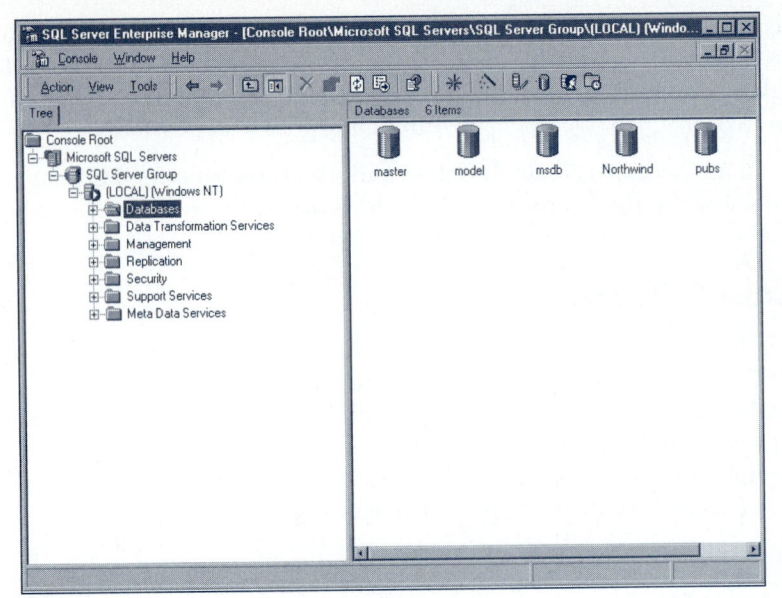

FIGURE 7.1 SQL Server Enterprise Manager

access to SQL Server features. In the Enterprise Manager, you can create databases, manage permissions, create tables and fields, set data types, create database diagrams, set primary key fields, and create views (and perform many other database design and management tasks).

The Enterprise Manager contains facilities for using SQL statements directly, and also contains a variety of useful visual tools. The table design facility allows you to create tables visually, by entering field names, data types, and field properties. You can set a field so that it automatically increments itself by changing its Identity property to "Yes", and you can set the field as a primary key by selecting the field and clicking on the Primary Key button.

The Query Builder is another example of a visual tool. The Query Builder allows you to select tables and views for inclusion in your queries visually (from a dialog box), and once selected you can create joins between tables, select fields to be retrieved in the results, and place criteria to be met. As you visually build your query, the Query Builder also writes and displays the appropriate SQL statements.

For ASP.Net Web applications, SQL Server makes a excellent tool for building the database support required to run your application, even when large numbers of users are coming to your site and using functions that make connections to the database and retrieve records.

Quick Check Questions

1. What structures in a database contain records?
2. What structures in a record contain data values?
3. What field type is always a good idea to include when you design a table?
4. How would you assign an auto-incrementing data type in SQL Server when you build a table?
5. How would you make a field into a primary key field in SQL Server?
6. What SQL reserved word would you use to start a SQL statement that retrieves records from a table?
7. What SQL reserved work would you use to begin placing criteria for records to meet in a SQL statement?
8. What are the four most commonly used types of SQL queries?
9. What SQL query type would you use to add records to a table?
10. What SQL query type would you use to edit records in a table?
11. What would you use to retrieve records from multiple tables in a SQL statement?

Summary

1. ASP.Net Web applications often require database support. While ordinary desktop database applications such as Microsoft Access can sometimes provide the necessary support, enterprise-grade database applications such as SQL Server are better at handling large numbers of users, records, and transactions. Therefore, SQL Server makes a good choice for back-end database support.
2. SQL Server, like most modern relational database management systems (RDBMSs), allows developers to build relational database applications. This means that the database designer builds individual tables for items to be tracked, such as customers, orders, and order items. The designer then establishes relationships between tracked items by means of primary key fields. Primary key fields are constrained to always contain unique values, so that each record has at least one field that identifies it uniquely from all the rest of the records. The primary key field is then duplicated in other tables to which the main table is related. In other tables, the primary key field is called the foreign key.
3. Tables may be related by a one-to-one, one-to-many, or many-to-many relationship. In a one-to-one relationship, the related tables act as one large table (each data value in a record is directly related to the data values in records in the related table). In a one-to-many relationship, each record in the main table (also called the parent table) is related to one or more records in

the "child" table. In a many-to-many relationship, each record in the main table may be related to one or more records in the foreign table, and vice versa, through a third table (called a junction table).
4. Most databases can be accessed using the appropriate database driver and Structured Query Language (SQL). Although there are numerous versions of SQL, they are so similar that using them is like using a standard language, with the differences easily overcome. Both Microsoft Access and SQL Server respond to basic SQL queries in the same way.
5. SQL statements can be used to create tables and set their fields, but more commonly used SQL statements are SQL queries. SQL queries include the SELECT, INSERT, UPDATE, and DELETE queries. The SELECT query is used to retrieve records in a result set. The fields retrieved and the table from which the records are retrieved can be set with the SELECT query.
6. The INSERT query can be used to add a record to a table. If a primary key field with an auto-incrementing data value is used, then there's no need to include the primary key field name or value in an INSERT query because this value will be automatically added when a record is inserted.
7. The UPDATE query can be used to edit existing records in a database. Typically, the primary key field will be used to specify the record to edit, although for edits involving multiple records another field may be used. The DELETE query can be used to delete one or more records from a table. The records to be deleted are specified in the same way as for the UPDATE query. The WHERE clause may be added to any query in order to restrict the records involved in the query to a subset of all the records in a table. SQL queries also can use relationships between tables as the basis for selecting records. Relationships are expressed as joins in SQL queries. SQL queries also can summarize results into groups of records, using aggregate queries with functions such as Sum and Count.
8. It is important to be familiar with SQL queries because written SQL statements are the basis for many of the database operations performed by your ASP.Net Web applications.

Exercise 7.1

1. Your assignment is to create the appropriate tables and relationships for managing aircraft and the maintenance work done on them. Your database must be able to track aircraft, mechanics, and maintenance tasks. List the tables you would create, the fields and data types in the tables, and what relationships the tables would have.
2. Using the tables created in Step 1, write a SQL query that selects all the aircraft you are tracking.
3. Using the tables created in Step 1, write a SQL query that adds a record to the aircraft table.
4. Using the tables created in Step 1, write a SQL query that deletes a record from the aircraft table.
5. Using the tables created in Step 1, write a SQL query that edits a record from the aircraft table.
6. Using the SELECT query you created in Step 2, add a WHERE clause that limits the aircraft records retrieved to only aircraft that have two engines (note: you may have to revise your aircraft table to include a field for the number of engines).

7. Create a SQL query that selects records from your mechanics table, and add a WHERE clause that selects only records in which the mechanic's last name starts with the letter "S".

8. Write a SELECT query that retrieves records from the aircraft table and from the maintenance table, so that each maintenance record for each aircraft is included.

9. Write a SELECT query that retrieves the total number of maintenance actions performed on each aircraft. Name the field retrieving the value "CountOfMaintenanceActions".

Building a Database with Enterprise Manager

In order to build database support for our OMPGame Web application, we will use the SQL Server Enterprise Manager to create a new database and add tables to it. We also will demonstrate how to build a database diagram, a visual map of the relationships we're going to establish between tables in our database.

CREATING A NEW DATABASE

1. If SQL Server Enterprise Manager is not already open, open it. Open nodes until you have the Databases node open. Right-click the Database node. You should see the shortcut menu shown in Figure 7.2.

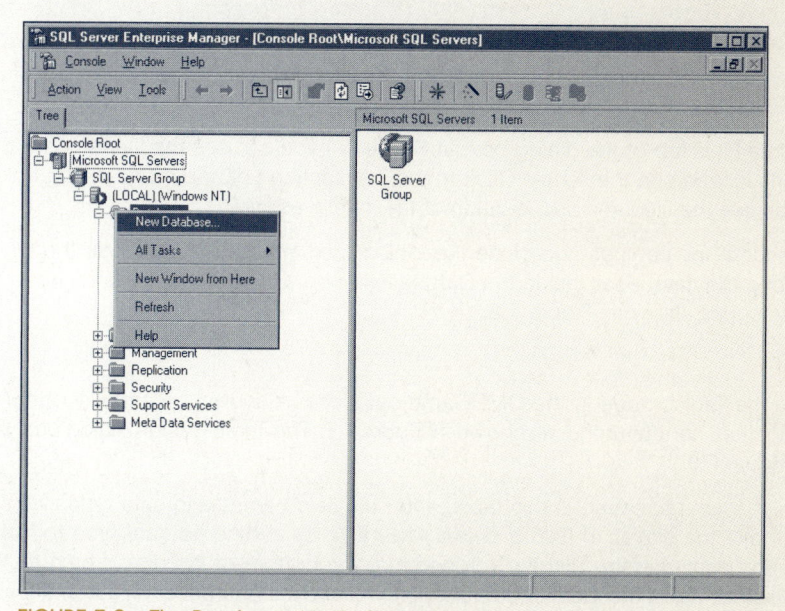

FIGURE 7.2   The Databases Node Shortcut Menu

2. Choose New Database. The Database Properties dialog box should open as shown in Figure 7.3. Enter "OMPGame" as the name of the database.

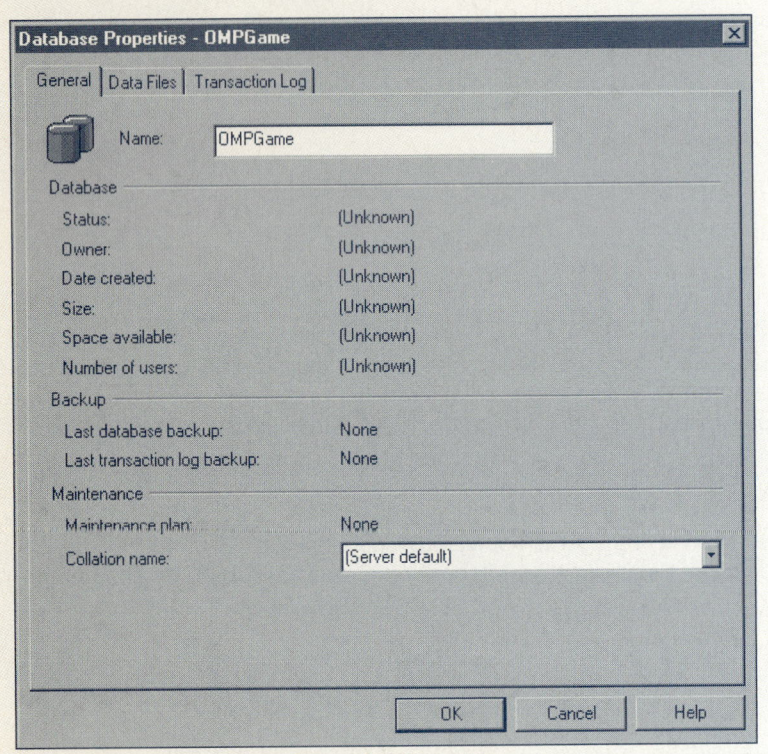

FIGURE 7.3 The Database Properties Dialog Box

3. Click to the Data Files tab of the dialog box. In Figure 7.4 you can see the filename for the database file and its location on the server. Click to the Transaction Log tab of the dialog box. In Figure 7.5 you can see the filename and location of the log file as well.

4. Click OK to accept the settings and close the dialog box. You should now see the OMPGame database among the databases inside the Databases node. Open the OMPGame node and you should see the nodes shown in Figure 7.6.

CREATING NEW TABLES

1. Right-click on the Tables node in the OMPGame database. A shortcut menu will open. Choose New Table from the shortcut menu, as shown in Figure 7.7. The Table Design dialog box will open, as shown in Figure 7.8.

2. We'll build the players table first. In this table, enter the field names and data types we specified in Table 7.1. Make the player_id field a primary key field by setting its data type to "int" with a length of "4" and changing its "identity" property (at the bottom of the dialog box) to "Yes", as shown in Figure 7.9. Using the Identity data property means the database will automatically increment the field value whenever a new record is inserted.

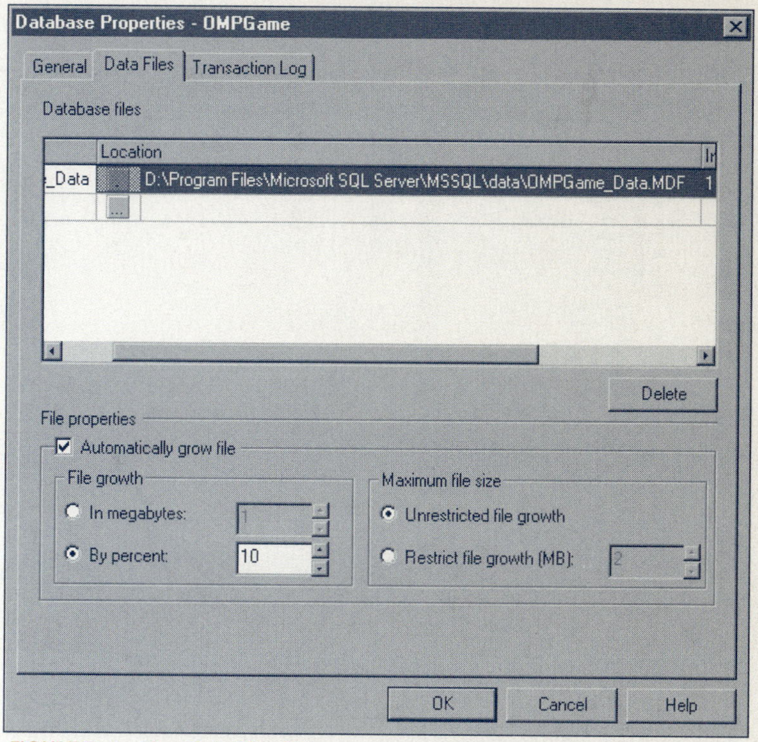

FIGURE 7.4 The Data Files Tab

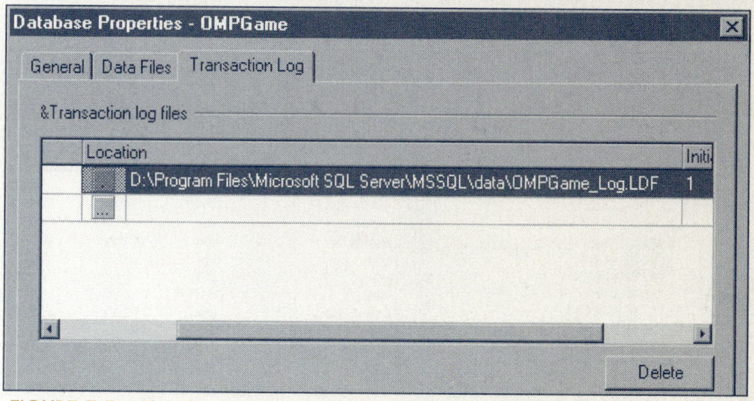

FIGURE 7.5 The Transaction Log Tab

CHAPTER 7 Databases and SQL

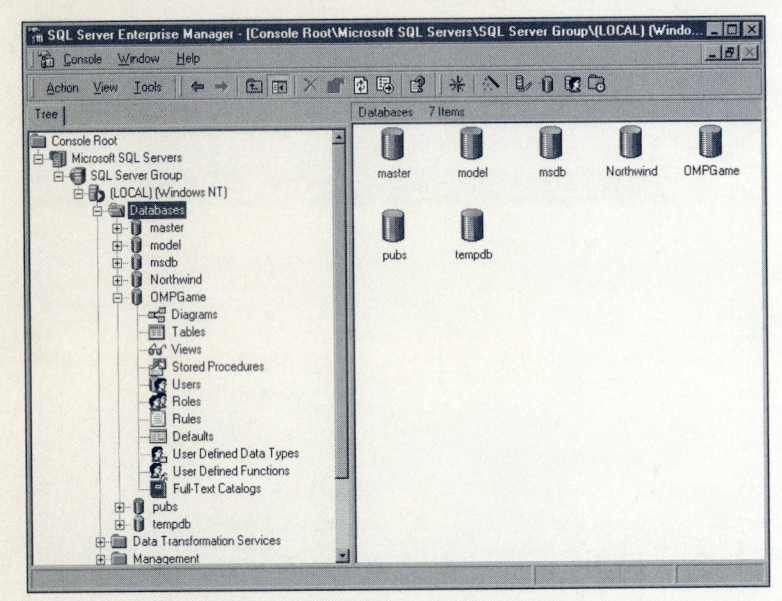

FIGURE 7.6 The Nodes Available in the OMPGame Database

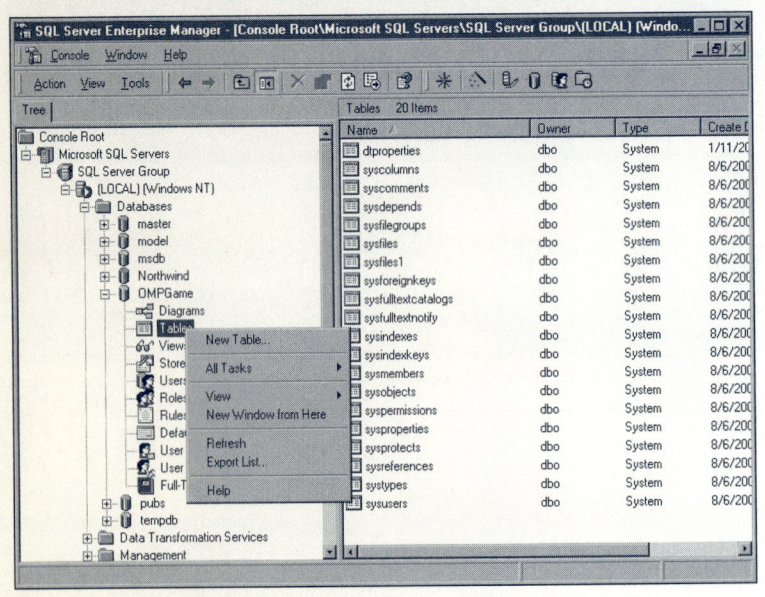

FIGURE 7.7 The Tables Shortcut Menu

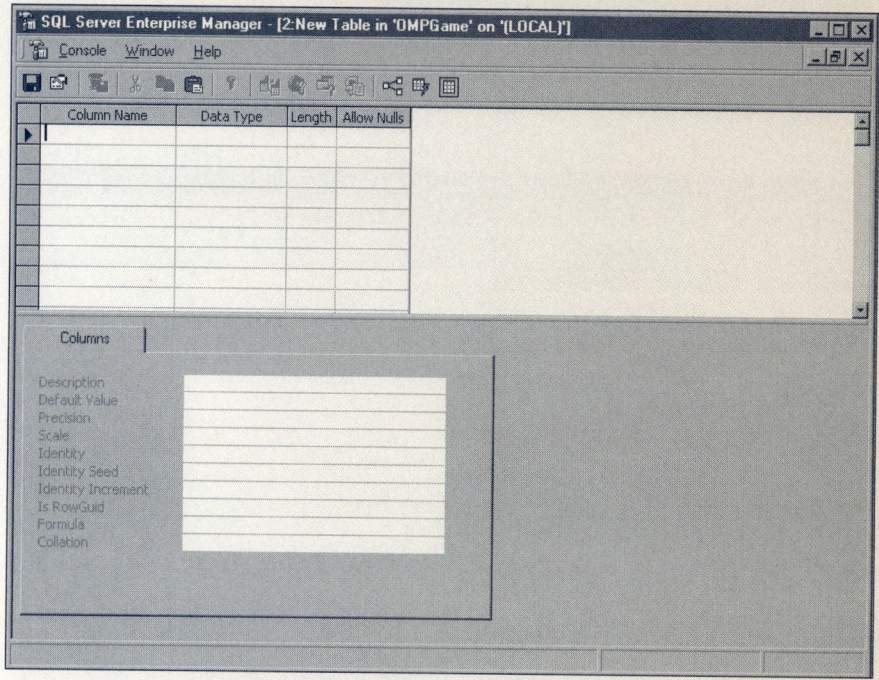

FIGURE 7.8 The Table Design Dialog Box

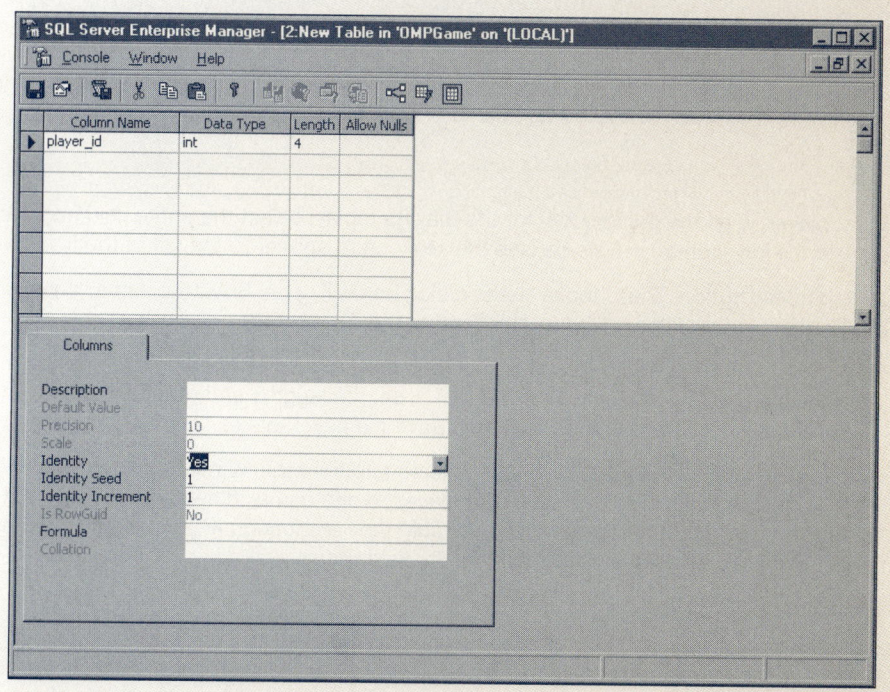

FIGURE 7.9 Creating the Primary Key Field for the Players Table

3. Add the rest of the fields specified in Table 7.1 A quick way to do this is to enter the field names first, and then go back and modify data types and field lengths all at once. Leave Allow Nulls "Yes" (checked) for all fields except the player_id field. Figure 7.10 shows some of the fields entered for the new table.

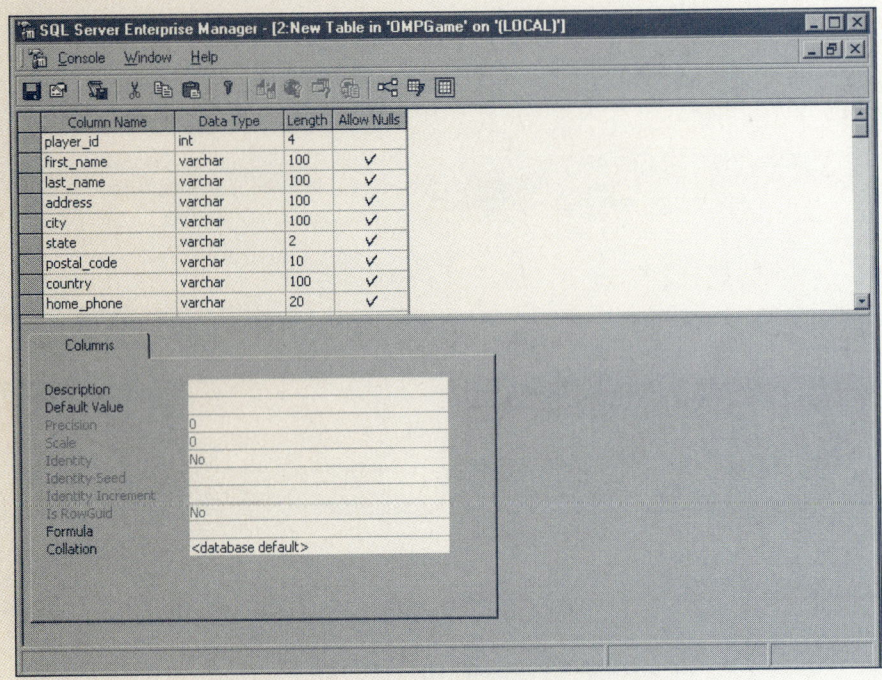

FIGURE 7.10 The Fields in the New Table

4. To set player_id as the primary key for the players tables, select the entire field and click the button with the key icon on it. This causes the key icon to appear to the left of the field name.

5. Click the Save button. The Choose Name dialog box will open. Enter the name "players" and click OK. The new table will be saved as "players" in the Tables node.

6. Right-click on the Tables node again and start the process of creating another table. Enter the field names and data types shown in Table 7.2, set the lengths and other properties as specified, and set the game_id field as a primary key. Save the new table as "games".

7. Right-click on the Tables node again and create another table named "games_played" as specified in Table 7.3. Make sure to include the player_id and game_id fields as integer data types, but don't reset their Identity properties. In this table they are foreign key fields and should not increment themselves automatically like an Identity field will.

BUILDING A DATABASE DIAGRAM

A database diagram is a visual representation of tables in a database and the relationships between them. Note that when you create relationships in this manner, you are actually creating a constraint on the database, meaning the database itself will now contain rules governing the manipulation of records in the affected tables. This is different from associating tables with one another in SQL queries with joins, which place conditions on the query as it runs but otherwise leaves the database unaffected.

Hands On Project

1. Right-click on the Database Diagrams node and choose New Database Diagram from the shortcut menu that appears. The Create Database Diagram Wizard will open, as shown in Figure 7.11.

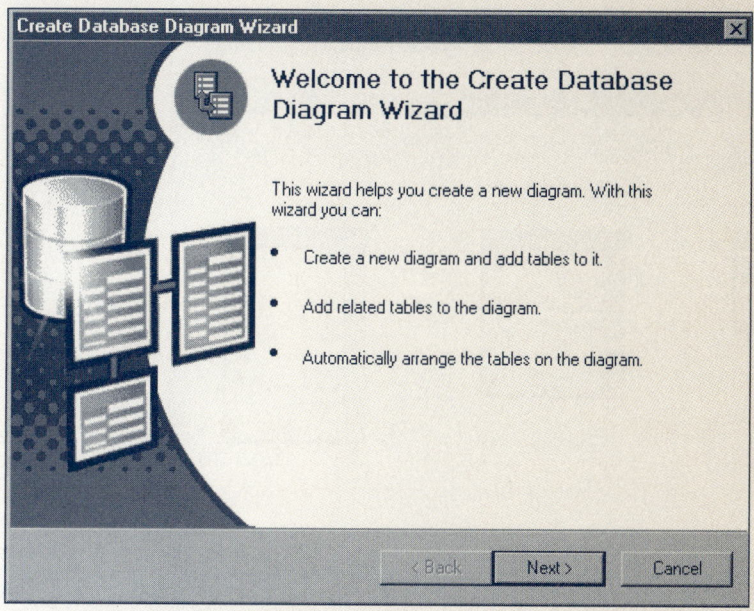

FIGURE 7.11 The Create Database Diagram Wizard, First Screen

2. The first screen of the Wizard is just information, so click Next.

3. On the second screen, add the games, games_played, and players tables from the Available tables side to the Tables to add to diagram side by selecting the tables and clicking the Add button, as shown in Figure 7.12.

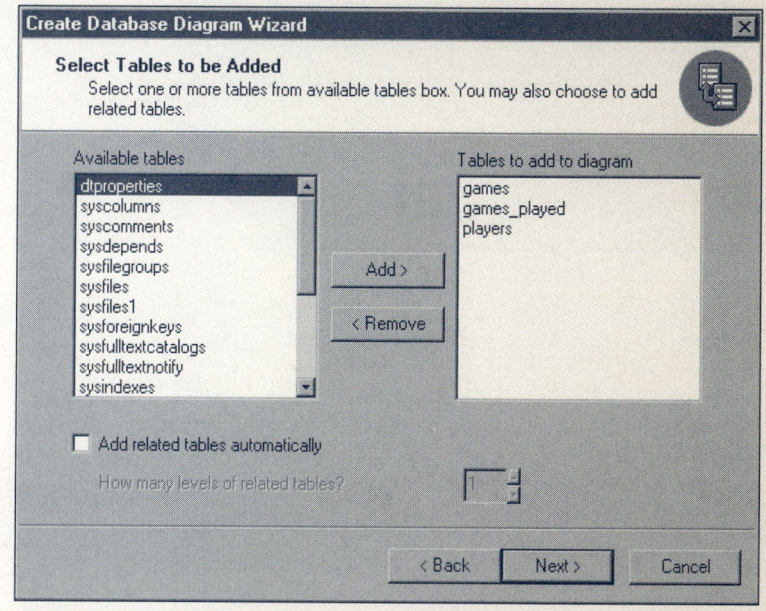

FIGURE 7.12 The Second Screen of the Wizard

CHAPTER 7 Databases and SQL

4. Click Next to go to the third screen. This screen is essentially information as well, so click Finish. The new database diagram will be displayed, as shown in Figure 7.13.

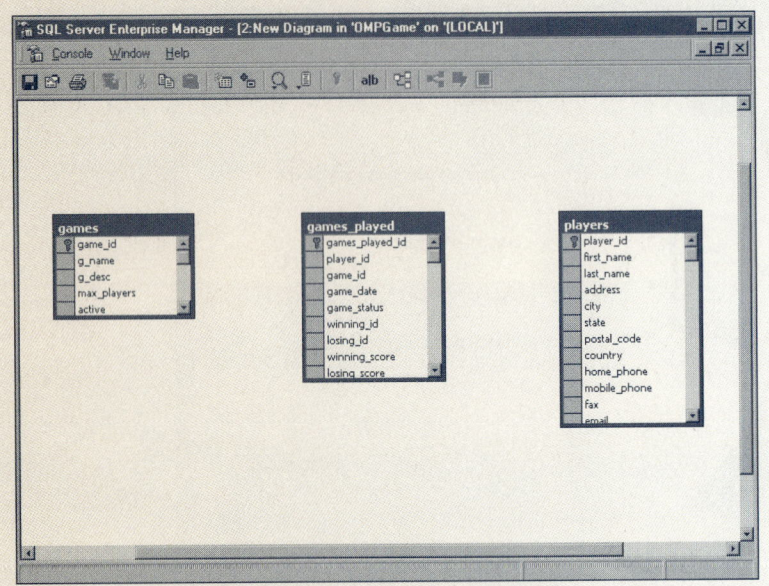

FIGURE 7.13 The New Database Diagram

5. Now it's time to establish relationships between the tables. There will be a one-to-many relationship between players and games_played, so click on the players.player_id field and drag it to the games_played.player_id field. The Create Relationship dialog box will open, as shown in Figure 7.14.

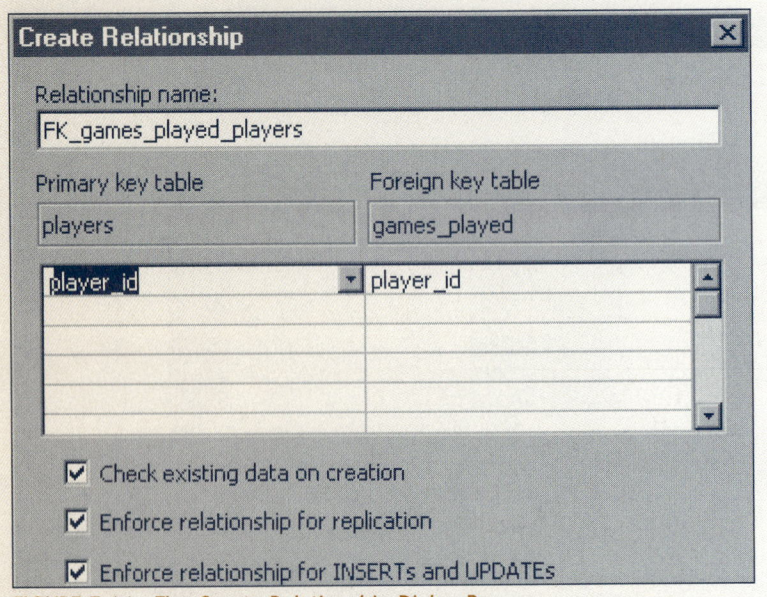

FIGURE 7.14 The Create Relationship Dialog Box

Hands On Project

6. The settings are fine as is. There are no existing data, but if there were, the data would be checked for anomalies and exceptions would be generated if any were found (such as "child" records without parent records). We won't be replicating the database, so the second setting doesn't matter. The third setting, "Enforce relationships for INSERTs and UPDATEs", allows us to make a rule in the database that when we make record modifications to parent records, such as deleting a parent record, all associated child records would be modified (deleted, in this case) as well. These are referential integrity constraints, and while we might want to set them once we're completely done with design work on the database, for now we'll leave them unchecked. Click OK to accept the settings and close the dialog box. You should see a line representing the relationship between the two tables now, as shown in Figure 7.15.

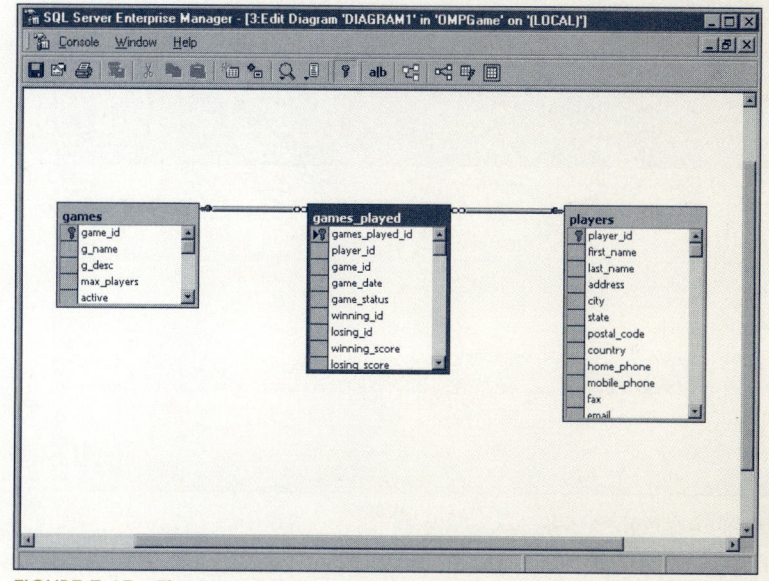

FIGURE 7.15   The New Relationship in the Database Diagram

7. Create a similar relationship between games.game_id and games_played.game_id.
8. Click the Save button and choose the default name for the database diagram. The new diagram is now saved in your database. Close the diagram.

Creating Views and Queries in SQL Server

SQL queries are the statements that perform record actions such as SELECT, INSERT, UPDATE, and DELETE. SQL Server Views are like queries and show the results of SELECT queries. There is a visual Query Designer in SQL Server that helps you write the appropriate query for the view. When you choose New View, the Query Designer opens, and when you run the query, the results are displayed as a View.

Although our SQL queries will run from the Web application (as SQL statements attached to ADO.Net objects, which we'll explorer in Chapter 8), the Query Designer in SQL Server is very helpful in writing them before we use them in the application. It's good practice to run some sample views or queries in SQL Server to ensure we're getting the right results before running those queries programmatically, especially if the queries change or delete multiple records.

CREATE VIEWS

1. Right-click the Views node to display the shortcut menu, and choose New View. The New View dialog box will open, as shown in Figure 7.16.

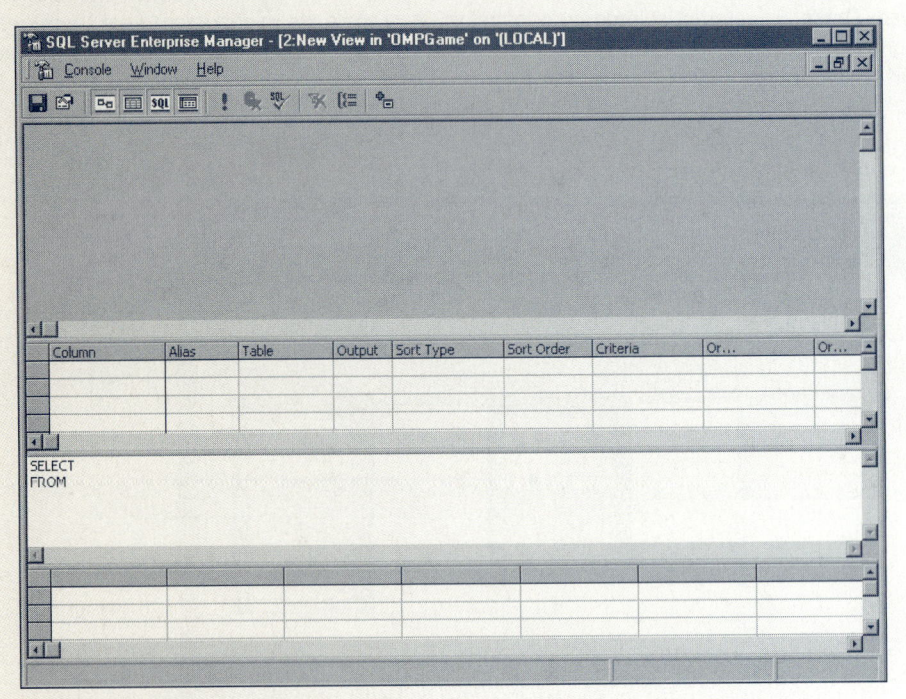

FIGURE 7.16 The New View Dialog Box

2. Click the Add Table button to display the Add Table dialog box, as shown in Figure 7.17.

3. Select the players table and click the Add button to add it to the query editor. Select the player_id, screen_name, username, and password fields to add them to the query grid, as shown in Figure 7.18. Adding these fields to the grid means they will be shown in the results (unless you unclick the Output column for that field).

4. The Query Designer allows us to visually create the query required to show several fields from the players table's records as a result (the results are shown in the Results pane) and shows the SQL code it is writing immediately. We can copy that code and use it later from VS.Net in our ASP.Net Web application. Here is the code:

```
SELECT player_id, screen_name, username, password
FROM dbo.players
```

5. As you see, the Query Designer is a useful tool for quickly extracting the SQL code we need to run from our Web application. There's no need to permanently save this view now, but it might be useful in the future, so save it with the default name "VIEW1".

Hands On Project

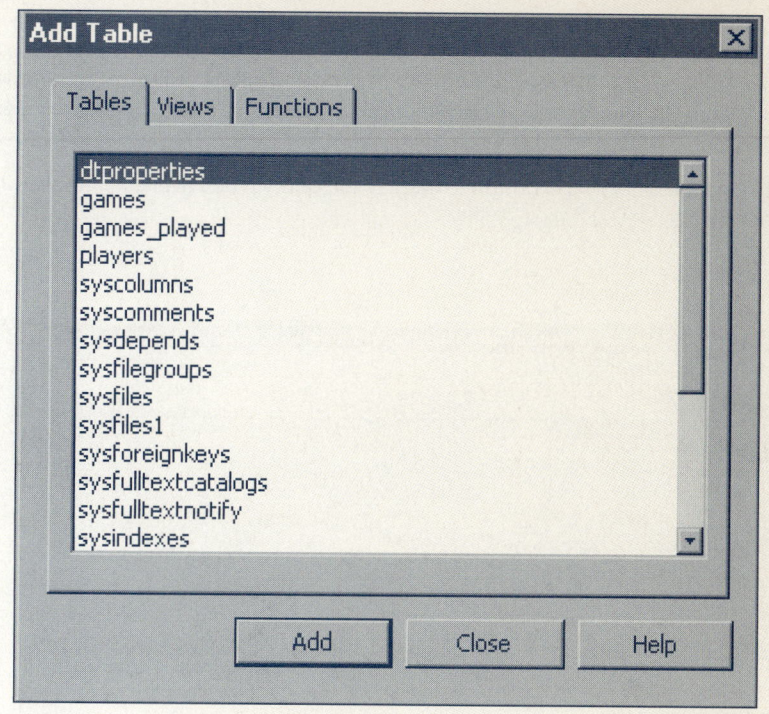

FIGURE 7.17 The Add Table Dialog Box

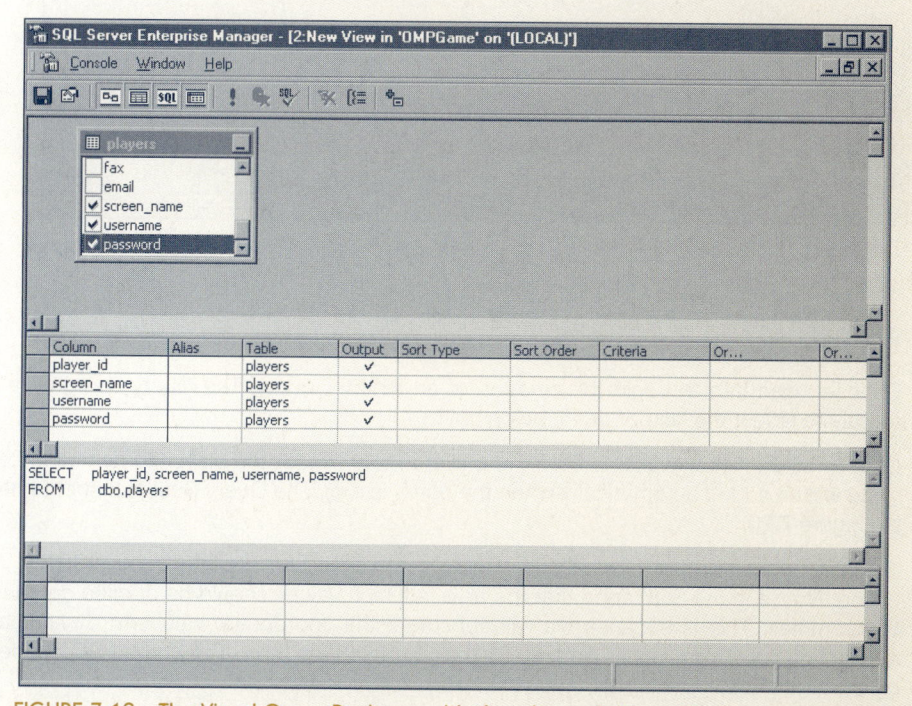

FIGURE 7.18 The Visual Query Designer with the players Table Added

CHAPTER 7 Databases and SQL

6. We also will have the need for inserting records in the players table when new players register. We can use the Query Designer again, but this time we start as though we're creating a query instead of a View. Click on the Tables node to select it, then right-click the players table to display the shortcut menu. Choose Open Table|Query from the shortcut menu. The Query Designer will open again, showing the players table.

7. Click the Change Query Type button to display the query types available, as shown in Figure 7.19.

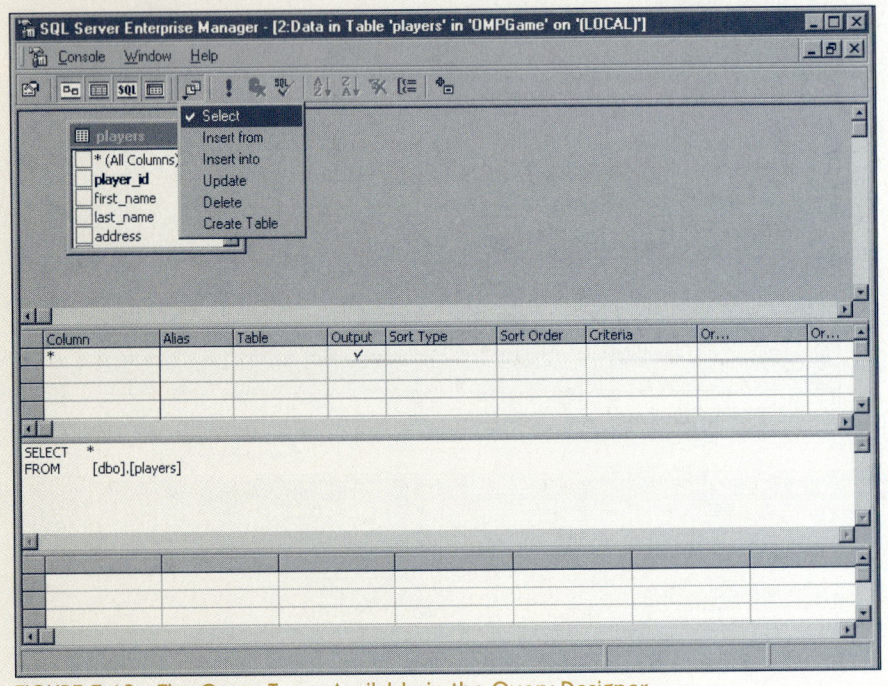

FIGURE 7.19 The Query Types Available in the Query Designer

8. Choose Insert into to begin the creation of an INSERT query. The Query Designer will change slightly to reflect the kind of query being built.

9. Choose all the fields available from the players table except the player_id field (this field and its value will be added automatically when the query is run). The Query Designer should now resemble Figure 7.20.

10. The SQL code is written for us. Once again, we can save it for use later in our ASP.Net Web application. Notice in the SQL code that the area in which values should be applied contains nothing but commas. This is because we will substitute the appropriate values in dynamically as the application runs, from values entered by the user in a Web form. The current SQL code is shown on the next page.

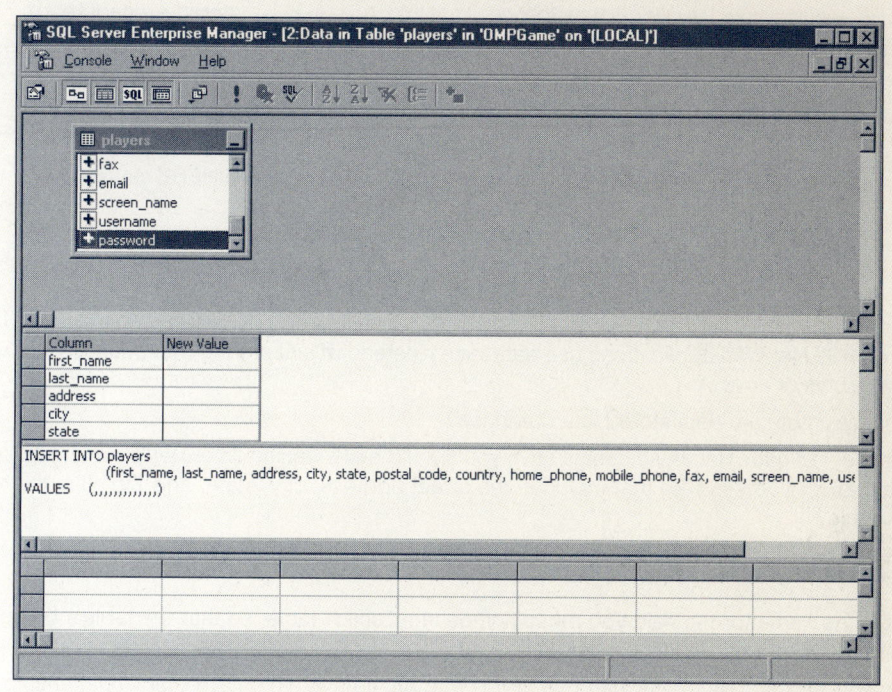

FIGURE 7.20 The INSERT INTO Query in the Query Designer

```
INSERT INTO players
(first_name, last_name, address, city, state, postal_code, country,
home_phone, mobile_phone, fax, screen_name, username, password, email)
VALUES (,,,,,,,,,,,,,,)
```

Database Structures   Database applications are made up of a number of basic structures, and from those structures many different types of database applications can be built. To store an individual chunk of data, the "field" is used. An example of the data stored in a single field is "LastName". Good database design dictates that data in fields should be atomic, meaning that you can't reasonably divide the data into smaller chunks. If you had stored both the first and last name in a single field (named "FullName", for instance), your data would not be atomic and would violate the rules of good database design.

Fields are connected to each other in rows (records) in a database structure called a table, and tables are connected to each other with relationships. You can think of the data in a single field, in multiple rows, as a column (much like a column in a spreadsheet). Not all tables in a database need to be connected for the database to be termed "relational." The basic structure of fields, records, and tables makes up most of what you need in a database, and the other components of a database application, such as queries, forms, reports, and stored procedures, are tools used for working with the data.

Key Terms

DELETE
equi-join
field
foreign key
INSERT
many-to-many
one-to-many
one-to-one
outer join
primary key
record
relational database
SELECT
stored procedure
Structured Query Language (SQL)
table
UPDATE
WHERE clause

Review Questions

1. Why do ASP.Net Web applications use databases instead of just storing the required data as application variables or arrays?
2. In what structure are data stored in a database?
3. One aspect of good database design says you should never design a field with many data elements in it, such as an address field that includes the street address, city, state, and Zip all in the same field. Why is this?
4. What is a primary key field, and what properties does it possess that make it valuable in designing a table?
5. What is the name for the field you must include in a "child" table, so that the table's parent table will have a one-to-many relationship with it?
6. When you design a database with two tables that must have a many-to-many relationship, you must design a third table called a junction table. What fields must this junction table have to support the many-to-many relationship?
7. What is the syntax for a SQL SELECT query?
8. What is the syntax for a SQL INSERT query?
9. What is the syntax for a SQL UPDATE query?
10. What is the syntax for a SQL DELETE query?
11. What is the syntax for a WHERE clause affecting only one field?
12. What is the syntax for a WHERE clause affecting two fields, if conditions for both fields must be met?
13. What is the syntax for a WHERE clause affecting two fields, if conditions for either field may be met?
14. What is the syntax for an aggregate query that produces the sum value for a particular field?

Introduction to ADO.Net

CHAPTER 8

LEARNING OBJECTIVES

Upon completion of this chapter, you will be able to:

1. Explain how ADO.Net and ASP.Net are related.
2. Describe the major ADO.Net structures and objects.
3. Make a connection to a SQL Server database from an ASP.Net application.
4. Retrieve records from a SQL server database.
5. Bind records to ASP.Net Web Server controls.
6. Build a registration and login process for a Web application.
7. Build a Web application that supports multiplayer games.

INTRODUCTION

ADO stands for Active Data Objects, Microsoft's technology for accessing data via a standard methodology. ADO.Net is the latest iteration of this technology and is designed to function well in the .Net Framework environment. Basically, ADO.Net is a set of objects you can call from your ASP.Net application (and others) that allow you to retrieve and manipulate records from a data store (such as SQL Server).

ADO.Net has been upgraded (from ADO) in such a way that you can work with the retrieved records in almost the same way that you would work with the data store directly, without the overhead of constant connections. Unlike previous versions, ADO.Net has objects representing not just sets of records, but entire tables and the relationships between them. This makes it convenient to bind ADO.Net objects to controls in your Web applications and use them as though your application were a database application.

The process you'll use in your Web application to work with database records involves making a connection to the database, retrieving the records you want to work with, binding them to specific controls, reading the records and making changes to them (or adding or deleting them), and feeding their results back to the database. There are ADO.Net objects, properties, and methods that assist in every step. In this chapter we cover ADO.Net and the objects it exposes, how to make connections to a SQL Server database, how to retrieve records, how to bind the controls, and how to make the desired changes.

In this chapter, we'll make a full-fledged ASP.Net Web application that plays Blackjack, but we'll hold off making it multiplayer until Chapter 10. Even so, the project to make the application takes up most of the chapter and involves lots of coding, so we don't include any Quick Check Questions or Exercises at the end of the chapter. You'll get plenty of exercise just coding the application, and plenty of practice with the concepts we cover in this chapter as well.

Data Providers

In Chapter 7 we discussed databases, how they are structured, and how the data they hold in such a structure lend themselves to many common ecommerce applications. Data in databases are actually stored in files, of course, and can be located on any accessible server, not just the local machine. To reach, retrieve, and manipulate the data, you use a data provider.

Database Engines

Microsoft's SQL Server contains a database engine, as does Microsoft Access (the Microsoft Jet Database Engine). Microsoft also provides a desktop version of SQL Server called the Microsoft Desktop Engine (MSDE). Often you will have a choice of database engine to use with any particular application you are building and can make your choice based on factors such as speed and efficiency of the engine for your particular requirements.

Middleware

You may have heard of applications discussed in terms of the number of "tiers" they utilize, such as two-tier, three-tier, and n-tier (n being an arbitrary number). The meaning of the term *tier* can be illustrated by examining the tiers making up a three-tier application.

In a three-tier application, the tier closest to the data is called the data tier. At this level are the database file and engine, and they take care of managing the physical storage of data, performing searches on the data, and so forth. On the other end is the presentation tier. The presentation tier consists of the applications (such as a browser) and rendered screens seen by the user. The presentation tier is responsible for displaying data to and for accepting input from the user.

In the middle is the business tier. In this tier your programming logic accepts input from the user, performs data processing, retrieves data from the data tier, and updates data back to the data tier. The business tier also contains **ADO.Net** and the data-oriented objects required to access data from the data tier, such as data connections, data adapters, and data sets. Software running anywhere between the data tier and the presentation tier is called middleware.

Communications between Tiers

When you enter data into a form on a Web page and click the Submit button, your data are formatted in the HTTP protocol. When your request (along with your data) reaches the server, the HTTP message you've sent is read (parsed) and the relevant data are then able to be used by the server, whether to simply fulfill a request for a page or to conduct more elaborate operations.

By the same token, when your Web application programming needs to get some records out of a database, it must use the proper protocol and format to "talk" to the database engine. First, it must make (or have open) a connection to the database. Most databases respond when the appropriate connection string is sent. A connection string consists of enough information to identify the database file and location, the driver to use, a username and password (if necessary), and so on. Not all database connections are required to have the same pieces of data, so the connection string is like the recipient's address you put on a letter. It may be formatted differently for delivery to different countries, but it is an address nonetheless. For example, you might use something such as the following to connect to a SQL database:

```
Dim dbConn As SqlConnection = New SqlConnection("Data
Source=localhost;Integrated Security=SSPI;" & "Initial
Catalog=mybusinessDB")
```

Notice the string (starting with "Data Source..."). This is the connection string. Whenever you need to get data from a database inside your application, you must know the correct connection string to use (although in Visual Studio.Net there are tools that help you build connection strings visually). And keep in mind that opening and maintaining data connections use quite a bit of overhead. Always close your data connections when you are done with them.

The actual retrieval, editing, and deletion of data from a database are done with SQL commands (SELECT, INSERT, UPDATE, DELETE) stored as strings as well. By manipulating ADO.Net objects that contain SQL commands, you can get any data records you like, process the data in them within your application, and format your resulting data for changes or storage back into the database. You can even bind the records you've retrieved to controls in the presentation layer, so that the user can make changes directly to the records as though they were using an ordinary desktop database application. This accounts for the power inherent in ADO.Net, and makes it a valuable addition to your applications capabilities. In the next few sections we'll discuss the capabilities of ADO.Net in much greater detail.

ADO.Net

Data are stored in databases in tables as rows of field values. For example, in a record from the players table we created in the last chapter, we would expect to find a First Name value in the first_name field if one had been entered when the player registered. If no value had been entered in the first_name field, we would expect that field to be NULL.

So if we retrieved this value from a Web application (and it didn't happen to be NULL), we would have a string of characters representing a first name. However, if we received this value alone, without any particular context or structure, it would have much less value than if we retrieved it with context and structure.

The point being made here is that it is often valuable to retrieve whole sets of records, along with their field names, and to work with them in a structured way. This is not an unusual requirement, and Microsoft has done quite a bit of work to make this possible. The result is Active Data Objects (ADO), of which ADO.Net is the latest iteration.

Like ASP.Net, ADO.Net is a set of classes from which objects can be derived. The classes include such things as Connections, Commands, DataAdapters, DataReaders, DataSets, DataTables, and so on. As you might guess from their names, the objects derived from these classes are optimized for retrieving and manipulating records with context and structure very similar to the database from which they are pulled. And these objects have properties and methods that let you create whole new database-like structures programmatically, inside your application. This section discusses ADO.Net objects and how to use them to retrieve and manipulate records from inside your ASP.Net Web application. Illustration 8.1 shows how the ADO.Net classes are related and how they work together.

Making Database Connections

ADO.Net Connection objects allow you to make a connection to a database in your Web application. Connections are made with connection strings, short strings of name-value pairs that identify the database file, location, username and password, and other data required to connect to and use a database. There are two types of Connection object available: the SqlConnection and the OleDbConnection. If you have SQL Server 7.0 or better available to your

ADO.Net

```
ADO.Net Classes – Functions, Properties, and Methods

Connection Object                    DataReader
 • Makes DB Connection                • Reads Data Stream
 • With ConnectionString

                                     DataAdapter uses Command
Command Object                        • Does SELECT
 • Implements Commands                • Does INSERT
 • CommandText                        • Does UPDATE
 • CommandType                        • Does DELETE
 • Connection                         • Fills DataSet
 • Parameters
 • ExecuteReader                     DataSet Contains
 • ExecuteNonQuery                    • DataTable
 • ExecuteScalar                      • DataRelation
                                      • DataRow
                                      • DataView
                                      • Data
```

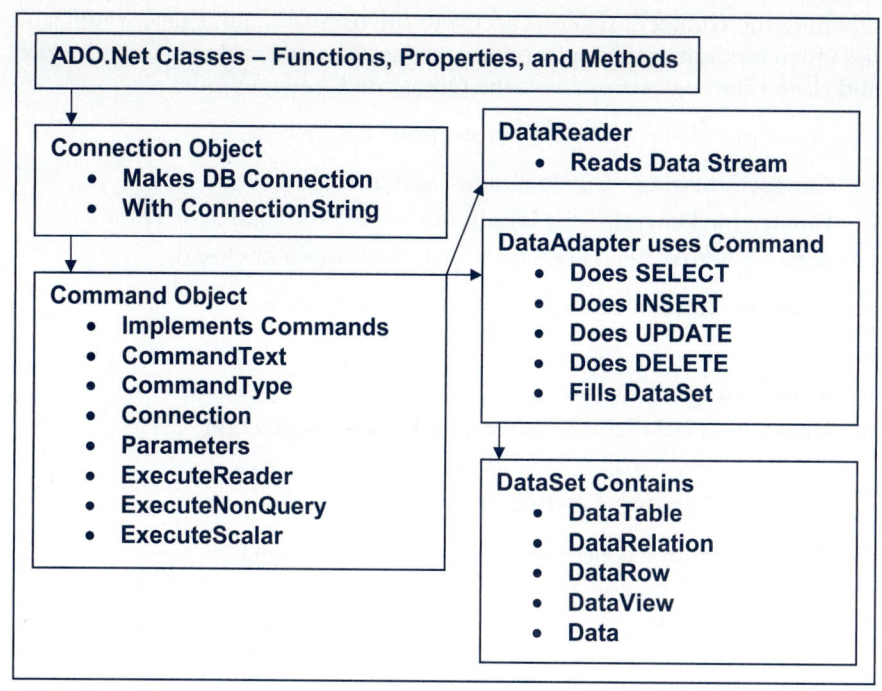

ILLUSTRATION 8.1   ADO.Net Classes

application, use the SqlConnection. Both connection object types are available in the VS.Net Toolbox when you are working in a Web application on a Web form.

The SqlConnection Object

As its name implies, the **SqlConnection** object is useful for making connections to SQL Server databases. Think of the connection as the same process you use when you log into and open a database file directly. The program you use to open the database file (such as SQL Server's Enterprise Manager) needs to know the name of the file and where it is located, and if a username/password is required, it needs to know that as well.

The SqlConnection object uses a connection string to connect to the database file, and the connection string contains the information just mentioned. It represents a unique session to a SQL Server database. Once it makes the connection, commands can be executed against the database file, in much the same way that you might manually retrieve or change records using Enterprise Manager. The results of both types of database manipulation may be the same, but the use of ADO.Net objects lets you perform database operations programmatically rather than manually.

When you add a SqlConnection object to a Web form, you are telling your application to create an instance of the object from the SqlConnection class.

Opening the connection allows access to the database and is performed with the Open method of the SqlConnection class. You must always explicitly open and close your connections with the Open and Close methods.

Important properties of the SqlConnection class include

- **ConnectionString**—the data to be used to make a connection.
- **ConnectionTimeout**—the length of time to try to make the connection.
- **State**—whether the connection is currently open or closed.

Important methods of the SqlConnection class include

- **Open**—opens the connection.
- **Close**—closes the connection.
- **Dispose**—releases the resources used by the connection.

Running Database Commands

Once a connection has been made, you can run commands against the database. Commands include SELECT, INSERT, UPDATE, and DELETE; as you may have guessed, these are defined by the SQL statements we learned in the last chapter. The **SqlCommand** and OleDbCommand objects are used to run commands, and are available in the Toolbox as well. Use the SqlCommand object if you have SQL Server 7.0 or better available.

There are several types of Execute method available with the SqlCommand object: ExecuteReader (returns a DataReader object), ExecuteScalar (returns a single value), ExecuteNonQuery (returns nothing but performs the action specified), and ExecuteXMLReader (returns an XMLReader object). When you run a command against a database, use the appropriate Execute method for the type of query you are performing. For example, if you run a SELECT statement that returns records, you'll want to use the ExecuteReader method.

The DataReader

A **DataReader** object is a forward-only stream of rows from a data source. When you only need to read records rapidly, in a forward-only fashion, the DataReader is very handy. You can access each record and each field (column), and also translate the data you retrieve into the appropriate data type. There are DataReaders specifically for SQL as well as OLE DB databases.

The DataAdapter

If you use the SqlCommand object, you can run commands against a database and you can create a DataReader object that allows you to read through records, but suppose you need to work with records from a database as though your application were a database application itself? Then you'll want to use a **DataAdapter** object. This object allows you to retrieve the entire structure of a database and manipulate it locally, and then update the remote database.

The DataAdapter uses Connection and Command objects (entered into **SelectCommand, InsertCommand, UpdateCommand,** and **DeleteCommand** properties of the DataAdapter object) to make a connection, retrieve, and manipulate records. If you fill a DataSet object from a DataAdapter, you can bind the DataSet of controls on your Web form, enabling users to easily work with the records.

DataAdapters have several methods for working with DataSets, such as Fill to put records in the DataSet and Update to send record changes from the DataSet back to the database. Once you have your records in a DataSet, you can use the properties, methods, and collections of the DataSet to work with records as though they were in a database. For example, there is a collection of **DataTable** objects that represents tables of records in your DataSet, and you can establish relationships between these DataTable objects (just like you would do between tables in an ordinary database) with DataRelation objects. All in all, the DataSet objects and its collections provide a very rich technology for working with database records.

The DataSet and Lower-Level ADO.Net Objects

The DataSet object is a memory-resident representation of the records (and their relationships) that were retrieved by the DataAdapter and filled into the DataSet. What this means is that the DataSet is not simply a set of records, but contains a collection of DataRelations (representing the relationships between tables), a collection of DataTables (representing the tables retrieved), and an ExtendedProperties collection (in which you can place special information such as the SELECT statement that retrieved the records).

The DataSet is also the parent object for each DataTable object in it. DataTable objects have their own properties and collections, such as the **DataRow** collection (which contains DataRow objects), the PrimaryKey object, and the DataColumn collection (which contains DataColumn objects).

The DataSet is independent of any data sources from which it retrieved data, and may contain data from the local application as well (data records and other data objects you have created programmatically while your application is running).

Creating a DataSet from a DataAdapter

All in all, ADO.Net contains enough objects and collections to provide a very rich set of functionality for working with records. Within a DataSet, you essentially have the objects and capabilities to work with what you've retrieved as though it were a mini-database application by itself. You can instantiate a DataSet and then fill it using the Fill method of your DataAdapter object (you can retrieve records for your DataAdapter using the SelectCommand property, which is in turn a Command object that contains a SQL SELECT statement). Essentially, the procedure works like this in your code:

1. Instantiate a Connection object (SQL or OLE DB) and apply the appropriate connection string to the Connection object's ConnectionString property.

2. Instantiate a DataAdapter object and apply the appropriate SQL SELECT, INSERT, UPDATE, and DELETE strings to the SelectCommand, InsertCommand, UpdateCommand, and DeleteCommands properties of the DataAdapter. Doing this will automatically create the underlying Command objects.

3. Instantiate a DataSet object and fill it using the Fill method of your DataAdapter object.

Discussion—ADO.Net

ADO.Net is a set of classes from which objects can be derived for use in ASP.Net Web applications. These objects provide an efficient mechanism for retrieving and manipulating records from databases. The objects include a Connection and a Command object, for making connections to databases and running commands (such as SELECT and UPDATE) on them. There is also a DataReader object for simply navigating through records and reading them.

For more elaborate manipulation of database records, there is the DataAdapter object, which can be used to retrieve records and place them in a DataSet. The DataSet is a high-level object that acts like an entire database represented as an object with collections of child objects for tables, relations, rows, and columns (the DataTable, DataRelation, DataRow, and DataColumn objects). When you use a DataAdapter to fill a DataSet, you then have the capability to work with records from the database as though you were directly manipulating the database (not just a set of records from one of its tables) and you also have the ability to programmatically create new tables, relations, rows, and columns in your application, as well as the ability to update the database later from your DataSet.

OMPGame Business Process

In Chapter 7 we began creating tables for our OMPGame, and we made some notes about the requirements for an application supported by this database.

Now it's time for us to be specific about the actual business process we want people to use and what screens they should see as they use our application to play games online.

Registration

Before players can log in and begin playing games, they must be registered. This means the application must treat all users who come to the site as anonymous until they either log in (if they've previously registered) or until they register. If they register, they should be automatically logged in at that time, but on subsequent visits they should be able to log in from the very first page they see.

If unregistered users (or users who are not logged in) attempt to navigate to any page that is reserved for registered/logged-in players, they should receive a warning message and be presented with the registration/login forms. The registration page should contain all the fields required for registration and should use validation methods to ensure required fields are filled in and screen_name, username, and password fields contain entries of the proper length before allowing them to be entered in the database.

Although we won't do it in this application, the registration process is ideal for collecting billing information and processing payments before allowing users to complete their registration (if this were a subscription-type service). Another handy feature would be to have the system send an email to the player who successfully registered, noting their username and password, as well as their screen name.

Login

Login processes typically start as a small block on all pages (perhaps only appearing when the user is not yet logged in) that has username and password fields and a submit button. There could be a bit of text that says something like "Login Here!" and labels for username ("Username"), password ("Password"), and the submit button ("Login"). Because people are becoming much more familiar with logging in, there's less and less need to explicitly label each textbox or button.

People do expect to see a nice warning message if they enter their usernames or passwords incorrectly, something that tells them the problem and also gives them another way to fix it (such as "Please call us to retrieve your password"). And when they log in correctly, it is helpful to tell them so. Finally, people like to see an explicit "Logout" button or link, even though they sometimes understand that simply closing their browser will log them out.

Game Selection and Start Notification

Once players are logged in, they will expect to see a list of the games available for play, and a list of other players looking to play one of the games. These two things could be separate screens, so that the player would first choose which game to play, and then choose to play him/herself or to play someone else who's looking for a partner.

This brings about an interesting situation, because while a player can log into the OMPGame application and indicate that he/she wants to play a certain game, how will the player be notified that another player is ready to play that game with him/her? The player could just sit there, repeatedly clicking a button to find out if someone else is ready, but few people will want to do that, not knowing if or when someone else will log in and accept his/her challenge.

The issue is that, with a Web-based online game system, there's no practical way for the server to communicate with the user unless the user initiates the communication. Just because someone has logged in to your Web application doesn't mean you can send that person a message anytime you want. You can only send an HttpResponse when someone submits an HttpRequest.

Therefore, we'll add a Javascript function to the Web form that can be used when the player selects whether he/she wants to play individually or with someone else. The Javascript function will automatically resubmit the form to itself on a periodic basis, each time checking to see whether someone else has accepted the challenge. If the challenge has been accepted, the Web form will beep and flash when it reappears, notifying the user that the game has started and telling him/her how much time until his/her turn is up.

In order to keep the material in this chapter reasonably simple, we'll add features for supporting more than one player in Chapter 10, and perform other optimizations to our OMPGame application as well. Note that often the first step to building a more complex application is to build basic features first and refine them later.

Game Play

When we build our two-player system in Chapter 10, we'll use Javascript to make the user's browser return to the server every so often and find out if the other player has responded yet. As the user takes a turn, he/she will make selections on a Web form and submit. The application tracks turns as they are taken, revises the score, determines if a win or loss has occurred, and readies itself for the next turn or notifies users of a Win or Loss. Once a user has taken a turn, another Javascript counts down the time allowed for the other player to take a turn. Depending upon the rules of the game (and whether it is operating in multiplayer mode), when the Javascript submits, it will find out if the other player has taken a turn or whether the other player has defaulted. If a player wins or loses on his/her turn, he/she will be notified immediately, but if a player wins or loses on the other player's turn, the first player will be notified by the Javascript submission after the appropriate time has elapsed for the other player to respond.

1. ADO.Net is Microsoft's latest iteration of Active Data Objects, a class from which objects can be derived that are highly useful in making database connections, running database commands, and retrieving records as results.
2. VS.Net comes with two types of ADO.Net connection and DataAdapter objects that can be called from ASP.Net Web applications code: the SqlConnection and OleDbConnection objects, and the **SqlDataAdapter** and OleDbDataAdapter objects.
3. Making a connection to the database requires a database to be available, but the DataAdapter Wizard can help with that process. When you add a SqlDataAdapter to your Web form in VS.Net, the Data Adapter Wizard opens, and on the second screen you will find a choice that lets you invoke a New Connection function that helps you establish a connection to any SQL Server databases you have available. Once you've created a SqlDataAdapter using the wizard, a SqlConnection is automatically created at the same time. Both controls are visible at the bottom of the screen.
4. During the process of creating a SqlDataAdapter, you also tell the wizard if you want queries built for the Select, Insert, Update, and Delete Command objects that come with the SqlDataAdapter. There is a Query Builder function built into the wizard to give you a visual query building interface. If you choose to have the wizard build SQL queries for you, it will also automatically fill in the **Parameters collection** for each type of command.
5. Once you're done creating the SqlDataAdapter object, you can programmatically change the SQL statements and parameters that are generated, so that you can use the same SqlDataAdapter over and over for different queries as your application runs.

Online Multiplayer Game (OMPGame)

We'll develop this application in steps, starting with the registration function, then the login function, and finally game play.

THE WELCOME PAGE

1. Open VS.Net and begin a new project named OMPGame (using the ASP.Net Web application template from the Visual Basic Projects node).
2. On the first page of the application, if this were a real Web site, we'd probably show a lot of information about the company and so forth. But we basically want the user to register, log in, and play, so on our first page we'll welcome them and invite them to register or log in.
3. Place a Label control at the top of the page and change its Text property to "Welcome to OMPGame".
4. Place two more Label controls, two TextBox controls, and a Button control on the surface of the form.
5. Rename the TextBox controls "username" and "password". Change the Text property of the Button to "Login" and rename it "LoginButton". Change the Text properties of the two new Label controls to "UN:" and "PS:".
6. Add a Link control to the form. Change its Link property to make it display "Click Here to Register As a Player", and make it link to "registration_form.aspx".

7. Modify the font properties of the Welcome label so the text is larger, bold, and Arial, and modify the Font properties of the rest of the controls so they are bold, Arial, and XX-Small.

8. Change the Background and Border colors of the Document, top Label, and Button so they create a pleasing effect, as shown in Figure 8.1.

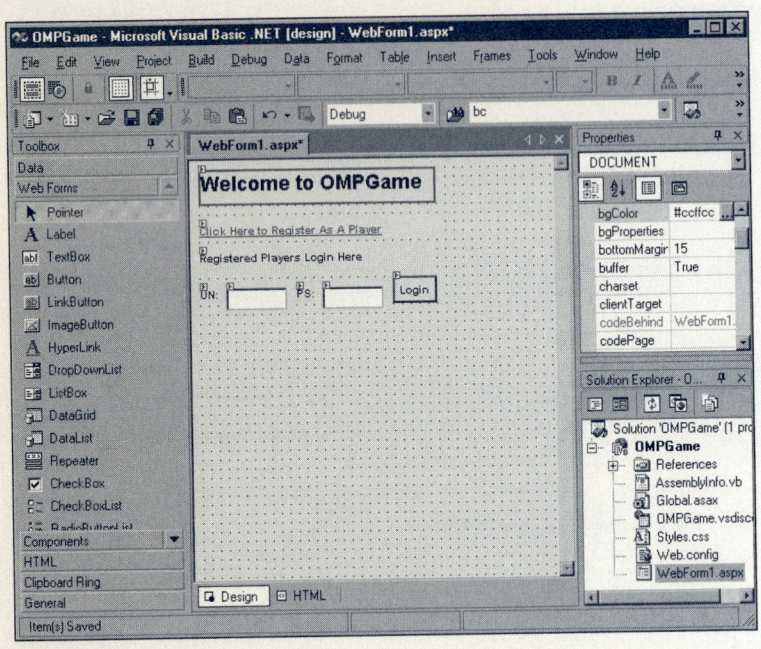

FIGURE 8.1 The Welcome Web Form

THE REGISTRATION PAGE

1. Add a new Web form to the project and name it "registration_form.aspx".

2. Add a Label control to the top and change its Text property to "Register Here".

3. Add Label controls and TextBox controls for each field in the players table (the table we created in our SQL Server OMPGame database in the last chapter) to the Web form. Name each TextBox control the same name as the field it represents (change the ID property of the First Name textbox to "first_name", and so on for all the textboxes).

4. Add a Button control to the form, change its Text property to "Register", and name it "RegisterButton".

5. Make the same kinds of changes to the font and color properties of this page as you made to the Welcome form. Your register form should now resemble Figure 8.2.

MAKING THE DATABASE CONNECTION

At this point we're going to begin making a database connection, using the SqlConnection and SqlDataAdapter controls. We'll need to do this because when users register using the Web form, we want to insert their information into our database. Once they are registered, we'll log them in automatically, and later when they return to the site they can log themselves in by entering their username and password. Since they'll be in the database, we have a means of looking them up.

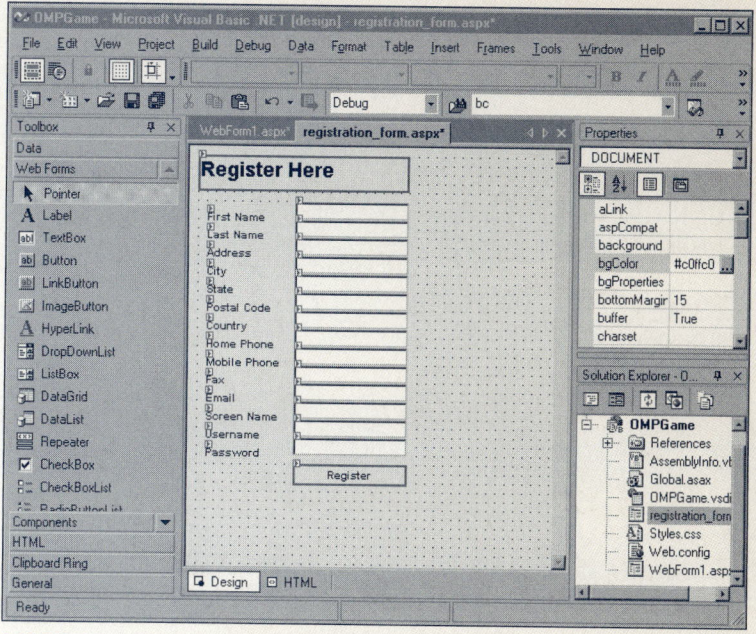

FIGURE 8.2 The Registration Form

1. On the Toolbox, click the Data section. The Toolbox should display a set of controls for working with data, including the SqlDataAdapter, SqlConnection, and SqlCommand controls. Drag a SqlDataAdapter control onto the surface of the form. The Data Adapter Configuration Wizard should appear, as shown in Figure 8.3.

FIGURE 8.3 The Data Adapter Configuration Wizard, First Screen

2. The first screen of the wizard is information only, so click Next. The second screen of the wizard will appear, as shown in Figure 8.4.

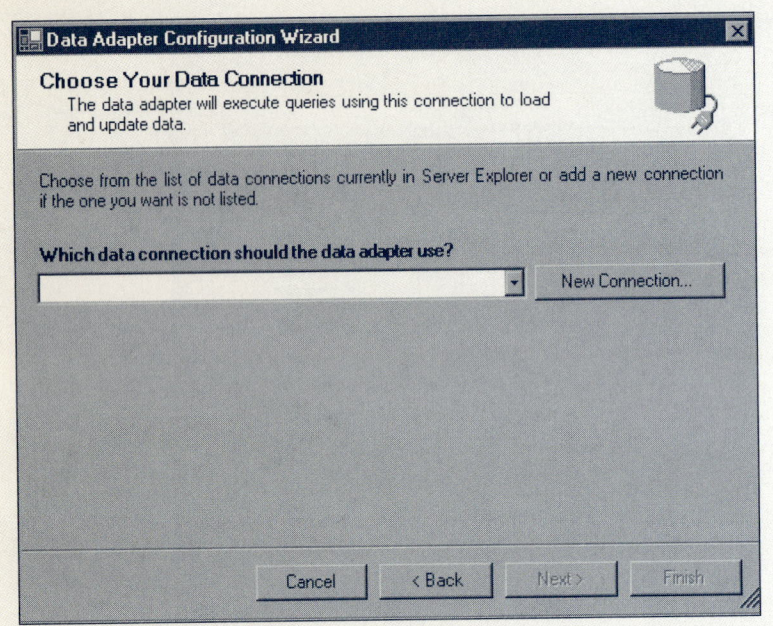

FIGURE 8.4 The Data Adapter Configuration Wizard, Second Screen

3. The second screen of the wizard allows you to choose either an existing database connection or a new one. Choose New Connection (unless you are directed to use an existing connection). The Data Link Properties dialog box will open.

4. The Data Link Properties dialog box should be open on the Connection tab. Fill out the options as is appropriate for your system. On our system, we select the server name, Use Windows NT Integrated Security, and the database (named "OMPGame") as shown in Figure 8.5. Make your selections and then click the Test Connection button. You should get a popup box telling you the Test connection succeeded.

5. If you click over to the Provider tab, you'll notice that the connection also specifies the database driver to use (in this case the driver is Microsoft OLE DB Provider for SQL Server). While no changes are necessary on this screen, it's good to be aware that the connection contains these data.

6. Click OK to set the new connection in the wizard, then click Next in the wizard. The third screen of the wizard should appear, as shown in Figure 8.6.

7. The third screen of the wizard allows you to choose how the Data Adapter will get records from the database: Use SQL statements, Create new stored procedures, or Use existing stored procedures. Stored procedures are like SQL statements (although they can be more elaborate) and they are prebuilt and stored in the database, not run from outside the database. For complex queries, they can be faster than externally run SQL statements. In this case, however, we will use SQL statements, so leave the default choice selected and click Next.

8. On the fourth screen of the wizard you can write your own SQL SELECT query and then have the wizard build INSERT, UPDATE, and DELETE queries based on the SELECT query. If you don't want to manually write the SELECT query, you can use the Query Builder. For our application,

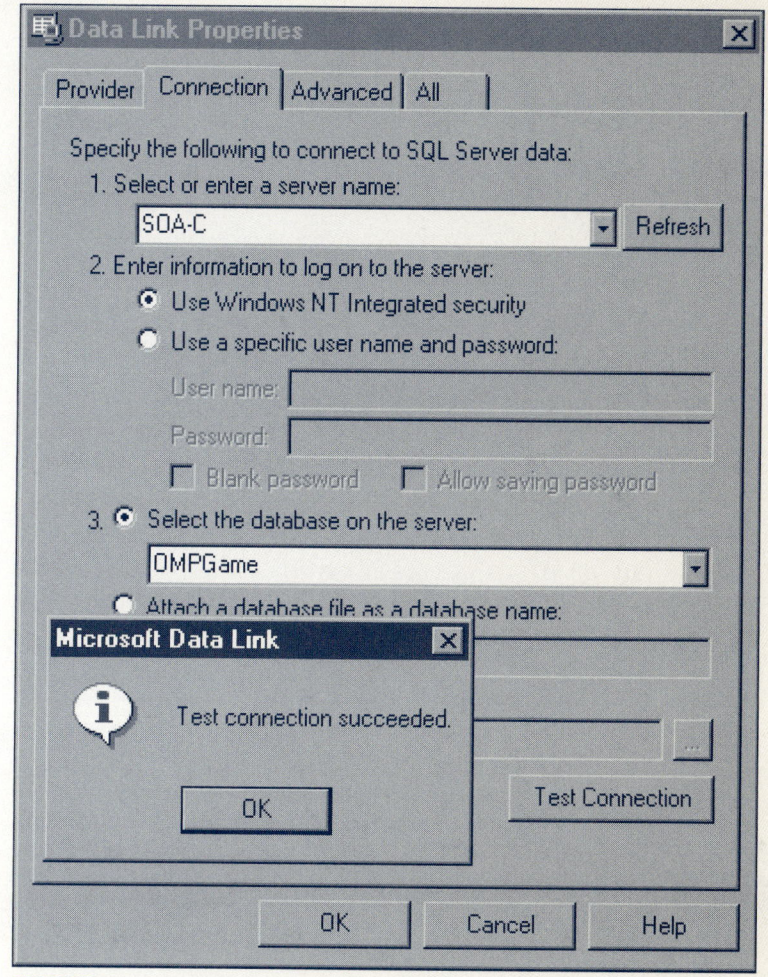

FIGURE 8.5 The Data Link Properties Dialog Box, on the Connection Tab

start by clicking the Advanced Options button. This will let you view and modify advanced options, as shown in Figure 8.7.

9. The Advanced Options dialog box has three choices. The first, Generate Insert, Update and Delete statements, will make the wizard generate these statements to go along with your SELECT statement. The second, Use optimistic concurrency, helps prevent problems with other users affecting the same records. The third choice, Refresh the DataSet, brings back data that you might need later, such as the new ID (the primary key) value for any records created by the INSERT statement. Leave all three choices selected and click OK.

10. From the fourth screen, click the Query Builder button. The Query Builder will open, as shown in Figure 8.8.

11. Select the players table and click the Add button. The players table will be added to the Query Builder screen. Close the Add Table dialog box.

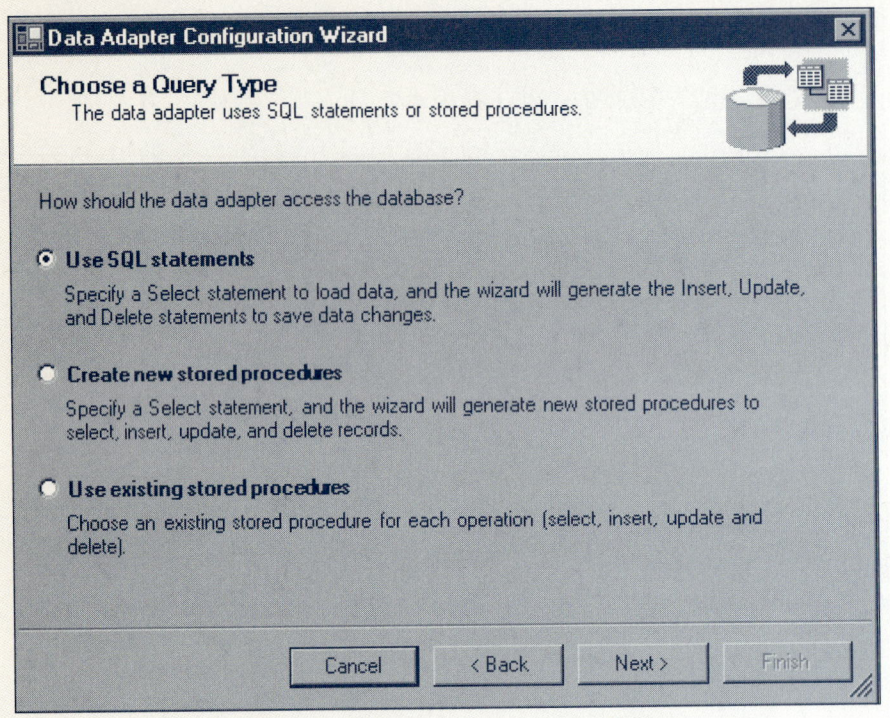

FIGURE 8.6 The Data Adapter Configuration Wizard, Third Screen

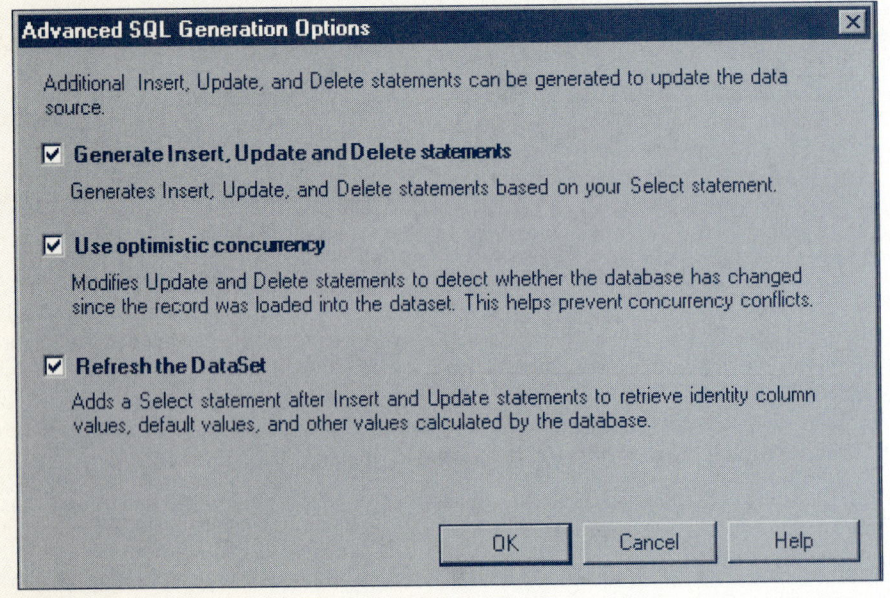

FIGURE 8.7 The Advanced Options Dialog Box

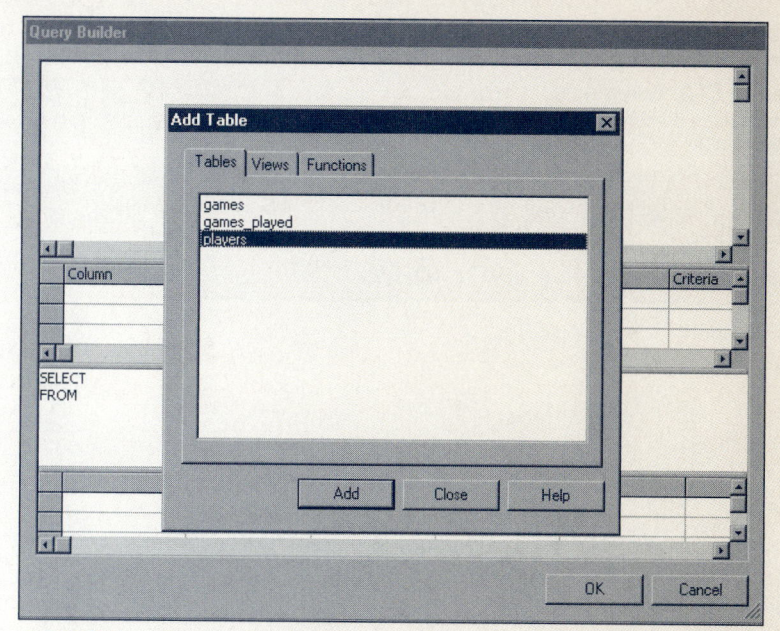

FIGURE 8.8 The Query Builder with the Add Table Dialog Box Open

12. Click the first row in the players table (* All Columns). The query should now read

    ```
    SELECT players.*
    FROM players
    ```

13. Click OK in the Query Builder. The fourth screen of the wizard should now resemble Figure 8.9.

14. Click Next, the fifth screen of the wizard should appear, telling you all the things it has done, such as Generated SELECT statement and so forth, as shown in Figure 8.10.

15. Click Finish to complete your SqlDataAdapter. The wizard should close, and you should be back in VS.Net with a SqlDataAdapter control and a SqlConnection control on the form, as shown in Figure 8.11.

THE REGISTRATION CODE

The next step in making our registration form work is to code the Register button's event handler. We'll open a connection to the database and use an INSERT statement to add a new record to the players table. We'll need to add the values entered by the user as parameters to the INSERT statement.

1. Add a Label control (you can copy the top label on the registration form) and change its Text property so that it displays no text). Name it "MessageLabel". Resize it so it takes up most of the right half of the form, as shown in Figure 8.12.

2. Double-click the Register button to begin an event handler in the code-behind page.

3. In the event handler for the Register button, dimension two variables to handle the checks for duplicate screen and usernames, and one to capture the player's new ID if he/she receives a valid registration, as shown on page 262.

CHAPTER 8 Introduction to ADO.Net

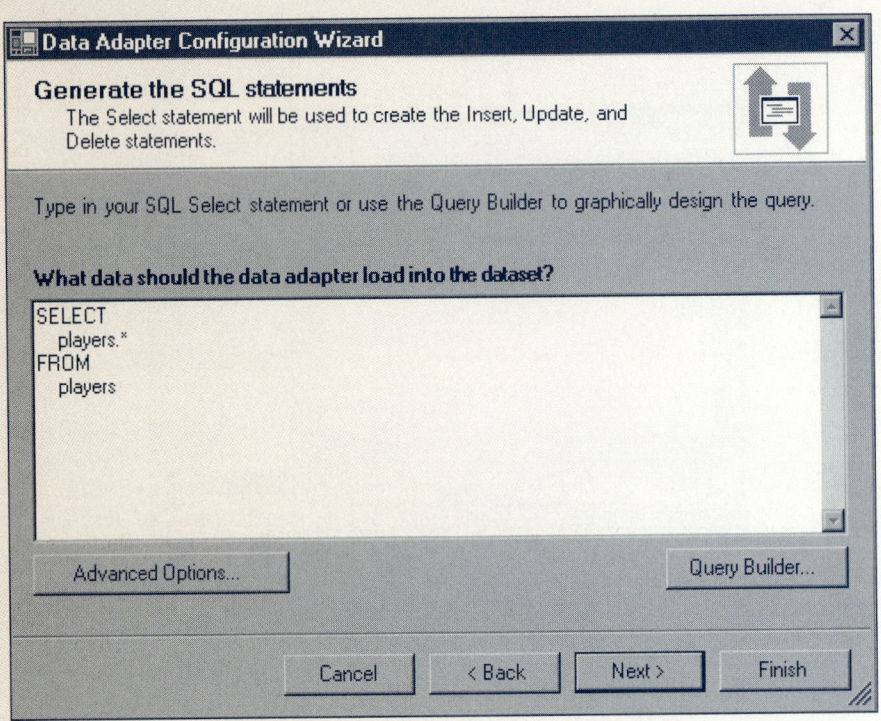

FIGURE 8.9 The Query Builder with the players Table Added and All Fields Selected

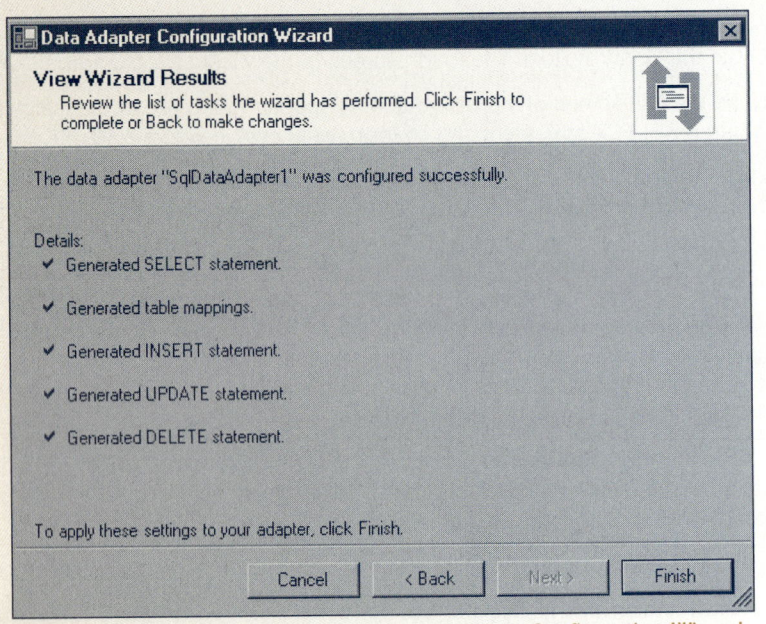

FIGURE 8.10 The Fifth Screen of the Data Adapter Configuration Wizard

Hands On Project

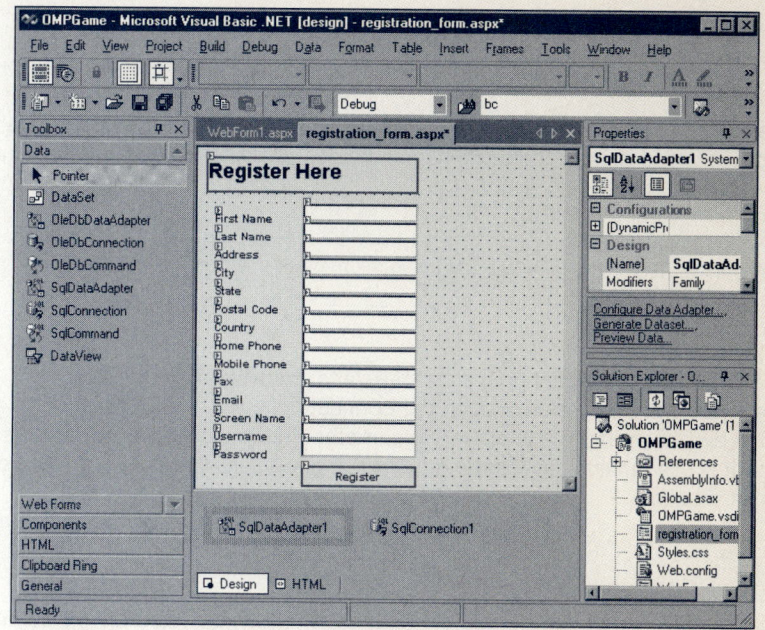

FIGURE 8.11 The Registration Web Form with SqlDataAdapter1 and SqlConnection1

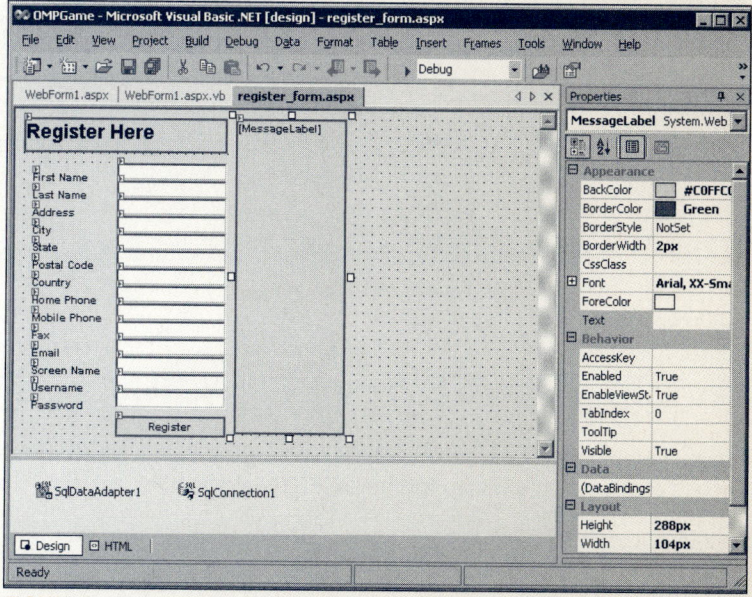

FIGURE 8.12 The Register Form with the MessageLabel Control

```
Dim SameSName As String
Dim SameUName As String
Dim NewPlayerID As Integer
```

4. Use the following code to revise the SqlDataAdapter1.SelectCommand's Text property so it will search for any records with the same screen name, returning only the screen_name field:

```
'set the select command text to retrieve any records with a
   matching screen name
SqlDataAdapter1.SelectCommand.CommandText = "SELECT screen_name FROM
   players WHERE screen_name = '" &
Request.Form.GetValues("screen_name")(0) & "';"
```

5. Now we'll open the connection to the database and execute our query using the SelectCommand's ExecuteScalar method. Once we open the connection, it will remain open until we close it at the end of the event handler. The ExecuteScalar method returns only one row and a single field value. Although it is used mainly for returning the result of an aggregate query, it is also appropriate for use in this situation.

```
SqlConnection1.Open()
SameSName = SqlDataAdapter1.SelectCommand().ExecuteScalar()
```

6. Once the query is executed, we can check to see if the result matches the screen name chosen by the user, and if it is, show an error message to the user, as shown here:

```
If SameSName = Request.Form.GetValues("screen_name")(0) Then
   'send user error and ask they try again
   MessageLabel.Text = "Please try a different screen name"
Else
```

7. If the screen names don't match, we can use similar code to check for duplicate usernames, like this:

```
'set the select command text to retrieve any records with a matching
   username
SqlDataAdapter1.SelectCommand.CommandText = "SELECT username FROM
   players WHERE username = '" & Request.Form.GetValues("username")(0)
   & "';"
'set the SameUName variable to the username if one is found
SameUName = SqlDataAdapter1.SelectCommand().ExecuteScalar()
If SameUName = Request.Form.GetValues("username")(0) Then
   'send user error and ask they try again
   MessageLabel.Text = "Please try a different username"
Else
```

8. If the usernames don't match, we can insert the new record. First we have to set the values of all the parameters created by the wizard for the INSERT statement, as shown in the following code:

```
'gather the entered values and place them in the parameters
SqlDataAdapter1.InsertCommand.Parameters(0).Value = Request.Form.
   GetValues("first_name")(0)
SqlDataAdapter1.InsertCommand.Parameters(1).Value = Request.Form.
   GetValues("last_name")(0)
```

```
SqlDataAdapter1.InsertCommand.Parameters(2).Value = Request.Form.
    GetValues("address")(0)
SqlDataAdapter1.InsertCommand.Parameters(3).Value = Request.Form.
    GetValues("city")(0)
SqlDataAdapter1.InsertCommand.Parameters(4).Value = Request.Form.
    GetValues("state")(0)
SqlDataAdapter1.InsertCommand.Parameters(5).Value = Request.Form.
    GetValues("country")(0)
SqlDataAdapter1.InsertCommand.Parameters(6).Value = Request.Form.
    GetValues("postal_code")(0)
SqlDataAdapter1.InsertCommand.Parameters(7).Value = Request.Form.
    GetValues("home_phone")(0)
SqlDataAdapter1.InsertCommand.Parameters(8).Value = Request.Form.
    GetValues("mobile_phone")(0)
SqlDataAdapter1.InsertCommand.Parameters(9).Value = Request.Form.
    GetValues("fax")(0)
SqlDataAdapter1.InsertCommand.Parameters(10).Value = Request.Form.
    GetValues("email")(0)
SqlDataAdapter1.InsertCommand.Parameters(11).Value = Request.Form.
    GetValues("screen_name")(0)
SqlDataAdapter1.InsertCommand.Parameters(12).Value = Request.Form.
    GetValues("username")(0)
SqlDataAdapter1.InsertCommand.Parameters(13).Value = Request.Form.
    GetValues("password")(0)
```

9. Now we can modify the SELECT statement that is included with the Insert query, so it only retrieves the new player_id. Do this by clicking over to the Web form and selecting the SqlDataAdapter1 control and finding the Insert command property in the Properties window. Open this property by clicking the plus sign, and click in the CommandText property. Open the Query Builder and modify the query by removing all field names from the SELECT part of the query except for the player_id field. Leave the WHERE clause as is.

10. We can now execute the query using the InsertCommand's ExecuteScalar method. While the Insert query portion returns no records, the Select portion returns the player_id value, showing only the player_id field, so ExecuteScalar works well in this situation.

```
'execute the query to insert the new record
SqlDataAdapter1.InsertCommand().ExecuteScalar()
```

11. Next we'll create two Session variables so that we can show the player is logged in and track the player's player_id (so we can store it with the games played records later).

```
'create Session variables for login status and player_id
    Session("LoggedIn") = "Yes"
    Session("PlayerID") = NewPlayerID
```

12. Because the player is now registered, we'll assume the player wants to go immediately to the page on which he/she can choose a game to play. Before adding the following code, add a Web form named "choose_game.aspx" to the project:

```
'redirect the player to the game choice screen
Response.Redirect("choose_game.aspx")
```

13. Finally, we will end both our If...Then...End If blocks, and then close the database connection:

    ```
    End If
    End If
    'and make sure to close the connection
    SqlConnection1.Close()
    ```

14. Test your code and your database connection by clicking back to the register_form.aspx Web form and choosing File|Build and Browse from the menu. To assist in the testing process (remember, you need to test for failed registrations as well as valid ones), add a record to the players table from the SQL Server Enterprise Manager and then try to register another player with the same screen name and the same username. In both cases, the Insert statement should not run and the MessageLabel should tell the user to try a different screen name or username.

THE LOGIN CODE

Back on the initial WebForm1.aspx page, we need to place code to allow registered users to log in when they come back to the site. We can do this by creating a SqlDataAdapter and SqlConnection on the form. Since the only purpose would be to log a registered player in, the DataAdapter only needs a SELECT statement retrieving the player_id if username and password match, a MessageLabel for informing the user if login fails, and a redirection to the choose_game.aspx page if login succeeds.

1. Add a SqlDataAdapter to WebForm1.aspx. When you get to the query screen, click the Advanced Options button and deselect the choices for building INSERT, UPDATE, and DELETE queries. Then click the Query Build button and deselect all fields from the players table except the player_id field. Put criteria in the grid next to the username and password fields so they will cause records to be selected only where `username = @username` and `password = @password` (the two parameters entered by the user).

2. Double-click the Login button to start an event handler in the code-behind page. In the handler, enter the following code to create a variable to hold the player_id value (if the login is successful), to capture the username and password entered by the user, and to open a database connection and run the select query:

    ```
    Dim PlayerID As Integer
    'capture the username and password and put them in parameters
    SqlDataAdapter1.SelectCommand.Parameters(0).Value = Request.Form.
       GetValues("username")(0)
    SqlDataAdapter1.SelectCommand.Parameters(1).Value = Request.Form.
       GetValues("password")(0)
    'open the connection
    SqlConnection1.Open()
    PlayerID = SqlDataAdapter1.SelectCommand().ExecuteScalar()
    ```

3. Now enter the code to test for a matching record (and thus a successful login) or not:

    ```
    'test if a matching record was returned
    If PlayerID > 0 Then
       'create Session variables for login status and player_id
       Session("LoggedIn") = "Yes"
       Session("PlayerID") = PlayerID
       'redirect the player to the game choice screen
       Response.Redirect("choose_game.aspx")
    ```

```
Else
    'if not, inform the user of the problem and suggest they register
    Label2.Text = "Login failed. Please try again or use the link above
to register"
End If
```

4. Finally, don't forget to close the database connection:

```
'close the connection
SqlConnection1.Close()
```

THE CHOOSE GAME PAGE

On the Choose Game page, we need to provide the user with the ability to choose from a dropdown list of the available games, and choose how many players they want to play with (individual, two players, three players, and so on). Once a game is selected, the player will go to the screen on which they play the game, but if they've selected two or more players, they will be informed that their browser will poll the system every 15 seconds until another player signs up for the same game.

For the sake of simplicity, we'll only develop one game, Blackjack, and only allow a maximum of two players, with the house (the dealer) as an automatic second or third player. As we mentioned earlier, we'll incorporate the second player in Chapter 10. The design rules we'll include in our Web application will be

- At the start of the game, the "deck" is shuffled once, and only one game is played per shuffle (we'll set up a marker for playing more than one game per shuffle in Chapter 10).
- Players may not bet and may not double-down.
- If a player gets Blackjack and dealer gets Blackjack, they push, but if one or the other gets Blackjack on the initial hand, he/she wins immediately.
- As they sign up to play, we'll add players to a list of players held in an application variable, and set the number of players for the game at the same time (in Chapter 10).
- If a player chooses "Individual", the game will start immediately, but if the player chooses multiple players, then when the number of players in the application variable reaches the number of players chosen, the game will commence.
- Upon commencing, the system will create a record in the games_played table, set the game status to "in_play", and set the winning and losing IDs and scores to zero.
- In Chapter 10, we'll add a feature that makes the system allow the first player a given amount of time to either make a move or forfeit the game.
- If any of the players wins or loses, it will be recorded. Wins, losses, and pushes will be recorded as "Closed-PlayerWin", "Closed-DealerWin", or "Closed-Push".
- Aces will start out as a value of 11, but this will automatically change if the player's score exceeds 21, until the player can no longer remain below 21.
- Players can either hit or hold, but if they win or lose, they will be able to select a "Play Again" button.
- The dealer must hit if the score is under 17.
    1. To set up the choose_game.aspx page, add a top label, two middle labels, a bottom label, two DropDownList controls, and a Button control. Set the background of each (and of the page) to "#FFCC66" (a light orange), and set the border color for the top label and the button to dark orange. Change the font properties of all labels and the button to Bold, Arial, and XX-Small (except for the top label, which you should set to Larger). See Figure 8.13 to get an idea of how these controls are laid out on the form.

CHAPTER 8 Introduction to ADO.Net

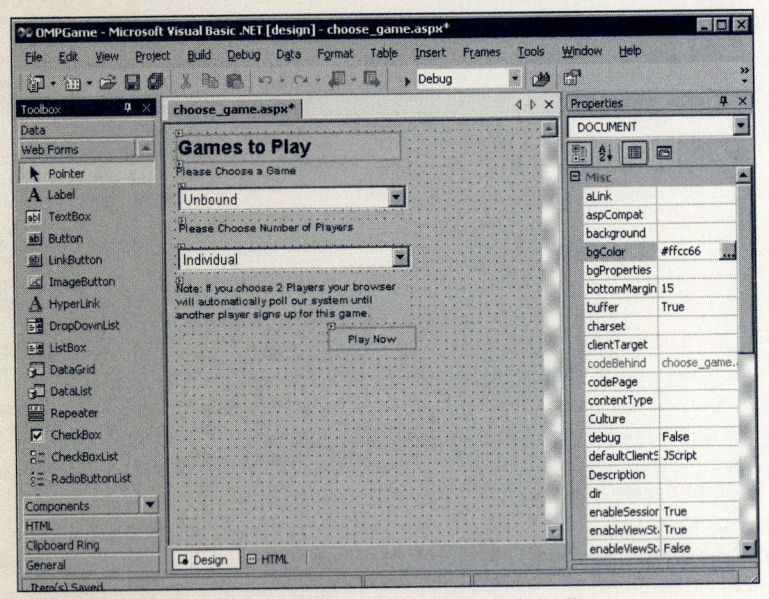

FIGURE 8.13 The Controls on the choose_game.aspx Form

2. Change the ID properties of the two dropdown lists to "DDLGameChoice" for the top one and "DDLNumberOfPlayers" for the bottom one. Select the DDLNumberOfPlayers control and in the Properties window find the Items collection. Click in the field to make the ellipsis button appear, and then add two items to the collection: "Individual" and "2 Players". Set the text value for these items as "Individual" and "2 Players", respectively, and set the Value values to "Individual" and "2 Players", respectively. Figure 8.14 shows how the ListItem Collection Editor should look.

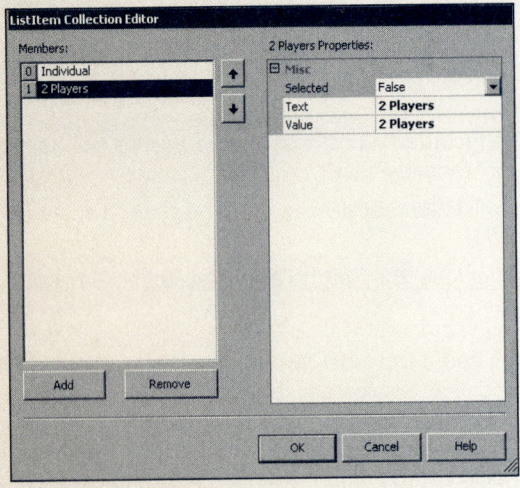

FIGURE 8.14 The ListItem Collection Editor

3. Change the ID property of the Button control to PlayNowButton.

4. Now we'll set up the code to fill up the Game Choice dropdown list box with the available games. We only need to do this once, when the page first opens, as we won't be refreshing the list every time the player reloads the page. The following code accomplishes the list generation the first time the page loads, in the Page_Load event:

```
'check to see if this is a postback
If Not IsPostBack() Then
  'dimension variables
  Dim GameChoicesDS As DataSet = New DataSet()
  Dim i As Integer
  Dim vItemText As String
  Dim vItemValue As Integer
  'perform the query
  SqlConnection1.Open()
  SqlDataAdapter1.Fill(GameChoicesDS, "games")
  'run through a For loop adding items to the dropdown list
  For i = 0 To (GameChoicesDS.Tables("games").Rows.Count - 1)
    vItemText = GameChoicesDS.Tables("games").Rows(i).Item("g_name")
    vItemValue = GameChoicesDS.Tables("games").Rows(i).Item("game_id")
    Me.DDLGameChoice.Items.Add(New ListItem(vItemText, vItemValue))
  Next
End If
```

5. Now we can design the code to allow the user to choose the game he/she wants to play and the number of players preferred. The player makes the choices from the initial Web server controls displayed on the GameChoice page and then clicks the Play Now button, so we'll start by creating an event handler for the PlayNowButton. Then we'll enter the following code:

```
Dim num_players As String
Dim game_to_be_played As String
'check first to see what number of players the player has selected
num_players = DDLNumberOfPlayers.SelectedItem.Value
game_to_be_played = DDLGameChoice.SelectedItem.Text
If num_players = "Individual" Then
  'check what game the player has selected
  If game_to_be_played = "Blackjack" Then
    Session("NumPlayers") = "Individual"
    Session("GamePlayed") = "Blackjack"
    Session("DealerID") = 1
    'redirect player to Blackjack Game page
    Response.Redirect("Blackjack.aspx")
  End If
End If
```

6. The code above dimensions two variables to capture the choices of the player: num_players (a string) and game_to_be_played (also a string). Then it sets the value of these two strings to the

"SelectedItem" property of the dropdown lists. We'll use the Text value for the SelectedItem property of the DDLGameChoice list (g_name from the database), but we could use the game_id value if we really were working with a large number of games and wanted to make sure we found the game unambiguously.

7. Next, the code simply checks to see how many players and what game was chosen, using an If...Then...End If block. Since there's only one game and only one number of players allowed (in this chapter), there's only one choice that actually does anything. The actions performed are the setting up of several Session variables to contain the choices of number of players and game, as well as the dealer's ID. Note that we have manually entered a record in players for the dealer. The final action is to redirect the player to another Web form named "Blackjack.aspx" and so our next step, obviously, is to create a new Web form in our project named "Blackjack.aspx". Figure 8.15 shows the choose_game.aspx page after Building and Browsing it in VS.Net.

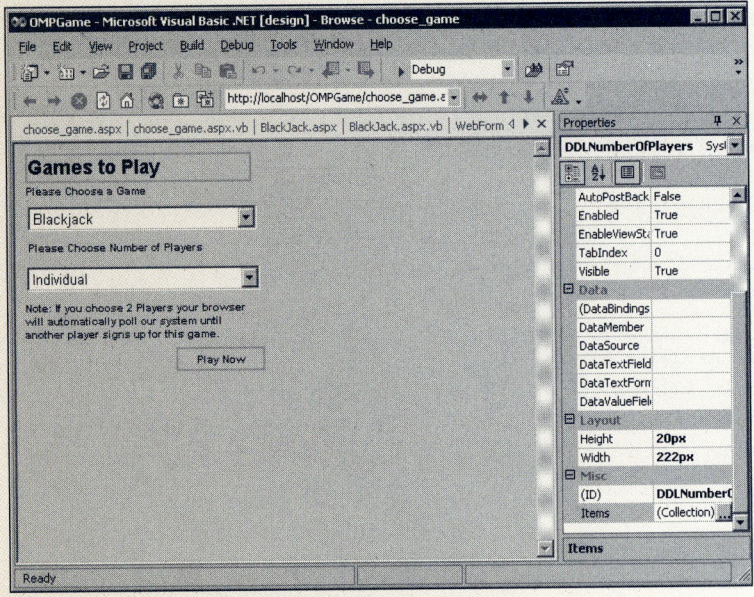

FIGURE 8.15 The choose_game.aspx Page

CREATING BLACKJACK.ASPX

Before we can create the page that actually allows the user to play the game, it is worthwhile to consider what we'll need for the page. First, we'll need graphic images for each of the cards. A deck of cards contains 52 cards, divided into four suits (hearts, spades, clubs, and diamonds) and while we could allow our graphic artists to be very creative, our current objective is to build the functionality of the game. Therefore, we'll use a simple graphic program to create card images using only a number or letter plus icons for the suits. The images included with this book were made in an old but quite functional graphic program (Microsoft Image Composer), and seem to work quite well. For the sake of simplicity, we are not going to make or use jokers. We also made a pattern for the back of a card, so the dealer's first card can be shown in the "down" position when first dealt. You can create your own images or use the ones provided on the CD. We'll discuss adding them to the project in the steps below.

As far as the functions used to play the game, we'll need a function that shuffles the cards before the first screen is shown, and this function will have to be stored as an array in a session variable. Fortunately, there's a Randomize function built into VB.Net, and all we have to do is make it create a set of 52 numbers in random order and not use the same number twice.

Once we have a set of 52 random numbers, we'll need to match those up with cards, so we can use another session variable array to store cards in sequence as the names of the card images (such as club01.gif, club02.gif, and so on). Finally, we can make another session variable array to hold the values of each card. When cards are "dealt," we'll just access the first array for the numerical index value to use on the other arrays to pick out the next card to deal.

In our session we also can keep a variable that determines the next card to deal from the deck and two variables that hold up to 11 cards (as the names of graphic images) representing the hand of the dealer and the hand of the player. While the game is being played, these variables will track cards to be dealt and the current cards in each hand, as well as provide the value for the hands so wins and losses can be determined.

1. Right-click the project name in Solution Explorer and choose Add Existing Item from the shortcut menu. Find all the graphic images on your hard drive (you should have either made them or used the ones provided on the CD) and add them to the project. Next, add another Web form to the project and name it "Blackjack.aspx". It should open up in Design view.

2. Add a SqlDataAdapter to the form, and use a simple query (such as SELECT * FROM games_played) as you progress through the wizard. You won't even need to generate any related SQL queries (such as Insert or Delete) as we will write these manually. Nor will you need any collections of parameters for the SelectCommand, InsertCommand, or the others that are automatically generated with the DataAdapter. Both the SqlDataAdapter and the SqlConnection should appear on your form.

3. Add six Label controls to the form. The top one will be informational, and the one to the right of it (named "Readout") will have red text; the next two (named NumberOfPlayersLabel and GameStatusLabel) will be for telling the player what game is being played (although the player should know from the top label) and how many players are playing, and the last two will be captions for the dealer's and player's hands. Figure 8.16 shows how to locate them and set their text and font properties.

4. Add 22 ImageButton controls. These are easy to programmatically change the images, and easy to place on the screen. The dealer will get 11 and the player will get 11, in rows. Set their Visible properties to "False", so only those that are specifically activated will show on the playing surface. You can do this all at once by selecting all the ImageButton controls at the same time. Also, if you're having trouble sizing or aligning them, use the format menu choices with the controls selected. Name these controls "DealerCard01", "DealerCard02", "PlayerCard01", "PlayerCard02", and so on.

5. Add three Button controls to the bottom of the form, named HitButton, HoldButton, and PlayAgainButton. Set their text properties accordingly, and their color and font properties as well. Figure 8.16 shows all the controls in Design view, and should be a good guide to the appropriate Property settings.

WRITING THE PAGE_LOAD CODE

When the game first starts, before the page is displayed, there are a few things that happen, so we'll need to use the Page_Load event and check for "IsPostBack()" before running our initial code. First, a record is made in the database indicating the game was started and who is playing. Both the dealer and the player get a record in the games_played table (we'll make a function to retrieve these values into a report in

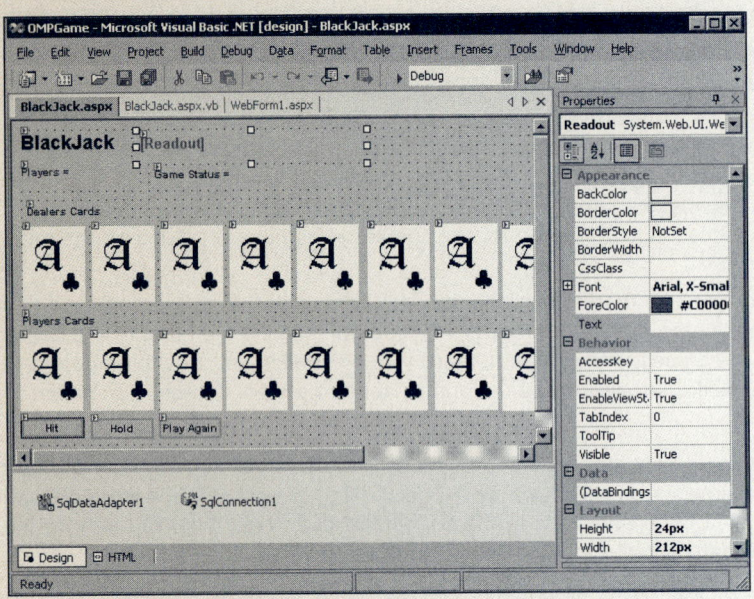

FIGURE 8.16 The Blackjack.aspx Web Form in Design view

Chapter 10). Next, we'll set up session variables to hold the hands of the dealer and the player. Then we'll shuffle the cards and deal the initial hand. If either or both players get Blackjack on the initial deal, we'll declare the game over and make a record of who won. All of these functions occur in the following code, so we'll break it down into bite-size chunks.

1. Double-click the form's surface in Design view to open the code-behind page and get inside the Page_Load event handler code block. Enter the following code to check to make sure we're not in a post back situation, and to start creating a record of the start of the game:

```
If Not IsPostBack() Then
    'record start of game in database
    Dim GameStartTime As Date
    GameStartTime = Now()
    Session("GameStartTime") = GameStartTime
```

2. Notice we're getting the GameStartTime from the Now() function. This function is built in to VB.Net, and gets both the date and the time. In our games_played table in SQL Server, we'll use this time as part of the unique ID of our game when we want to update the records created later with win or loss information. Therefore, we'll also save the GameStartTime as a session variable.

3. The following code opens a database connection and then gets the player's ID number (remember, it is stored as a session variable when the player logs in).

```
'open the database connection
SqlConnection1.Open()
'Insert record for player
```

```
'Insert record for dealer
Dim vPlayerID As Integer
vPlayerID = CInt(Session("PlayerID"))
```

4. Now we can set custom queries in the InsertCommand (a property of the SqlDataAdapter). To do this, we specify the SQL query as a string in the InsertCommand's CommandText property. To include the PlayerID value and the GameStartTime value in the SQL query, we'll break off the string at the appropriate points and use the variable value, then begin the string again. We do this by terminating the string with a quote (") mark, putting in the ampersand symbol (&), and then using the variable name, as shown here:

```
SqlDataAdapter1.InsertCommand.CommandText = "Insert Into games_played
(player_id,game_id,game_date,game_status) values(" & vPlayerID & ",1,
    '" & GameStartTime & "','started')"
```

5. Once we've set up our SQL query as a string, we can execute the query, and since it returns no records, we can use the ExecuteNonQuery() method. We'll do it once for the player using the value in the vPlayerID variable, and once for the dealer using the value 1 (because we already know the Dealer's ID will be 1 in every case, although if there was a question about this, we could use the Dealer ID that was stored as a session variable).

```
SqlDataAdapter1.InsertCommand.ExecuteNonQuery()
SqlDataAdapter1.InsertCommand.CommandText = "Insert Into games_played
(player_id,game_id,game_date,game_status) values(1,1,'" & GameStartTime
    & "','started')"
SqlDataAdapter1.InsertCommand.ExecuteNonQuery()
```

6. Next, we'll set the Text properties for the number of players and game choice labels:

```
'set the labels for the game
NumberOfPlayersLabel.Text = "Players = " & Session("NumPlayers")
GameStatusLabel.Text = "Game Status = In Play"
```

7. Now we're ready to create a few variables for our For loops, our randomization function, and our arrays of card values, images, and players' hands. We also create a few for use as we're working through the code:

```
'create a few variables
Dim i As Int16
Dim i2 As Int16
Dim vArrNum As Int16
Dim arrCardSeq(52) As Int16
Dim arrCardImages(52) As String
Dim arrCardValues(52) As Integer
Dim arrPlayerHand(10) As Integer
Dim arrPlayerHandImages(10) As String
Dim arrDealerHand(10) As Integer
Dim arrDealerHandImages(10) As String
Dim vFlag As Int16
Dim vCardUpDown As String
Dim vReadout As String
```

8. The following code fills the arrays for holding the dealer and player hands, and creates Session variables of them:

```
'create session hand arrays
For i = 0 To 10
    arrPlayerHand(i) = 0
    arrPlayerHandImages(i) = ""
    arrDealerHand(i) = 0
    arrDealerHandImages(i) = ""
Next i
Session("arrPlayerHand") = arrPlayerHand
Session("arrPlayerHandImages") = arrPlayerHandImages
Session("arrDealerHand") = arrDealerHand
Session("arrDealerHandImages") = arrDealerHandImages
```

9. Now it's time to shuffle the deck. VB.Net has a Randomization function but needs some extra code to create a set of 52 random numbers, and to make sure not to use the same number twice. These numbers will be stored in an array (named arrCardSeq) and used as index numbers for other arrays that hold card image file names and card values. The following code accomplishes these tasks (use the comments as a guide to what the code does):

```
'to shuffle the deck
'create a set of 52 numbers in random order
vFlag = 0
i = 1
i2 = 0
'call the Randomize function
Randomize()
arrCardSeq(0) = Int(52 * Rnd() + 1)
'randomize again
Randomize()
'run this routine 52 times
For i = 1 To 51
    vArrNum = Int(52 * Rnd() + 1)
    'check to see if the same number has been used
    For i2 = 0 To 51
      If arrCardSeq(i2) = vArrNum Then
         vFlag = 1
      End If
    Next
    'if not, add the number to the array
    If Not vFlag = 1 Then
       arrCardSeq(i) = vArrNum
    Else
       If i > 0 And i < 52 Then
          i = i - 1
       End If
    vFlag = 0
```

```
        End If
    Next
'put the array minus 1 (the array index starts at zero) in the Session
    array
Session("arrCardSeq") = arrCardSeq
For i = 0 To 51
    Session("arrCardSeq")(i) = Session("arrCardSeq")(i) - 1
Next
```

10. The deck has been shuffled, but the indexes created need other arrays to "deal" cards from. Use the following code to create an array of card image names and an array of card values, named arrCardImages and arrCardValues, respectively. Note that all the aces start with a value of 11.

```
'create an array of 52 cards by image name
arrCardImages(0) = "club01.gif"
arrCardImages(1) = "club02.gif"
arrCardImages(2) = "club03.gif"
arrCardImages(3) = "club04.gif"
arrCardImages(4) = "club05.gif"
arrCardImages(5) = "club06.gif"
arrCardImages(6) = "club07.gif"
arrCardImages(7) = "club08.gif"
arrCardImages(8) = "club09.gif"
arrCardImages(9) = "club10.gif"
arrCardImages(10) = "club11.gif"
arrCardImages(11) = "club12.gif"
arrCardImages(12) = "club13.gif"
arrCardImages(13) = "heart01.gif"
arrCardImages(14) = "heart02.gif"
arrCardImages(15) = "heart03.gif"
arrCardImages(16) = "heart04.gif"
arrCardImages(17) = "heart05.gif"
arrCardImages(18) = "heart06.gif"
arrCardImages(19) = "heart07.gif"
arrCardImages(20) = "heart08.gif"
arrCardImages(21) = "heart09.gif"
arrCardImages(22) = "heart10.gif"
arrCardImages(23) = "heart11.gif"
arrCardImages(24) = "heart12.gif"
arrCardImages(25) = "heart13.gif"
arrCardImages(26) = "diamond01.gif"
arrCardImages(27) = "diamond02.gif"
arrCardImages(28) = "diamond03.gif"
arrCardImages(29) = "diamond04.gif"
arrCardImages(30) = "diamond05.gif"
arrCardImages(31) = "diamond06.gif"
arrCardImages(32) = "diamond07.gif"
```

```
arrCardImages(33) = "diamond08.gif"
arrCardImages(34) = "diamond09.gif"
arrCardImages(35) = "diamond10.gif"
arrCardImages(36) = "diamond11.gif"
arrCardImages(37) = "diamond12.gif"
arrCardImages(38) = "diamond13.gif"
arrCardImages(39) = "spade01.gif"
arrCardImages(40) = "spade02.gif"
arrCardImages(41) = "spade03.gif"
arrCardImages(42) = "spade04.gif"
arrCardImages(43) = "spade05.gif"
arrCardImages(44) = "spade06.gif"
arrCardImages(45) = "spade07.gif"
arrCardImages(46) = "spade08.gif"
arrCardImages(47) = "spade09.gif"
arrCardImages(48) = "spade10.gif"
arrCardImages(49) = "spade11.gif"
arrCardImages(50) = "spade12.gif"
arrCardImages(51) = "spade13.gif"
'create a session array for card image names
Session("arrCardImages") = arrCardImages
'create an array of 52 card values
arrCardValues(0) = 11
arrCardValues(1) = 2
arrCardValues(2) = 3
arrCardValues(3) = 4
arrCardValues(4) = 5
arrCardValues(5) = 6
arrCardValues(6) = 7
arrCardValues(7) = 8
arrCardValues(8) = 9
arrCardValues(9) = 10
arrCardValues(10) = 10
arrCardValues(11) = 10
arrCardValues(12) = 10
arrCardValues(13) = 11
arrCardValues(14) = 2
arrCardValues(15) = 3
arrCardValues(16) = 4
arrCardValues(17) = 5
arrCardValues(18) = 6
arrCardValues(19) = 7
arrCardValues(20) = 8
arrCardValues(21) = 9
arrCardValues(22) = 10
arrCardValues(23) = 10
```

```
arrCardValues(24) = 10
arrCardValues(25) = 10
arrCardValues(26) = 11
arrCardValues(27) = 2
arrCardValues(28) = 3
arrCardValues(29) = 4
arrCardValues(30) = 5
arrCardValues(31) = 6
arrCardValues(32) = 7
arrCardValues(33) = 8
arrCardValues(34) = 9
arrCardValues(35) = 10
arrCardValues(36) = 10
arrCardValues(37) = 10
arrCardValues(38) = 10
arrCardValues(39) = 11
arrCardValues(40) = 2
arrCardValues(41) = 3
arrCardValues(42) = 4
arrCardValues(43) = 5
arrCardValues(44) = 6
arrCardValues(45) = 7
arrCardValues(46) = 8
arrCardValues(47) = 9
arrCardValues(48) = 10
arrCardValues(49) = 10
arrCardValues(50) = 10
arrCardValues(51) = 10
'create a session array for card values
Session("arrCardValues") = arrCardValues
```

11. Now make a Session variable that tracks the card played and set it to zero (because it is also going to be used as an index, and the first card to be dealt will be at index position zero).

```
'make the Session Next Card To Deal Counter
Session("NextCardToDeal") = 0
```

12. We can now deal the initial hand. Basically, the deal starts by dealing a card to the player, then one to the dealer, then one to the player. The dealer's first card is dealt down, but the Session array for holding the dealer's hand will contain the correct value and card image, regardless. Notice how the Session array variables are "nested" so that the appropriate index number is used for each card dealt. Also, note that when the dealing is done for each card, the ImageButton representing the card is made Visible.

```
'deal the initial hand
' start by dealing one card to the Player
PlayerCard01.ImageUrl =
    Session("arrCardImages")(Session("arrCardSeq")(Session
```

```
       ("NextCardToDeal")))
Session("arrPlayerHandImages")(0) = _
   Session("arrCardImages")(Session("arrCardSeq")(Session _
   ("NextCardToDeal")))
Session("arrPlayerHand")(0) = Session("arrCardValues") _
   (Session("arrCardSeq")(Session("NextCardToDeal")))
Session("NextCardToDeal") = Session("NextCardToDeal") + 1
PlayerCard01.Visible = True
'deal a card to the Dealer and set first dealer card down
DealerCard01.ImageUrl = "cardback.gif"
Session("arrDealerHandImages")(0) = Session("arrCardImages") _
   (Session("arrCardSeq")(Session("NextCardToDeal")))
Session("arrDealerHand")(0) = Session("arrCardValues") _
   (Session("arrCardSeq")(Session("NextCardToDeal")))
Session("NextCardToDeal") = Session("NextCardToDeal") + 1
   DealerCard01.Visible = True
   'deal another card to the player
PlayerCard02.ImageUrl = Session("arrCardImages") _
   (Session("arrCardSeq")(Session("NextCardToDeal")))
Session("arrPlayerHandImages")(1) = _
Session("arrCardImages")(Session("arrCardSeq") _
   (Session("NextCardToDeal")))
Session("arrPlayerHand")(1) = _
   Session("arrCardValues")(Session("arrCardSeq") _
   (Session("NextCardToDeal")))
Session("NextCardToDeal") = Session("NextCardToDeal") + 1
PlayerCard02.Visible = True
'deal another card to the Dealer and set second dealer card up
DealerCard02.ImageUrl = Session("arrCardImages") _
   (Session("arrCardSeq")(Session("NextCardToDeal")))
Session("arrDealerHandImages")(1) = _
   Session("arrCardImages")(Session("arrCardSeq") _
   (Session("NextCardToDeal")))
Session("arrDealerHand")(1) = _
   Session("arrCardValues")(Session("arrCardSeq") _
   (Session("NextCardToDeal")))
Session("NextCardToDeal") = Session("NextCardToDeal") + 1
DealerCard02.Visible = True
```

13. Before the user can choose to Hit or Hold, we need to check for a Win, Loss, or Push, based on whether anyone got Blackjack. We can do this pretty easily, as Blackjack is the only hand that adds up to 21 after two cards are dealt. We just check total hand values by adding them together. However, since there are a number of outcomes, and if the player has 22 (two aces), we need to reset the player's hand to 12 (one ace and one 11), the same blocks of code are repeated several times to account for all the varieties of outcomes:

```
'check for a Win on the initial hand
If Session("arrPlayerHand")(0) + Session("arrPlayerHand")(1) = 21 Then
```

```
            If Session("arrDealerHand")(0) + Session("arrDealerHand")
              (1) = 21 Then
              'set dealer first card up
              DealerCard01.ImageUrl = Session("arrDealerHandImages")(0)
              'declare a push
              Readout.Text = "Push"
              'record the push in the database
               'Update record for player
              'Update record for Dealer
              Dim vPlayerID2 As Integer
              vPlayerID2 = CInt(Session("PlayerID"))
              SqlDataAdapter1.UpdateCommand.CommandText =
                "Update games_played set game_status = 'Closed-Push',
                 winning_player_id = 0, losing_player_id = 0, winning_player_score
                  = 21 WHERE game_date = '" & Session("GameStartTime") & "' and
                 player_id = " & vPlayerID2 & ";"
              SqlDataAdapter1.UpdateCommand.ExecuteNonQuery()
              SqlDataAdapter1.UpdateCommand.CommandText = "Update games_played
                set game_status = 'Closed-Push', winning_player_id = 0,
                losing_player_id = 0, winning_player_score = 21 WHERE game_date
                = '" & Session("GameStartTime") & "' and player_id = 1;"
              SqlDataAdapter1.UpdateCommand.ExecuteNonQuery()
              'show player play again button and remove the Hit and Hold buttons
              HitButton.Visible = False
              HoldButton.Visible = False
              PlayAgainButton.Visible = True
          Else
              'set dealer first card up
              DealerCard01.ImageUrl = Session("arrDealerHandImages")(0)
              'declare player win and game over
              Readout.Text = "Player Wins - Game Over"
              'record the win in database
              Dim vPlayerID2 As Integer
              vPlayerID2 = CInt(Session("PlayerID"))
              SqlDataAdapter1.UpdateCommand.CommandText = "Update games_played
                set game_status = 'Closed-PlayerWin', winning_player_id = " &
                vPlayerID2 & ", losing_player_id = 1, winning_player_score = 21
                WHERE game_date = '" & Session("GameStartTime") & "' and
                player_id = " & vPlayerID2 & ";"
              SqlDataAdapter1.UpdateCommand.ExecuteNonQuery()
              SqlDataAdapter1.UpdateCommand.CommandText = "Update games_played
                set game_status = 'Closed-PlayerWin', winning_player_id = " &
                vPlayerID2 & ", losing_player_id = 1, winning_player_score = 21
                WHERE game_date = '" & Session("GameStartTime") & "' and
                player_id = 1;"
              SqlDataAdapter1.UpdateCommand.ExecuteNonQuery()
              'show player play another game button and remove the Hit and Hold
```

```
            buttons
        HitButton.Visible = False
        HoldButton.Visible = False
        PlayAgainButton.Visible = True
      End If
    ElseIf Session("arrPlayerHand")(0) + Session("arrPlayerHand")
      (1) < 21 Then
      If Session("arrDealerHand")(0) + Session("arrDealerHand")
         (1) = 21 Then 'set dealer first card up
        DealerCard01.ImageUrl = Session("arrDealerHandImages")(0)
        'declare a dealer win and game over
        Readout.Text = "Dealer Wins - Game Over"
        'record win in database
        Dim vPlayerID2 As Integer
        vPlayerID2 = CInt(Session("PlayerID"))
        SqlDataAdapter1.UpdateCommand.CommandText = "Update games_played
          set game_status = 'Closed-DealerWin', winning_player_id = 1,
          losing_player_id = " & vPlayerID2 & ", winning_player_score = 21
          WHERE game_date = '" & Session("GameStartTime") & "' and
          player_id = " & vPlayerID2 & ";"
        SqlDataAdapter1.UpdateCommand.ExecuteNonQuery()
        SqlDataAdapter1.UpdateCommand.CommandText = "Update games_played
          set game_status = 'Closed-DealerWin', winning_player_id = 1,
          losing_player_id = " & vPlayerID2 & ", winning_player_score = 21
          WHERE game_date = '" & Session("GameStartTime") & "' and
          player_id = 1;"
        SqlDataAdapter1.UpdateCommand.ExecuteNonQuery()
        'show player play another game button and remove the Hit and Hold
          buttons
        HitButton.Visible = False
        HoldButton.Visible = False
        PlayAgainButton.Visible = True
      ElseIf Session("arrDealerHand")(0) + Session("arrDealerHand")
         (1) = 22 Then
        'set the first dealer Ace from 11 to 1
        Session("arrDealerHand")(0) = 1
        'continue playing
        Readout.Text = "Continue Playing"
      ElseIf Session("arrDealerHand")(0) + Session("arrDealerHand")
         (1) < 21 Then
        Readout.Text = "Continue Playing"
      End If
    ElseIf Session("arrPlayerHand")(0) + Session("arrPlayerHand")
      (1) = 22 Then
      'set the first player Ace from 11 to 1
      Session("arrPlayerHand")(0) = 1
```

```
            If Session("arrDealerHand")(0) + Session("arrDealerHand")
              (1) = 21 Then
            'set dealer first card up
            DealerCard01.ImageUrl = Session("arrDealerHandImages")(0)
            'declare dealer wins and game over
            Readout.Text = "Dealer Wins - Game Over"
            'record the win in database
            Dim vPlayerID2 As Integer
            vPlayerID2 = CInt(Session("PlayerID"))
            SqlDataAdapter1.UpdateCommand.CommandText = "Update games_played
              set game_status = 'Closed-DealerWin', winning_player_id = 1,
              losing_player_id = " & vPlayerID2 & ", winning_player_score = 21
              WHERE game_date = '" & Session("GameStartTime") & "' and
              player_id = " & vPlayerID2 & ";"
            SqlDataAdapter1.UpdateCommand.ExecuteNonQuery()
            SqlDataAdapter1.UpdateCommand.CommandText = "Update games_played
              set game_status = 'Closed-DealerWin', winning_player_id = 1,
              losing_player_id = " & vPlayerID2 & ", winning_player_score = 21
              WHERE game_date = '" & Session("GameStartTime") & "' and
              player_id = 1;"
            SqlDataAdapter1.UpdateCommand.ExecuteNonQuery()
            'show player play another game button and remove the Hit and Hold
              buttons
            HitButton.Visible = False
            HoldButton.Visible = False
            PlayAgainButton.Visible = True
          ElseIf Session("arrDealerHand")(0) + Session("arrDealerHand")
              (1) = 22 Then
            'set the first dealer Ace from 11 to 1
            Session("arrDealerHand")(0) = 1
            'continue playing
            Readout.Text = "Continue Playing"
          End If
        End If
```

14. Now that all the possible outcomes for the initial hand have been accounted for, we can close the database connection:

```
      End If
      SqlConnection1.Close()
```

WRITING THE HIT BUTTON CODE

Once the inital hand has been dealt, if neither the dealer nor player wins, the player can then hit until he/she either busts or decides to hold. The Hit button lets the player hit. In order to hit, the function must deal the player a card and not only place it in his/her cards on the screen but place it in his/her Session variables for the hand as well. Then, if the player busts, it must declare the player a loser and the game over. If the player has 21, the game must tell the player to hold, and if the player is under 21, the game must let the player Hit again or Hold.

1. First we'll declare some variables as counters for our For loops (some of the loops are embedded and require their own counters rather than reusing existing counters).

    ```
    Dim i As Integer
    Dim i2 As Integer
    Dim i3 As Integer
    Dim PlayerHandTotal As Integer
    ```

2. Next, we'll start a For loop and declare some more variables inside the loop. Then we'll deal a card to the first empty card in the player's hand (remember, all cards in the player's hand, held as a Session array variable, were initialized when the game started). In order to reset the proper control, when we don't know the name of the next ImageButton control, we'll figure out what the name should be using a small If...Then...End If block, and then find that control using the FindControl method:

    ```
    'determine the name of the next empty card in the Player's hand
    For i = 0 To 10
    Dim vPCNum As Integer
    Dim vPCNumString As String
    Dim vCurrPCIBName As String
    Dim vImageButton As ImageButton
    If Session("arrPlayerHandImages")(i) = "" Then
      'figure out dealer card image button name
      vPCNum = i + 1
      If vPCNum < 10 Then
        vPCNumString = "0" & CStr(vPCNum)
      Else
        vPCNumString = CStr(vPCNum)
      End If
      vCurrPCIBName = "PlayerCard" & vPCNumString
        vImageButton = FindControl(vCurrPCIBName)
    ```

3. Now we can deal the card, using code much like the code we used in the Page_Load event handler.

    ```
    'deal the card
    vImageButton.ImageUrl = Session("arrCardImages")
      (Session("arrCardSeq")(Session("NextCardToDeal")))
        Session("arrPlayerHandImages")(i) = Session("arrCardImages")
          (Session("arrCardSeq")(Session("NextCardToDeal")))
        Session("arrPlayerHand")(i) =
    Session("arrCardValues")(Session("arrCardSeq")
      (Session("NextCardToDeal")))
    Session("NextCardToDeal") = Session("NextCardToDeal") + 1
    vImageButton.Visible = True
    ```

4. After dealing a card, we can get out of the loop. If a card wasn't dealt, we remain in the loop until we find the first empty card in the player's hand.

```
         'get out of the loop
            Exit For
         End If
      Next
```

5. Once out of the loop, we recalculate the total value of the player's hand.

```
      For i2 = 0 To 10
         PlayerHandTotal = PlayerHandTotal + Session("arrPlayerHand")(i2)
      Next
```

6. If the player has more than 21, we check to see if they have any aces, on the assumption that they will want one of their aces to count as 1 instead of 11.

```
   'if player hand more than 21
   If PlayerHandTotal > 21 Then
   'does player have any 11s
      For i3 = 0 To 10
         If Session("arrPlayerHand")(i3) = 11 Then
            Session("ArrPlayerHand")(i3) = 1
            Exit For
         End If
      Next
```

7. If the player had any aces and we could recalculate, we do and then if the player is still over 21 (this would happen only if the player didn't have any aces, but we need to recalculate anyway), then the player has busted and the game is ended and recorded in the database:

```
      'recalc player hand total
      i = 0
      PlayerHandTotal = 0
      For i2 = 0 To 10
         PlayerHandTotal = PlayerHandTotal + Session("arrPlayerHand")(i2)
      Next
      'check again for over 21
      If PlayerHandTotal > 21 Then
         'player loses
         'declare game over
         Readout.Text = "You Busted - Game Over"
         'record loss
         SqlConnection1.Open()
         Dim vPlayerID2 As Integer
         vPlayerID2 = CInt(Session("PlayerID"))
         SqlDataAdapter1.UpdateCommand.CommandText = "Update games_played
            set game_status = 'Closed-DealerWin', winning_player_id = 1,
            losing_player_id = " & vPlayerID2 & ", losing_player_score = "
            & PlayerHandTotal & " WHERE game_date = '" & Session
            ("GameStartTime") & "' and player_id = " & vPlayerID2 & ";"
         SqlDataAdapter1.UpdateCommand.ExecuteNonQuery()
```

```
        SqlDataAdapter1.UpdateCommand.CommandText = "Update games_played
          set game_status = 'Closed-DealerWin', winning_player_id = 1,
          losing_player_id = " & vPlayerID2 & ", losing_player_score = "
          & PlayerHandTotal & " WHERE game_date = '" & Session
          ("GameStartTime") & "' and player_id = 1;"
        SqlDataAdapter1.UpdateCommand.ExecuteNonQuery()
        SqlConnection1.Close()
        'show player play again button
        HitButton.Visible = False
        HoldButton.Visible = False
        PlayAgainButton.Visible = True
    End If
End If
```

8. If the player's hand value is exactly 21, we tell the player to Hold, and if under 21 we tell the player to Hit or Hold:

```
        If PlayerHandTotal = 21 Then
         'show player Hold button but remove Hit button
         HitButton.Visible = False
         Readout.Text = "You have 21 - Please Hold"
        ElseIf PlayerHandTotal < 21 Then
         'if still under 21, player may hit again or hold
         Readout.Text = "Please Hit Again or Hold"
        End If
```

WRITING THE HOLD BUTTON CODE

The Hold button code actually affects only the dealer's hand. If the dealer's hand value is under 17, it makes the dealer hit until reaching 17. If the dealer's hand value goes above 17 (or starts above 17), it checks to see if the dealer is over 21, and if so whether the dealer has any aces that can be converted to a value of 1. Once all the dealer's options are exhausted, it compares the dealer's total score to the player's total score to see who won, lost, or pushed, and then it records the outcome in the database and offers the player a chance to play again. Much of the code is similar to what happens when the user plays, and the comments are a good guide to what specific parts of the code are doing.

1. Enter the following code in the Hold button's event handler:

```
Dim i As Integer
Dim i2 As Integer
Dim i3 As Integer
Dim i5 As Integer
Dim i6 As Integer
Dim DealerHandTotal As Integer
Dim PlayerHandTotal As Integer
'check dealer total
For i = 0 To 10
   DealerHandTotal = DealerHandTotal + Session("arrDealerHand")(i)
Next
'if dealer under 17, hit dealer
```

```
If DealerHandTotal < 17 Then
  For i2 = 0 To 10
    Dim vDCNum As Integer
    Dim vDCNumString As String
    Dim vCurrDCIBName As String
    Dim vImageButton As ImageButton
    If Session("arrDealerHandImages")(i2) = "" Then
      'figure out dealer card image button name
      vDCNum = i2 + 1
      If vDCNum < 10 Then
        vDCNumString = "0" & CStr(vDCNum)
      Else
        vDCNumString = CStr(vDCNum)
      End If
      vCurrDCIBName = "DealerCard" & vDCNumString
      vImageButton = FindControl(vCurrDCIBName)
      'deal the card
      vImageButton.ImageUrl = Session("arrCardImages")
        (Session("arrCardSeq")(Session("NextCardToDeal")))
  Session("arrDealerHandImages")(i2) = Session("arrCardImages")
    (Session("arrCardSeq")(Session("NextCardToDeal")))
  Session("arrDealerHand")(i2) = Session("arrCardValues")
    (Session("arrCardSeq")(Session("NextCardToDeal")))
  Session("NextCardToDeal") = Session("NextCardToDeal") + 1
      vImageButton.Visible = True
      'check to see if over 17
      DealerHandTotal = 0
      For i3 = 0 To 10
        DealerHandTotal = DealerHandTotal + Session("arrDealerHand")
          (i3)
      Next
      If DealerHandTotal >= 17 Then
        'check to see if over 21
        If DealerHandTotal > 21 Then
          'if over 21, does dealer have any 11s
          Dim i4 As Integer
          For i4 = 0 To 10
            'if yes, change oldest 11 to 1
            If Session("arrDealerHand")(i4) = 11 Then
              Session("arrDealerHand")(i4) = 1
              Exit For
            End If
          Next

          'recalc DealerHandTotal
          DealerHandTotal = 0
```

```vbnet
            For i5 = 0 To 10
                DealerHandTotal = DealerHandTotal + Session _
                    ("arrDealerHand")(i5)
            Next

            If DealerHandTotal >= 17 Then
                Exit For
            End If
         Else
            Exit For
         End If
         Exit For
      End If
    End If
  Next
End If

'if greater than 17 - decide winner
'check dealer total
DealerHandTotal = 0
For i6 = 0 To 10
   DealerHandTotal = DealerHandTotal + Session("arrDealerHand")(i6)
Next
i6 = 0
'check player total
For i6 = 0 To 10
   PlayerHandTotal = PlayerHandTotal + Session("arrPlayerHand")(i6)
Next

If DealerHandTotal > 21 Then
   'dealer loses
   'set dealer first card up
   DealerCard01.ImageUrl = Session("arrDealerHandImages")(0)
   Readout.Text = "Player Wins - Game Over"
   'record results
   SqlConnection1.Open()
   Dim vPlayerID2 As Integer
   vPlayerID2 = CInt(Session("PlayerID"))
   SqlDataAdapter1.UpdateCommand.CommandText = "Update games_played set
      game_status = 'Closed-PlayerWin', winning_player_id = " &
      vPlayerID2 & ", losing_player_id = 1, winning_player_score = " &
      PlayerHandTotal & " WHERE game_date = '" & Session("GameStartTime")
      & "' and player_id = " & vPlayerID2 & ";"
   SqlDataAdapter1.UpdateCommand.ExecuteNonQuery()
   SqlDataAdapter1.UpdateCommand.CommandText = "Update games_played set
      game_status = 'Closed-PlayerWin', winning_player_id = "
```

```
              & vPlayerID2 & ", losing_player_id = 1, winning_player_score = "
              & PlayerHandTotal & " WHERE game_date = '" & Session
              ("GameStartTime") & "' and player_id = 1;"
            SqlDataAdapter1.UpdateCommand.ExecuteNonQuery()
            SqlConnection1.Close()
            'show Play Again button
            HitButton.Visible = False
            HoldButton.Visible = False
            PlayAgainButton.Visible = True

        Else
            If DealerHandTotal > PlayerHandTotal Then
                'dealer wins
                'set dealer first card up
                DealerCard01.ImageUrl = Session("arrDealerHandImages")(0)
                'do readout
                Readout.Text = "Dealer Wins - Game Over"
                'record in database
                SqlConnection1.Open()
                Dim vPlayerID2 As Integer
                vPlayerID2 = CInt(Session("PlayerID"))
                SqlDataAdapter1.UpdateCommand.CommandText = "Update games_played
                    set game_status = 'Closed-DealerWin', winning_player_id = 1,
                    losing_player_id = " & vPlayerID2 & ", winning_player_score = "
                    & PlayerHandTotal & " WHERE game_date = '" & Session
                    ("GameStartTime") & "' and player_id = " & vPlayerID2 & ";"
                SqlDataAdapter1.UpdateCommand.ExecuteNonQuery()
                SqlDataAdapter1.UpdateCommand.CommandText = "Update games_played
                    set game_status = 'Closed-DealerWin', winning_player_id = 1,
                    losing_player_id = " & vPlayerID2 & ", winning_player_score = "
                    & PlayerHandTotal & " WHERE game_date = '" & Session
                    ("GameStartTime") & "' and player_id = 1;"
                SqlDataAdapter1.UpdateCommand.ExecuteNonQuery()
                SqlConnection1.Close()
                'show play again button
                HitButton.Visible = False
                HoldButton.Visible = False
                PlayAgainButton.Visible = True

            ElseIf DealerHandTotal < PlayerHandTotal Then
                'player wins
                'set dealer first card up
                DealerCard01.ImageUrl = Session("arrDealerHandImages")(0)
                'do readout
                Readout.Text = "Player Wins - Game Over"
                'record in database
```

```vb
        SqlConnection1.Open()
        Dim vPlayerID2 As Integer
        vPlayerID2 = CInt(Session("PlayerID"))
        SqlDataAdapter1.UpdateCommand.CommandText = "Update games_played set
           game_status = 'Closed-PlayerWin', winning_player_id = " &
           vPlayerID2 & ", losing_player_id = 1, winning_player_score = " &
           PlayerHandTotal & " WHERE game_date = '" & Session("GameStartTime")
           & "' and player_id = " & vPlayerID2 & ";"
        SqlDataAdapter1.UpdateCommand.ExecuteNonQuery()
        SqlDataAdapter1.UpdateCommand.CommandText = "Update games_played set
           game_status = 'Closed-PlayerWin', winning_player_id = " &
           vPlayerID2 & ", losing_player_id = 1, winning_player_score = " &
           PlayerHandTotal & " WHERE game_date = '" & Session("GameStartTime")
           & "' and player_id = 1;"
        SqlDataAdapter1.UpdateCommand.ExecuteNonQuery()
        SqlConnection1.Close()
        'show play again button
        HitButton.Visible = False
        HoldButton.Visible = False
        PlayAgainButton.Visible = True

    ElseIf DealerHandTotal = PlayerHandTotal Then
       'push
       'set dealer first card up
       DealerCard01.ImageUrl = Session("arrDealerHandImages")(0)
       'do readout
       Readout.Text = "Push - Please Play Again"
       'record in database
         SqlConnection1.Open()
         Dim vPlayerID2 As Integer
         vPlayerID2 = CInt(Session("PlayerID"))
         SqlDataAdapter1.UpdateCommand.CommandText = "Update games_played
            set game_status = 'Closed-Push', winning_player_id = 0,
            losing_player_id = 0, winning_player_score = 0 WHERE game_date =
            '" & Session("GameStartTime") & "' and player_id = " & vPlayerID2
            & ";"
         SqlDataAdapter1.UpdateCommand.ExecuteNonQuery()
         SqlDataAdapter1.UpdateCommand.CommandText = "Update games_played
            set game_status = 'Closed-Push', winning_player_id = 0,
            losing_player_id = 0, winning_player_score = 0 WHERE game_date =
            '" & Session("GameStartTime") & "' and player_id = 1;"
         SqlDataAdapter1.UpdateCommand.ExecuteNonQuery()
         SqlConnection1.Close()
         'show play again button
         HitButton.Visible = False
         HoldButton.Visible = False
```

```
            PlayAgainButton.Visible = True
        End If
    End If
```

THE PLAY AGAIN BUTTON CODE

The code for the Play Again button is very simple; it just redirects the player back to the "choose_game.aspx" page. When the player picks this option, he/she goes back to the page where he/she can choose a game, and if the player chooses Blackjack, he/she goes back to the Blackjack.aspx page, at which time the system reshuffles the deck and starts over.

1. Enter the following code in the Play Again button's event handler:

```
Response.Redirect("choose_game.aspx")
```

Blackjack and Other Card Game Rules You can find a great source for card game rules on the Web at www.pagat.com. Go to www.pagat.com/alpha for an alphabetical listing of links to the rules for hundreds of card games, including blackjack.

ADO.Net
DataAdapter
DataReader
DataRow
DataTable

DeleteCommand
InsertCommand
Parameters collection
SelectCommand
SqlCommand

SqlConnection
SqlDataAdapter
UpdateCommand

Review Questions

1. What kinds of data does a database connection contain?
2. Once a database connection is made, what can be done with it?
3. Why should you always close database connections when you are finished with them?
4. What commands can be run against a database through a database connection?
5. What objects are used to open a database connection in an ASP.Net Web application?
6. What objects are used to run commands against a database?
7. What commands can be run against a database?

8. What types of query can be executed with these commands?
9. How does a DataAdapter execute commands against a database?
10. Where does a DataAdapter store results it retrieves from a database?

XML Web Services

CHAPTER 9

LEARNING OBJECTIVES

Upon completion of this chapter, you will be able to:

1. Explain what XML Web Services are.
2. Search for XML Web Services in a UDDI registry.
3. Open and modify a WSDL file.
4. Build a WSDL file.
5. Explain how Simple Object Access Protocol (SOAP) relates to XML Web Services.
6. Build an ASP.Net XML Web Service file.
7. Build XML Web Services in VS.Net.
8. Connect a Web application to a Web Service in VS.Net.

INTRODUCTION

ASP.Net Web applications, in their basic form, allow users to interact with your application over the Internet, instead of having to have the application reside on their local computer. This takes the notion of "Web site" to a new level, and brings much more functionality to the Web. It allows developers to use the Internet to provide their programming expertise to millions of users in a new way, and to eliminate costs in the process.

XML Web Services represent another step forward in this trend of designing applications to work across the Internet. In traditional applications, all functionality was programmed into a single application. If you create an ASP.Net Web application that utilizes XML Web Services, some of the programmatic functionality may reside in one or more Web Services located anywhere on the Internet. Then, several of your programs can share access to the Web Service functions. Such sharing of resources reduces overhead and duplication of programming effort.

While the concept of Web Services is fairly straightforward, there are a few practical requirements that must be addressed, and these requirements add a layer of complexity to the process. The first step forward was the XML specification, which defines a highly useful method for applying context to any data. The XML Schema, Web Services Description Language (WSDL), Simple Object Access Protocol (SOAP), and several other standards all make Web Services feasible (note that there are competing standards in several areas, and that all issues have not been settled yet). Finally, some of VS.Net's built-in tools address development issues related to these requirements and make the process less difficult.

In this chapter we discuss the nature of XML Web Services, how they are written and exposed across the Internet, WSDL and SOAP, UDDI, and how all of these things are used to develop ASP.Net Web applications in VS.Net that connect to XML Web Services.

XML Web Services and ASP.Net

Anytime you go to a Web site and use it to perform some kind of data processing (such as when you use a mortgage calculator to find out what your new loan payments might be) you are using a Web service. **XML Web Services** differ from ordinary Web services in that they are meant to be accessed by Web applications from within the code of the application. Communication between a Web application and an XML Web Service is a good example of machine-to-machine communication and requires a machine-to-machine interface, not an ordinary user interface.

Using your browser, you communicate with an ordinary Web Service with the HTTP protocol. The browser just provides an easy-to-use visual interface so you can specify the HTTP to send without having to know HTTP. If you want the code in your ASP.Net Web application to make calls to procedures that are contained externally in an XML Web Service, your application must convert ordinary function calls into calls using other protocols: Web Services Description Language (WSDL) and Simple Object Access Protocol (SOAP). Fortunately, VS.Net has tools that do the conversion for you, and even allow you to include calls in your application that work like ordinary calls to procedures in the Source Code Editor. We'll cover how to make such calls from your code, as well as explore WSDL and SOAP, later in this chapter.

XML Web Services Development Process

During the course of developing an ordinary ASP.Net Web application (or any application, for that matter), you might find it useful to create a number of functions that are repeatedly called while your application processes data.

These functions are a good starting point for deciding if you need to build XML Web Services. For example, if you need to store a piece of data in a database several times as a user uses the application, you might want to make the data storage function into an XML Web Service, so that many company Web sites can use the same function independently. However, there are a few more factors to consider in the design of XML Web Services:

- XML Web Services should be designed to be used by potentially many applications. While you may not initially be aware all of the applications that could use your XML Web Service, by their nature they lend themselves to reuse by many different applications across the Internet. Try to avoid designing your XML Web Services in such a way that only your single application can use them.
- XML Web Services are available to other XML Web Services (one Web Service can talk to another, if the developer allows it). Therefore, you can have a whole series of XML Web Services, not necessarily all developed or hosted by a single company, working together to form ad hoc "applications" as necessary. Although this can be fairly complex, it also can be a great way to leverage all the work done by the individual companies involved, rather than the unnecessary duplication that is currently the case.
- XML Web Services can be accessed by Windows applications as well as Web applications. You can develop ordinary desktop applications that retrieve data or perform processing via XML Web Services.
- The capabilities of XML Web Services can be sold to other organizations. With a little extra effort you can publish your XML Web Services for use on a subscription basis (see the section on UDDI below), thereby generating revenue. You may not want to do this initially, or for some services, but the fact that this capability exists should make you consider the possibility of doing so at the design stage.

Due to these additional considerations, the design and development of XML Web Services should include steps that attempt to mold them into small, reusable, discrete functions, some of which could be resold outside your organization. And since other organizations also might have Web Services available, whether or not to develop them in-house should be taken into consideration.

Discussion—XML Web Services Design

Most of us use Web Services in one form or another everyday. For example, we often use search engines, and search engines are considered a Web Service because they allow us to perform some kind of data processing on the Web. However, one subcategory of Web Service is designed specifically for machine to machine communication (without a user interface), and Microsoft refers to these Web Services as XML Web Services.

The "XML" part of the name is applied because communication takes place with XML-based protocols. There are several popular XML-based languages (WSDL and SOAP) that provide a standardized format for calling data processing functions across the Web.

XML Web Services perform data processing the way any function or procedure processes data: they accept input, process it, and return output. Designing XML Web Services is similar to the design of any function as well: outline the problem, decide what inputs are necessary to solve it efficiently, and write and debug the code. However, since using XML Web Services ordinarily occurs within the process of designing and developing a Web application, there are additional questions to answer concerning the need to use XML Web Services, their reliability and security, and whether or not they should be developed in-house or bought from an outside company.

XML Web Services Protocols

Imagine for a moment that you have written the code for an algorithm that solves a common problem in a unique way. You've designed and tested the code, and it seems bulletproof, highly efficient, very fast, scalable, and perhaps even patentable. But the algorithm accepts only certain data values and is more suited to supplying input to other algorithms than as something a person would use directly. How would you make it available to other people who might want to use it?

Over the years, many programmers have faced this challenge. The great variety of programs in place, and the need to share some of their processing results with other programs, has resulted in many man-hours spent on integration. The term *integration* is used whenever work needs to be done to help programs communicate with each other. Ideally, there would be no need to translate data or functionality between programs.

In the real world, it can be very difficult to translate data, because data are kept in many formats and their meaning is often undocumented. The use of XML-based languages to document the meaning of data goes a long way toward assigning meaning to data in a standard way. Functionality benefits from the application of standard, XML-based protocols and formats as well. In this section, we discuss some of the more popular formats for publicizing and using functionality across the Web.

Specific Problems Facing XML Web Service Developers

If you are writing a function within a Web application, you simply write the code you need and call the function whenever you wish. But if you write a function to use as an XML Web Service, or use an external XML Web Service in your application, there are a number of concerns you should address. As the developer of an XML Web Service, will your Web Service be for use by only your application, or will it be published and used within your entire organization, or perhaps even sold to clients or the public? The use your service gets may affect your own application's ability to use it.

Other important concerns, from either the developer's or user's point of view, are the security and reliability of the XML Web Service. If the service is sold outside the developing organization, measures must be taken to ensure security and limit users to only those who are authorized. And if the service is sold to the general public, dramatic increases in use may make the service unusable. Finally, payment for service can be even more difficult to track than the service itself.

Not all these problems have ready answers, but there are a few protocols in use that address some of them. **Universal Description, Discovery, and Integration (UDDI)** is a standard method for publishing Web Services to make them available for external subscribers. **Web Services Description Language (WSDL)** is an XML-based protocol for describing the functionally of Web Services. And **Simple Object Access Protocol (SOAP)** is an XML-based protocol for communicating functionality (for calling functions and returning results) across the Web.

Universal Description, Discovery, and Integration (UDDI)

If you want to find a Web site that has information about a particular subject, you can use a search engine. While not every site located through a search engine will necessarily be what you are looking for, search engines are nonetheless a very good tool for finding relevant Web sites, and the better the user is at using a search engine, the more profitable a search will be. We take it for granted that just about any subject is discussed at some site on the Internet, and expect search engines to catalog most of them.

But how do you find an XML Web Service that suits your needs? First of all, you need to have the equivalent of a search engine to help you find available services. Because XML Web Services don't really have a user interface, searching with a search engine is not practical. XML Web Services directories are an attempt to provide search capability for XML Web Services.

UDDI is a set of standards that specify a common format for registering XML Web Services in an XML Web Service directory. One such directory is located at www.uddi.org, and Microsoft maintains a node at uddi.microsoft.com. In an XML Web Service directory **(UDDI registry),** you can register your information about your service including business information, service information, binding information, and specifications for what the service does.

Discovery Files

Once you have created and registered a Web Service, you may want to have a discovery file located on your server to enable potential users to programmatically discover your Web Service. Such files end with the extension .disco. Discovery files are XML-based documents that provide information about where in your site WSDL data are located. The WSDL data, in turn, describe the available Web Services. Discovery files are essentially a roadmap to any Web Services you are making available to the public and operate like your own Web Services directory. You can see from the following contents how they work:

```xml
<?xml version="1.0" encoding="utf-8" ?>
<dynamicDiscovery xmlns="urn:schemas-
dynamicdiscovery:disco.2000-03-17">
<exclude path="_vti_cnf" />
<exclude path="_vti_pvt" />
<exclude path="_vti_log" />
<exclude path="_vti_script" />
<exclude path="_vti_txt" />
<exclude path="Web References" />
</dynamicDiscovery>
```

The dynamicDiscovery element specifies (or excludes) folder locations in the site that may or may not contain WSDL files. You also can add discovery elements of your own, including service descriptions, XML schemas, and so forth, by including discoveryRef, contractRef, and schemaRef elements, as shown in this example:

```xml
<discoveryRef ref="/sub_folder/newwebservice.disco"/>
<contractRef ref="http://server/webservicename.asmx?WSDL"
    docRef="newwebservice.html"
xmlns="http://schemas.xmlsoap.org/disco/"/>
<schemaRef ref="newwebschema.xsd"
xmlns="http://schemas.xmlsoap.org/disco/schema/"/>
```

Web Services Description Language (WSDL)

The WSDL specification is XML-based. The purpose of WSDL documents is to provide a means by which XML Web Services can be communicated with programmatically. Therefore, the format of WSDL follows a predictable pattern. In a WSDL document, there are elements and attributes that define all features of your XML Web Service, including how they can be bound to the service and what data types they accept.

WSDL Document Sections

Any location on a network or the Internet could either read, process, or write data, and therefore could be an endpoint for a Web Service. WSDL documents describe Web Services in terms of what each endpoint may do with the service, the type of data the service requires for processing, and how to bind to the service. There are specific sections in WSDL documents that provide this information in the appropriate format:

- **Binding.** Binding translates communications into the format that the endpoint can understand. Essentially, binding is a protocol and data format specification for the Port Type.

- **Ports.** Endpoints and ports are synonymous. The port "listens" for any messages sent.
- **Types.** Types are containers for data with a specific data type.
- **Messages.** Messages are the data being communicated.
- **Operations.** Operations are the processing that happens to the data.
- **Port Type.** The Port Type is a set of operations.

A WSDL Example In our Hands On Project at the end of this chapter, we create a Web Service that calculates odds for a Blackjack hand. VS.Net provides a means by which you can test Web Services as you work on them, and, as part of the testing, WSDL documents representing the service are created and displayed. In the following code is an example of the WSDL document created for our Web Service (you'll see it in action as you do the project) broken into sections, with a short explanation of each section.

```
<?xml version="1.0" encoding="utf-8" ?>
<definitions xmlns:s1="http://blackjack.com/AbstractTypes"
xmlns:http="http://schemas.xmlsoap.org/wsdl/http/"
    xmlns:soap="http://schemas.xmlsoap.org/wsdl/soap/"
xmlns:s="http://www.w3.org/2001/XMLSchema"
    xmlns:s0="http://blackjack.com/"
xmlns:soapenc="http://schemas.xmlsoap.org/soap/encoding/"
xmlns:tm="http://microsoft.com/wsdl/mime/textMatching/"
xmlns:mime="http://schemas.xmlsoap.org/wsdl/mime/"
    targetNamespace="http://blackjack.com/"
xmlns="http://schemas.xmlsoap.org/wsdl/">
```

WSDL documents begin with the XML version (as good XML documents do) followed by the root element "definitions." Also included are the namespaces of the elements and attributes in the document and, as you can see, the default namespace location for VS.Net applications (tempuri.org) has been changed to blackjack.com, a made-up namespace.

```
<types>
<s:schema elementFormDefault="qualified" targetNamespace=
    "http://blackjack.com/">
<s:element name="ExactOdds">
<s:complexType>
<s:sequence>
<s:element minOccurs="1" maxOccurs="1" name="vNumCardsDlt"
    type="s:int" />
<s:element minOccurs="0" maxOccurs="1" name="vCards"
    type="s0:ArrayOfInt" />
</s:sequence>
</s:complexType>
</s:element>
<s:complexType name="ArrayOfInt">
```

```xml
<s:sequence>
<s:element minOccurs="0" maxOccurs="unbounded" name="int"
  type="s:int" />
</s:sequence>
</s:complexType>
<s:element name="ExactOddsResponse">
<s:complexType>
<s:sequence>
<s:element minOccurs="0" maxOccurs="1"
  name="ExactOddsResult" type="s:string" />
</s:sequence>
</s:complexType>
</s:element>
<s:element name="string" nillable="true" type="s:string" />
</s:schema>
<s:schema targetNamespace="http://blackjack.com/
  AbstractTypes">
<s:complexType name="StringArray">
<s:complexContent mixed="false">
<s:restriction base="soapenc:Array">
<s:sequence>
<s:element minOccurs="0" maxOccurs="unbounded" name=
  "String" type="s:string" />
</s:sequence>
</s:restriction>
</s:complexContent>
</s:complexType>
</s:schema>
</types>
```

Next come the definitions of types in our service, and you'll notice they include "vNumCardsDlt" as an integer and "vCards" as an array.

```xml
<message name="ExactOddsSoapIn">
<part name="parameters" element="s0:ExactOdds" />
</message>
<message name="ExactOddsSoapOut">
<part name="parameters" element="s0:ExactOddsResponse" />
</message>
<message name="ExactOddsHttpGetIn">
<part name="vNumCardsDlt" type="s:string" />
<part name="vCards" type="s1:StringArray" />
</message>
<message name="ExactOddsHttpGetOut">
<part name="Body" element="s0:string" />
</message>
```

```
<message name="ExactOddsHttpPostIn">
<part name="vNumCardsDlt" type="s:string" />
<part name="vCards" type="s1:StringArray" />
</message>
<message name="ExactOddsHttpPostOut">
<part name="Body" element="s0:string" />
</message>
```

The message elements define how the service uses HTTP GET, HTTP POST, and SOAP as communication protocols.

```
<portType name="ExactOddsCalcSoap">
<operation name="ExactOdds">
<input message="s0:ExactOddsSoapIn" />
<output message="s0:ExactOddsSoapOut" />
</operation>
</portType>
<portType name="ExactOddsCalcHttpGet">
<operation name="ExactOdds">
<input message="s0:ExactOddsHttpGetIn" />
<output message="s0:ExactOddsHttpGetOut" />
</operation>
</portType>
<portType name="ExactOddsCalcHttpPost">
<operation name="ExactOdds">
<input message="s0:ExactOddsHttpPostIn" />
<output message="s0:ExactOddsHttpPostOut" />
</operation>
</portType>
```

The Port Type elements define the operations and input/output formats for each protocol.

```
<binding name="ExactOddsCalcSoap" type="s0:
   ExactOddsCalcSoap">
<soap:binding transport="http://schemas.xmlsoap.org/soap/
   http" style="document" />
<operation name="ExactOdds">
<soap:operation soapAction="http://blackjack.
   com/ExactOdds" style="document" />
<input>
<soap:body use="literal" />
</input>
<output>
<soap:body use="literal" />
</output>
</operation>
```

```xml
    </binding>
    <binding name="ExactOddsCalcHttpGet" type="s0:
      ExactOddsCalcHttpGet">
    <http:binding verb="GET" />
    <operation name="ExactOdds">
    <http:operation location="/ExactOdds" />
    <input>
    <http:urlEncoded />
    </input>
    <output>
    <mime:mimeXml part="Body" />
    </output>
    </operation>
    </binding>
    <binding name="ExactOddsCalcHttpPost" type="s0:
      ExactOddsCalcHttpPost">
    <http:binding verb="POST" />
    <operation name="ExactOdds">
    <http:operation location="/ExactOdds" />
    <input>
    <mime:content type="application/x-www-form-urlencoded" />
    </input>
    <output>
    <mime:mimeXml part="Body" />
    </output>
    </operation>
    </binding>
```

The Binding element specifies the binding method, operation, and input/output types.

```xml
    <service name="ExactOddsCalc">
    <port name="ExactOddsCalcSoap" binding="s0:
      ExactOddsCalcSoap">
    <soap:address location="http://localhost/BlackJackHands/
      ExactOddsCalc.asmx" />
    </port>
    <port name="ExactOddsCalcHttpGet" binding="s0:
      ExactOddsCalcHttpGet">
    <http:address location="http://localhost/BlackJackHands/
      ExactOddsCalc.asmx" />
    </port>
    <port name="ExactOddsCalcHttpPost" binding="s0:
      ExactOddsCalcHttpPost">
    <http:address location="http://localhost/BlackJackHands/
      ExactOddsCalc.asmx" />
```

```
</port>
</service>
</definitions>
```

The service name identifies the service and the ports associated with it, and the last line finishes the "definitions element."

Generating or Linking to WSDL documents

While you're working on a Web Service, you can bring up the WSDL document just using the facilities in VS.Net. But if you want to automatically generate a WSDL document when the service is accessed directly, add "?WSDL" to the URL you enter in the browser (or from a link). The WSDL document will be returned in XML format in your browser. You also can add a link from the start page of a Web application. The link should reference the disco file for the Web Service.

Simple Object Access Protocol (SOAP)

WSDL documents provide a way to "call" programmatic functions over the Web. Still, you need to have a means of exchanging "calls" in a standard format. Simple Object Access Protocol (SOAP) fills this need. It "wraps" calls to objects over the Internet in an XML-based language. SOAP messages may contain the following parts:

- **Envelope**—defines what is in the message, who or what should process the message, and whether such processing is optional or mandatory.
- **Encoding Rules**—defines a serialization mechanism for communicating instances of application-defined data types.
- **Procedure Call Conventions**—defines a standard means of calling procedures remotely.

SOAP messages must contain an envelope element and a body element and may or may not contain SOAP headers. The body contains the information for the user application or service.

Discussion—WSDL and SOAP

In order to create an XML Web Service, you need to create the programmatic functionality for the service, and then create WSDL and SOAP documents that provide the mechanism to format and communicate the service across the Web in a standard way. WSDL stands for Web Services Description Language, and it describes the Web Service and connection methods in terms of messages, port types, and operations. SOAP stands for Simple Object Access Protocol and calls to services are made using the SOAP envelope schema.

Building Web Services

Developers have the option of building ASP.Net XML Web Services manually, writing out the code in a text editor, or using the templates in VS.Net to get a jumpstart on building their service. The following sections describe both methods.

Building XML Web Services Manually

VS.Net has many built-in tools and templates for creating XML Web Services and for connecting them to an ASP.Net Web application. But you can build XML Web Services manually as well. In the simplest terms, you can create XML Web Services by making a file with an .asmx extension. Then put a **@ WebService directive** in the file and define the functions that service performs in code.

Files with an .asmx extension on the name are taken to be ASP.Net XML Web Services by the Common Language Runtime (CLR). The following code shows an example of the directive and class declaration for an .asmx file:

```
<%@ WebService Language="VB" Class="NewWebService" %>
Imports System
Imports System.Web.Services
Public Class NewWebService :Inherits WebService
<WebMethod()> Public Function NewWebService() As String
Return("This is a new Web Service")
End Function
End Class
```

The @ WebService directive is on the first line of code, followed by a few Import statements importing the appropriate classes into the service. The class is named "NewWebService", and the WebMethod line indicates it is a public function that returns a string once processing is complete.

The WebMethodAttribute Class

You can use this class to make a function you've written in your Web application into a public function that can be called by remote Web clients. As we mentioned, you must add the WebService directive to the page. There are a number of interesting properties associated with this class, several of which are listed here:

- **Description**—describes what the service does.
- **EnableSession**—indicates whether session state is enabled for the service.

Using VS.Net to Build Web Services

VS.Net has project templates for building XML Web Services, and these can be added to any existing solution or created as part of a new solution. In the

Hands On Project, we'll first create a new Web application to calculate the odds of getting any given hand in our Blackjack game, and then we'll create a Web Service that does much of the processing separately.

Quick Check Questions

1. What is a Web Service? What is an XML Web Service?
2. How can you publish Web Services you've created for others to use?
3. What does a discovery file do for your Web Service?
4. In an ASP.Net XML Web Service, what extension is used for the filename?
5. What is the name of the directive used to make an ASP.Net file a Web Service?
6. What is the name of the attribute added to the Class declaration in the code-behind file to expose it as a Web Service?
7. What is the root element of a WSDL document?
8. What HTTP protocol methods can be used with a WSDL document for Web Service communications?
9. When would you place "?WSDL" on the end of a URL, if you were accessing the Web Service in a browser?
10. What part of a SOAP message carries the data to be processed?

Summary

1. XML Web Services are equivalent to functions in Web applications, in the sense that you can programmatically pass them data and they will return answers, without the need for a user interface or human interaction. The development process for creating XML Web Services is much the same as for Web applications (at least the data processing part), but you need to think about what data must be passed to the service, rather than in terms of user interaction with a Web form.
2. For Web Services to work, a good Internet or network connection must be available, but this is usually not a problem. However, if you allow outside users to use your Web Services, there are additional concerns about security, reliability, and payment that must be addressed.
3. Developers of Web Services can publish those services for others to find, perhaps using a UDDI Web Services directory. WSDL acts as a description language for Web Services, and SOAP acts as a language for formatting calls to and responses from Web Services.
4. Visual Studio.Net has templates for building Web Services in solutions and projects, and tools for discovering and making references to them in Web applications.

Exercise

1. You have been assigned to create a Web application that will calculate what your company charges to ship the specialized goods your company produces. Your company performs its own shipping because of the special nature of the products, and shipping charges are based on quantity, weight, size, shelf life, hazardous material content, due date, and customer. The shipping charges change frequently as the shipping department updates its cost basis and new variations of the products are

added. Many different departments across your company use the shipping costs as part of their own internal calculations of costs. Answer the following questions:
- Do you think your Web application should include a Web Service? Why?
- If so, how would you split up the Web application and what might you name the Web Service function?
- What parameters do you think would need to be sent to the Web Service so the answer could be processed?
- What processing do you think the Web Service would do?
- You have estimated that your application will cost $10K to develop as specified. How might this cost be defrayed?

Creating an XML Web Service

The project will supplement our existing OMPGame ASP.Net Web application, and we will attach the resulting XML Web Service to our OMPGame application to demonstrate how to make Web references. In this project, we will define the XML Web Service we intend to build as follows:

"This service will be available on an internal network to our application, but not generally across the Internet. A page in the OMPGame application will provide an interface by which the application will accept input from users, and that page will also display the returned output. The purpose of this service is to calculate the odds of any particular hand appearing in a card game, based on the suits, card values, and total number of cards in the deck."

Inputs from the user will consist of card choices by value for up to seven cards. Card choices allowed will be

1. Any card with a value of 1, 2, 3, 4, 5, 6, 7, 8, or 9 (each of these choices will be separate).
2. Any card with a value of 10.
3. Any card with a value of 11.

The total number of cards will start at 52, but the number will decrease each time a card is "dealt," and the number of remaining cards of a given value also will decrease as each value is "used."

Output will be the probability of getting the hand in question on the deal. Output will be given in exact order and in any order (the probabilities of each exact order are added to give any order).

We will start our project by creating a new ASP.Net Web application from the Visual Basic projects template. In this project we will create a form for submitting inputs, and then we will create an XML Web Service that processes the inputs and returns the answers. The Web Service will then be connected to the project via a Web Reference, and the form will display the answer to the user.

CREATING THE NEW WEB APPLICATION

1. Open VS.Net and create a new project (from the Visual Basic projects template for ASP.Net Web applications) named BlackjackHands. A blank Web form should open on your screen.

2. Place four Label controls on the form. Put one at the top and change its Text property to read "Blackjack Hand Odds Calculator". Put another below the top label and to the left, and put the message in Figure 9.1 in it. Put the other two below that and change their Text properties to read "Exact Order =" and "Any Order =". Name these last two labels ExactOrderLabel and AnyOrderLabel.

3. Place 12 more Label controls on the form in a column from top to bottom. Change their Text properties to read "Number Of Cards Dealt", "Value of Card 1", "Value of Card 2", and so on.

4. Place 12 DropDownList controls on the screen in a column from top to bottom, to the right of the 12 Labels. Start by placing the first Label, then before you add the rest, create a set of items in the Items collection of the first DropDownList control. The items should be indexed from zero to eleven, and their Text and Values properties should be exactly the same as their index number (Item index 0 should have a Text value of 0 and a Values value of 0, and so on). Now copy the remaining 11 DropDownList boxes from the first one. Doing it this way avoids having to rebuild the Items collection for each new DropDownList control.

5. Place two Button controls at the bottom of the form. Set the Text property for the first one to read "Clear", and for the second one to read "Calculate Odds".

6. Set the background color of the form to Black and set the background, border, and foreground colors of the controls as shown in Figure 9.1.

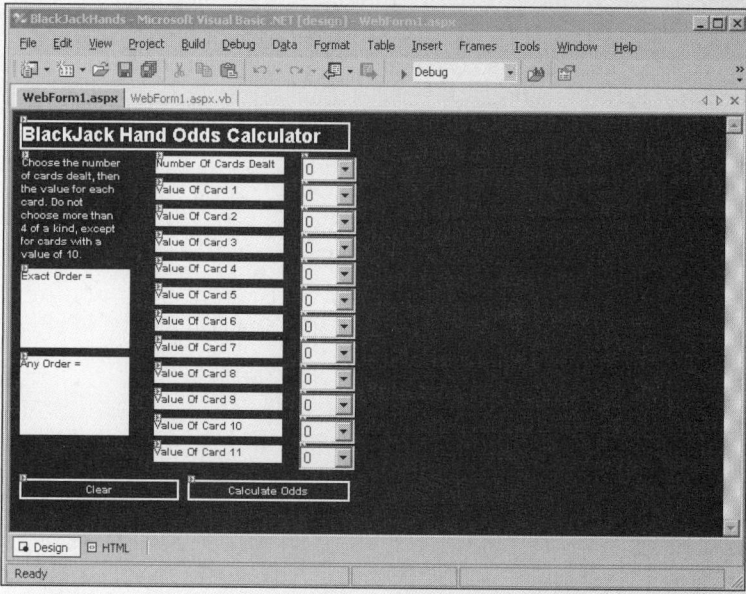

FIGURE 9.1 The BlackjackHands Web Form in Design View

WRITING THE CODE TO CALCULATE HANDS

Before we create our XML Web Service, we'll write and debug the code as part of our ASP.Net Web application. Although we could, of course, use the application without going through the problem of converting the code into an XML Web Service, our reasoning for creating the service might be so that we can resell the same service to anyone, without having to allow them access to our Web application. Note that once we've written and debugged the code here, we'll have to make some significant changes so that it will work properly as an XML Web Service.

To calculate the odds of the appearance of a particular hand, we need to track the number of cards dealt (we could deduce this from the value of selected items, but this just makes our job easier), the number of each card value available (there are four 2s, four 3s, and so on, except there are 16 cards with a value of 10 and we need to account for the fact that four aces can be either 1 or 11), and the actual cards chosen by the user. We also need to build in a mechanism for ending the calculation if the user has chosen more than four of a kind (like choosing five 2s). Then we can calculate the odds for each hand showing up in the exact order, and from that we can calculate the odds of the same hand appearing in any order. Finally, we need to create the label text for the ExactOrderLabel and the AnyOrderLabel controls to tell the user what the odds were found to be.

1. Create an event handler for the "Calculate Odds" button (either Button1 or Button2). Enter the following code to dimension variables for the application:

```
'dimension some variables for cards dealt, odds, cards, and so on
Dim NumberOfCardsDealt As Integer
Dim i As Integer = 1
Dim ExactOrderOdds As Double = 1
Dim AnyOrderOdds As Double = 0
Dim arrCards(11) As Integer
Dim vTotalCards As Integer = 52
Dim vMoreThan4Flag As Boolean
```

Enter the following code to reset the ExactOrder and AnyOrder labels, in case the user is returning to the page for another calculation:

```
'reset the odds labels, just in case
ExactOrderLabel.Text = "Exact Order = "
AnyOrderLabel.Text = "Any Order ="
```

2. Enter the following code to set up the array of card values:

```
'set up the cards array for available card values
    'there are four of each kind, except there are 16 cards with 10 value
    arrCards(0) = 0
    arrCards(1) = 4
    arrCards(2) = 4
    arrCards(3) = 4
    arrCards(4) = 4
    arrCards(5) = 4
    arrCards(6) = 4
    arrCards(7) = 4
    arrCards(8) = 4
    arrCards(9) = 4
    arrCards(10) = 16
    arrCards(11) = 4
```

3. Enter the following code to capture value of the number of cards dealt, and to check to see if it is zero:

```
'set this variable to the value for the number of cards dealt
NumberOfCardsDealt = DDLNumberOfCardsDealt.SelectedItem.Value
'if the number of cards dealt is zero, remind the user
If NumberOfCardsDealt = 0 Then
    ExactOrderLabel.Text = "Please select Number Of Cards"
    AnyOrderLabel.Text = "Any Order ="
Else
```

Hands On Project

4. Enter the following code to start a For loop and dimension more variables for inside the loop:

```
'go thru a loop for the number of cards dealt times
For i = 1 To NumberOfCardsDealt
    'dimension some variables for finding the DDLCard control
    Dim vCardNum As Integer
    Dim vCardNumStr As String
    Dim vCardName As String
    Dim vDDL As DropDownList
    Dim i2 As Integer = 1
```

5. Enter the following code to figure out the name of the current DropDownList control the user has selected a card value in:

```
'figure out card number and find the control
vCardNum = i
If vCardNum < 10 Then
    vCardNumStr = "0" & CStr(vCardNum)
Else
    vCardNumStr = CStr(vCardNum)
End If
vCardName = "DDLCard" & vCardNumStr
vDDL = FindControl(vCardName)
```

6. Enter the following code to start an inner For loop that will check any of the 11 choices the user can make for this DropDownList:

```
'go though a loop for each potential card value
For i2 = 1 To 11
```

7. Enter the following code to see which card value was selected and determine whether there are any of those card values left in the deck. This code sets the flag and exits the loop if more than four of a kind were chosen:

```
    'if the value is the same as the loop number
If vDDL.SelectedItem.Value = i2 Then
'check to see if there are any of these card values left
If arrCards(i2) < 1 Then
    'if not, set a flag and exit the inner loop
    vMoreThan4Flag = True
    Exit For
```

8. Enter the following code for action if there are card values of this kind left. This code calculates the ExactOrderOdds value by dividing the number of cards with this value (that are left) by the total number of cards that are left, and then multiplying that value times any previously calculated odds. The code then decrements the number of card values by 1, except if the card was an ace (card value 1 or 11), in which case it decrements both types of card value by 1.

```
Else
        'if so, calculate odds of this card occurring, times any odds
already calculated
```

```
            ExactOrderOdds = ExactOrderOdds * (arrCards(i2) / vTotalCards)
            'if the card value was 11 or 1
            If i2 = 11 Or i2 = 1 Then
               'remove the appropriate values from the array
               arrCards(1) = arrCards(1) - 1
               arrCards(11) = arrCards(11) - 1
               'decrement total cards by one
               vTotalCards = vTotalCards - 1
            Else
               'remove the appropriate value from the array
               arrCards(i2) = arrCards(i2) - 1
               'decrement total cards by one
               vTotalCards = vTotalCards - 1
            End If
         End If
      End If
   Next
```

9. Enter the following code to exit the outer loop if more than four of a kind have been chosen:

```
   'if the flag is set exit the outside loop
   If vMoreThan4Flag = True Then
      Exit For
   End If
```

10. Enter the following code to notify the user if more than four of a kind were chosen, or else calculate the AnyOrderOdds value and then display the ExactOrder and AnyOrder labels. This code also calculates the number of hands that would have to be dealt for this hand to show up:

```
   'if the flag is set, notify the user about more than 4 of a kind
   If vMoreThan4Flag = True Then
      ExactOrderLabel.Text = "Can't get more than 4 of a kind"
      AnyOrderLabel.Text = "Please try again"
   Else
      'calculate odds of cards in any order
      AnyOrderOdds = ExactOrderOdds * NumberOfCardsDealt
      'set the Exact and Any Order Labels
      ExactOrderLabel.Text = "Exact Order = " & CStr(ExactOrderOdds) & " or 1 out of " & CStr(CInt(1 / ExactOrderOdds)) & " hands"
      AnyOrderLabel.Text = "Any Order = " & CStr(AnyOrderOdds) & " or 1 out of " & CStr(CInt(1 / AnyOrderOdds)) & " hands"
   End If
End If
```

11. Create an event handler for the "Clear" button. Enter the following code to reset things for another calculation (this is not necessary, but may make the user feel more comfortable):

```
'reset things for another calculation
ExactOrderLabel.Text = "Exact Order = "
AnyOrderLabel.Text = "Any Order = "
```

```
DDLNumberOfCardsDealt.SelectedIndex = 0
DDLCard01.SelectedIndex = 0
DDLCard02.SelectedIndex = 0
DDLCard03.SelectedIndex = 0
DDLCard04.SelectedIndex = 0
DDLCard05.SelectedIndex = 0
DDLCard06.SelectedIndex = 0
DDLCard07.SelectedIndex = 0
DDLCard08.SelectedIndex = 0
DDLCard09.SelectedIndex = 0
DDLCard10.SelectedIndex = 0
DDLCard11.SelectedIndex = 0
```

12. Go back to WebForm1.aspx in Design view and choose File|Build and Browse from the menu. Check to make sure you're getting the correct answers. For example, the odds of getting a card valued at 10 in the first card is 16/52 (about 0.3077) and the odds of getting a card valued at 11 on the second card is 4/51 (about 0.078, because there are now only 51 cards left). The odds of getting these two cards in this exact order is about 0.3077 * 0.078 = 0.2413, or one out of every 42 hands, and the odds of getting these two cards in any order is about one out of 21 hands. Figure 9.2 shows how the form looks in use, with this calculation.

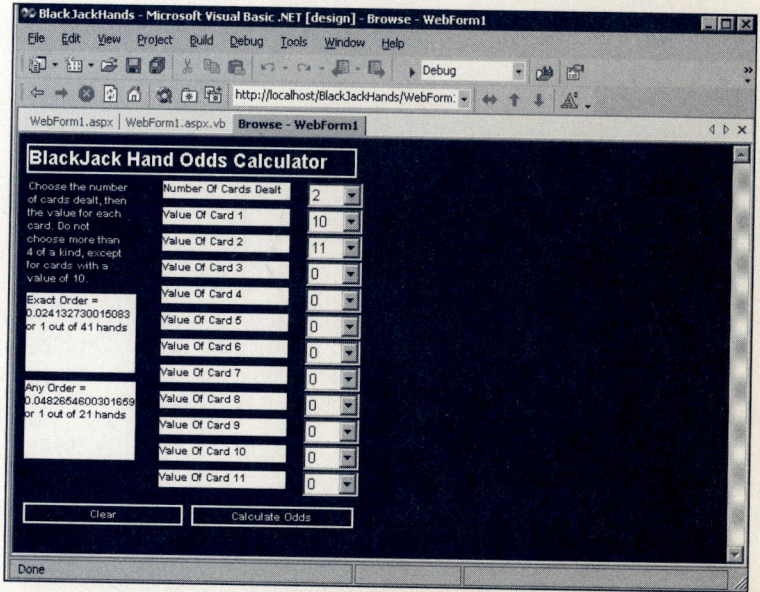

FIGURE 9.2 The Web Application in Use

CREATING AN XML WEB SERVICE FOR CALCULATING BLACKJACK HANDS

To create an XML Web Service from this procedure in Visual Basic, we need to pass the service a set of values that can be processed in a like manner and yield the same result. In order to do this, we'll have to pass the NumberOfCards value and the value of the DropDownList controls representing card values, and create in the XML Web Service the card value array and the variable that holds the total number of cards. Then we'll have to recreate much of the processing that is done by the Web application.

TESTING THE HELLO WORLD EXAMPLE WEB SERVICE

1. If VS.Net is not open, open it, open the BlackjackHands project (with WebForm1.aspx open), and display the Solution Explorer.

2. Right-click the project name in Solution Explorer and choose Add|Add Web Service from the shortcut menu. The Add New Item dialog box should open.

3. The Web Service template should be selected. Rename the service "ExactOddsCalc.asmx". Click Open. A new Web Service file named ExactOddsCalc.asmx.vb should open on your screen, as shown in Figure 9.3.

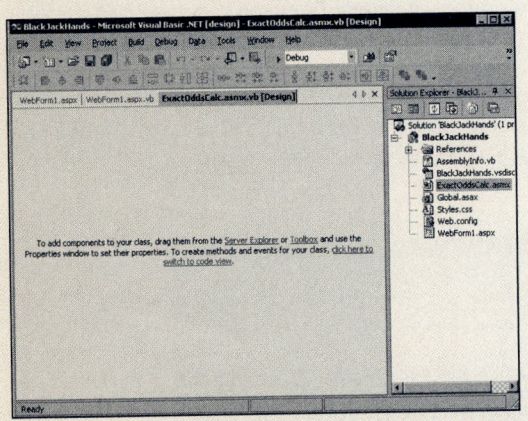

FIGURE 9.3 The New Web Service File in Design View

4. Notice on the surface of the file you have the ability to put components from the Toolbox in the service, and if you were going to do so you would need to open the Toolbox. In this case we're simply going to add code, so there's no need to open the Toolbox. Instead, click the link that puts the file into Code view. Figure 9.4 shows what the code-behind file looks like.

5. The ExactOddsCalc.asmx file contains ASP.Net code, including a directive. In the Solution Explorer, view the code by right-clicking the ExactOddsCalc.asmx file (not the .asmx.vb file) and choosing Open With from the shortcut menu. The Open With dialog box will open, as shown in Figure 9.5.

6. Choose Source Code (Text) Editor and click the Open button. The ExactOddsCalc.asmx file will open and display the following code:

```
<%@ WebService Language="vb" Codebehind="ExactOddsCalc.asmx.vb"
Class="BlackJackHands.ExactOddsCalc" %>
```

7. As we mentioned earlier, this code has the WebService directive, and also specifies the language, the name of the code-behind file, and the name of the class for the Web Service. We're not going to make any changes, so close the file.

Hands On Project

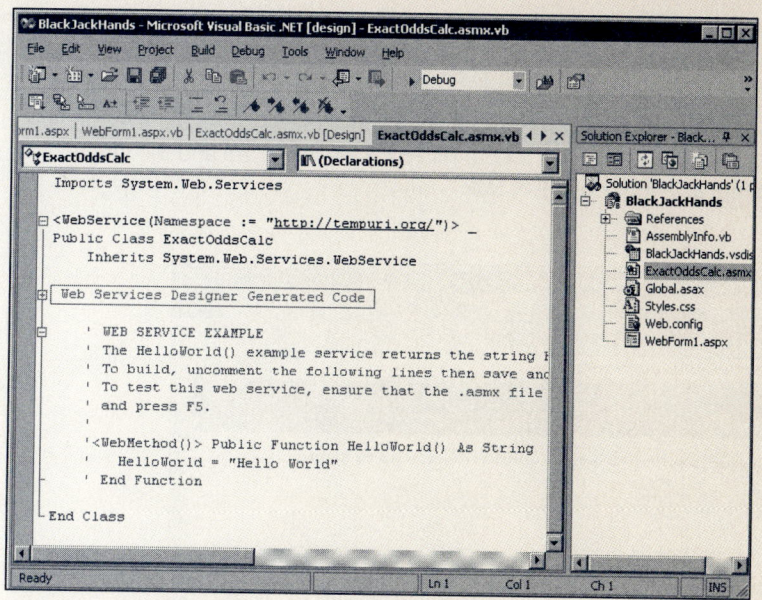

FIGURE 9.4 The Web Service Code-Behind File

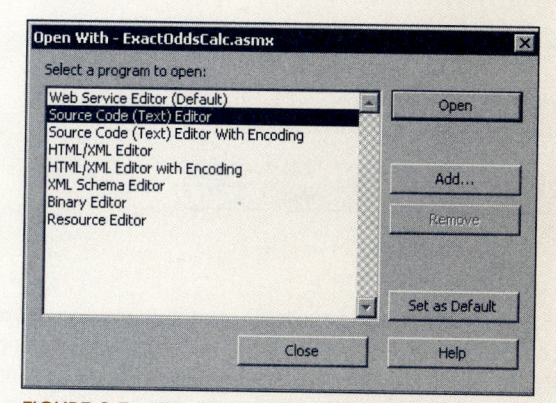

FIGURE 9.5 The Open With Dialog Box

8. Back in the ExactOddsCalc.asmx file, notice the comments that include an example Web Service function. Remove the comment markers from the function, so the code is the same as this:

```
<WebMethod()> Public Function HelloWorld() As String
    HelloWorld = "Hello World"
End Function
```

9. Notice this code starts with the WebMethod() attribute and is declared as a Public Function. This means the code will be exposed as part of the Web Service. Later, when we reference the Web Service from our Web application, we could have several functions available.

10. Notice also that the function returns a string (with the words "Hello World"). That's the entire processing the function performs, and it accepts no values as input. Basically, if you call this function, you get the words "Hello World" back.

11. To test the Web Service, right-click the ExactOddsCalc.asmx file in Solution Explorer and choose it as the Start Page from the shortcut menu. Hit F5 on the keyboard and the function will become available for testing, as shown in Figure 9.6.

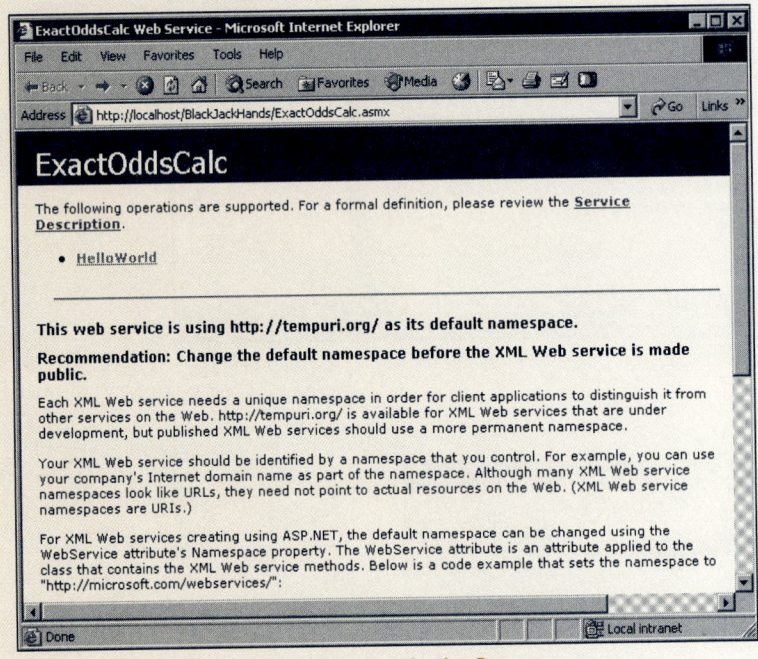

FIGURE 9.6 The Hello World Function in the Browser

12. In the browser you can see that the Hello World service is available, and that you can get a formal definition of the service in the Service Description. Below that, note the there is a warning about using the tempuri.org default namespace. This is because the namespace is the default for everyone, and if your Web Service is made public, using this namespace could conflict with someone else's namespace.

13. Close the browser. In the code-behind file, change the WebService code as shown here (notice the line continuation symbol at the end of this line of code):

```
<WebService(Namespace:="http://blackjack.com/")> _
```

14. Now hit the F5 key again. The browser should open with the function available, but without the warning, as shown in Figure 9.7.

15. Click the Service Description link. This automatically generates and displays a WSDL file, as shown in Figure 9.8. The code was used earlier in our discussion of WSDL.

16. Click Back in the browser. Click the Hello World link. A page allowing you to invoke the function should appear, as shown in Figure 9.9.

Hands On Project

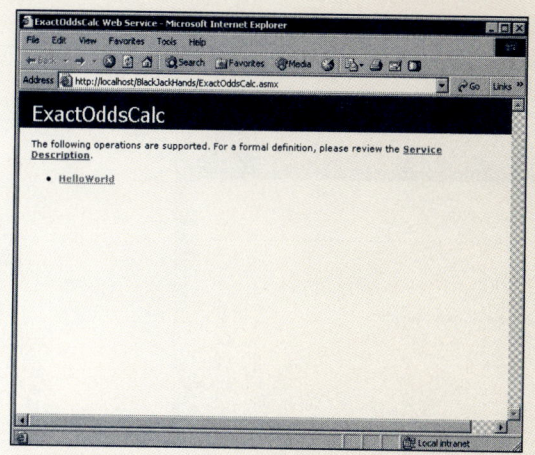

FIGURE 9.7　The Hello World Function without the Warning

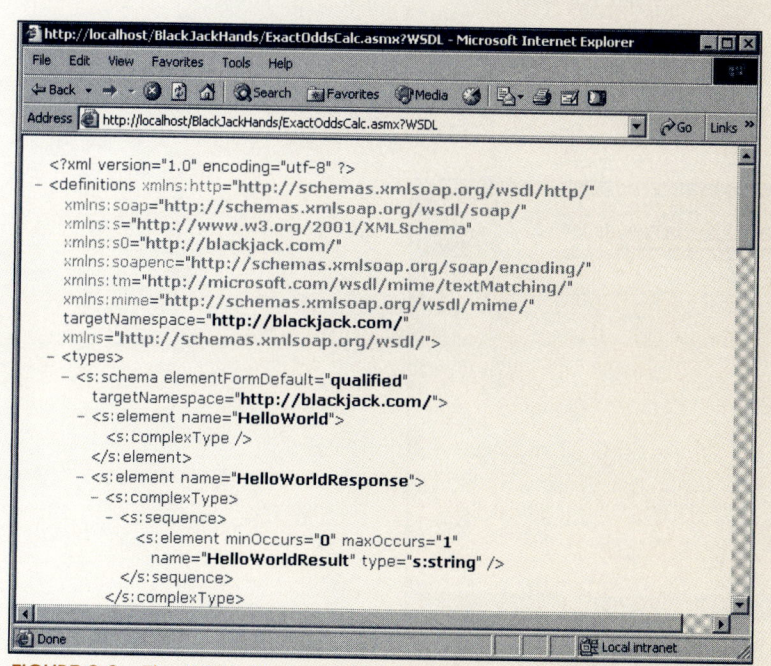

FIGURE 9.8　The WSDL File for Hello World

17. Click the Invoke button. A response showing the string Hello World in an XML document should appear, as shown in Figure 9.10.
18. Close the browser window with the XML response. Close the browser window with the Invoke button. In VS.Net, close the Output window (this window comes open by default as the service is processed).

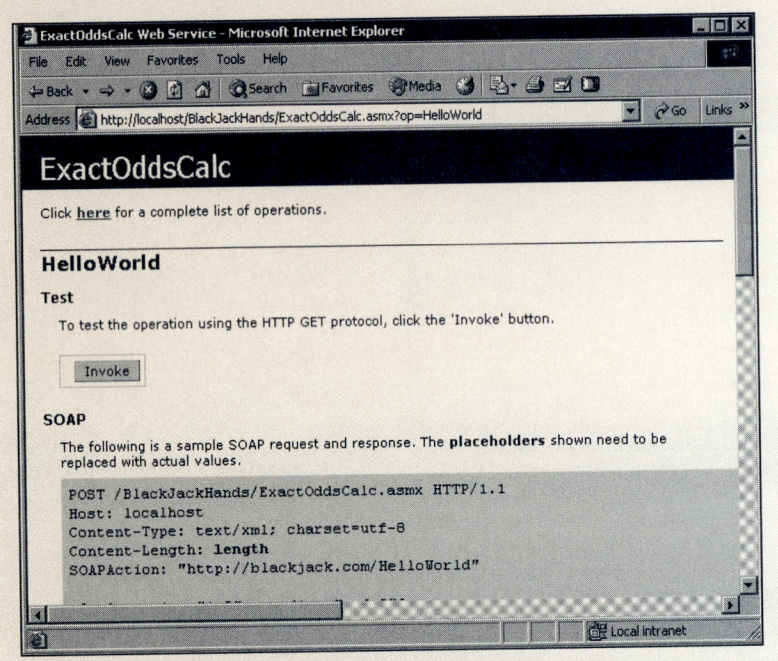

FIGURE 9.9 The Invoke Page

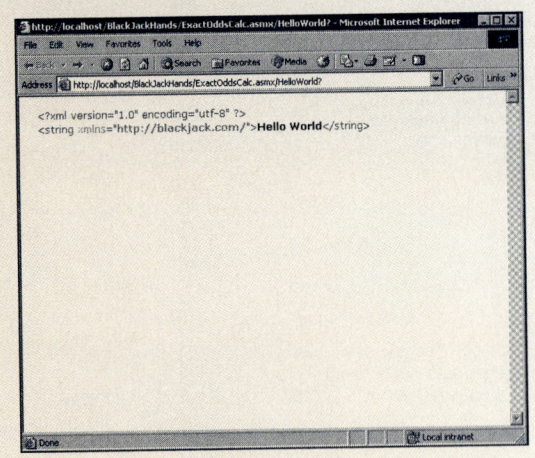

FIGURE 9.10 The XML Response with the String "Hello World"

Coding the ExactOddsCalc Function

1. We can start coding the ExactOddsCalc function by making some changes to the Hello World function. First, rewrite the first line as follows:

   ```
   <WebMethod()> Public Function ExactOdds(ByVal vNumCardsDlt As Integer, ByVal vCards() As Integer) As String
   ```

Hands On Project

2. In the code above, we've renamed the function "ExactOdds", and we've included two variables to be passed to the function by value: vNumCardsDlt as an integer and an array named vCards, also as an integer. The result will be a string passed back to the Web application code.

3. Next, we can copy most of the code from the Web application code-behind page with some slight modifications. First, we dimension some variables the same way we did in the Web application:

```
'dimension the card values array and other variables
Dim arrCards(11) As Integer
Dim NumberOfCardsDealt As Integer = vNumCardsDlt
Dim vMoreThan4Flag As Boolean
Dim vTotalCards As Integer = 52
Dim ExactOrderOdds As Double
Dim AnyOrderOdds As Double
Dim vArrCards(11) As Integer
Dim i As Integer
For i = 0 To 11
   vArrCards(i) = vCards(i)
Next
'set up the cards array for available card values
'there are four of each kind, except there are 16 cards with 10 value
arrCards(0) = 0
arrCards(1) = 4
arrCards(2) = 4
arrCards(3) = 4
arrCards(4) = 4
arrCards(5) = 4
arrCards(6) = 4
arrCards(7) = 4
arrCards(8) = 4
arrCards(9) = 4
arrCards(10) = 16
arrCards(11) = 4
```

4. In the code above, we've dimensioned some variables the same as in the Web application, but have added vArrCards(11), the array that replaces the DropDownList controls in the Web application. The For loop sets the new array to the same values as the array that was passed in (vCards()) so that each item in the vArrCards array will mimic the value of each DropDownList control that represents a card value in the Web application. Of course, this means we'll have to put some code in the Web application to set up the values in the array being passed to the Web Service (and we'll have to dimension that array as well). Finally, we duplicate the arrCards array for available card values.

5. The rest of the code is very similar to the Web application code, except that we don't need to use the FindControl function to find the DropDownList control or get its value. We already have these values in our vArrCards array, so we can simply iterate through the array to get all the values.

```vb
        'Calculate the exact odds
'go through a loop for the number of cards dealt times
For i = 1 To NumberOfCardsDealt
    'dimension another counter
    Dim i2 As Integer = 1
    'go though a loop for each potential card value
    For i2 = 1 To 11
        'if the chosen value is the same as the loop number
        If vArrCards(i2) = i2 Then
            'check to see if there are any of these card values left
            If arrCards(i2) < 1 Then
                'if not, set a flag and exit the inner loop
                vMoreThan4Flag = True
                Exit For
            Else
                'if so, calculate odds of this card occurring, times any odds
                    already calculated
                ExactOrderOdds = ExactOrderOdds * (arrCards(i2) / vTotalCards)
                'if the card value was 11 or 1
                If i2 = 11 Or i2 = 1 Then
                    'remove the appropriate values from the array
                    arrCards(1) = arrCards(1) - 1
                    arrCards(11) = arrCards(11) - 1
                    'decrement total cards by one
                    vTotalCards = vTotalCards - 1
                Else
                    'remove the appropriate value from the array
                    arrCards(i2) = arrCards(i2) - 1
                    'decrement total cards by one
                    vTotalCards = vTotalCards - 1
                End If
            End If
        End If
    Next
    'if the flag is set exit the outside loop
    If vMoreThan4Flag = True Then
        Exit For
    End If
Next
'if the flag is set, notify the user about more than 4 of a kind
If vMoreThan4Flag = True Then
    ExactOdds = "Can't get more than 4 of a kind. Please try again."
Else
    'calculate odds of cards in any order
    AnyOrderOdds = ExactOrderOdds * NumberOfCardsDealt
    'set the Exact and Any Order Labels
```

```
        ExactOdds = "Exact Order = " & CStr(ExactOrderOdds) & " or 1 out of "
            & CStr(CInt(1 / ExactOrderOdds)) & " hands. "
        ExactOdds = ExactOdds & "Any Order = " & CStr(AnyOrderOdds) & " or 1
            out of " & CStr(CInt(1 / AnyOrderOdds)) & " hands."
    End If
```

6. Since we're only passing one string value back to the Web application, we combine the values for the ExactOrderOdds and AnyOrderOdds labels into the returnString value and send that back. In our Web application, we'll resize the ExactOrderOddsLabel to accommodate the entire answer in one label.

REBUILDING THE WEB APPLICATION CODE TO CALL THE WEB SERVICE

1. In order to call a Web Service from the code in the Web application, you first create a Web Reference. This serves as a proxy for the calls to the Web Service in your code. To create a Web Reference, choose Add Web Reference from the Project menu. A browser-type window will open with some information about making Web References. Enter the URL for your Web Service files (http://localhost/BlackjackHand/ExactOddsCalc.asmx) and hit Enter. The ExactOddsCalc Web Service will be displayed, as shown in Figure 9.11.

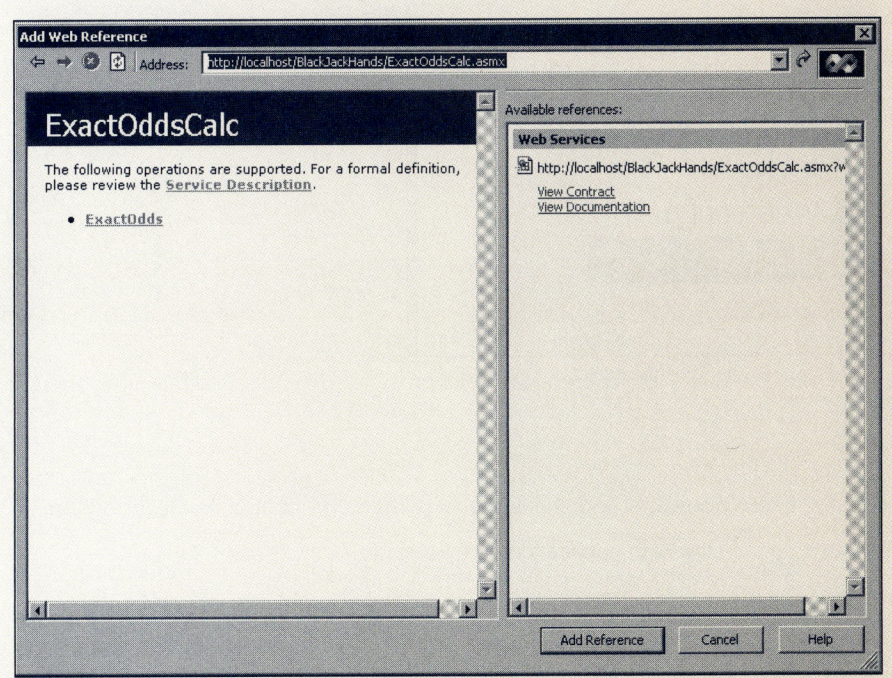

FIGURE 9.11   The ExactOddsCalc Web Service Ready for Web Reference

2. Click Add Reference. The browser-type window will disappear, and a new Web Reference will appear in Solution Explorer, as shown in Figure 9.12.

3. Now you can call the Web Service function by name: ExactOddsCalc( ).

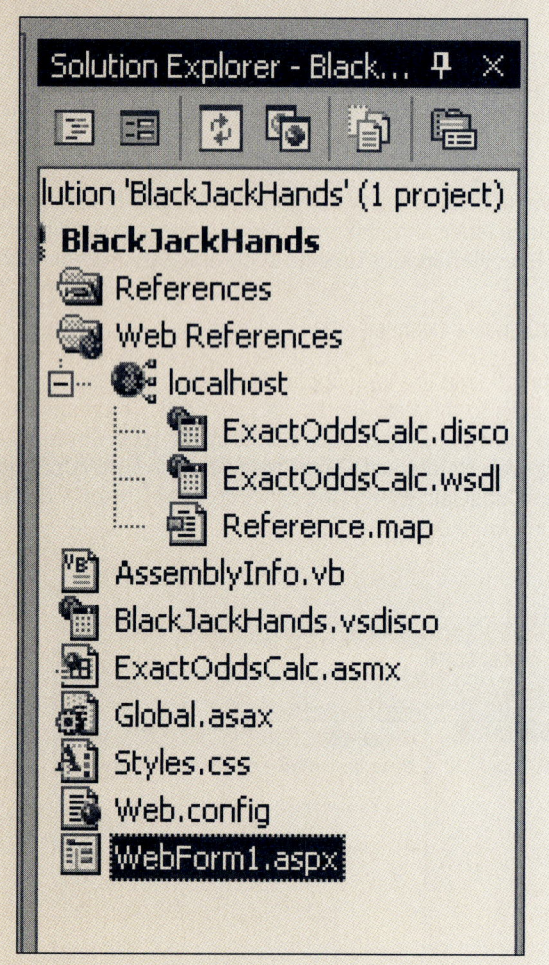

FIGURE 9.12 The New Web Reference in Solution Explorer

4. Enlarge the ExactOrderLabel and shrink the AnyOrderLabel control on the Web form.

5. Rewrite the code in the Web application as follows:

```
'dimension some variables for cards dealt, and so on
Dim NumberOfCardsDealt As Integer
Dim i As Integer = 1
Dim EOCWS As New ExactOddsCalc()
Dim vNumCardsDlt As Integer
Dim vCards(11) As Integer
'reset the odds labels, just in case
ExactOrderLabel.Text = "Exact Order = "
```

```
AnyOrderLabel.Text = ""
'set this variable to the value for the number of cards dealt
NumberOfCardsDealt = DDLNumberOfCardsDealt.SelectedItem.Value
vNumCardsDlt = NumberOfCardsDealt
'if the number of cards dealt is zero, remind the user
If NumberOfCardsDealt = 0 Then
   ExactOrderLabel.Text = "Please select Number Of Cards"
   AnyOrderLabel.Text = "Any Order ="
Else
```

6. The code above is essentially the same as the code from the original Web application, except for a few less variables initialized, and a few new variables (EOCWS for the Web Service function and vCards to mimic the DropDownList controls on the Web form). There is also an extra line setting vNumCardsDlt equal to the number of cards dealt.

7. The For loop now just captures the DropDownList control values and inserts them in the vCards array.

```
   'go through a loop for the number of cards dealt times
For i = 1 To NumberOfCardsDealt
   'dimension some variables for finding the DDLCard control
   Dim vCardNum As Integer
   Dim vCardNumStr As String
   Dim vCardName As String
   Dim vDDL As DropDownList
   'figure out card number and find the control
   vCardNum = i
   If vCardNum < 10 Then
      vCardNumStr = "0" & CStr(vCardNum)
   Else
      vCardNumStr = CStr(vCardNum)
   End If
   vCardName = "DDLCard" & vCardNumStr
   vDDL = FindControl(vCardName)
   vCards(i) = vDDL.SelectedItem.Value
Next
```

The final step is to send the data to the Web Service. The Web Service does the rest of the processing and returns a string representing the answer for both Exact and Any order of cards.

```
   ExactOrderLabel.Text = EOCWS.ExactOdds(vNumCardsDlt, vCards)
End If
```

8. Set WebForm1.aspx as the Start Page again, and choose Build and Browse from the menu. Test your Web Service using two cards dealt (a 10 and an 11) and see if you get the same answers as before.

Key Terms

@ WebService directive
Public Class
Simple Object Access Protocol (SOAP)
UDDI registry
Universal Description, Discovery, and Integration (UDDI)
Web Services Description Language (WSDL)
XML Web Services

Review Questions

1. Accessing a Web Service could take longer than accessing the same processing from inside your Web application, and this could slow performance. What other factors might still make it desirable to create some of your data processing functions as Web Services?
2. You have been told to create a Web Service for sale to other companies across the Internet. What operations should you include in the service to sell it to other companies?
3. What protocols are included in the WSDL file you receive if you access a Web Service and include "?WSDL" on the end of the URL?
4. How can you create a user interface for a Web Service? Do you need to?
5. What is added to a Web application to connect it to a Web Service?
6. How would you create a Web Service in VS.Net, if you already had a solution going?
7. What must you do prior to building and running a Web Service in VS.Net, if you have Web Form pages already present in the solution?
8. What VB.Net keyword is used when you dimension the function for a Web Service?
9. How do you define variables that are passed in to a Web Service?
10. How do you define the return value data type for a Web Service, if it returns a value?

CHAPTER 10

ASP.Net Optimizing and Debugging

LEARNING OBJECTIVES

Upon completion of this chapter, you will be able to:

1. Review and optimize an ASP.Net Web application.
2. Learn about threads and thread models.
3. Learn how to add Javascripts to ASP.Net Web applications.
4. Explain testing and debugging issues in application development.
5. Debug a Web application.
6. Explain deployment considerations in Web application development.
7. Deploy a Web application.

INTRODUCTION

As an application developer, you will probably start by writing code to support some particular application requirement. For example, you may write the code for the part of a project that places a customer and his/her order into a database. Later, you may design the database for holding customer and order records. Eventually, you may build the entire application. In each case, you will (hopefully) be working from some kind of project specification.

The project specification is like a translation. It translates broad objectives (we want to be able to provide customers with a catalog of our products and allow them to order our products online) into specific, doable tasks. Doable means the requirements can be programmed. Since there are multiple ways to program just about anything, the project specification often will include direction about *how* to accomplish certain tasks, in addition to *what* to accomplish.

Building a project specification starts with identifying the broad objectives of the project's sponsor, and then making decisions about what to accomplish and how. Often teams of experts will work together to assemble a good project specification, and it's not uncommon to see the specification revised even as the project is underway. Project specifications are working documents that guide application design. Once the functionality of a project has been assembled and developed, there is often a need to optimize the application so that it can run efficiently in a production environment.

Along with project optimization, testing protocols are devised to ensure the application meets performance, accuracy, and security goals along the way. Testing protocols work hand-in-hand with debugging procedures to make an application clean and efficient.

Once an application is complete, the final step is to deploy the application. Deployment is a separate process that has a number of special considerations of its own. In this chapter we look at how application design and development proceed from a project specification, and also how the project specification is created in the first place. We'll also create an example application using many of the ASP.Net Web application components we created in earlier chapters, and proceed from design, to development and optimization, to debugging, and finally to deployment.

Optimizing an ASP.Net Web Application

Building a Web application that displays the correct pages, with the correct data on them, is just one aspect of Web application development. While displaying the correct pages is a fundamental requirement, responding to the user quickly and efficiently is also important, particularly as more users use the application. For any given project, the budget for hardware is finite, and part of the return-on-investment (ROI) calculation is based on spending only a certain amount to support a certain number of users. Slow Web applications frustrate users, sometimes to the point they don't come back or can't do their own work efficiently, which in turn negates the reason for the Web application in the first place. Inefficient Web applications can consume or overwhelm a hardware/bandwidth budget quickly, making the project into a money-loser. Both slow and inefficient Web applications can be helped by optimization techniques. The process of optimizing a Web application includes measuring performance, making changes, and measuring again, an iterative process similar to debugging.

ASP.Net Specific Performance Improvements

There are a number of things you should remember to check for and do whenever you are ready to prepare an ASP.Net Web application for production use. The following list outlines some basic steps you should always take (in addition to following an optimization process as described next), and we cover these steps in more detail later in the chapter:

1. Turn off debug mode.
2. Use page and data caching.
3. Use stored procedures and data readers.
4. Disable sessions for pages that don't need it.

Measuring Web Application Performance

The first step in optimizing a Web application involves measuring how well the application currently performs. Note that basic debugging, code documentation, and code optimization should already have taken place. Some code improvements are obvious, and as the code is programmed, the programmer is probably making notes in comments about what to fix before the application is debugged or optimized. Following the basic development process, as part of the optimization process, performance measurements will be conducted and a baseline established. Only with a baseline can you tell whether changes you've made have resulted in an improvement.

Performance Measures

Web application performance can be measured in several ways. The time it takes to process a request and begin delivering the response is one **performance measure**, and the time it takes to complete processing and complete delivery of the response is another. There is a difference between these measures because often a preliminary response can be sent by flushing current output, which appeases the user until the entire response can be completed and sent. These measures are called **execution time** and **response time**.

Another measure of performance is **throughput**, the number of requests that can be processed and responded to in a given amount of time (usually requests per second). Throughput depends not just on processor speed but on bandwidth as well. After all, even the fastest server can only respond to so many requests per second before the available bandwidth is overwhelmed.

Performance Factors

Factors that affect the performance of a Web application, the **performance factors**, include number of processors, processor speed and available RAM, operating system, the Web application's use of resources and the efficiency of its code, the form of persistent data storage, and available bandwidth. Performance targets are usually set as response times to the user, meaning the user is able to interact with the application in a reasonable time, no matter what other loads are being placed on the application.

Optimization Decisions

Deciding what and how to optimize in the entire mix of factors affecting Web application performance is not necessarily straightforward. For example, if there is a rush project with an extremely short deadline, perhaps it would be better to spend more money on a "brute force" approach to optimization that simply involves buying more and more powerful equipment to make up for inefficient code. Of course, while this is sometimes necessary and the idea is always "we'll clean it up later," keep in mind that once something is working, there is often little incentive to "clean up" unless a problem crops up.

On the other hand, it can sometimes be more cost-effective, from a maintenance standpoint as well as efficiency, to build better code before the application goes into production. Better code is optimized, uses the least amount of resources possible, and is well documented. Not only does it run faster and with fewer errors, it is easier to maintain.

Finally, other factors affect Web application performance. For example, well-thought-out graphic design can play a major role in reducing bandwidth requirements. Too many graphics, large graphics, or a large graphic file format can make it difficult to respond quickly to some users, even when the code has completed processing.

Performance Testing

Web applications are usually built in response to a recognized need, for a target audience. This being the case, as a developer you should investigate who the target audience is, what platforms (or browsers) they will be using to access the application, and how many of them are expected in the first month, quarter, and year. Then you can test application performance under conditions that may actually be encountered. For example, you can estimate what kinds of requests are typically going to be made of the application, as well as the number of users as the application becomes more well-known and more heavily used. You also can increase the users until the server fails to determine the total capacity of the application. Keep in mind that users sometimes use applications in unexpected ways, and that even the best testing is still just an approximation of what the application will face in actual use.

ASP.Net Web Application Testing Tools

ASP.Net contains several tools that are helpful in performance testing. Microsoft provides a tool named the Web Application Stress (WAS) tool. You can find it on the Microsoft site by entering "Web Application Stress tool" in the site search function on the home page. If you download and install this tool, it gives you the capability to easily simulate hits on your site, and to vary the number of connections, the number of users, the format of cookies and HTTP response headers, and so on. Because it is quite versatile, it makes simulating fairly realistic loads much easier.

Built-in ASP.Net Web Application Performance Counters

There are quite a few counters available for ASP.Net applications, both in total and per application. Broadly categorized, these counters inform you about activity for anonymous requests, cache, errors, output cache, requests, sessions, and transactions. Using a little logic and common sense, these counters can reveal much about how your application is performing and how well it is responding to use under varying conditions.

ASP.Net Tracing

The **ASP.Net Trace** feature allows developers to follow the path of execution as a Web application performs, and to write statements in your code that will become part of the Trace information. Chapter 6 began a discussion of the Trace feature, and in this section we will explore in more detail the **Trace object** and how it provides Trace information.

Setting Tracing in the Web.config File You can set the entire application to show trace information by making a change in the application's Web.config file. The following section from a Web.config file shows how:

```
<configuration>
<system.web>
<trace enabled="true" requestLimit="40" localOnly="false"/>
</system.web>
</configuration>
```

Notice that the trace element is a self-terminated XML element. The allowable attributes for this element are

- **enabled.** The default value is "false", and setting this attribute to "true" causes trace information to be collected and made available.
- **pageOutput.** The default is "false", and setting this attribute to "true" causes trace information to be displayed both on the page and in the "trace.axd" file.
- **requestLimit.** The default is "10", and you can set this attribute as high as you like. Once the maximum is reached, the server stops storing trace information.
- **traceMode.** The default is "SortByTime", and you also can set this attribute to "SortByCategory".
- **localOnly.** The default is "true", and setting this attribute to "false" means the "trace.axd" file can be found in locations besides the local server.

If you want to enable tracing for only a single page (or individual pages instead of the whole application), use the Trace attribute.

The Trace Attribute As we mentioned in Chapter 6, ASP.Net tracing can be turned on and off by including the Trace attribute in an @ Page directive and setting its value to True, as shown in this code:

```
<% @ Page Trace="true" %>
```

Once this is done, the page will display trace information when pulled up in your browser. However, any pulling up the page will get the trace information, so be sure to disable this attribute or remove it before putting the application into production.

There is also a TraceMode attribute that can be included in the @ Page directive (as well as the Trace attribute). The TraceMode attribute has several allowable values: SortByTime and SortByCategory. Setting the TraceMode attribute to one of these enumerated values will cause the trace information messages to be sorted accordingly. The following code shows how to set trace information enabled and sorted by category:

```
<% @ Page Trace="true" TraceMode="SortByCategory" %>
```

The Trace Object A Trace object is included in ASP.Net. Like the Request and Response objects, it has properties and methods that allow you to work with it. For example, you can write custom trace messages to the trace log using the **Trace.Write** method. There is also a **Trace.Warn** method that will write custom trace messages, but color them in red so they are easier to find. The Trace.Write method accepts three arguments: the category, the message, and any error messages (the exceptions). If you include the category and use the TraceMode value "SortByCategory", your custom trace messages will be sorted by this category.

Trace Information Tables Trace information, as displayed on the page or in the trace viewer file (trace.axd) includes many common values and indicators that help you determine exactly what is happening between the browser and the client for each request. This information is reported in the following tables:

- The Request Details table contains the Session ID (if sessions are operating), the time of the request, the character encoding type for the request and response, the Request type (GET or POST), and the HTTP Status code.
- The Trace Information table contains the custom category you specified, the custom message you specified, and the time since the first and last message were displayed.
- The Control Tree table contains the ID value and type for each control, plus the render size and viewstate size in bytes.
- The Cookies Collection table contains the name, value, and size of any cookies.

- The Headers Collection, Form Collection, and Server Variables tables contain the name and value of any headers, form fields, and server variables available.

Threads

When a computer processes data, the CPU does the main processing. Lower-level systems, such as circuitry on the hard drive, may perform low-level processing functions, but the bulk of the work is performed by the CPU. When the CPU is processing a Web application, it is using a "thread" of operation. Until the work being performed by the thread is complete, the rest of the application must wait.

Therefore, the ability to use more than one thread to perform data processing functions in an application can speed up the application under some circumstances. However, the use of threads is somewhat complex from a programming standpoint.

ASP.Net Web Application Debugging

Like any application, ASP.Net Web applications often require **debugging**. Some debugging takes place as you are writing the application. Some takes place as you are optimizing the application. Later, as you make your final changes and later still, when you respond to user bug reports (sometimes generated in beta testing) or post-release modifications, you will be debugging again. Debugging is a constant part of application development, and ASP.Net and Visual Studio.Net provide numerous tools that are very helpful with the debugging process.

The Debugging Process

Except for very simple applications, it may be impossible to know all the possible ways in which an application can fail. Errors in coding that lead to compilation or execution problems are usually easy to find, even though some of them may be hard to fix. These are called semantic errors because they reflect poor use of keywords, code structures, code syntax, naming conventions, or other programming language rules. Errors in output, when the application seems to run properly, are called logic errors because the program runs correctly but produces the wrong answer. Both can be resolved by changing the application in some way, but logic errors tend to be harder to detect and fix because there may be no obvious error message.

The Testing Protocol

Before the application is built, some thought should be given to the expected outputs for given inputs, and a testing protocol devised. A **testing protocol** is a set of tests with certain values that can be expected to produce certain output values or conditions. As you might imagine, it's difficult to guess in advance all the entries a user might make, but it's a little easier to define what the outputs should be. For example, if a user is expected to enter his/her username and password in form fields, the application is expected to search a database for these values and log the user in if a match is found. Although the user might enter any combination of characters (or even noncharacters in some cases), the application should restrict the entry to legal characters with a limited length, and should then accurately search for and find the correct record in the database.

In this particular case, one of the testing protocol tests might be to feed in random characters and random string lengths and see if the application is unable to handle the requests or responds improperly to them (such as by allowing login for unacceptable usernames and passwords). Note that this particular test could identify problems with the database or with the application code, and if the location of the problem was not apparent, you might have to do further testing to isolate the problem.

The development of testing protocol tests is partly based on the specifications of the application and partly on intuition and experience on the part of the developers. As the application is developed, debugged, and optimized, new tests often must be devised to ensure the most recent changes can be tested for. Once a good testing protocol is in place, formal debugging can proceed.

Basic Debugging

Debugging an application starts with the identification of bugs, either through formal testing or simply feedback from beta testers or users. Once a bug has been identified, it must be isolated, meaning that the code, logic, data store structure, data, or other factor making up the erroneous output is found. Sometimes debugging reveals problems in more than one area. Once the culprits are found, it's best to eliminate them one by one and retest. Debugging can be thought of as a cycle of testing, making changes, and retesting until all known bugs are found. In cases where performing a complete fix is not feasible, mitigating the problem with specialized error messages may be a better course.

Fixing Bugs with Troubleshooting

When an electronics technician works on an elaborate piece of electronic gear, often the approach is to isolate the circuit board causing the problem by testing its individual outputs. The fix is to replace the faulty circuit board. Although you may not replace entire sections of code or databases when you fix bugs, the approach is the same. Troubleshooting applications is a process of checking each variable value, object property, or database record, while the application runs, to see at what point bad values are cropping up.

In order to troubleshoot efficiently, you should have some knowledge of how the program works and what it is expected to do at each stage. This is one reason it's important to document your code with comments. Even if you are troubleshooting your own code, comments are still very helpful.

When you're not exactly sure how a bug is being generated, you'll need to make a guess and start there, perhaps by making a small change and seeing what happens to the output. Essentially, this is a trial-and-error approach, but, like the game of 20 questions, it can let you rapidly zero in on the problem and fix it.

ASP.Net Debugging Tools in VS.Net

Any good Integrated Development Environment (like VS.Net) contains debuggers and other features that assist in the debugging process. VS.Net contains an ASP.Net debugger that you can set to run when using debug mode.

When running in debug mode in VS.Net, you can set breakpoints. **Breakpoints** are markers in your code that pause execution (when execution reaches the marker) so you can examine current variable and property values. A common method of debugging is to start with a variable or property value that is incorrect and work your way back through the program until you figure out why the value is incorrect. The ability to view variable or property values while the program executes helps you make your way through the application efficiently.

VS.Net's debugging tools include several windows that display variable and property values, as well as other important information about the overall status of the running application. These Windows include the **Autos window** (shows current property values) and the **Breakpoints window** (shows all breakpoints and any conditions on them).

Discussion—Debugging

Debugging is the process of finding and eliminating bugs (errors) in your application. Some errors are obvious and can be fixed right away; others are subtle and can only be found with a good testing protocol. The amount of effort to be put into fixing errors depends in part on how serious they are; errors that rarely appear and cause no serious problems are in a sense cosmetic and may not be fixed but "patched" with an error message.

Bugs are generally categorized as semantic, meaning they are the result of incorrect coding, or logical, in which a properly coded application produces erroneous output under some circumstance. Semantic errors are usually found and fixed during programming, while logic errors are sometimes more difficult to find and some may only be found as the result of a good testing protocol.

A testing protocol is a set of tests designed to subject an application to usage patterns and inputs similar to what might occur once the application is in production, plus extreme conditions, in order to detect any unforeseen error conditions or problems. Developing a testing protocol is partly an art, because experience and intuition play a role in the development of good application tests.

VS.Net contains an ASP.Net debugger, and running in debug mode is a good way to troubleshoot and debug your ASP.Net Web application. Several Debug windows are provided in the VS.Net debugger, thereby helping you isolate and fix bugs.

Deploying an ASP.Net Web Application

The informal process of deploying ASP.Net Web applications is little more than transferring the Web application files from your development server to the production server. Once the files are copied in and any required changes made to Web.config files or the Web server, the application will run properly (assuming ASP.Net has been loaded on the server, of course).

But you can do a formal **deployment** if you desire. Deploying an application built with Visual Studio.Net involves adding a new project called a deployment project to your existing solution, and then using the settings available in the deployment project to manage the actual installation of files on the designated server. For Web applications, the deployment projects are called Web Setup projects. The files for these projects (and the Setup projects for other types of applications as well) have an extension of .msi (meaning these files are Windows installer files). Adding a Web Setup project can be helpful when you are not sure exactly how the receiving server is configured and want to make sure things are handled properly. The second Hands On Project at the end of this chapter demonstrates how to add a deployment project and set some of its properties.

Quick Check Questions

1. What two things should you do to every ASP.Net Web application before you deploy it?
2. How is the Performance Console opened?
3. How do you add ASP.Net Application Performance Counters to the Performance Console?
4. What two broad categories of bugs are found in applications?
5. Why is it hard to find all logic errors?
6. What process is used to isolate and identify bugs in applications?
7. How are Project Property Pages set?

1. Like any application, ASP.Net Web applications are optimized, debugged, and deployed following the bulk of the development work. There are specific things you can do to optimize ASP.Net Web applications, such as turning off debug mode and using stored procedures, and you also can follow a predefined testing/optimization process to measure performance and improve it.
2. Debugging goes hand-in-hand with optimization. Semantic (code syntax or use) errors are often caught during coding as error messages will be generated and the application may not compile or run properly. Logic errors are more difficult to catch because the application will run fine but produce incorrect answers under some circumstances. Creating a testing protocol means building one or more test procedures for the application that hopefully subject it to nearly normal operating conditions with a full range of inputs in order to detect any errors that might occur.
3. ASP.Net Web applications are sometimes developed on the same server on which they are intended to be deployed, and sometimes their files are transferred into the production server. In either case, deployment is more a process of copying the appropriate files than of "installation" per se, although in some cases differences in database connections or configuration files cause some work on the developer's part.

Exercise 10.1

There are a number of performance counters available with ASP.Net to help you determine how well your Web application is performing, and whether your changes have made any performance improvement. In order to use them (and to perform the following project) you must be working on the server and have access to Administrative tools. The following steps demonstrate how to view ASP.Net Application performance counters.

1. Choose Start|Programs|Administrative Tools|Performance from the desktop. The screen shown in Figure 10.1 will appear.

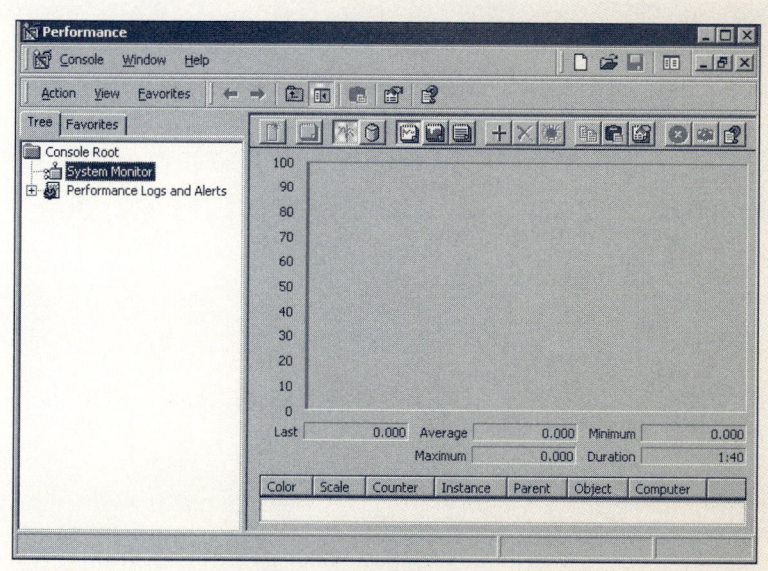

FIGURE 10.1   The Performance Console

CHAPTER 10 ASP.Net Optimizing and Debugging

2. On the right side of the screen, above the chart, click the button for View Report (this caption will appear when you place the cursor above the correct button, seventh from the left). Click the Add button, just to the right of the View Report button. The Add Counters dialog box will appear, as shown in Figure 10.2.

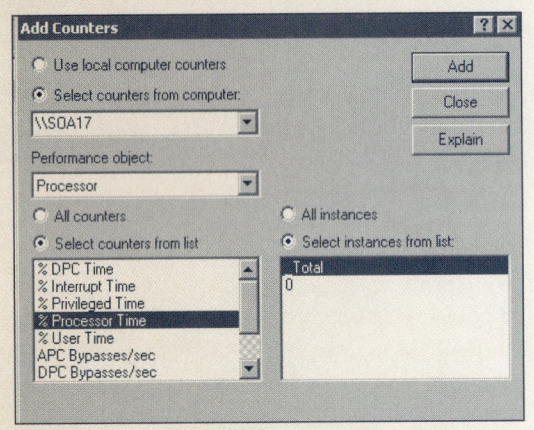

FIGURE 10.2 The Add Counters Dialog Box

3. From the dropdown list of performance objects, select ASP.Net Applications, and check the All counters radio button so that all ASP.Net Applications counters will be included. Click the Add button to add all the counters.

4. From your desktop, open Internet Explorer and open the BlackjackHands Web application's WebForm1.aspx. This should open the application. Go back to the Performance Console and you should see a report resembling Figure 10.3.

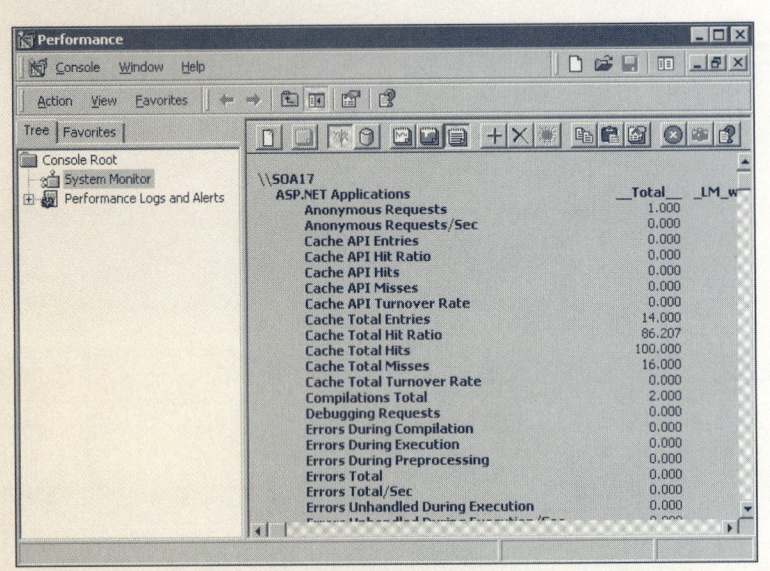

FIGURE 10.3 The Report Showing Counter Data for the BlackJackHands Web Application

5. Click the button with the caption "View Histogram" in the Performance Console. The screen should now display the histogram shown in Figure 10.4. Notice the color-coded lines at the bottom of the histogram, identifying the measure each line represents. Clicking the "View Chart" button shows the same data over time.

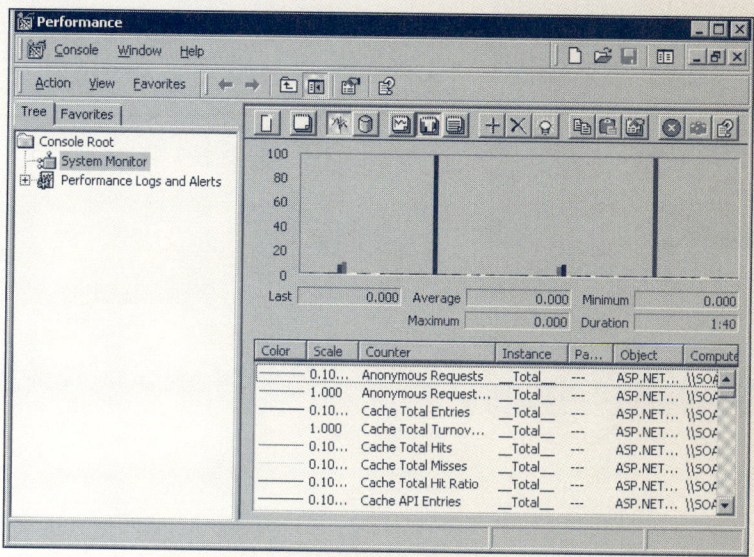

FIGURE 10.4 The Histogram of Counter Data

6. Click on the View Report button again. Right-click "ASP.Net Applications" in the report and choose Properties from the shortcut menu. The System Monitor Properties dialog box should open, as shown in Figure 10.5.
7. On the General tab, display properties can be set, including how often to update the display and in what format to show data. The Source tab allows you to choose where to get data, and the Data tab shows the counters available. The Graph, Colors, and Fonts tabs all give you options for rendering your data.
8. Close the System Monitor Properties dialog box and close the Performance Console.

Exercise 10.2

In this exercise, we will expand upon the use of trace begun in Chapter 6 and write several of our own custom trace messages. To conduct this exercise, we will create a simple ASP.Net Web application called Trace.

1. Open VS.Net and create a new Visual Basic ASP.Net Web Application project from the template provided. Name the new project Trace. A blank Web form should appear on your screen.
2. Double-click the surface of the form to enter the code-behind page in the Page_Load event handler. In the event handler code block, enter the following code:

```
Trace.Write("Test", "This is a test of the Trace Write Function")
Trace.Warn("Test", "This is a test of the Trace Warn Function")
```

3. Save the Web form and close it, then right-click it in Solution Explorer and choose Open With|Source Code (Text) Editor. Add a Trace attribute to the @ Page directive and set it to "true".

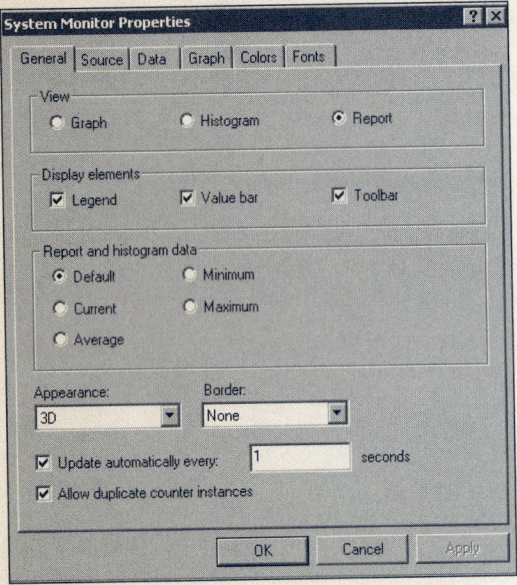

FIGURE 10.5 The System Monitor Properties Dialog Box

4. Choose File|Build and Browse from the menu to see the result of your work. You should see a page in your browser view resembling Figure 10.6, with the two customer messages you specified.

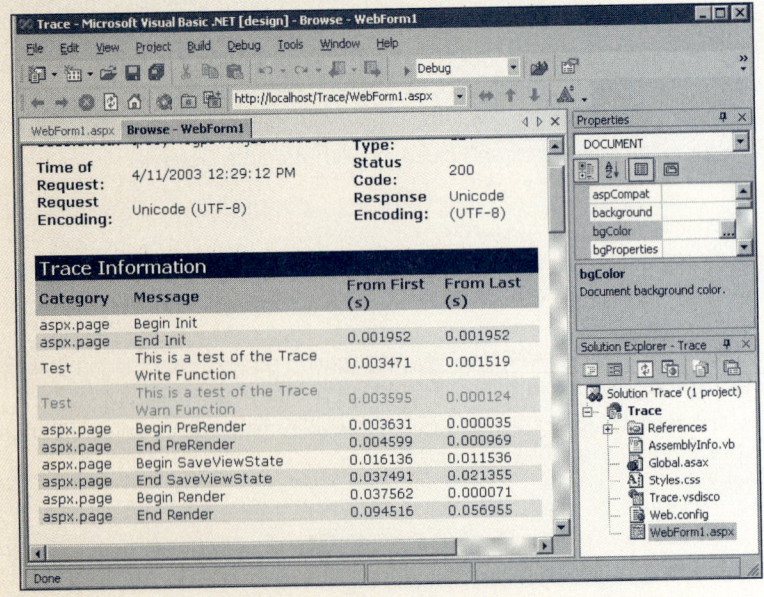

FIGURE 10.6 Custom Trace Messages

Debugging a Multiple-Player Online Game

For this project, we will extend the functions of our online multiplayer game to accommodate two simultaneous players. We also will use this project as an example for performing debugging.

To accommodate multiple players, the application will employ several timers to restrict

- The amount of time that can elapse before two players must be signed up.
- The amount of time that can elapse before a player's turn is up.

Once a player has signed in and notified the system that he/she is looking for another player, the system will count down three minutes (we'll use 30 seconds for testing purposes, so we can test more quickly). A Javascript in the player's browser will resubmit every 15 seconds (we'll use 10 seconds for testing purposes) until three minutes are up to see if someone else has agreed to play. If someone has, the system will deal the hand to both players. If no one has, the system will notify the first player to try again later or try another game.

If we incorporated this functionality into our OMPGame, once the hand was dealt, the first player would have 15 seconds to Hit or Hold. If the player chooses Hit, he/she would have another 10 seconds to Hit or Hold again until his/her hand is done. If the player chooses Hold, the system will wait until the second player's Javascript resubmits, and then notify the second player that he/she has the opportunity to Hit or Hold (within the same time limits as the first player had). If either player didn't Hit or Hold within 15 seconds, the system would assume they both Hold and move on. Once both players have played, the system would deal to the dealer and the hand would be over. For this project, we'll implement only the functionality that gets the players into the game, because that demonstrates how the timing functionality would work.

As we develop the functionality specified above, we'll also demonstrate some common ASP.Net Web application debugging features. Note that in order to debug your application, you must have administrator privileges on the server.

STARTING THE PROJECT AND SETTING UP THE GLOBAL.ASAX FILE

1. Open VS.Net and create a new ASp.Net Web Application from the Visual Basic Projects template. Name the project OMPDebugging. A blank Web form should open in VS.Net.

2. Check to make sure the project is in debug mode (debug mode is the default) by opening Solution Explorer and right-clicking the Web.config file and opening it with the HTML/XML Editor. When the Web.config file opens, scroll down to the section shown here:

   ```
   <compilation defaultLanguage="vb" debug="true" />
   ```

3. The compilation element shown above has a debug attribute, set to "true". When we are ready to deploy this project, we'll set the debug attribute to "false". Close the Web.config file. Note that there is a dropdown list on the Standard toolbar that displays the debug setting, and it can be changed here as well.

4. In Solution Explorer, double-click the Global.asax file to open it in Design view. Open the Toolbox and place two Timer components on the Design surface of the file. These will be named Timer1 and Timer2 by default. The Global.asax file in Design view should now look like Figure 10.7.

5. Double-click the Global.asax file in Design view to open the code-behind file. In the event handler for the Application_Start event, enter the following code:

   ```
   'create an array named arrGame with 5 cells
   Dim arrGame(5) As String
   'create a variable for the Interval of Timer2
   ```

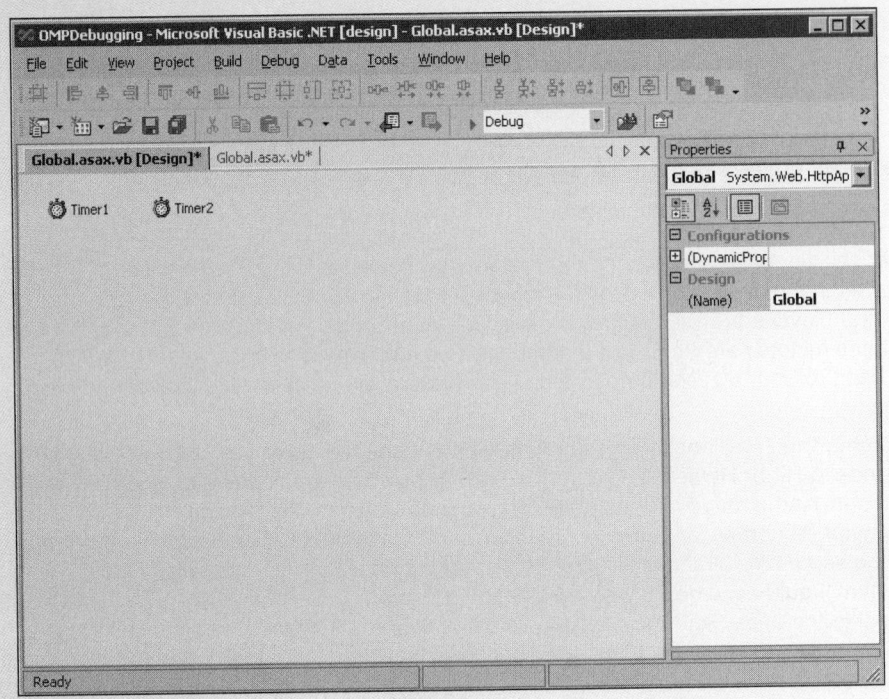

FIGURE 10.7 The Global.asax File in Design View

```
Dim appTimer2Interval As Integer
'set the Application variables equal to the variables just created
Application("arrGame") = arrGame
Application("appTimer2Interval") = appTimer2Interval
'start timer1 and set timer 2 interval
Timer1.Interval = 1000
Timer1.Start()
Timer2.Interval = 1
```

6. The code above creates two variables: arrGame, with five cells to hold game data, and appTimer2Interval, to hold the interval value for Timer2 (that will be set and started when Player01 signs in). The code then sets the Application object version of these variables, sets the Timer1 interval, starts Timer1, and initializes Timer2's interval to a value of 1. Because Timer1's interval is set to 1000, its "Elapsed" event will be raised every one second. We'll use Timer1 to check to see if a player has logged in, and if so to start Timer2, so Timer2 can check for three minutes to see if another player has signed in.

7. In the Session_Start event handler, enter the following code:

```
Session("message") = "Click the button above to start, and when another
   player has signed up you will be notified."
```

8. This code sets a message within the session so we can communicate with each player.

DESIGNING WEBFORM1.ASPX

1. WebForm1.aspx should still be open and blank. Click back over to it in Design view.

2. On this form, we'll assume that Player01 has logged in and simply needs to click a button to choose Blackjack with two players (rather than make choices from a dropdown list, as in OMPGame). Clicking this button will sign the player up and begin the wait for another player to log in, click the button, and agree to play.

3. Add a Label control to the form and make it read "Welcome". Add a Button control to the form and make it read "Start 2 Player Blackjack". Add another Button control to the form and make it read "Enter Existing Game", and set its Visible property to "false". Add another Label control and blank out its Text property. Name this last label "MessageLabel". Change background and font properties of the form and its controls so the form looks better, like Figure 10.8.

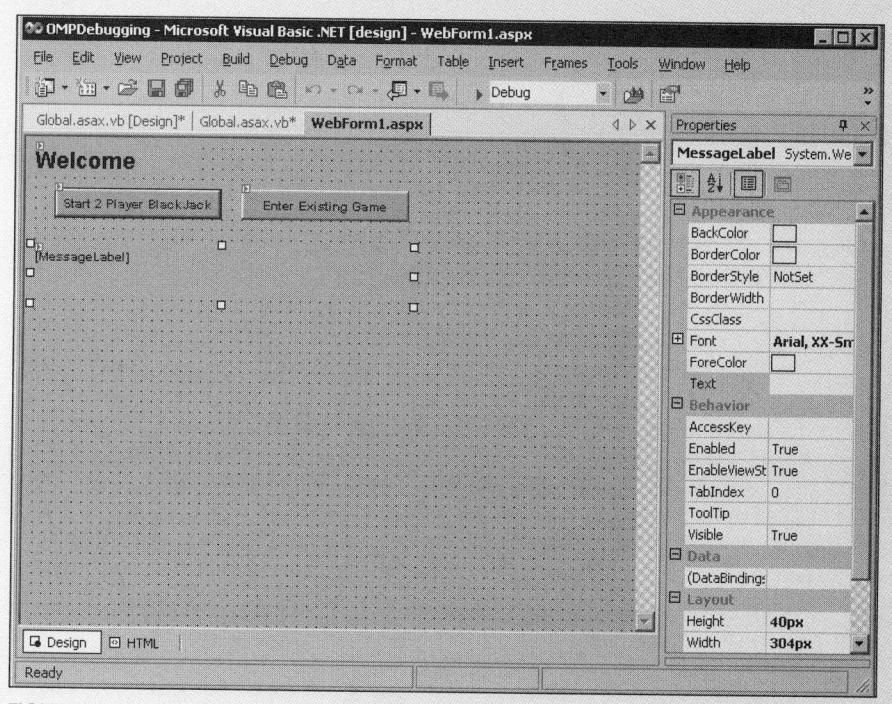

FIGURE 10.8 WebForm1.aspx in Design View

4. Double-click the surface of the form to enter the code-behind page in the Page_Load event handler. Enter the following code:

```
If Application("arrGame")(0) = "Not Started" Then
   Button2.Visible = True
End If
If Not Page.IsPostBack Then
    'the zero index indicates whether the game is available but not yet
      started
   Application("arrGame")(0) = "Not Started"
```

```
        'the one index indicates whether Timer2 has timed out
    Application("arrGame")(1) = "Not TimedOut"
        'the two index indicates the gameID
    Application("arrGame")(2) = "1"
        'the three index indicates Player01's ID
    Application("arrGame")(3) = "1"
        'the four index indicates Player02's ID
        'but is initialized at 0 to indicate Player02 isn't signed up yet
    Application("arrGame")(4) = "0"
End If
MessageLabel.Text = Session("message")
```

5. This code first checks the value of our application-level array named "arrGame", in the zero index, to see whether the game has been started. If there is no value, it doesn't show Button2, but if the value reads "Not Started", then it shows Button2. What this means is, only Player02 will see this button, and therefore only Player02 can enter a game that is available but not yet started.

6. Next, the code checks to see whether this is a post back, and if not (if this is the first time the page has been displayed), it initializes the Application("arrGame") array values as noted in the comments. Last, this code sets the MessageLabel control's Text value to the initial session message.

7. Click back over to WebForm1.aspx in Design view and double-click Button1. In the event handler that opens, enter the following code:

```
'set the Application appTimer2Interval variable to 3 minutes
Application("appTimer2Interval") = 30000
'redirect Player01 to a page that resubmits every 15 seconds
Response.Redirect("GameStatusChecker.htm")
```

8. When Player01 clicks this button, the interval for Timer2 (in the application) will be set to 30 seconds, for testing purposes. After we complete the project, we can set it to its correct value, 180,000 milliseconds (three minutes). Then Player01 is redirected to an HTML Web page named "GameStatusChecker.htm". This Web page contains a Javascript that automatically resubmits every 15 seconds to check whether or not another player has signed up to play the game.

CREATING THE GAMESTATUSCHECKER.HTM WEB PAGE

1. In Solution Explorer, right-click on the project and choose Add|Add HTML Page from the shortcut menu. When the Add New Item dialog box opens, name the page "GameStatusChecker.htm" and click the Open button. The new Web page will open in Design view.

2. Click the HTML button at the bottom of the page to view the HTML code. Add the following Javascript inside the HTML, before the ending "head" tag (</head>):

```
<script language="Javascript">
<!--
  function timedSubmit()
{
  var my_timeout = setTimeout("submitForm();", 10000);
}
  function submitForm()
{
```

```
    document.Form1.submit()
}
-->
</script>
```

3. This code creates a function named "timedSubmit" that runs the "submitForm()" function every 10 seconds (this is for testing purposes; it can be changed to 15 seconds when the project is ready to be deployed). The submitForm function submits the form continuously until either Timer2 is timed out or another player signs up to play.

4. Add an "onload" event to the beginning "body" tag, like this:

```
<body MS_POSITIONING="GridLayout" onload="timedSubmit()">
```

5. The "onload" event starts the "timedSubmit" function when the page first loads.

6. In the body of the page, add the following code:

```
<form name="Form1" action="check_game_started.aspx" method="POST"
  ID="Form1">
  <p>Still checking</p>
  <input type="hidden" name="game_status" value="check" ID="Hidden1">
</form>
```

7. This code creates an HTML form and a hidden field named "game_status" with a value of "check". In this project all that's required is to submit the form to the appropriate Web form (in this case, a form named "check_game_started.aspx"), but if we wanted to create a more elaborate checking process, the hidden field would come in handy. Notice the form is named "Form1", so the Javascript line "document.Form1.submit()" submits the right form. Also, we've included the text "Still checking" as a notice to the player.

8. Save the page and click back to Design view. The page should now resemble Figure 10.9. Close the page.

CREATING THE WEB FORM CHECK_GAME_STARTED.ASPX

1. In Solution Explorer, right-click the project and add a new Web form named "check_game_started.aspx". The form will open in Design view.

2. Double-click the surface of the form to open the Page_Load event handler in the code-behind page. Enter the following code:

```
If Application("arrGame")(1) = "TimedOut" Then
  Session("message") = "Sorry, no one else has signed up yet. Please
    try again"
  Response.Redirect("WebForm1.aspx")
Else
  If Application("arrGame")(4) > "0" Then
    Response.Redirect("GameStarted.aspx")
  Else
    Response.Redirect("GameStatusChecker.htm")
  End If
End If
```

CHAPTER 10 ASP.Net Optimizing and Debugging

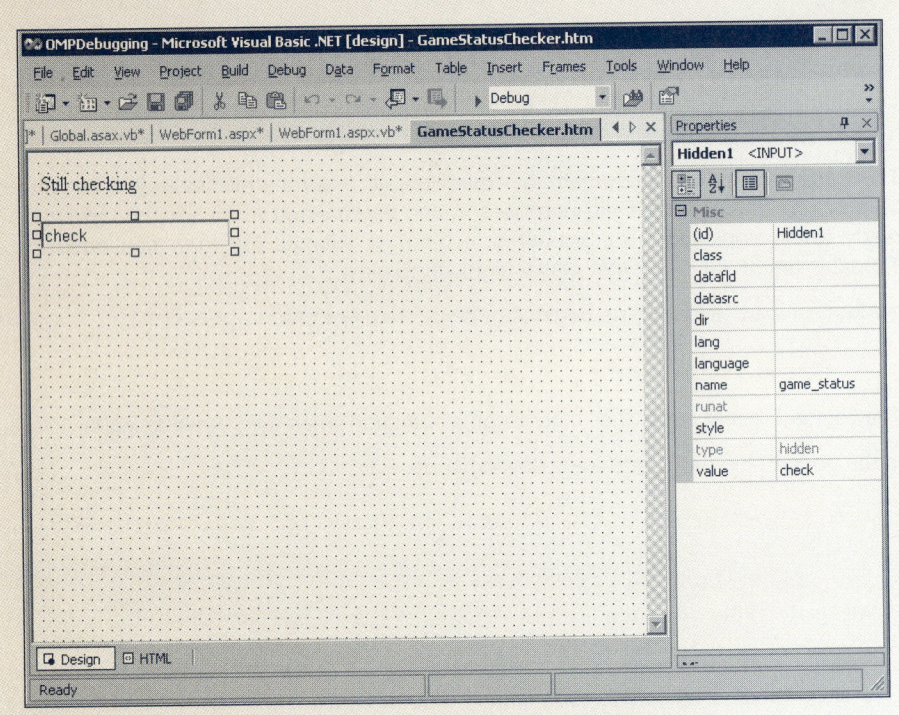

FIGURE 10.9 The GameStatusChecker.htm Web Page in Design View

3. This code checks to see if the value for Application("arrGame")(1) (the one index of the array) is "TimedOut", and, if so, redirects the player back to the original Web form (WebForm1.aspx) with a Session message telling the player that no one else has signed in, so please try again. The code to set this array index value will be placed in the Global.asax file in the next section.

4. If the array index value is not "TimedOut", another If...Then...End If block checks to see if the Player02 ID (the four index of the array) is greater than zero. The idea is that if another player has signed in, his/her ID value would have been placed in the array, and it would always be greater than zero. If this value is greater than zero, Player01 is redirected to the Game Started form, named "GameStarted.aspx". But if another player has not yet signed in (if the Player02 ID is still zero), then the player is redirected back to GameStatusChecker.htm to wait another 15 seconds before resubmitting and checking again.

5. That's all the code this Web form needs. Save it and close it.

FINISHING GLOBAL.ASAX AND CREATING GAMESTARTED.ASPX

1. Click back over to the Global.asax file in Design view and double-click Timer1. This will open an event handler in the code-behind page for Timer1's Elapsed event.

2. In the Timer1 Elapsed event handler, enter the following code:

```
If Application("arrGame")(0) = "Not Started" Then
    If Application("appTimer2Interval") > 0 Then
        If Timer2.Interval = 1 Then
            Timer2.Interval = Application("appTimer2Interval")
```

```
            Timer2.Start()
        End If
    End If
End If
```

3. This code first checks to see whether the game is "Not Started". If so, it checks to see whether the value for the application variable named "appTimer1Interval" is still zero. If Player01 has signed in, this value should now be "30000".

4. If the appTimer2Interval value is greater than zero, the code checks to see if the Timer2 interval is still one. If it is (this condition occurs only when Timer2 has not yet been set), then the code sets the interval for Timer2 and starts Timer2. If none of these conditions applies, Timer1 starts counting down one second again and rechecks.

5. Click back over the Design view and double-click Timer2 to open its Elapsed event handler in the code-behind page. Enter the following code:

```
If Application("arrGame")(4) = "0" Then
    Application("arrGame")(1) = "TimedOut"
        Application("arrGame")(0) = ""
Else
    Timer2.Stop()
    Application("arrGame")(0) = "Started"
End If
```

6. This code checks to see whether Player02 has signed in, and if not sets the one index of the array to "TimedOut" and sets the zero index to "" (a blank string). But if Player02 has signed in (and thereby set his/her ID value to something other than zero), it stops Timer2 and sets the game status (the zero index of the array) to "Started".

7. Now enter the following code in the Session_End event handler:

```
Timer1.Stop()
Timer2.Stop()
Dim i As Integer
For i = 0 To 4
    Application("arrGame")(i) = ""
Next
```

8. This code stops both Timers and resets all Application("arrGame") array values to a blank string. Note, however, that this only occurs when the Session itself times out, and the default for this is 20 minutes.

9. In Solution Explorer, create a new Web form and name it "GameStarted.aspx". When it opens in Design view, add a Label control that reads "GameStarted" in bold.

10. Double-click the surface of the form and enter the following code in the Page_Load event:

```
Application("arrGame")(0) = "Started"
```

11. This code makes sure the zero index of the array is set to Started, even if Timer2 hasn't timed out yet.

FINISHING WEBFORM1.ASPX

1. Click back over to WebForm1.aspx and double-click Button2 to open its Click event handler in the code-behind page. Enter the following code:

```
Application("arrGame")(4) = 2
Response.Redirect("check_game_started.aspx")
```

2. This code sets the Player02 ID value to "2" and redirects the player to the check_game_started.aspx Web form, which then checks to see if the Player02 index value of the array is set higher than 0. In this project, we could probably send the players straight to the GameStarted.aspx file, but we've sent them first to the check_game_started.aspx form because if more players were needed, they'd go there first.

DEBUGGING THE PROJECT

Now we're ready to debug the project. The code has been checked already, but we may find a few things we want to change as we go through it again. We'll at least demonstrate how to use the built-in Debugging tools in VS.Net.

1. Save and close all the files except WebForm1.aspx and WebForm1.aspx.vb.

2. In Solution Explorer, right-click the project and choose Properties from the shortcut menu. This will open the Project Property pages, as shown in Figure 10.10.

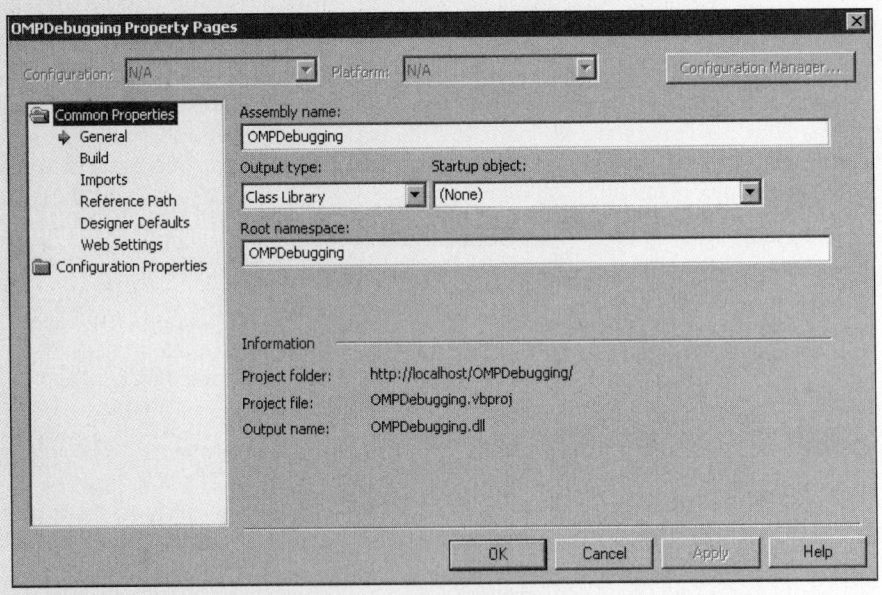

FIGURE 10.10   The Project Property Pages Dialog Box

3. On the Common Properties node, on the General tab you can see the Assembly name, Output type, Startup object, and so on. On the Build tab you can see the compiler defaults (Option Explicit is On and Option Strict is Off). On the Reference Path, Designer Defaults, and Web Settings tabs are a few more interesting settings, but we'll make no changes.

4. On the Configuration Properties node, on the Debugging tab (shown in Figure 10.11), you can see what happens when Start is chosen on the Debug menu. The WebForm1.aspx file opens first and

the application is started. At the bottom you also can see that the ASP.Net Debugger is started. The other tabs contain some interesting information as well, but we'll make no changes. Close the Project Property Pages dialog box.

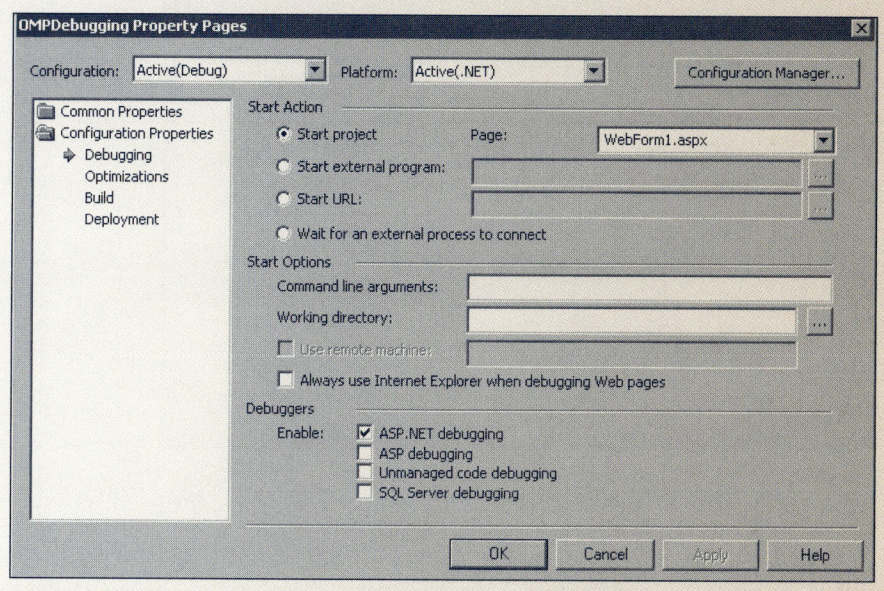

FIGURE 10.11 Setting the Page in Which to Start the Project

5. In the code-behind page for WebForm1.aspx, click on the gray bar running down the left side of the screen, next to the code line "MessageLabel.Text = Session("message")".

6. Clicking in the gray bar on the left side in a code file sets a breakpoint. Breakpoints cause the program to stop (while running) at that point in execution, so we can see what has happened to variables in the program. This is an extremely valuable debugging tool that helps identify where bugs occur (by viewing incorrect values in variables and object properties), thereby allowing you to isolate and fix the problem.

7. Once you've set the breakpoint, you should see a red dot on the gray bar, and a red line should highlight the entire line of code.

8. Click back over to WebForm1.aspx in Design view and choose Debug|Start from the menu. The application will start, the Autos window will open, the Task List window will open, the browser will open and begin displaying the page, and the code-behind page will appear with the breakpoint line highlighted in yellow, as shown in Figure 10.12.

9. Close the Task List window and you'll see the Output window underneath it. The Output window shows everything that has happened so far.

10. Close the Output window and you'll see the Call Stack window showing all the calls that have been made. Close the Call Stack window and you'll see the Breakpoints window, showing the breakpoint that has been set with No Conditions. Close the Breakpoints window and you'll see the Command window—immediate window with nothing in it. Close the Command window and you're left with the Autos window.

CHAPTER 10 ASP.Net Optimizing and Debugging

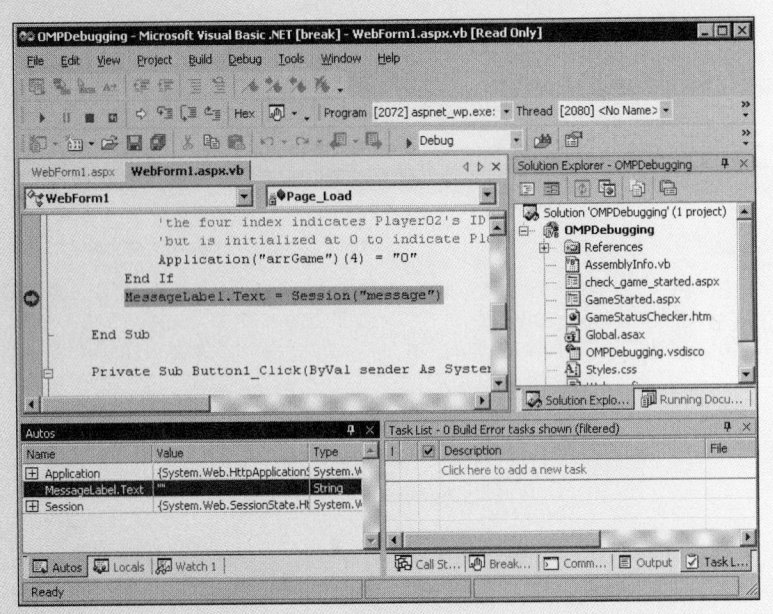

FIGURE 10.12 VS.Net Showing the Breakpoint and Associated Windows

11. In the Autos window, click the plus sign next to the Application node. This opens the node to reveal all the properties and objects in the Application object, so you can see what their values currently are. Being able to determine what these values are, at any stage of execution, makes it much easier to determine where bugs are.

12. Close the browser (it's probably underneath VS.Net in a separate window). The Outputs window will again display itself. Close the Outputs window. Remove the breakpoint from the code by clicking again on the red dot.

RUNNING THE APPLICATION WITHOUT A BREAKPOINT

Now we'll run the application without a breakpoint, to see if we detect any bugs.

1. Choose Debug|Start from the menu and run the application.

2. When WebForm1.aspx opens, click the first button. The GameStatuschecker.htm page should open, and it should say "Still checking".

3. Wait 10 seconds to see if it submits itself. It should submit itself and come back to the same page. Wait a total of 30 seconds, and you should be redirected back to WebForm1.aspx with the message "Sorry, no one else has signed in. Please try again".

4. Close the application again, then start the application again. This time click the first button, and then open another browser window and browse to WebForm1.aspx on the local server. You should see both buttons on the form this time. Click the second button as though you were Player02 entering an existing game. You should see the words "Game Started" in bold.

5. Go back to the other browser window, and the next time it submits you should be redirected to the Game Started form as well.

Adding a Deployment Project

This project will demonstrate adding a Web Setup project to a new Solution. Although the Web application project is quite simple, the Web Setup project used to deploy the Web application is the same as would be used for more complex Web applications.

1. Create a new ASP.Net Web application (using the VB.Net template) and name it WebDeploy. A blank Web form should open.

2. Change the background color of the form to blue, so it will be easily recognizable.

3. Open the Solution Explorer (if not already open) and right-click the Solution. Choose Add|New Project from the menu. The New Project dialog box will open. Choose the Web Setup Project from the Setup and Deployment Projects node, as shown in Figure 10.13. Leave the name WebSetup1 and click OK. The File System Editor for the WebSetup1 project will open in VS.Net, as shown in Figure 10.14.

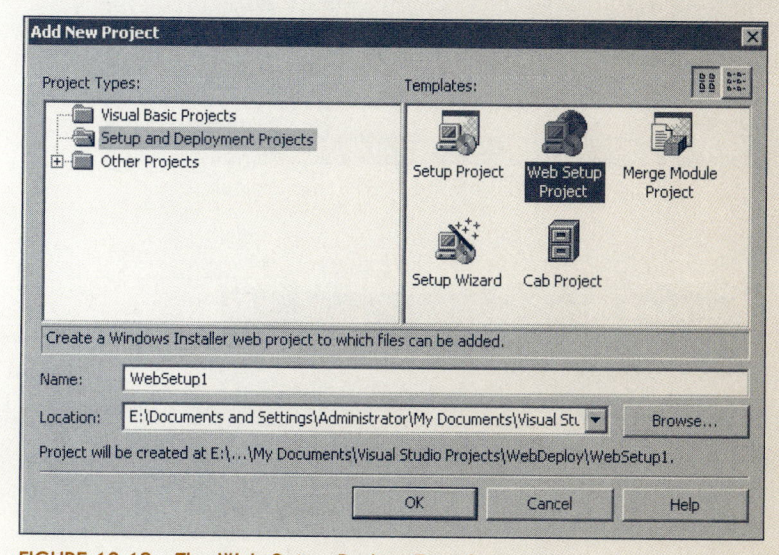

FIGURE 10.13 The Web Setup Project Template

4. To add the files from your WebDeploy Web application, click on (select) the WebApplication Folder on the left side of the screen, and then choose Action|Add|Project Output from the menu. The Add Project Output Group dialog box will open, as shown in Figure 10.15. If you click the drop-down box next to "Project:" you'll notice that WebDeploy is the only project available. Select Primary output and Content Files from the list below Projects: and click OK. These items will be added to your project.

5. Click on the WebSetup1 project, open the Properties window (if not already open), and set the ProductName to "My Web Application". Select the Web Application Folder and set the Virtual Directory property to "MyWebApp". Set the DefaultDocument property to "WebForm1.aspx".

6. You are now ready to build the application, and you can, at this point, change the application configuration to Release (from Debug) if you like. To build the Web Setup project, choose Build|WebDeploy from the menu. The notes on page 345 will appear in your Output screen in VS.Net.

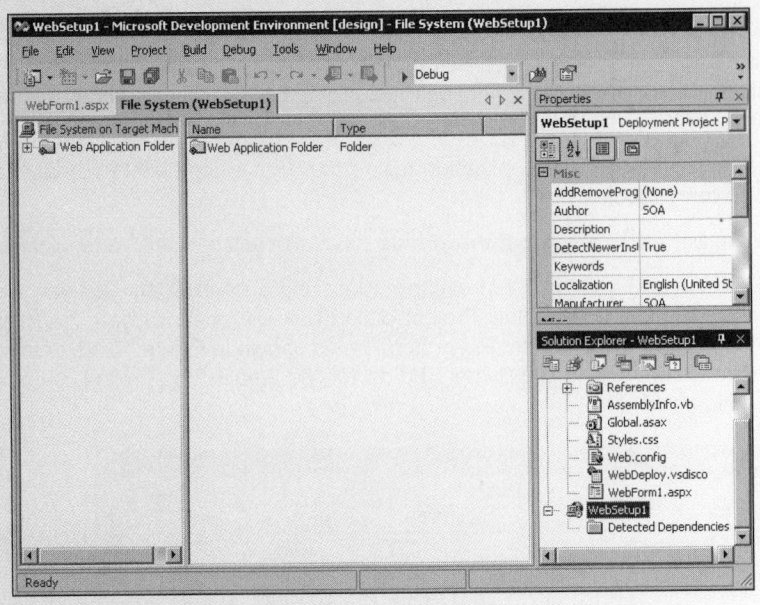

FIGURE 10.14 The File System Editor in the Web Setup Project

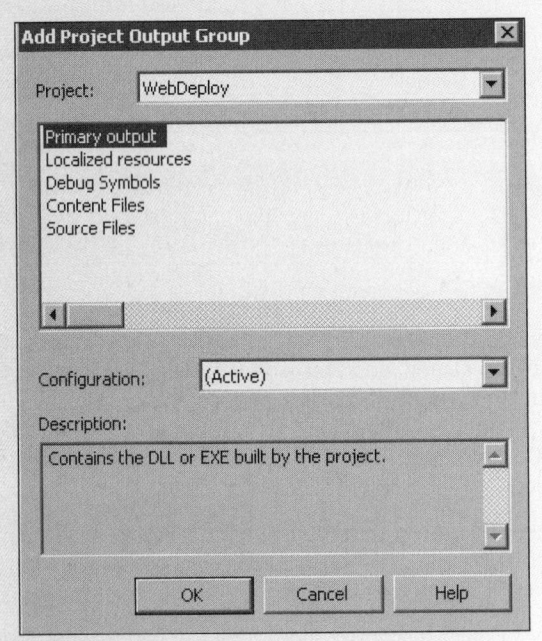

FIGURE 10.15 The Add Project Output Group Dialog Box

```
----- Build started: Project: WebDeploy, Configuration: Debug .NET -----
Preparing resources...
Updating references...
Performing main compilation...
Building satellite assemblies...

----- Starting pre-build validation for project 'WebSetup1' -----
----- Pre-build validation for project 'WebSetup1' completed -----
----- Build started: Project: WebSetup1, Configuration: Debug -----
Building file 'E:\Documents and Settings\Administrator\
   My Documents\Visual Studio Projects\WebDeploy\WebSetup1\Debug\
   WebSetup1.msi'...
WARNING: This setup does not contain the .NET Framework which must be
   installed on the target machine by running dotnetfx.exe before this
   setup will install. You can find dotnetfx.exe on the Visual Studio
   .NET 'Windows Components Update' media. Dotnetfx.exe can be
   redistributed with your setup.
Packaging file 'Setup.Exe'...
Packaging file 'InstMsiW.Exe'...
Packaging file 'Global.asax'...
Packaging file 'WebDeploy.dll'...
Packaging file 'Web.config'...
Packaging file 'WebForm1.aspx'...
Packaging file 'InstMsiA.Exe'...
Packaging file 'Styles.css'...

--------------------- Done ---------------------
   Build: 2 succeeded, 0 failed, 0 skipped
```

7. Note that you get a warning message saying that the target machine must have .Net Framework installed (which you can ensure by packaging "dotnetfx.exe" with your application). However, you should always make sure the server has the .Net Framework, as well as the proper version of IIS, installed before even attempting to install the application.

8. You can install the application on any server for which you have permission by copying the files and folders that have been created in the WebSetup1 folder to the server and double-clicking the Setup.exe file. You'll find the completed Web Setup project in the Visual Studio Projects folder (under My Documents, under Administrator), not in the IIS wwwroot folder.

ASP.Net Trace	deployment	testing protocol
Autos window	execution time	throughput
breakpoint	performance factors	Trace object
Breakpoints window	performance measures	Trace.Warn
debugging	response time	Trace.Write

Review Questions

1. Why is it important to turn off debug mode before final deployment?
2. What is the purpose of performance measurement? Why is it important to measure performance for an ASP.Net Web application before making changes to the application?
3. How is tracing enabled for an ASP.Net Web form?
4. What file can you examine from your browser to find trace information?
5. What Trace tables are available?
6. How is a breakpoint set?
7. How is a breakpoint removed?
8. In what window can you find Application object properties when running an ASP.Net Web application in debug mode?
9. What is the general process by which debugging is performed?

Index

A

AcceptTypes property, 94
Active Data Objects.Net (ADO.Net), 63, 210. *See also* Active Server Pages
  DataAdapter, 248–250
  database commands, 248–249
  database connections, 246–248
    SqlConnection object, 247–248
  DataReader, 248
  discussed, 250
  in general, 246
  introduction, 243–244
Active Server Pages (ASP). *See also* Active Server Pages.NET
  compared to ASP.NET, 1–2, 2–3, 48–50, 64
    Common Language Runtime, 48–49
    Microsoft Intermediate Language Specification, 49
    .NET structures and languages, 48
  defined, 30
  migrating from ASP to ASP.NET, 49–50
Active Server Pages.NET (ASP.NET). *See also* Visual Studio.Net
  application development
    building and hosting, 11–13
    discussed, 5–7, 13–14
    in general, 4–5
  ASP.NET Trace, 323
  compared to ASP, 1–2, 2–3, 48–50, 64
    Common Language Runtime, 48–49
    Microsoft Intermediate Language Specification, 49
    .NET structures and languages, 48
  control functions, dot-notation syntax for addressing controls, 90–92
  control objects, 89–90
  defined, 4, 30
  described, 2
    how ASP and ASP.NET are processed, 2–4
  directives
    coding directives, 66–68
    in general, 65–66
  exercises
    coding ASP.NET server controls in Web form, 69
    creating virtual directory in IIS, 69–72
  HTML server controls, 90
  installation
    acquiring ASP.NET, 8–9
    in general, 8
    system requirements, 8
  introduction, 1–2
  migrating to from ASP, 49–50
    ASP.NET server controls, 49

page directives, 49
variable declaration and data types, 50
VB.Net syntax, 50
optimizing, in general, 320
page processing
  compilation process, 64
  discussed, 64–65
  in general, 63–64
  page life cycle, 65
  render, 64
performance measurement
  in general, 321
  optimization decisions, 322
  performance measures, 321
  performance testing, 322
  specific performance improvements, 320–321
performance testing tools
  ASP.Net Trace, 323–325
  built-in performance counters, 323
  in general, 322
sessions
  in general, 162
  session methods, 163–164
  session properties, 163
state, 154–157
Web application
  application structure, 51–63
  in general, 50
Web server controls, 91
Web.config file, 195–198
what does it do?
  ASP.Net objects, 9–11
  in general, 9
AddCacheItemDependency method, 102
AddFileDependency method, 102
AddHeader method, 102
ADO.Net. *See* Active Data Objects.Net
ADO.Net class, 15
AdRotator control, 91
AllErrors property, 93
AllKeys property, 96
Animation, 116
Apache, 13
AppendHeader method, 102
Application. *See also* Application development; Middleware; Session; Web application
  adding variables to, 161–162
  desktop application, compared to Web application, 81–82
  discussed, 164–165
  using, 167–177
Application development. *See also* Template; Web application
  building and hosting, 11–13
  building and testing, 43

business application example, 7
  in general, 4–5
    desbch_ktop application, 4–5
    development solution, 5
    project management program, 6
    project plan, 5–6
  interactivity, 44
  process, 5–7, 13
  Web application, 4
    add Textbox control and Button Control, 41–42
    ASP.NET Web application template, 29–30
    change document properties for Webform1.ASPX, 34–36
    change label control, 40–41
    create Event Handler, 42–43
    developing, 13
    examine HTML and ASP.NET elements in Webform1.aspx, 36–38
    find Solution file and Web application file, 31–33
    hosting, 12–13
    open Solution Explorer, 34
    open Toolbox and put label control on form, 38–40
    open VS.Net and create Solution, 31
    Solutions and Projects, 29
Application event, 55
  discussed, 157–158
Application-Level Trace Logging, 197
Application object, 92. *See also* Object
  intrinsic application object, 160–162
Application programming tools, 7
  Integrated Development Environment, 7
  Visual Studio.Net, 7
Application property, 93. *See also* Properties
Application tracing. *See also* Trace
  web.config file, 201–203
ApplicationPath property, 94
Arithmetical operators, 130
ASP. *See* Active Server Pages
.asp file extension, 3
ASP.NET. *See* Active Server Pages.NET
ASP.NET object. *See also* Object
  in general, 9–10
    server object, 10
  using, 10–11
ASP.NET Trace, 323–325. *See also* Trace
Assembly, 54
  references and, 53
Assembly attributes, 55
AssemblyInfo.vb, 30
  discussed, 54–55
  settings, 73–75
@ Assembly directive, 67

INDEX

@ Control directive, 67
@ Implements directive, 67
@ Import directive, 67
@ OutputCache directive, 67–68, 192
@ Page directive, 49, 62, 66–67
@ Register directive, 67
@ WebService directive, 300
Attributes, 121
AutoEventWireup, 79
Autos window, 327

B

Bin folder, discussed, 54
BinaryRead method, 100
Bit, in compiled languages, 129
Blackjack.aspx, creating, 268–269
Breakpoints, 327. *See also* Breakpoints window
    running application without, 342
Breakpoints window, 327
Browser. *See* Web browser
Browser property, 94
Buffer attribute, page buffering, 67
Buffer property, 100
BufferOutput property, 101
Business process
    OMPGame, 250–252
    user interface, 185
Button control, 89, 91
    adding, 41–42
Byte types, in compiled languages, 129

C

C#, 13, 49, 115, 126
C++, 13, 49, 119
Cache object, 92
Cache property, 93, 101
CacheControl property, 101
Caching
    data caching, 192, 193–194
    discussed, 194
    in general, 192
        Cache object, 192
        output caching, 192–193
Calendar control, 91
Cascading Style Sheet (CSS), 58
    declaration, 58
    external stylesheets, 60
    selector, 58
    setting CSS styles, 75–78
Central processing unit (CPU), 118
CheckBox control, 91
CheckBoxList control, 91
Check_Game_Started.aspx, 337–338
Class. *See also* Http class; HttpContext class;
        HttpRequest class
    ADO.Net class, 15
    base class
        objects and, 87–88
        properties, 88
    customized, 88
    references and, 29
    SQL class, 15
    Windows Forms class, 15
    writing your own, 87
    XML class, 15
Class View menu, 20. *See also* View menu
Clear method, 102
ClearContent method, 102
ClearHeaders method, 102
Client-side management. *See also* Client-side
        processing
    discussed, 156–157
        hidden form fields, 156–157
        ViewState property, 156
Client-side processing, vs. server-side
        processing, 44
ClientCertificate property, 94–95
Close method, 102
CLR. *See* Common Language Runtime
Code-behind file, 2, 89. *See also* Code-behind
        page
    WebForm1.aspx, 62
Code-behind page, 3, 49, 115
Code editor, 7, 15, 26
Collection
    cookies, 95
    discussed, 95
Colors, HTML, 150
Common Language Runtime (CLR), 13, 15,
        63–64
    discussed, 48–49
    VB.NET and CLR data types, 129
Comparison operators, 130–131
Compilation, 118
Compilation process, ASP.NET, 64
Compiled languages. *See also* Programming
        languages
    bit and byte types, 129
    comments in code, 127–128
    control flow structures, 131–132
    data types, 128–130
    dates, 129
    defining variables, 127
    expressions, 131
    in general, 119, 126, 132–133
    keywords, 131
    object data type, 129
    operators, 130–131
Computers, 118
ContentEncoding property, 95
ContentLength property, 95
ContentType property, 95, 101
Control, in ASP.NET application, 92
Control Execution Lifecycle, Page event, in
        general, 188
Control flow structures, 4
    in compiled languages, 131–132
        Do...Loop, 132
        For Each...Next, 132
        For...Next, 132
        Select Case structure, 132
        While...Wend structure, 132
        With structure, 132
Control function. *See also* Control object
    dot-notation syntax for addressing
        controls, 90–92
    focus, 92
Control object. *See also* Object

ASP.Net and, 89–90
    Document Object Model, 89
    in general, 188
Cookies. *See also* Cookies property
    state and, 156
Cookies property, 95–96, 101
    collection of cookies, 95
CPU. *See* Central processing unit
CreateObject method, 103
CSS. *See* Cascading Style Sheet
CurrentExecutionFilePath property, 96
Customize menu, 25. *See also* Visual
        Studio.Net

D

Data types
    discussed, 128–130
        common type system, 128
        Integer type, 128
        String type, 128
    numerical data types, 128–129
    object data type, 129
    Strings and, 128
    user-defined data type, 130
    variables and, 127
    VB.NET and CLR data types, 129
DataAdapter, 248–250
    DataSets, 249
        creating, 249–250
    DataTable, 249
Database, 154. *See also* Database engine;
        Structured Query Language; Table
    creating, with Enterprise Manager,
        229–237
    defined, 210
    design
        discussed, 214–215
        field, 212
        in general, 211–212, 222
        OMPGame application, 222–224
        record, 212, 213
        table, 212–213
        tables, 222–224
    ecommerce applications, 211
    in general, 210–211
    relational database, 211
    relational database management system,
        215
    structures, 241
Database diagram, building, 234–237
Database engine
    in general, 224, 244
    Microsoft Access, 224–225
    Microsoft Jet Database Engine, 244
    Microsoft SQL Server, 225
    selecting, 224
DataGrid control, 91
DataReader, 248
DataRow, 249
DataSets, 249
    ADO.Net objects and, 249
    creating, from DataAdapter, 249–250
DataTable, 249
DataList control, 91

Index

Dates
    in compiled languages, 129
    in VB.Net, 144–148
Debugger, 7. *See also* Debugging
Debugging. *See also* Debugging tools; Error message; Performance measurement
    Application-Level Trace Logging, 197
    discussed, 327–328
    in general, 325
    OMPGame, 333–342
    process
        basic debugging, 326
        fixing bugs with troubleshooting, 326–327
        in general, 325
        testing protocol, 325–326
Debugging tools, 15
    VS.Net, 27, 327
        Autos window, 327
        breakpoints, 327
        Breakpoints window, 327
Declaration, CSS, 58
DELETE query, 219. *See also* Structured Query Language
DeleteCommand property, 249
Deployment. *See also* Deployment project
    Web application, 328
Deployment project, Web application, adding, 343–345
Desbch_ktop application programs, 4–5, 7, 13
Development solution, 5
Dim keyword, 127, 135
Directives
    coding directives, 66–68
        @ Assembly directive, 67
        @ Control directive, 67
        @ Implements directive, 67
        @ Import directive, 67
        @ Output Cache directive, 67–68
        @ Page directive, 49, 62, 66–67
        @ Reference directive, 68
        @ Register directive, 67
    in general, 65–66, 68
.disco files, 293–294
Discovery files, XML Web Services, 293–294
.dll. *See* Dynamic link library
DOCUMENT file, 21
Document Object Model (DOM), 89
Document Type Definition (DTD)
    HTML and SGML, 121, 133
        attributes, 121
        elements, 121
        XML, 122
Do...Loop structure, 132
DOM. *See* Document Object Model
Dot-notation syntax, controls, 90–92
DropDownList control, 91, 107
DTD. *See* Document Type Definition
Dynamic link library (.dll), 54, 64

E

Edit menu
    VS.Net, 16
        discussed, 18–19

Element, DTD, 121
Encapsulation, in OOP, 87
Encoding, ContentEncoding property, 95
End method, 102
Enterprise Manager, 225–226
    creating database with, 229–237
Error message. *See also* Debugging
    custom error message, 197
    404 Not Found message, 84
    storage, 58
Event. *See also* Event handler
    defined, 85
    in general, 85–86
    objects and, 89
    session event, 55
Event handler, 157. *See also* Event handling
    ASP.NET, 49, 86
    creating, 42–43
    Global.asax file, 158–160
    purpose, 89
Event handling, page processing, 65
ExactOddsCalc function, coding, 312–317
Examples, organization of, 27–28
Execute method, 104
Expires property, 101
ExpiresAbsolute property, 101
Expressions, in compiled languages, 131

F

Field. *See also* Database
    database, 212
File menu
    VS.Net, 16
        discussed, 18
FilePath property, 96
Files property, 96
Find and Replace, Edit menu, 19
Flash, 116
Flush method, 102
Focus, 92
For Each...Next structure, 132
For Next loop, 109
Form. *See also* Web application; WebForm1.aspx
    coding ASP.NET server controls in Web form, 69
    creating Check_Game_Started.aspx, 337–338
    hidden form fields, 156–157
    label control, 38–40
    login form, creating, 200
    setting up Web form, 106–110, 167–168
        DropDownList control, 107
        For Next loop, 109
        ListBox control, 107
        Select Case code block, 109
    Web forms, 115
        adding, 72–73
Form property, 96
For...Next structure, 132

G

Game. *See* OMPGame

GamesStatusChecker.htm Web page, creating, 336–337
GameStarted.aspx, 338–339
GET and POST methods, HTTP and, 84, 97, 98
Global.asax file, 30, 48, 153, 165
    discussed, 55–58, 158–160
        application event, 55
        session event, 55
        Source Code Editor, 58
    event handlers, 158–160
    finishing, 338–339
    opening, 56–58
    setting up, 168–170, 333–334
    variables, 161

H

Hard drive, RAID system, 13
Header fields, HTTP, 84–85
Headers property, 97
Help menu. *See also* Visual Studio.Net
    discussed, 25–26
Hit button, writing, 279–282
Hold Button, writing, 282–287
Hot-keys, discussed, 44
HTML. *See* Hypertext Markup Language
HTML Decode method, 104
HTML Designer, discussed, 27
HTML Encode method, 104
HTTP. *See* Hypertext Transfer Protocol
Http class, discussed, 104–105
HttpApplication class, 153, 160
HttpApplicationState class, 153, 160
HttpContext class. *See also* Class; HttpContext properties; HttpRequest class
    in general, 92
HttpContext object, 104
HttpContext properties. *See also* HttpRequest properties
    discussed, 92–93
        AllErrors property, 93
        Application property, 93
        Cache property, 93
        Request and Response properties, 93
        Session property, 93
        Trace property, 93
HttpMethod property, 97
HttpRequest class. *See also* Class; HttpRequest properties
    discussed, 93
    member, 93
HttpRequest methods. *See also* HttpRequest properties
    discussed, 99–100
        BinaryRead method, 100
        MapImageCoordinates method, 100
        MapPath method, 100
        SaveAs method, 100
        ToString method, 100
HttpRequest properties. *See also* HttpRequest methods
    discussed, 93–99
        AcceptTypes property, 94
        AllKeys property, 96

INDEX

ApplicationPath property, 94
Browser property, 94
ClientCertificate property, 94–95
ContentEncoding property, 95
ContentLength property, 95
ContentType property, 95
Cookies property, 95–96
CurrentExecutionFilePath property, 96
FilePath property, 96
Files property, 96
Form property, 96
Headers property, 97
HttpMethod property, 97
IsAuthenticated property, 97
IsSecureConnection property, 97
Params property, 97
Path property, 98
PathInfo property, 98
PhysicalApplicationPath property, 98
QueryString property, 98
RawURL property, 98
RequestType property, 98
ServerVariables property, 99
TotalBytes property, 99
URL property, 99
URLReferer property, 99
UserAgent property, 99
UserHostName property, 99
HttpResponse class. *See also* HttpResponse methods; HttpResponse properties
discussed, 100
HttpResponse methods. *See also* HttpResponse class; HttpResponse properties
AddCacheItemDependency method, 102
AddFileDependency method, 102
AddHeader method, 102
AppendHeader method, 102
Clear method, 102
ClearContent method, 102
ClearHeaders method, 102
Close method, 102
End method, 102
Flush method, 102
Redirect method, 103
RemoveOutputCacheItem method, 103
Write method, 103
WriteFile method, 103
HttpResponse properties. *See also* HttpResponse class; HttpResponse methods
Buffer property, 100
BufferOutput property, 101
Cache property, 101
CacheControl property, 101
ContentType property, 101
Cookies property, 101
Expires property, 101
ExpiresAbsolute property, 101
IsClientConnected property, 101
Status property, 102
StatusCode property, 102
StatusDescription property, 102
HttpServerUtility class, in general, 103
HttpServerUtility methods, 103
CreateObject method, 103

Execute method, 104
HTML Decode method, 104
HTML Encode method, 104
MapPath method, 104
Transfer method, 104
URL Decode method, 104
URL Encode method, 104
HttpServerUtility ScriptTimeout property, 103
HttpSessionState, 160
Hyperlink control, 91
Hypertext Markup Language (HTML)
ASP and, 2–4, 89, 115
code-behind file, 2
ASP.NET and, HTML server controls, 90
colors, 150
features, 116–117
links, 116
in general, 44, 83, 119, 120, 132–133
HTTP 1.1, 83
GET and POST methods, 84
header fields, 84–85
HTML document creation
adding hyperlinks, 140
adding tables and images, 141–144
in general, 138–140
HTML tag, 121
SGML and, 119–121
VS.Net and, 15
XHTML and, 3
Hypertext Transfer Protocol (HTTP), 13
discussed, 44, 104
Internet communications and, 82–83

I

IDE. *See* Integrated Development Environment
IIS. *See* Internet Information Server
Image, adding to HTML document, 141–144
Image control, 91
Inheritance, in OOP, 87
INSERT query, 218–219. *See also* Structured Query Language
InsertCommand property, 249
Integer data type, 128
Integrated Development Environment (IDE), 7, 14, 26, 28, 47, 327
Interactivity, in application development, 44
Internet communications, HTTP and, 82–83
Internet Information Server (IIS), 8, 13
creating virtual directory in, 69–72
Interpretation, 118
Interpreted languages. *See also* Programming languages
in general, 119, 125, 132–133
Javascript, 125–126
IP address, 117
IsAuthenticated property, 97
IsClientConnected property, 101
IsPostBack property, 189
IsSecureConnection property, 97

J

J#, 126
Javascript, 115, 119

discussed, 125–126, 133
Jscript, 115

K

Key
foreign key, 213
primary key, 212
Keywords
in compiled languages, 131
Dim keyword, 127

L

Label control, 91
form, 38–40
changing, 40–41
LAN. *See* Local Area Network
Link
HTML hyperlinks, 116
adding, 140
HyperText link, 151
Linux, 13
ListBox control, 91, 107
Literal control, 91
Local Area Network (LAN), 82
Login function, coding, 200–201

M

Machine.config file, 195
Macros menu, 24. *See also* Visual Studio.Net
MapImageCoordinates method, 100
MapPath method, 100, 104
Markup languages. *See also* Programming languages
in general, 118–119, 132–133
HTML and SGML, 119–121
Document Type Definition, 121
XML and XHTML, 121–124
MDAC. *See* Microsoft Data Access Components
Member, 93
Menu. *See also* Help menu; Toolbar; View menu; *other specific menus*
VS.Net, 15–16
Methods
in general, 85–86
objects and, 88–89
session methods, 163–164
Microsoft
MSDN site, 8
.NET Framework technology, 1–2
Microsoft Access, 224–225
Microsoft Data Access Components (MDAC), 8, 14
Microsoft Data Engine (MSDE), 224
Microsoft Intermediate Language Specification (MSIL), discussed, 49
Microsoft Jet Database Engine, 244
Microsoft SQL Server, 8
discussed, 225–226
SQL Server Enterprise Manager, 225–226
Microsoft Word, 182

Index

Middleware. *See also* Application
 discussed, 244–246
 tiers, 244
  communication between, 245–246
MIME. *See* Multipurpose Internet Mail Extension
MSDE. *See* Microsoft Data Engine
Multipurpose Internet Mail Extension (MIME), 94
 MIME types, 113

N

Name/Value pairs, discussed, 44
Namespaces
 discussed, 44
 VB.Net, 150
 XML namespace, 123
.NET Framework, 1–2
 classes
  ADO.Net classes, 15
  SQL classes, 15
  Windows Forms classes, 15
  XML classes, 15
 discussed, 14–15
Notepad, 65, 119

O

Object. *See also* ASP.NET objects; Control object; Object-oriented programming; *specific objects*
 base classes and, 87–88
 built-in objects, 7
 creating, 30
 defined, 4, 85
 Document Object Model, 89
 events, 89
 in general, 85–86
 methods, 88–89
 properties, 88
Object data type, 129
Object-oriented programming (OOP), 85
 discussed, 86–87
  encapsulation, 87
  inheritance, 87
  polymorphism, 87
OleDbCommand object, 248
OMPGame. *See also* Web application
 application, 222–224
 business process, 250–252
  game play, 252
  game selection and start notification, 251–252
  login, 251
  registration, 251
 chose game page, 265–268
 creating Blackjack.aspx, 268–269
 database connection, 254–259
 debugging, 333–342
 Hit button, 279–282
 Hold Button, 282–287
 login code, 264–265
 Page_Load code, 269–279
 Play Again Button, 287
 registration code, 259

 registration page, 254
 welcome page, 253–254
OOP. *See* Object-oriented programming
Operating system (OS), 8, 11
Operators
 arithmetical operators, 130
 comparison operators, 130–131
 concatenation operators, 131
 discussed, 130–131
Options menu, 25. *See also* Visual Studio.Net
OS. *See* Operating system
OSI Reference model, layers, 82
Other Windows menu, 23

P

Page event. *See also* Event
 Control Execution Lifecycle
  in general, 188
  IsPostBack property, 189
  Page_Load event, 189
  saving state, 189
Page object. *See also* Object
 in general, 188
Page_Load code. *See also* Page_Load event
 writing, 269–279
Page_Load event, 189, 192
Panel control, 91
Params property, 97
Path property, 98
PathInfo property, 98
.pdb file. *See* Program Debug Database file
Pending Checkins, 23
Percent-sign delimiter, ASP code, 3
Performance measurement. *See also* Debugging; Performance measures
 optimization decisions, 322
 performance factors, 321
 performance measures, 321
 performance testing, 322
Performance measures
 ASP.NET, 321
  execution time, 321
  response time, 321
  throughput, 321
Perl, 13
Php, 13
 discussed, 125
PhysicalApplicationPath property, 98
PlaceHolder control, 91
Play Again Button, writing, 287
Polymorphism, in OOP, 87
Private keyword, 135
Program Debug Database (.pdb) file, 54
Programming, practice notes, 113
Programming languages
 compiled languages, 119, 126, 132–133
 discussed, 132–133
 in general, 2, 118
  compilation, 118
  interpretation, 118
 interpreted languages
  compared to compiled language, 125
  in general, 119, 125, 132–133
  Php and VBScript, 125
  scripting languages, 125

markup languages
 in general, 118–119, 132–133
 HTML and SGML, 119–121
Project. *See also* Application development
 defined, 29
 VB.Net Project, 51
Project management program, 6
Project plan, 5–6
Properties. *See also* Properties window
 discussed, 88
 in general, 85–86
 HttpContext properties, 92–93
 session properties, 163
Properties window. *See also* Visual Studio.Net
 discussed, 21
  DOCUMENT file, 21
 VS.Net, 15
Protocols, 83. *See also* Hypertext Transfer Protocol
Public keyword, 135
Python, 13

Q

Query Builder, 226
Query string. *See also* String
 state, 156, 157
QueryString property, 98

R

RadioButton control, 91
RadioButtonList control, 91
RAID. *See* Redundant array of inexpensive drives
RawURL property, 98
RDMS. *See* Relational database management system
Record. *See also* Database
 database, 212
 adding, 213
Redirect method, 103
Redundant array of inexpensive drives (RAID), 13
References
 Classes and, 29
 Web application, 52–54
 assemblies, 53
Regular expressions, 191
Relational database management system (RDMS), 215
RemoveOutputCacheItem method, 103
Repeater control, 91
Request and Response objects, 2, 3–4, 9, 92. *See also* Request and Response properties
 discussed, 104–105
 HttpRequest class, 87, 88
Request and Response properties, 93. *See also* Request and Response properties and methods
Request and Response properties and methods
 in general, 106
 RequestObject methods, 111–113
 RequestObject properties, 110–111

INDEX

setting up Web form, 106–110
Request for Comment 2616, 83
RequestType property, 98
Resource View, 21. *See also* View menu

S

SaveAs method, 100
Scope
   discussed, 136
   in general, 133–134
   in VB.NET, 134–135
Scripting languages, 125. *See also* Programming languages
Select Case code block, 109
Select Case structure, 132
SELECT query. *See also* Structured Query Language
   discussed, 216–218
      WHERE clause, 217–218
SelectCommand property, 249
Selector, CSS, 58
Server Explorer, 21
Server object, 10, 105. *See also* ASP.NET objects
Server-side processing, vs. client-side processing, 44
ServerVariables property, 99
Session. *See also* Application; Session event; Session object
   adding variables to, 161–162
   ASP.NET session, 162–164
   discussed, 164–165
   using, 167–177
Session event, 55
   discussed, 157–158
Session object, 92
   intrinsic session object, 160–162
Session property, 93
SGML. *See* Standard Generalized Markup Language
Simple Object Access Protocol (SOAP), 293
   XML Web Services, 299
SOAP. *See* Simple Object Access Protocol
Solution. *See also* Solution Explorer
   application development, 29
      creating, 31
      projects, 29
   find Solution file, 31–33
Solution Explorer, 65
   opening, 20, 34
Source Code Editor
   Global.asax file, 58
   VS.Net, 2
SQL. *See* Structured Query Language
SQL classes, 15
SqlCommand object, 248
SqlConnection object, 247–248
Standard Generalized Markup Language (SGML), HTML and, 119–121, 133
Standard Toolbar. *See also* Toolbar; Visual Studio.Net
   discussed, 26
Start button control, WebForm1.aspx, 170–171
State

ASP.NET Web application state, 154–157
   stateless nature of Web, 155–156
client-side management, 156–157
   cookies, 156, 157
   hidden form fields, 156
   query strings, 156, 157
   ViewState property, 92, 156
defined, 154
in general, 154
saving state, 189
Status property, 102
StatusCode property, 102
StatusDescription property, 102
Stored procedures, SQL, 221
String. *See also* Query string
   data type and, 128
String data type, 128
Structured Query Language (SQL), 116, 210. *See also* Database
   aggregate query, 220–221
   creating views and queries, 237–241
   discussed, 221–222
   in general, 215
   Microsoft SQL server, 225–226
   SQL queries
      DELETE query, 219
      in general, 215–216
      INSERT query, 218–219
      joining tables, 219–220
      SELECT query, 216–218
      UPDATE query, 219
   stored procedures, 221
Style.css, 30
   discussed, 58–60
Stylesheet. *See* Cascading Style Sheet
Summary Validation Control, 190. *See also* Validation

T

Table. *See also* Database
   adding to HTML document, 141–144
   creating, 230–234
   database, 212
      many-to-many relationship, 213
      one-to-many relationship, 213
      one-to-one relationship, 213
      primary key, 212
   joining in SQL query, 219–220
      equi-join, 220
      outer-join, 220
   OMPGame application, 222–224
   Trace information table, 324–325
Table control, 91
TableCell control, 91
TableRow control, 91
TCP/IP, 82
Template. *See also* Application development
   ASP.NET Web application template, 29–30, 50
      AssemblyInfo.vb, 30
      Global.asax, 30
      References, 29
      Style.css, 30
      VSDISCO. file, 30
      Web.config, 30

WebForm1.aspx, 30
   VB.Net ASP.Net template, 65
   Web site template, 10
Template file, 7
Text Editor, 2, 26
TextBox control, 89, 91
   adding, 41–42
Tic Tac Toe, 167–177
Tier
   communication between, 245–246
   middleware, 244
Toolbar. *See also* Menu; Toolbox
   standard toolbar, 26
   VS.Net, 15–16
Toolbox
   discussed, 22–23
   opening, 38–40
Tools menu, 23–25. *See also* Visual Studio.Net
ToString method, 100
TotalBytes property, 99
Trace. *See also* Trace object; Trace property
   set tracing in Web.config file, 323
   threads and, 325
   Trace attribute, 324
   Trace information table, 324–325
Trace object, 323. *See also* ASP.NET Trace; Object; Trace property
Trace property, 93
TraceContext object, 92
Trace.Warn method, 324
Trace.Write method, 324
Tracking, user numbers, 177–179
Transfer method, 104
Troubleshooting. *See also* Debugging
   fixing bugs with troubleshooting, 326–327

U

UDDI. *See* Universal Description, Discovery, and Integration
UI. *See* User interface
Undo, Edit menu, 18
Universal Description, Discovery, and Integration (UDDI), 293
Unix, 13
UPDATE query, 219. *See also* Structured Query Language
UpdateCommand property, 249
URL, absolute URL vs. relative URL, 151
URL Decode method, 104
URL Encode method, 104
URL property, 99
URLReferer property, 99
User interface (UI). *See also* Web application
   basic requirements, 183
   customizing, 204–205
   design
      business process, 185
      control and menu layout, 184
      in general, 183
      hints, 186–187
      security considerations, 184
      user demographics, 183–184
   development, in general, 185–186
   discussed, 191–192

Index

in general, 182–183
practicing techniques, 200–205
UserAgent property, 99
UserHostName property, 99

V

Valid document, XML, 121
Validation. *See also* Validation controls; Web application
  ASP.Net validation controls
    in general, 190
    Summary Validation Control, 190
  in general, 189–190
  regular expressions, 191
  server-side and client-side validation, 190–191
    available validation controls, 190–191
    enabling validation, 190
Validation controls, 90
  using, 205–208
Variables
  adding, to application or session, 161–162
  calling, 134
  declaring, 50, 127
  defined, 127
    data type, 127
    Dim keyword, 127
  defining, compiled languages, 127
VB.Net. *See* Visual Basic.Net
VB.Net Project, 51. *See also* Project
VBScript, 13, 50
  discussed, 125, 133
View, creating, 237–241
View menu. *See also* Visual Studio.Net
  discussed, 19–23
    Class View menu, 20
    Properties window, 21
    Resource View, 21
    Server Explorer, 21
    Solution Explorer, 20
ViewState property, 92
  discussed, 156
Virtual directory, creating, in IIS, 69–72
Visual Basic.Net (VB.Net), 2, 13, 15, 49, 115, 119. *See also* Compiled languages
  CLR data types, 129
  dates, 144–148
  discussed, 133
  namespaces, 150
  scope, 134–135
    block scope, 135
    module scope, 135
    namespace scope, 135
    procedure scope, 135
  syntax, 50
Visual Studio.Net (VS.Net), 2, 47, 86
  application development
    add Textbox control and Button Control, 41–42
    ASP.NET Web application template, 29–30
    building and testing, 43
    change document properties for Webform1.ASPX, 34–36
    change label control, 40–41
    create Event Handler, 42–43
    examine HTML and ASP.NET elements in Webform1.aspx, 36–38
    find Solution file and Web application file, 31–33
    open Solution Explorer, 34
    open Toolbox and put label control on form, 38–40
    open VS.Net and create Solution, 31
    Solutions and Projects, 29
  building XML Web Services, 300–301
  debugging tools, 327
  discussed, 7
  editors and tools
    Code Editor, 26
    debugging tools, 27
    in general, 26
    HTML Designer, 27
    Text Editor, 26
    XML Designer, 27
  features, 15, 28
    Properties window, 15
  in general, 15–16
  installing and configuring, 14
    opening, 16–17
  menus and toolbars
    Customize menu, 25
    Edit Menu, 16, 18–19
    File Menu, 16, 18
    in general, 15–16, 18
    Help Menu, 25–26
    Macros menu, 24
    Options menu, 25
    Other Windows menu, 23
    Pending Checkins, 23
    Standard Toolbar, 26
    Toolbox, 22–23, 38–40
    Tools Menu, 23–25
    View menu, 19–23
    Web browser menu, 23
    Windows menu, 25–26
  .NET Framework, 14–15
  Source Code Editor, 2
  template, VB.Net ASP.Net template, 65
.vsdisco file, 30
  WebAppStructure.vsdisco file, discussed, 61
VS.Net. *See* Visual Studio.Net

W

W3C. *See* World Wide Web Consortium
WAS. *See* Web Application Stress
Web application, 4. *See also* Active Server Pages.NET; Application; Form; OMPGame; User interface; Validation; Web site; XML Web Services
  add Textbox control and Button Control, 41–42
  application structure
    Assembly attributes, 55
    Assemblyinfo.vb file, 54–55
    bin folder, 54
    in general, 51
    Global.asax file, 55–58
    references, 52–54
    Styles.css file, 58–60
    WebAppStructure.vsdisco file, 61
    Web.config file, 60–61
    Webform1.aspx file, 61–63
  ASP.NET applications
    adding Web forms, 72–73
    assemblyinfo.vb setttings, 73–75
    setting CSS styles, 75–78
  ASP.NET Web application template, 29–30
  change document properties for Webform1.ASPX, 34–36
  change label control, 40–41
  configuration, 194–198
    practicing configuration techniques, 200–205
  create Event Handler, 42–43
  creating, 153–154, 302–303
  defined, 154
  deployment, 328
  deployment project, adding, 343–345
  developing, 13
  examine HTML and ASP.NET elements in Webform1.aspx, 36–38
  find Solution file and Web application file, 31–33
  in general, 50
  hosting, 12–13
  how they work, 117–118
  languages, 132–133
  open Solution Explorer, 34
  open Toolbox and put label control on form, 38–40
  open VS.Net and create Solution, 31
  running without breakpoints, 342
  Solutions and Projects, 29
  state, 154–157
Web Application Stress (WAS), 322
Web application structure. *See* Web application
Web browser, VS.Net menu, 23
Web page. *See also* Web site
  dynamic vs. static Web page, 10–11
  index, 117
Web server, 117
Web server controls, 91
Web Services Description Language (WSDL)
  document sections, 294–295
  in general, 293, 294
  generating or linking to WSDL documents, 299
  WSDL example, 295–299
Web site. *See also* Web application
  in general, 116
  how they work, 116–117
WebAppStructure.vbproj file, 52, 53–54
WebAppStructure.vsdisco file, discussed, 61
Web.config file, 30, 195
  application tracing, 201–203
  ASP.NET configuration file, 195–198
  discussed, 60–61

tracing settings, 323
WebForm1.aspx, 30, 89. *See also* Form
   change document properties, 34–36
   designing, 335–336
   discussed, 48, 61–63
      coding controls into Web form manually, 63
      Webform1.aspx.resx, 61
      Webform1.aspx.vb, 61
   examine HTML and ASP.NET elements, 36–38
   finishing, 340
   Image button control, 171–173
   Start button control, 170–171
WebMethodAttribute class, 300
Well-formed document, XML, 121
WHERE clause, SELECT query, 217–218
While...Wend structure, 132
Windows 2000, 3, 8
Windows Forms classes, 15
Windows menu. *See also* Visual Studio.Net
   discussed, 25–26
Windows XP, 8
With structure, 132
World Wide Web Consortium (W3C), 120
   Request for Comment 2616, 83
Write method, 103
WriteFile method, 103

WSDL. *See* Web Services Description Language

X

XHTML, 3, 115, 117, 133
   discussed, 121–124
      making XHTML document XML-compliant, 123–124
XML
   data-oriented vs. document-oriented, 122
   discussed, 121–124
      valid document, 121
      well-formed document, 121
   DTD, 122
   Schema Language, 122–123
      XML namespaces, 123
   VS.Net and, 15
   XML document, creating, 148–150
XML classes, 15
XML Designer, discussed, 27
XML namespaces, 123
XML schema, 121, 198
   creating, 148–150
   discussed, 90
XML Web Services. *See also* Web application
   building
      manually, 300
      with VS.Net, 300–301
   WebMethodAttribute class, 300
   creating
      in general, 302
      new Web application, 302–303
      writing code, 303–307
      writing code for Blackjack hands, 307–312
   design, 291–292
   development process, 290–291
   introduction, 289–290
   protocols, 292
      integration, 292
   Simple Object Access Protocol, 299
   specific problems facing XML developers, 292–294
      discovery files, 293–294
      Simple Object Access Protocol, 293
      Universal Description, Discovery, and Integration, 293
      Web Services Description Language, 293
   Web Services Description Language document sections, 294–295
      in general, 293, 294
      generating or linking to WSDL documents, 299
      WSDL example, 295–299